NATO ASI Series

Advanced Science Institutes Series

A series presenting the results of activities sponsored by the NATO Science Committee, which aims at the dissemination of advanced scientific and technological knowledge, with a view to strengthening links between scientific communities.

The Series is published by an international board of publishers in conjunction with the NATO Scientific Affairs Division

A Life Sciences B Physics	Plenum Publishing Corporation London and New York
C Mathematical and Physical Sciences D Behavioural and Social Sciences E Applied Sciences	Kluwer Academic Publishers Dordrecht, Boston and London
F Computer and Systems Sciences G Ecological Sciences H Cell Biology I Global Environmental Change	Springer-Verlag Berlin Heidelberg New York London Paris Tokyo Hong Kong Barcelona Budapest

NATO-PCO DATABASE

The electronic index to the NATO ASI Series provides full bibliographical references (with keywords and/or abstracts) to more than 30000 contributions from international scientists published in all sections of the NATO ASI Series. Access to the NATO-PCO DATABASE compiled by the NATO Publication Coordination Office is possible in two ways:

- via online FILE 128 (NATO-PCO DATABASE) hosted by ESRIN, Via Galileo Galilei, I-00044 Frascati, Italy.
- via CD-ROM "NATO-PCO DATABASE" with user-friendly retrieval software in English, French and German (© WTV GmbH and DATAWARE Technologies Inc. 1989).

The CD-ROM can be ordered through any member of the Board of Publishers or through NATO-PCO, Overijse, Belgium.

Series F: Computer and Systems Sciences Vol. 85

The ASI Series Books Published as a Result of Activities of the Special Programme on ADVANCED EDUCATIONAL TECHNOLOGY

This book contains the proceedings of a NATO Advanced Research Workshop held within the activities of the NATO Special Programme on Advanced Educational Technology, running from 1988 to 1993 under the auspices of the NATO Science Committee.

The books published so far as a result of the activities of the Special Programme are:

Vol. F67: Designing Hypermedia for Learning. Edited by D. H. Jonassen and H. Mandl. 1990.

Vol. F76: Multimedia Interface Design in Education. Edited by A. D. N. Edwards and S. Holland. 1992.

Vol. F78: Integrating Advanced Technology into Technology Education. Edited by M. Hacker, A. Gordon, and M. de Vries. 1991.

Vol. F80: Intelligent Tutoring Systems for Foreign Language Learning. The Bridge to International Communication. Edited by M. L. Swartz and M. Yazdani. 1992.

Vol. F81: Cognitive Tools for Learning. Edited by P. A. M. Kommers, D. H. Jonassen, and J. T. Mayes. 1992.

Vol. F84: Computer-Based Learning Environments and Problem Solving. Edited by E. De Corte, M. C. Linn, H. Mandl, and L. Verschaffel. 1992.

Vol. F85: Adaptive Learning Environments. Foundations and Frontiers. Edited by M. Jones and P. H. Winne. 1992.

Vol. F86: Intelligent Learning Environments and Knowledge Acquisition in Physics. Edited by A. Tiberghien and H. Mandl. VIII, 285 pages. 1992. *(AET)*

Adaptive Learning Environments

Foundations and Frontiers

Edited by

Marlene Jones

Advanced Computing and Engineering
Alberta Research Council
6815 8 St. N.E.
Calgary, Alberta
Canada T2E 7H7

Philip H. Winne

Faculty of Education
Simon Fraser University
Burnaby, British Columbia
Canada V5A 1S6

With the assistance of
Carol Tubman

Springer-Verlag
Berlin Heidelberg New York London Paris Tokyo
Hong Kong Barcelona Budapest
Published in cooperation with NATO Scientific Affairs Division

Proceedings of the NATO Advanced Study Institute on Syntheses of Instructional Science and Computing Science for Effective Instructional Computing Systems, held in Calgary, Canada, July 15–27, 1990.

ISBN-13:978-3-642-77514-7 e-ISBN-13:978-3-642-77512-3
DOI: 10.1007/978-3-642-77512-3

Softcover reprint of the hardcover 1st edition 1992

Typesetting: camera ready by authors

45/3140-543210 – Printed on acid-free-paper

Preface

During July 1990, a two-week Advanced Study Institute, "Syntheses of Instructional Science and Computing Science for Effective Instructional Computing Systems," was held at the University of Calgary. Approximately sixty-five researchers from Canada, the United States, the United Kingdom and Europe participated in the Institute. This book is an outgrowth of the presentations and discussions that took place at the Advanced Study Institute.

Adaptive Learning Environments can be viewed as the intersection of two traditionally distinct areas of research: instructional science and computational science. As such, Adaptive Learning Environments (ALEs), encompass Intelligent Tutoring Systems (ITSs), Interactive Learning Environments (ILEs), and Situated Learning Environments (SLEs). There have been recent significant advances within both fields (as illustrated by the chapters herein). There is increasing interest for effective instructional systems from several sectors: education, industry, military, and government. There is growing interest in the field from graduate students. All this is coupled with recent advances in hardware architecture and a reduction of hardware costs. The time is right to share resources, particularly our expertise and knowledge, and to define the next steps in research and development of Adaptive Learning Environments.

At the Advanced Study Institute, six broad topics were addressed:

- Systems and Architectures for Instruction
- Representing Curriculum and Designing Instructional Tasks
- Environments to Support Learning
- Diagnosing Students' Learning and Adjusting Plans for Instruction
- Models of Students' Metacognition, Motivation and Learning Strategies
- Student-System Interactions.

Each topic was addressed in several ways: lectures, working groups, plenary sessions, and synthesis.

The Institute was sponsored and funded by NATO's Advanced Educational Technology Programme, the Alberta Research Council, and Simon Fraser University.

We would like to acknowledge the efforts of many people in making the Institute a success: our co-organizers Peter Goodyear and Elliot Soloway; the speakers, synthesizers and participants; and the local arrangements team from the Alberta Research Council: Janet McCracken, Alice Grimsen, Kar-Ling Cheng, and Julia Driver. Two graduate students from the University of Saskatchewan handled many of the day-to-day tasks during the Institute: Carl Gutwin and Permanand Mohan.

In producing this volume, Carol Tubman handled much of the preparation and proofreading. Her hard work and perseverance are gratefully acknowledged. Additional proofreading assistance provided by Mary Mark and Nancy Perry is greatly appreciated.

Marlene Jones

Philip H. Winne

Table of Contents

Introduction

Introduction

Marlene Jones

Advanced Computing and Engineering, Alberta Research Council, Calgary, Canada

This volume is the outgrowth of a two-week Advanced Study Institute, "Syntheses of Instructional Science and Computing Science for Effective Instructional Computing Systems," held at the University of Calgary in July 1990.

Adaptive Learning Environments can be viewed as the intersection of two traditionally distinct areas of research: instructional science and computational science. As such, Adaptive Learning Environments (ALEs)[1] encompass Intelligent Tutoring Systems (ITSs), Interactive Learning Environments (ILEs), and Situated Learning Environments (SLEs). Significant advances have been made recently within both instructional science and computational science (as illustrated by the chapters herein).

The goal of the Advanced Study Institute was to bring together researchers from the two fields of instructional and computational sciences whose work linked to or directly addressed the field of Adaptive Learning Environments, and to spend two weeks building bridges to join the two research areas. These bridges consist of learning about each field's current research paradigms and goals, as well as defining threads or themes within six particular topics of interest to both fields. It is the belief of the Institute organizers that future research gains will be more easily achieved through the coordination of research efforts across these two fields. Coordinated efforts should see the merging of ideas and the development of more effective instructional systems as well as the breaking of further research ground.

At the Advanced Study Institute, six broad topics were addressed:

- Systems and Architectures for Instruction
- Representing Curriculum and Designing Instructional Tasks
- Environments to Support Learning
- Diagnosing Students' Learning and Adjusting Plans for Instruction

[1] The acronym ALE is copyrighted by Peter Goodyear and Helen Pain, 1990.

NATO ASI Series, Vol. F 85
Adaptive Learning Environments
Edited by M. Jones and P. H. Winne

- Models of Students' Metacognition, Motivation and Learning Strategies
- Student-System Interactions.

Each topic was addressed in several ways: lectures, working groups, plenary sessions, and synthesis. Lecturers were explicitly paired so that each topic was presented from two perspectives: instructional science and computational science. In addition, each lecturer presented issues for further discussion within small working groups. Each working group then presented the results of their discussions in a plenary session. The task of synthesizing the discussions of each week fell to Benedict du Boulay and Peter Goodyear, and Ellen Mandinach and Jim Greer. Synthesizers from the two fields of instructional science and computational science were teamed to capture the two perspectives.

The format of the book mirrors that of the Institute. The first six parts correspond to the six broad topic areas. Each part contains two chapters, authored by the two Institute lecturers and their colleagues. Each part contains an introduction to the two chapters written by one of the teams of synthesizers. The seventh and final part of the book contains a chapter which captures much of the debate that took place at the Institute.

Throughout this book several terms are employed to denote sophisticated instructional systems which are built employing techniques from both computational science and instructional science. We employ the term Adaptive Learning Environments (ALEs) in the title of the book, throughout the introductory chapter, and throughout the final chapter. We have chosen not to edit the terminology employed by the books' other contributors. Their terminology includes the terms Intelligent Tutoring Systems (ITSs), Interactive Learning Environments (ILEs), and the umbrella term Instructional Computing Systems (ICSs).

Overview of the Chapters

As mentioned earlier, the book consists of seven parts, each of which is briefly described here.

Systems and Architectures for Instruction. The two chapters in this first part of the book are by Thomas Shuell and Stellan Ohlsson. Shuell's paper, "Designing Instructional Computing Systems for Meaningful Learning," is an excellent paper for computational scientists working in this area. Shuell reminds us that the goal of every instructional system is to facilitate student learning. Hence, it is important to understand how students learn, the relationships between instruction and learning, and means for incorporating this knowledge into ALEs. An apt warning, however, is that it is easy to oversimplify the relevant processes of learning when faced with incorporating such principles into an ALE.

Shuell also reminds the reader that every instructional system embodies a model of learning. Unfortunately, too often such models are implicit, based on opinion, or adopted with little awareness of their validity or consideration of the psychological literature. Shuell's chapter provides a starting point for reasoned consideration of the research literature. He proposes twelve learning functions that are necessary for meaningful learning. These functions can be initiated either by the instructional agent (e.g., the ALE) or by the learner, and can be performed in a variety of equally valid and effective ways.

The latter part of Shuell's chapter is a preliminary discussion of how the proposed principles of learning can be incorporated in developing ALEs. The Institute's participants would agree that the research community needs to foster further discussions along such lines. A goal should be to develop ALEs which are pedagogically sound; they must be based on our best understanding of how students learn from instruction.

Stellan Ohlsson's chapter, "Artificial Intelligence: A Method for Relating Learning Theory to Instructional Design," nicely complements that of Shuell. Rather than examining general principles of learning, Ohlsson puts forward a method for evaluating the cognitive complexity of different instructional strategies. The approach involves the development of runnable simulation models of learning. These simulation models can be taught a particular concept and the resulting learning processes can be examined. This provides the teacher or ALE developer with a technique for comparing different teaching methods. The assumption is that the method which is learned most easily will be then employed for instructing students. The example Ohlsson employs in his chapter is teaching subtraction.

This approach of teachable simulation models provides the research community with a tool for linking learning theory to instructional decisions. This is just one example of the many tools needed in order to facilitate decisions regarding instructional system design.

Representing Curriculum and Designing Instructional Tasks. Chapters by Gordon McCalla and Roger Hartley address the notion of curriculum from different aspects. McCalla starts with a traditional definition of curriculum as, "the selection and sequencing of material for purposes of instruction," and expands this to a more appropriate definition for ALEs: "Curriculum is the selection and sequencing of knowledge for the purposes of achieving instructional goals appropriate to the current context and the individual being tutored." The latter definition captures the dynamic aspect of curriculum, placing emphasis on knowledge rather than material, on the individual student, and on the current context of learning.

McCalla documents the evolution of the notion of curriculum within ALEs, evolving from an externally imposed syllabus to knowledge about which the systems reason. But curriculum is more pervasive within ALEs than that. Curriculum is not an isolated component. Rather it arises from interactions from among several system components, and is intimately tied to the pedagogical decision-making of instructional planning.

Hartley's view of curriculum encompasses delivery as well as selecting and sequencing of instruction. Curriculum is both the plan designed for a learner to allow for achievement of particular goals, and the instructional tasks to ensure delivery of the goals. The instructional tasks provide a framework for the instructional tactics to be employed. Hartley goes one step further in stating that the learner must be an equal participant in the interactions. The learner must have the ability to negotiate over the curriculum. Hartley employs the EUROHELP system as an example of how this can be achieved, admitting to the difficulty of accomplishing all this within a computer-based system.

Both chapters emphasize the dynamic nature of curriculum, the need for curriculum to be individualized, and illustrate how to incorporate pedagogical decision making within ALEs. Yet the authors differ in their treatment of student models. McCalla feels that student modelling is crucial to the notion of curriculum in order to accomplish the individualization that is required. In contrast, Hartley believes we can eliminate the student model through the use of Dialog Game (DG) theory. He states, "DG provides a framework for representing, planning, and controlling educational interactions in ways which permit initiatives from the student but in a restricted form that is more computationally tractable."

Environments to Support Learning. The two chapters in this part are based on presentations made by Patrick Dickson and Elliot Soloway at the Advanced Study Institute. The chapter by Dickson and colleagues, "Exploratory Multi-Media Environments," discusses their efforts to build computer-based exploratory environments.

The work has grown out of Dickson's interest in museums and his examination of which museums and exhibits attract attention from visitors, particularly young visitors. In recent years museums have become increasingly "hands-on" and interactive. Unlike classrooms, within museums there is learner choice; hence, uninteresting activities in museums are neglected. By examining what visitors choose to explore and how, Dickson and his colleagues have gained insights which they are applying to the development of their exploratory environments.

The philosophy underlying their systems is that motivation and curiosity are central educational objectives. This differs from the more typical philosophy that motivation and curiosity are enabling factors which are important only in that they facilitate the learning of the specified subject matter. Such computer-based exploratory environments are an attempt to create enclaves in classrooms that allow children to go exploring without leaving the classroom.

The chapter also includes descriptions of particular environments that the authors have developed and a discussion of the authors' experience of placing their exploratory environments within a classroom setting.

The chapter by Elliot Soloway and colleagues is entitled "Technology Support for Learning and Doing of Design." In his presentation at the Advanced Study Institute, Soloway passionately argued that schools must change. He wants to see students who are both confident and passionate. Without passion for learning or a field of study, one simply has the accumulation of facts or knowledge, and this is not a sufficient educational goal. This belief has motivated Soloway's recent work and is reflected in his contribution to this book.

In their chapter, Soloway and colleagues argue that a major transition is happening in classrooms, from a more traditional didactic instructional approach to a constructivist, project-oriented approach. The underlying philosophy of the constructionist approach is that one learns by constructing some type of artifact. Hence, Soloway and his colleagues are exploring technology that provides learners with necessary supports to undertake such constructions. They have developed several Computer-Aided Design (CAD) systems in which learners can generate alternative designs, undertake comparisons, and engage in structured exploration. Soloway's group discusses the experience obtained while designing and developing such systems. In particular, they examine the demands of two types of students' activities, learning and doing design, and the implications of each.

Diagnosing Students' Learning and Adjusting Plans for Instruction. The two chapters in this part are written by Beverly Woolf and Diana Laurillard. Woolf's chapter, "Towards a Computational Model of Tutoring," addresses the central theme of the Institute, namely the successful symbiosis of instructional science and computational science. The two key issues discussed by Woolf are:

- the need to identify and articulate elements of cognitive principles for use in computational models
- how the process of building ALEs might be clarified to facilitate the participation of instructional designers in the development of such systems.

Woolf stresses the need to provide appropriate tools for developing ALEs: tools that are appropriate for use by instructional designers, curriculum developers, and computer scientists. She advocates the development of tools that facilitate identifying and representing tutoring knowledge, and tools that allow for a variety of system components, teaching styles, and intervention strategies. She draws on the research of herself and colleagues to illustrate the power of this approach to instructional system development.

Laurillard's chapter describes a research paradigm unfamiliar to many computational scientists: phenomenographic research. The premise of this paradigm is that learning and context should *not* be decoupled. Rather, researchers need a methodology that examines the way phenomena are experienced or learned. In brief, the methodology involves the generation of questions to probe a selection of students' understanding of the given topic, interviewing students, sorting protocols into categories, and refining the categories. The process is illustrated in the chapter which includes an example of employing the phenomenographic approach to capture and diagnose students' understanding of Newton's Third Law.

The power of the phenomenographic approach lies in the ability to develop diagnostic strategies and student models for ALEs. Laurillard argued at the Institute that resulting categorizations are sufficiently complete to provide the developer with an understanding of the underlying conceptions that students have. The strength of the approach comes from its focus on one concept at a time in situ, rather than learning in general. It provides a means of examining how the learner is thinking about a specified concept or phenomenon, and hence provides insight into how to teach that concept. The description is at a level one can exploit: the level at which instruction should occur.

Models of Students' Metacognition, Motivation and Learning Strategies. This section contains chapters by Sharon Derry and Pierre Dillenbourg. Both authors stress the importance of metacognitive skills; convincing arguments are contained in the opening remarks of each chapter. Derry also effectively illustrates the cost of metacognitive failures with what are unfortunately every day examples.

The chapter authored by Derry stresses the need to design more sophisticated metacognitive intelligence into cognitive systems, including the cognitive systems within children and ourselves, as well as the large corporate cognitive systems such as the post office. Metacognition has two important aspects: a system's — learner or ALE — intelligence about itself, and the system's ability to regulate and control its own operation.

The chapter examines two models of interactive learning which emphasize metacognitive intelligence: a neo-Piagetian model and a model based on Vygotskian psychology. In the former, the student is characterized as a "reflective explorer." The latter stresses the importance of mentoring, placing the student in the role of a cognitive apprentice who gradually assumes increased responsibility for problem-solving.

A large portion of the chapter describes the "artificially-intelligent" cognitive mentorship system, TAPS, which is based on the Vygotskian approach to promoting metacognitive intelligence.

Like Derry, Dillenbourg examines means for designing ALEs that facilitate the student's acquisition of metacognitive skills. He strives to transfer increased control in the problem-solving process to the learner. To illustrate his intentions, Dillenbourg applies a pyramid metaphor to the design of ALEs. The pyramid consists of a small number of distinct levels depending upon the domain, with transition from the current level to the next higher level representing the learner's internalization of metacognitive concepts at the current level. The goal is to achieve the highest level. As the learner moves up the pyramid, acquiring new metacognitive skills, the ALE needs to encourage the use of such skills. Hence, the ALE must provide new problem solving tools to the learner at each level of the pyramid.

To answer the implicit question of how useful is the pyramid metaphor, Dillenbourg briefly discusses MEMOLAB, a learning environment in the area of experiment development, currently being developed to explore these ideas. He also relates this work to three existing ALEs: ALGEBRALAND, the GEOMETRY TUTOR, and Derry's TAPS system.

Student-System Interactions. The final pair of lectures at the Advanced Study Institute were presented by Stefano Cerri and Philip Winne. Although the two presented diverse aspects of student-system interactions, the chapters share a common theme: the need for appropriate tools for use by developers and researchers.

The chapter authored by Cerri and his colleagues focusses on the acquisition of student models within ALEs. He describes a prototypic knowledge acquisition system for developing formal representations of student misconceptions (bugs). As is typical of knowledge acquisition methodologies, the proposed methodology is iterative, a gradual process of refinement and extension.

One of the techniques employed is that of inverted dialogues. The dialogues are used to extend the set of student models, and to validate the models proposed by the system designer. The system relieves the expert of having to directly construct the student models.

Winne approaches the topic of student interactions and tools for research from a different perspective. Winne is concerned with developing an instructional environment which is both a research tool for instructional scientists and a learning environment for students. Winne puts forward a theory of cognition and draws on education literature for supporting evidence to develop a theory of instruction. This then becomes the underlying basis for a proposed learning environment.

From the learner's perspective, Winne's ALE is serving two purposes. The student is simultaneously studying knowledge of a subject matter domain, and knowledge of strategies for comprehension and recall. From the perspective of the researcher, the ALE is a tool for collecting further empirical data on topics such as feedback, motivation, and learning preferences, and so forth. The proposed system is a tool for bootstrapping instructional psychology research, providing a means for undertaking studies that previously would have been infeasible due to lack of resources. It allows a means of collecting data over time and at an appropriate grain size.

Synthesis. The final chapter, "Synthesizing Instructional and Computational Sciences," is authored by the four synthesizers — Benedict du Boulay, Peter Goodyear, Jim Greer and Ellen Mandinach — and me. The chapter tries to capture the essence of the debates that took place at the Advanced Study Institute. To do so, the chapter indicates why synthesis of two traditionally distinct research areas is a worthwhile goal, outlines some impediments to synthesis, and suggests that by addressing our differences we can begin to understand them and bridge them. A discussion follows, outlining several common themes that are interwoven through the Advanced Study Institute and this book: simplifying assumptions, the role of the learner, and a shift in perspective on pedagogical knowledge. The chapter contains a discussion of research and collaboration goals, and gives examples of steps we must take to achieve success. Two important steps are the development of tools to facilitate research and development, and the integration of ALEs within educational institutions. The chapter concludes with a brief discussion of the research and development associated with Adaptive Learning Environments viewed as a field of study.

Part 1

Systems and Architectures for Instruction

Systems and Architectures for Instruction

Peter Goodyear[1] and Benedict du Boulay[2]

[1]Department of Educational Research, Lancaster University, Lancaster, England
[2]School of Cognitive and Computing Sciences, University of Sussex, Falmer, Brighton, England

The papers by Stellan Ohlsson and Thomas Shuell epitomize the themes of the Calgary Institute and highlight the gulf yet to be traversed between an artificial intelligence approach (as practiced by a highly competent psychologist) and an educational approach (as exemplified by a highly technically literate psychologist). Like Winne [this volume], Ohlsson is seeking to find a principled way to derive effective instructional behaviour from a descriptive theory of learning. His methods are, however, very different from those of an educationalist.

Ohlsson asks us to evaluate two claims. He proposes a general method for resolving specific instructional design questions by testing alternative instructional methods on a runnable computer simulation model of learning. He exemplifies the method through tests of four types of instruction in the skill of subtraction (using augmentation and regrouping, either "mechanically" or with conceptual understanding). As a result of these tests, he claims that learning regrouping is more difficult than learning augmentation and that learning subtraction conceptually is more difficult than learning it mechanically, an outcome which contradicts the orthodox line in maths education, at least in the U.S.

Of course, we must not be simple-minded about the relationship between these two claims. Our view on the success of the specific example necessarily underdetermines our appraisal of the general method, and it is surely the latter which is more significant. Nevertheless, the example is open to some criticisms, which can, in fact, be turned on the method itself.

At the heart of the matter is the contention that "learning mechanically" is less computationally complex, less cognitively demanding, than "learning with conceptual understanding." Ohlsson presents an elegant, precise and penetrating account of what can be discovered by rendering this question in computationally tractable form. The operational definitions of "learning with and without conceptual understanding" are implemented in his HS learning system. Various measures of the computational behaviour of HS allow comparative judgements to be made about the demands of the four instructional treatments. The greater demands of "learning with conceptual understanding" are clearly shown.

But this is not an experiment in the relative efficiency of machine learning methods. The purpose is to use the data from this experiment in "artificial instruction" to answer a question about instructional design: how should we teach subtraction to human beings? In attending to the underlying assumption about the transferability of results from the artificial to the human,

NATO ASI Series, Vol. F 85
Adaptive Learning Environments
Edited by M. Jones and P. H. Winne

Ohlsson gives an outline defence against the charge that HS might be an inaccurate model of human learning. There is one crucial way in which it is inaccurate, through omission, that Ohlsson does not mention. This can be put most clearly as a question: how plausible is it to conceive of human beings engaging in meaningless learning?

We have many reasons for seeing the learner as an inveterate meaning-maker, as an active participant in the educational process. Winne speaks of "the learner as artisan." But the point is stronger than merely acknowledging that new learning must be brought into relation with existing (declarative) knowledge. We have many accounts of the importance of the learner's interpretation of the learning task as a key element in determining the learning processes they engage in, and the outcomes of their learning. From problem-solving studies, we know that the learning of procedures (such as those necessary to operate an unfamiliar device) is accompanied by spontaneous generation of mental models, however bizarre and fragmentary, of the device, [e.g., 4]. It should be contended, then, that learners being taught "mechanical" methods of subtraction spontaneously generate their own meanings for the tasks they are being asked to do. More accurately, it would be unreasonable to assume that they do not. Such meanings may include "myths" that make some sense of the operations required in "borrowing." Others may be attempts to make sense of the activity of subtraction (as something that takes place in the outside world). Others may be transient or volatile accompaniments to blocks or failures in carrying out a part-mastered procedure [cf 3].

Now if this is the case — if "meaningless learning" is not an activity in which people engage — then the comparison Ohlsson is asking us to make is not between "meaningful" and "mechanical" but between "teacher-provided" and "learner-invented" meanings. And there are all sorts of speculations it would be reasonable to make about the relative cognitive cost of inventing one's own meanings.

A second issue concerns the *content* of the conceptual understanding with which HS is provided. When engaged in "conceptual", rather than "mechanical" learning, HS uses some instructor-provided mathematical principles. Ohlsson makes the useful distinction between such principles of mathematics (e.g., the associative law) and the principles that underlie particular algorithms. He rightly observes that mathematical principles underdetermine mathematical action. But he doesn't explore its corollary — that HS could have been provided with other conceptual knowledge that *does* more closely determine or constrain action. For example, there should be no major difficulty in representing some of the conceptual basis for the relative efficiency in performance of the various (mathematically legitimate) subtraction methods.

In Winne's terms, the confusion is between "knowledge of" and "knowledge about" the domain of subtraction. More accurately, one could say that the domain itself has been unhelpfully defined — that it *should* centre on the activity of subtraction rather than on the mathematics of subtraction. There may also be differences between North American and other traditions of teaching arithmetic in that notions of "expediency" and algorithm efficiency are indeed regarded as legitimate parts of the domain of mathematics, even at Primary (Elementary School) level [e.g., 1].

Further experiments with HS would be valuable, especially if, having already learned how to do subtraction effectively, it were to be extended to deal with other areas of arithmetic. It is possible that the extra effort required to learn subtraction under certain conditions might well have later payoffs in easier learning of subsequent topics. Related to this (and the mechanical/meaningless distinction) is the further issue of motivation and sense in mathematics instruction. The debate about whether mechanical or conceptual instruction is more effective in teaching a procedure cannot be conducted as if the enterprise takes place in an educational vacuum. One of the issues concerns what Shuell calls expectations, motivation and attention. Now it may be possible to factor out some parts of these "learning functions" in a theoretical comparison of learning efficiencies, but it may not be possible to disregard their effect altogether.

Another of the problems of teaching a procedure mechanically (whatever its other virtues) is that it may offer the pupil a message about the wider purposes and content of (mathematics) education — namely that (mathematics) education is merely an accumulation of such arbitrary procedures, which have to be learned by rote. Such a message is damaging in terms of how the pupil may approach other parts of mathematics as well as for the pupil's self-image as a pupil. Of course, mechanical rote learning has a place, but the pupil needs to understand that place. Ohlsson's reference here to the spiral curriculum is spot on.

We have been rather critical of the specifics of Ohlsson's claim; what of his more general argument? If we are to take Cognitive Science seriously, Ohlsson must be right in his general enterprise. Maybe HS embodies (as yet) too simple a model of human cognition and maybe (as yet) the model of learning is psychologically underdeveloped. Nevertheless, conducting learning experiments on models of students has a strong future. In any case the work provokes focussed debate on exactly what HS lacks as a plausible model — a debate which helps to cross the divide between education and artificial intelligence methods. There are also possibilities in the approach for intelligent tutoring systems, in that such a system might dynamically conduct a similar experiment on its stored student model in order to determine its own best course of future action.

A significant motivation for Ohlsson's work is his belief that general principles of learning and instructional design (ID) give very little help in answering the specific questions that make up the bulk of the ID task (or the on-line decision-making tasks of an intelligent tutoring system). Shuell is more sanguine on this issue. Like Ohlsson, he is very concerned to use reliable knowledge about learning as a guide to instructional design. Also like Ohlsson, and unlike many psychologists, Shuell emphasizes the special character of *learning from instruction*. He admits, quite rightly, that the knowledge base on learning from instruction is a small subset of our knowledge about learning more generally. Our knowledge about learning from computers, and about learning from intelligent tutoring systems, are even smaller subsets. We find ourselves in a vicious circle. We would like our work in designing intelligent tutoring systems to be informed by relevant learning theory. And, as Shuell implicitly suggests, the most relevant learning theory will draw on learning with intelligent tutoring systems. There are few such systems around — at least in a state to be used with real learners. Our best option at the moment is a highly iterative design and implementation process, which allows rapid incremental testing and improvement of individual systems. But this seems a poor way to make a general advance. Consequently, there must be strong arguments for much greater involvement in well-designed empirical studies, using mock-ups and/or partial prototypes of intelligent tutoring systems.

Shuell sees a bridge between learning theory and instructional design consisting of "Learning Functions." These are psychological processes which are activated in the learner, either at their own initiative or in response to some action by an instructional agent. Examples of such processes are "comparison," "evaluation," "monitoring," and "integration." Shuell's psychological processes are worth comparing with those postulated by Winne. Each emphasizes the centrality of the *learner's* activity.

Shuell makes a crucial point that learning functions can be performed in different yet equally valid ways. Consequently, "there is no single 'best way' to provide instruction." The challenge is to design instruction, or equip an instructional agent, so that a number of alternate ways of initiating learning functions are available. This is refreshing to hear. The high price of implementing an intelligent tutoring system has led a number of researchers on the wild goose chase of optimized instruction. Asking "what's the best method of teaching x? (and can you prove it?)" should no longer be taken as a serious question. It is hard enough to generate a repertoire of acceptable teaching action for this to be a perfectly appropriate goal for pedagogic knowledge engineering.

Shuell is perhaps too sanguine about the implementation issue. He says that writing production systems for stimulating learning functions is not difficult. He cites Wasson's work as an example [2]. But nice and "state-of-the-art" though this work is, it still does not really get to the bottom of key issues such as motivation. It is not that intelligent tutoring systems researchers possess the technology but have failed to apply it; the difficulty is that theories at the right level of granularity do not yet exist ready for implementation.

It could be that Shuell underestimates the interpretive task faced by an instructional agent (a) in gauging the right conditions for an instructional action (such as suggesting a comparison), and (b) in instantiating an instructional action appropriate to the prevailing conditions. Such interpretation is likely to need some equivalent of Shuell's "implicit model of learning (which) resides in every instructional system." There are some significant advances still to be made in the intelligent tutoring system field before we have anything functionally equivalent to such a model.

References

1. Association of Teachers of Mathematics: *Notes on Mathematics in Primary Schools.* Cambridge: Cambridge University Press 1969
2. Brecht (Wasson), B.: Determining the Focus of Instruction: Content Planning for Intelligent Tutoring Systems, PhD Thesis, Dept. of Computational Science, University of Saskatchewan 1990
3. Payne, S & Squibb, H.: Algebra malrules and cognitive accounts of errors. *Cognitive Science,* 14, pp. 445-481 (1990)
4. Shrager, J & Klahr, D.: Instructionless learning about a complex device. *International Journal of Man-Machine Studies,* 25, pp. 153-189 (1986)

Designing Instructional Computing Systems for Meaningful Learning

Thomas J. Shuell

Department of Counselling & Educational Psychology, State University of New York at Buffalo, NY, USA

Abstract: The design of instructional computing systems is discussed within the context of current psychological theories of meaningful learning and teaching. It is suggested that twelve "learning functions" must be engaged by either the instructional agent or the student if effective learning is to occur and that each function can be elicited in a number of equally effective ways. Examples are provided of ways in which these learning functions can be incorporated into an instructional computing system, and the instructional design process as it relates to instructional computing is discussed.

Keywords: alternate instruction, assessment, attention, audience consideration, combination, comparison, encoding, evaluation, expectations, explicit implementation, feedback, field testing, hypothesis generation, implicit implementation, instructional design, instructional goal, integration, learning functions, meaningful learning, monitoring, motivation, prior knowledge, repetition, synthesis, understanding.

Introduction

There is little doubt that computers will change the way in which we live. They also will change the way in which education is conducted and, quite likely, the way in which we learn. Instructional computing, however, is in its infancy, and the exact nature of these changes remains hidden in the thick fog of the future. Who would have predicted in the early days of the automobile, for example, that this wonderful new machine would result in sprawling suburbs or change our courting and sexual practices?

Nevertheless, changes are likely to occur more gradually and encounter more resistance than some seem to think — i.e., they are likely to be more evolutionary than revolutionary. The wise use and wide-spread implementation of computer based instructional systems depend on

NATO ASI Series, Vol. F 85
Adaptive Learning Environments
Edited by M. Jones and P. H. Winne

many factors, including psychological and educational factors related to learning and cognition. Developers of intelligent tutoring systems (ITSs) are beginning to address issues related to learning [31], and a systematic consideration of how the rich psychological literature on human learning and teaching relates to instructional computing would appear to be a timely effort. This chapter represents a step in that direction by addressing some of the issues involved in designing instructional computing systems (ICSs) that possess educational and instructional validity.

The chapter consists of four main sections. The first section discusses current theories of cognitive learning and the role of learning in the design of ICSs. Included in this initial section — which provides a foundation for the subsequent sections — are a consideration of implicit models of learning that people have and a discussion of the nature of meaningful learning. The second section presents twelve "learning functions" that must be engaged if students are to learn from instruction. These functions, based on evidence presented in the preceding section, provide a useful set of guidelines for designing effective instruction, including the development of ITSs. The third section includes a general discussion of various issues related to the design of instructional computing systems which will facilitate student learning, while the fourth section addresses the instructional design process itself. A concluding section summarizes key points from the chapter and discusses some of the problems and issues that are encountered when a concern for student learning is incorporated into instructional computing systems.

The Primacy of Learning

The goal of every instructional system — whether live teacher, textbook, or computer — is to facilitate student learning. Thus, an understanding of how students learn, the relationship between teaching and learning, and various ways in which these concerns can be incorporated into the design of an ITS is essential if the resulting system is to be effective from an educational point of view.

But learning — especially learning from instruction — is not a simple phenomenon. A great deal is known about the complexities involved in the relevant processes, but it is easy to oversimplify them when faced with the difficult task of incorporating them into a computer system. For example, the notion that there are several different types of learning which result in different types of outcomes and require different instructional conditions is an old one [20], but one that is still relevant. The reality of different types of learning means that different kinds of ICSs and software design are required for achieving different types of outcomes (e.g., microworlds and didactic computer-aided instruction embody conditions suitable for different types of outcomes). Furthermore, not everyone learns in the same way, and there is not a single best way in which all students "should" learn. The learning process depends on the student's prior knowledge and the type of outcome that he or she is trying to achieve. In addition, learning from instruction involves metacognitive and affective processes as well as the cognitive processes that most commonly come to mind.

This section first considers several implicit models of learning frequently held by teachers and other individuals who design instruction. Next, some of the changes that have occurred in recent years with regard to psychological theories of learning will be explored, including a discussion of meaningful learning and how it can be assessed. Then, metacognitive and affective aspects of learning will be discussed. The section concludes with a discussion of different types of learning and knowledge.

Some Implicit Models of Learning

Every teacher, instructional designer, and developer of instructional software has an implicit model of learning. This model of learning influences the wide variety of instructional decisions that must be made with regard to the way in which new information is presented to the learner and the cognitive and affective processes thereby elicited. Thus, *an implicit model of learning resides in every instructional system.*

The difficulty with these implicit models of learning is twofold. They often are: (a) unconscious and implemented with little awareness of their validity for various types of instructional situations and (b) based more on opinion or philosophical belief than on a thoughtful consideration of the large body of psychological research (both theoretical and empirical) on student learning. Personal models of learning need to be examined and reflected upon within the context of relevant psychological research. In this way, the developer can have a conscious rationale for making the various decisions regarding the learning tasks presented to the student. The system is likely to be more effective if it is based on the best possible understanding of the teaching-learning process.

The following four implicit models are representative of those commonly encountered among teachers and developers. The brief description of each model is intended to encourage self-reflection; a detailed critique of each is beyond the scope of this chapter.

Passive reception. This model has been prevalent in education for so long that many individuals do not fully realize the extent to which it permeates our thinking about educational practices and instructional systems. In fact, it is so ingrained in our thinking that we often fail to recognize the many assumptions and implications related to the model. Although some would argue that this model represents a behaviourist approach to learning, such a characterization is not totally accurate, and in any case the model involves far more than a simple behavioural theory of learning. An image that may come to mind is of a student sitting in a classroom listening to a teacher or at a desk reading a book — an image of a mind waiting to be filled with the pre-existing knowledge of experts. A corollary of the model is a belief that knowledge is an entity that can be passed, more-or-less intact, from one individual to another. Consequently the teaching-learning process proceeds in a largely top-down, didactic manner with "teaching by telling" being the predominate mode of instruction.

Discovery. The discovery model of learning is virtually the converse of the passive reception model. According to this model, students learn little from didactic instruction, from being given pre-digested knowledge. Rather, it is essential that students "discover" knowledge and develop an understanding of it on their own. In the extreme case, virtually any exploration on the part of the student is permissible. Explicit intervention on the part of the teacher or instructional system is often viewed as inappropriate or counterproductive. Consequently, very little effort has been invested in developing a systematic understanding of ways in which instructional environments can best facilitate this type of learning. Developers of microworlds often subscribe to this model of learning to varying degrees.

Knowledge deficit and accrual. This model of learning is based on the notion that a person learns by gradually accruing an already existing body of knowledge (e.g., the one held by experts in the field) in something approximating a "brick-by-brick" manner. In applying this model, the student's current knowledge is assessed to determine what he or she currently knows (or doesn't know), and the missing knowledge is supplied. In certain ways, this model is similar to the passive reception model, but one important difference is that a number of individuals who appear to hold this model seem to ascribe to cognitive, even constructivist, models of learning. One notable characteristic of this model is that typically more emphasis is placed on the logical and discipline-based knowledge of experts than on the psychological nature of knowledge possessed by novices. In addition, there is usually little overt concern for the *learning process* itself (according to this model, learning consists of little more than the accumulation of knowledge and its associated understandings).

Guided construction. Guided construction represents the model most consistent with current cognitive theories of learning. According to this model, it is necessary for the learner to construct his or her own knowledge (often by a discovery-like process), but in contrast to the pure discovery model discussed previously, this model recognizes that instructional guidance facilitates the process of learning. For example, in their analysis of ALGEBRALAND and GEOMETRY tutor, Collins and Brown [12] make a case for the value of students floundering (learning by discovery) and reflecting on their pattern of responses, but they go on to note that:

> We need to create environments where ... the system helps students profit from this floundering by making it explicit and, if necessary, by having coaching systems highlight the floundering and help students discover or understand better metacognitive strategies grounded on their particular experience. (p. 9)

Other examples of ITSs based on a guided construction model of learning include SHERLOCK [28] and SMITHTOWN [50]. The specific way in which instructional guidance is provided varies from system to system, but in each case it is the instructional guidance that differentiates this model from the pure discovery model discussed previously. Although microworlds are often based on the strict discovery model, they can also be based on guided construction models, as is evident in the work of G. Fischer and others [16] on increasingly complex microworlds. For example, G. Fischer [16, p. 142] suggests the following ways of providing instructional support for the user:

1. A critic should "look" over a user's work and make suggestions for improvements.
2. A tutoring component (using some of our visualization techniques) can illustrate the advice given.
3. An explanation component can provide the rationale that leads to the improvement.

Cognitive Conceptions of Learning

For many decades, prevailing psychological theories viewed learning as something that happened to you — from the outside in, so to speak. The learner encounters a stimulus (perhaps presented by a teacher or other instructional agent), makes a response (perhaps elicited by the stimulus), and the consequences of the response (i.e., reinforcement) determine whether there is an increase (or decrease) in the likelihood that the learner will repeat the response. This view of learning is still around — as evident in the passive reception model discussed in the preceding section — but substantial changes have occurred in psychological conceptions of human learning, prompted largely by the advent of the cognitive sciences.

Today's cognitive theories have reversed this orientation, emphasizing that learning occurs from the inside out rather than the other way around. The importance of the learner's environment has not been excluded, but the emphasis has shifted from the pre-eminence of external factors to the pre-eminence of internal, cognitive factors. The prevailing metaphor is one of problem solving [1, 4, 49, 56]. These cognitive conceptions of learning stress that learning is an active, constructive, cumulative, self-regulated, and goal-oriented process in which the learner plays a critical role [22, 46, 47]. Let's examine each of these characteristics and their implications in a little more detail.

Learning is *active* in the sense that the learner must carry out various cognitive operations on newly encountered information in order for it to be acquired in a meaningful manner. Note that the emphasis is on cognitive activity rather than physical activity (learning-by-doing in the absence of mental reflection). When all is said and done, *the type of cognitive processing in which the learner engages is the single most important determiner of what he or she will learn* — more important by far than the activities of the teacher or instructional system with which the learner is interacting. This is not to say that the latter are not important. They are very important, for it is their job to insure that students are engaged with the instructional material in meaningful and appropriate ways.

Learning is *constructive* in the sense that every learner creates his or her own knowledge in a somewhat idiosyncratic manner. Knowledge is not an entity that is passed from one person (or instructional agent such as a textbook or ICS) to another (the learner). New information is perceived and interpreted in a more-or-less unique manner based on the learner's prior knowledge and other factors. In order for a person to retain simple information and understand complex material, the learner must elaborate the new information and relate it to other information (both his or her prior knowledge and other information in the collage of new material). Thus, meaningful learning involves more than simply reproducing material in essentially the same form in which it was presented, and due to the constructive nature of meaningful learning, no two students have exactly the same perception of the instructional situation or end up with exactly the same understanding of the material being acquired.

Learning does not occur on the proverbial "blank slate." Rather, all learning is *cumulative*, with new learning building upon and being influenced by the learner's prior knowledge. This prior knowledge is a major determiner of what and how much a student learns. A rolling snowball provides a good metaphor for the cumulative nature of learning, although in the case of prior knowledge the effect can either facilitate or inhibit new learning. One example of the potent influence that prior knowledge has upon learning is the large body of literature on the way in which prior conceptions (many of which are misconceptions) affect meaningful learning and the difficulty that is experienced in overcoming misconceptions [11, 39].

To say that meaningful learning is *self-regulated* recognizes the important role played by the learner in managing and controlling the learning process. As learning progresses, various decisions must be made regarding what the learner does next (e.g., rehearse a particular piece of information, relate one piece of information to another, or seek an answer to a question that just came to mind). In addition, it is important to monitor the learning process, with periodic checks being made of how well the student understands the material being learned. Traditional conceptions of instruction often depict the teacher as the one performing these activities, but cognitive theories of learning recognize the necessity for the student to perform them, perhaps with the assistance of the instructional agent. This self-regulation of the learning process is primarily a metacognitive activity related to the types of issues discussed by Derry and Dillenbourg [this volume], and is consistent with a problem-solving conception of learning. Emphasis on self-regulation and studying places a refreshingly different perspective on traditional concerns for didactic teaching, a perspective more aligned with cognitive conceptions of learning [14, 34, 43, 44].

Meaningful learning is most likely to be successful if it is *goal oriented* — i.e., if the learner is aware of the goal (at least in a general sense) toward which he or she is working and possesses expectations appropriate for attaining the desired outcome. There are many ways in which this goal orientation can be established and maintained. Pre-defined instructional objectives, such as those advocated by many instructional design theorists, are one — but certainly not the only — way in which appropriate goals and/or expectations can be established. In many instructional situations, it is more appropriate for students to develop and/or discover goals on their own. Note, however, that the current approach emphasizes the need for the *students* to formulate their own goals. Due to the constructive nature of learning, the mere statement of objectives or goals by the teacher (instructional agent) is not sufficient for effective learning to occur. Unless the learner adopts the objectives/goals as his or her own, they will have little, if any, impact on the learning process.

Other Considerations

Several other considerations are germane to a comprehensive understanding of current cognitive conceptions of meaningful learning. One such consideration is the extent to which learning is situational and culturally specific rather than a phenomenon that is largely independent of the specific domain and situation in which it occurs. It has been suggested, for example, that meaningful learning is situated in a particular cultural context (culture on a small, not large, scale), that knowledge evolves by being used in "authentic" activities [8], and that there are substantial differences between school learning and learning in the real world [e.g., 8, 37, 41, 58].

Some controversy and unresolved issues currently surround these ideas. For example: (a) What is the nature of knowledge if it resides in a particular situation or inter-personal interaction (does not some residue have to remain in the mind of each individual); (b) if all knowledge is situated, how is it possible for an individual to use it in a different situation; and (c) what is the relationship between mediated learning (in which students acquire knowledge already discovered by other individuals) and situated learning? Nevertheless, many of the ideas have been incorporated into the cognitive apprenticeship model, a model that has served as the theoretical base for several successful ITSs [8, 13, 23].

The cognitive apprenticeship model provides a fresh and useful way to think about certain aspects of meaningful learning from instruction. For example, Collins et al. [13] suggest a framework for designing learning environments in which students: (a) observe and model the desired performance in an environment similar to the ones in which the performance is to occur; (b) receive external support from a tutor or expert in the form of coaching and/or conceptual scaffolding; (c) experience the gradual fading of that support; (d) articulate and reflect upon the knowledge, reasoning, and problem-solving processes in the domain being studied; and (e) are forced to explore new ways in which the knowledge or skill can be used. The learning experience is sequenced with regard to: (a) increasing complexity, (b) increasing diversity, and (c) the acquisition of global before local skills.

What is "Meaningful" Learning?

Throughout this chapter, reference is made to meaningful learning. Some attempt must be made to define what is meant by "meaningful" and how meaningful learning differs from other kinds of learning. Generally speaking, meaningful learning is concerned more with understanding than with behavioral change, although *definitions* of learning by cognitive psychologists are remarkably similar to traditional definitions of learning [46]. However, there are considerable differences in the way cognitive psychologists talk about or *describe* the learning process. For example, John Seely Brown [7] offers a description of learning that I particularly like (note that the following is a *description* rather than a definition of learning in the strictest sense):

> Learning is much more an evolutionary, sense-making, experiential process of development than of simple acquisition.

It is difficult to define "understanding" in a rigorous sense, but certain characteristic features of the concept can be identified. For example, a body of knowledge must be structured or organized in order for it to be meaningful and therefore capable of being understood [46]. Most people would say that one cannot understand a phone number, although one can certainly learn, know, and remember one [32]. Thus, relationships among concepts and facts are an integral part of understanding a body of knowledge, and there are several ways in which understanding can be assessed [26]. For example, an individual can demonstrate that he or she understands something by: (a) paraphrasing it, (b) summarizing it, (c) answering questions about it, and/or (d) performing a transfer task. Soloway [this volume] talks about the need for the learner to design and construct an artifact. Although such a procedure is a good way to encourage and assess meaningful learning, it is also true that we can learn without producing an artifact.

In helping students to engage in meaningful learning, it is important to remember that the material must be meaningful to, or made meaningful by, the learner. It is easy for teachers and developers to think of meaningful learning in terms of the way in which material is presented to the learner — e.g., the instructional agent articulates and demonstrates how various facets of the material are interrelated, the use of organizational devices such a tree diagrams and matrices, or requiring students to paraphrase or summarize the material. However, it is possible for these instructional acts to be performed without any meaningful learning on the part of the students. In fact, it can be argued that meaningful learning can only be defined in terms of appropriate assessment (i.e., assessment that assesses understanding rather than rote recall) of what the students are acquiring.

Metacognitive and Affective Aspects of Learning

It is understandable that the cognitive sciences have focussed almost exclusively on cognitive processes and their role in learning and human behaviour. The equally important contributions of affective and/or motivational factors have either been ignored or studied as separate topics. In the real world of teaching and learning, however, cognitive processes do not operate in isolation; affective, motivational, and metacognitive factors occur simultaneously and interact with cognitive processes in significant ways [35, 38, 55]. (Since the Derry and Dillenbourg chapters in this volume deal extensively with the role of metacognition, the present discussion will focus on affective and motivational factors.)

Students function as whole individuals, and consequently they bring more than prior content knowledge and learning skills with them to a given learning task. For instance, a person sitting down at a terminal to work on a task has certain perceptions relevant to his or her performance on the task. These perceptions, which may or may not be consistent with more objective ones, include perceptions of what the task requires and his or her own personal needs, interests, and ability to complete the task. The person's evaluation of these perceptions of task and self determines the effort that he or she puts into the task and the manner in which the information is processed [35, 55]. An example of how important these non-cognitive factors can be is afforded by a study which indicates that interest can account for up to 30 times more variance in the recall of sentences than readability, a more traditional index of task difficulty [3].

Similarly, there is a large body of knowledge concerned with ways in which emotion influences cognitive functioning, although virtually all of it focusses on factors that have a negative effect on performance (e.g., text anxiety). It seems likely that emotions can interfere with some cognitive processes while enhancing others, but so far there have been extremely few attempts to analyze the psychological mechanisms that produce such effects [54, 55]. In this regard, however, there is some evidence that anxiety interferes with the learning process by impairing the students' organization and retrieval processes [36].

With regard to motivation, it is sometimes assumed, or so it appears, that working with computers is so intrinsically motivating that no special concern needs to be given to motivation in developing an ICS. Nothing could be further from the truth. Many individuals, of course, have experienced that totally "caught-up" feeling in which several hours of work with a computer have passed in what seems like a few minutes. But the experience is not inherent in the machine any more than our preoccupation with a novel or professional article is inherent in the book or journal we happen to be reading. For many users, the motivating characteristic of computers resides in either the novelty of computers (and novelty can wear off) or the fact that the user is engaged in solving a problem and is making reasonable progress toward that end. In the latter case, the locus of the motivation is clearly in the program or the task. If the user fails to make satisfactory progress toward reaching the desired goal, he or she is likely to give up in frustration in exactly the same way as would be the case with any other instructional medium. The interactive and visual nature of computers offers the potential for motivating students in new ways, but steps must be taken to capitalize upon that potential; it does not occur automatically.

For example, WEST [9] was constructed in accordance with specific principles of motivation. It was hypothesized that a decrement in motivation would be likely to occur if the learner experienced a series of failures. Thus, in order to avoid the feelings of punishment or boredom that might result from such failures, the play strategy and criteria for winning were changed every time a failure occurred. Other ways in which motivation can be incorporated into the design of an ITS will be discussed in the subsequent instructional design section of this chapter.

Lepper and Chabay [29, pp. 243-244] argue that "*motivational* components of tutoring strategies are as important as cognitive components, and more generally, that truly personalized instruction must be individualized along motivational as well as cognitive dimensions." Consideration must be given to affective components as well. One major challenge that faces us during the next decade is finding ways to *integrate* the cognitive, metacognitive, affective, and motivational factors responsible for effective learning into instruction. The planning and design of instructional systems must make provisions for engaging all four types of processes in a meaningful way.

Different Types of Learning and Knowledge

There is a tendency at times to think that there is only one type of learning or that all knowledge about a particular topic is the same. Unfortunately, we are faced with a more complex situation.

For example, cognitive psychologists make a distinction between procedural and propositional (or declarative) knowledge, and imagery/spatial knowledge could certainly be added to that list. Gagné [20] originally identified eight types of learning, and the well-known Bloom's taxonomy [5] implies six types of learning. Although there is considerable agreement that there is more than a single type of learning, there is little consensus on exactly how many types should be specified. For present purposes, it is sufficient for developers to be aware that there is more than one type of learning and that each type is served best by different environmental conditions and instructional procedures.

In a similar manner, it is worthwhile to realize that there is not a single body of knowledge about a particular topic. One aspect of this realization involves the difference between the logical type of knowledge typically associated with a given discipline and the psychological nature of knowledge held by learners. The two are not necessarily the same, and the latter as well as the former must be taken into account in designing instructional material and/or activities. In addition, knowledge resides in several different locations relevant to the teaching-learning process. While these bodies (notice the plural) of knowledge are related, each is different from the others in ways that are important for the planning of instructional experiences. In their discussion of scientific knowledge relevant to the teaching of science, Gilbert, Watts, and Osborne [21] identify five "locations" where such knowledge exists: (a) scientists' science, (b) curricular science, (c) teachers' science, (d) children's science, and (e) students' science. This taxonomy is the most complete I have encountered, and it appropriately represents the various sources of knowledge that should be considered in trying to understand how knowledge is represented in a school setting. These differences have important implications for curriculum planning and the way in which content is presented.

Learning Functions

In order for a student to learn from instruction, various psychological processes (e.g., attention, motivation, comparison) must occur in the learner. These learning functions provide a productive means of linking learning theory with instructional practices. They can be incorporated into ICSs both directly (e.g., incorporating them into the program as computational rules) and indirectly (e.g., designing programs and interfaces in ways that increase the likelihood that the various functions will be engaged), and both of these approaches will be discussed in a subsequent section of this chapter. The functions possess two characteristics that make them powerful yet flexible tools for planning experiences that will result in meaningful learning [47].

The first characteristic is that they can be performed in a number of *equally valid and effective* ways. Thus, there is no single "best" way to provide instruction. Although each function must be performed if meaningful learning from instruction is to occur in an effective manner, each may be accomplished in a variety of equally appropriate and effective ways. Depending on the specific instructional situation being considered (content being learned, type of students, etc.), attention, for example, can be accomplished in any of the following ways: highlighting that part of the display to which the learner should pay attention (by using a boldface or italic font, putting a border or circle around part of the display, etc.), animating part of the display, using a dynamic graph to plot algebraic coordinates, or presenting a verbal statement to notice some aspect of the material being presented. The important thing is *not how* the function was performed, *but whether* the learner paid attention to relevant aspects of the material being acquired.

The second characteristic is that the various functions can be initiated by either the instructional agent (teacher, textbook, computer, etc.) or by the student. This characteristic acknowledges the dynamic, interactive nature of the teaching-learning process. In designing an ITS (or any instructional computing system), the developer should insure that the various functions are performed in an appropriate manner. In the real world, however, people frequently find themselves in situations in which they must learn with less than optimal instructional support (such as those notorious instruction sheets provided with items warning that "some assembly is required," or in understanding a particular passage in a textbook or a novel, etc.). In these situations, the functions must be initiated by the learner if the outcome is to be accomplished. It is easy for teachers and instructional designers to become preoccupied with the teacher-initiated side of things and lose sight of the fact that students can become overly dependent on the instructional agent for initiating the learning functions. In such cases, students often fail to learn how they can initiate the functions on their own in those situations that require it. Thus, we have a responsibility to help students acquire appropriate ways of initiating the various functions on their own..

The following discussion suggests twelve learning functions, summarized in Table 1. These twelve functions are neither exhaustive nor mutually exclusive. They are suggested by the author on the basis of current theory and research on the teaching-learning process. Ways of incorporating learning functions into instructional computing systems will be discussed in the next major section of the chapter.

Expectations

Meaningful learning is most effective when the learner has some idea of what he or she is trying to accomplish. The anticipated outcome, however, does not have to be a set of pre-defined instructional objectives. In some instructional situations (e.g., when the concern is for inquiry

Function	Teacher Initiated	Learner Initiated
Expectations	Provide overview (map, diagram); statement of purpose	Identify purpose for using the program
Motivation	Opportunities for interaction; interesting material	Personal interest; look for ways to make personally relevant — make it a game
Prior Knowledge Activation	Remind learner of prerequisite information, etc.	Ask self what is already known about the topic
Attention	Highlights; animation; audio supplements	Identify key features; record notes
Encoding	Provide diagrams and/or multiple examples/contexts; suggest mnemonics, etc.	Generate mnemonics, images and/or multiple examples/contexts
Comparison	Encourage comparison with diagrams/charts/questions	Look for similarities; draw diagrams/charts
Hypothesis Generation	Encourage student to think of and try various alternative courses of action	Generate possible alternatives and corresponding solutions
Repetition	Guided practice and/or reflection; multiple perspectives/examples	Systematic reviews
Feedback	Provide instructionally relevant feedback and correctives	Seek answers to self-posed questions
Evaluation	Have next action by student based on an *evaluation* of the feedback received	Ask, "What do I currently know?" "What do I need to know?"
Monitoring	Check for understanding	Monitor performance; self testing
Combination, Integration, Synthesis	Provide ways to combine and integrate information — e.g., with graphics or multimedia	Establish categories; construct tables; seek higher-order relationships

Table 1: Examples of Ways in Which Learning Functions Can Be Engaged by the Instructional Agent and by the Learner

teaching or for the discovery learning inherent in microworlds), the instructional outcome is difficult or impossible for either the teacher or the student to identify ahead of time. In many instances — and not just those that involve discovery learning — the student's perception of the instructional goal evolves in significant ways as learning progresses. Thus, concern for developing appropriate expectations in the student does not end with the presentation of clearly defined objectives at the onset of an instructional unit. Rather, it continues throughout the learning process, and in some cases, it may be best to provide a statement of the instructor's goals/objectives later in the lesson rather than at the beginning.

It is also important to keep in mind that the active, constructive view of meaningful learning discussed earlier in this chapter suggests that it is the learner's objectives and goals — not those of the teacher — that actually influence the learning process. Obviously, it is the role of the instructional agent to help the student establish appropriate goals, but the stated goal of the teacher and the actual goal of the learner do not always correspond [2].

As noted earlier, meaningful learning involves affective as well as cognitive factors, and consequently, attention should be given to affective as well as cognitive expectations. Expectations having to do with a variety of affective factors play a critical role in determining what and how much the learner acquires as a result of the instructional experience. For example, the perceived difficulty of the task by the learner, as well as expectations regarding his or her ability to complete the task in a successful manner, influence the amount and type of effort that is invested in the task. Expectations regarding the extent to which the material/task will be interesting and/or relevant to his or her personal life also influence the activities in which the learner engages, thereby determining the type and amount of material that is acquired.

Appropriate expectations may be established through a variety of different techniques. For example, the instructional agent may provide: (a) an overview (e.g., an outline, either graphical or verbal, of what the student will encounter in working with the program); (b) a brief statement of the purpose for engaging in the instructional activity and/or the goal that the learner may reasonably expect to achieve or move toward; (c) a list of instructional objectives; or (d) a request for the learner to articulate (e.g., write down — either on paper or with a note-keeping utility incorporated into the ICS — his or her expectations (both cognitive and affective) regarding the instructional experience). These attempts to accomplish the expectation function can be initiated at any time during the lesson, and it may be desirable to provide them at various points in the program, not just at the beginning.

Motivation

Motivation is concerned, of course, with an individual's willingness to persist and contribute effort to the task in which he or she is engaged. This function is obviously related to expectations, especially the more affective aspects of expectations such as perceived interest and one's ability to complete the task successfully. In fact, three of the fifteen motivational techniques in teaching suggested by Gage and Berliner [19] (begin the lesson by giving students a reason to be motivated, tell students exactly what you want accomplished, and have students set short-term goals), although worded in a more rigid manner than I would prefer, are clearly concerned with establishing appropriate expectations. But incorporating motivational concerns into an ICS is neither as easy nor as automatic as it might appear. Instructional software can be as boring, especially after the novelty wears off, as it can be exciting. Specific ways of engaging this function will be discussed at greater length in the instructional design section of this chapter.

Prior Knowledge Activation

Meaningful learning is cumulative, with new learning building on prior knowledge. The typical learner knows a considerable amount that is relevant to the instructional task, but unless appropriate knowledge structures are in working memory (i.e., the relevant knowledge is available for use), the learner is unable to build upon or use that prior knowledge to his or her advantage in learning the new material. Thus, in order for learning to be efficient, steps need be taken to ensure that both cognitive and affective prerequisites (including the needs, goals, and everyday experiences of the learner) are available for use by the learner.

The initiation of this function might involve reminding the learner of information in a previous lesson — e.g., "Yesterday (or in the preceding lesson) we considered such-and-such; today we will use that information to solve a new kind of problem." Or, "what are some of the things you know/feel about (the topic to be addressed in the current lesson)." Although technology may not be currently available to handle open-ended queries such as the latter one on-line, it may prove beneficial, depending on the level and maturity of the students with which one is working, to use such prompts either as a basis for discussion prior to actual use of the ICS or as a prompt which *may be* sufficient for eliciting the desired knowledge. This learning function is important even with less structured ICSs such as microworlds, and careful consideration needs to be given to appropriate ways of initiating it.

Attention

In any situation giving rise to meaningful learning, so much information is available that it is impossible for the learner to attend to all of it. As a result, he or she attends to some of the information and ignores the rest. From an instructional point of view, however, the many pieces of information that are available differ greatly with regard to their relevance in helping the learner acquire the desired understandings. If the learner pays attention to irrelevant information, he or she may fail to achieve the desired instructional goal due to the acquisition of inappropriate material (e.g., the learner thinks an appropriate instructional goal has been achieved when such is not the case), lost opportunity (e.g., interest dwindles when the learner discovers that he or she is not making headway), or even increased difficulty in achieving the goal as a result of negative transfer from having acquired an inappropriate understanding that conflicts with the desired one.[1] Thus, it is important for the learner to pay attention to important features of the instructional task and to ignore features that are irrelevant.

The way in which this function is engaged will differ somewhat for different types of computer learning environments. In more didactic situations, for example, the developer often has a fairly clear idea of the relevant features to which the student should attend. In these situations, the instructional agent might highlight certain features (e.g., portions of a diagram or graphic display) of the material presented. Such highlighting could be accomplished by using lines of various widths, different colors and shades, or a host of other specific techniques.

In more open-ended situations, however, such as microworlds or the exploratorium described by Pat Dickson [this volume], other techniques for focussing attention are more appropriate. In these situations, initiation of the various learning functions is more the responsibility of the learner than the instructional agent, although some instructional intervention is usually desirable. Although some use of the highlighting techniques mentioned in the preceding paragraph may be appropriate, other techniques are likely to be more consistent with the instructional goals of these programs. For example, it may be appropriate, either on- or off-line, to ask the learner to indicate what he or she thinks are the key features to which attention should be paid, perhaps as part of a planning phase in which the learner plans for an up-coming instructional experience or as part of an intermediate or terminal phase during which the learner is asked to evaluate and critique the learning experience just completed. Information obtained from such inquiries could be used by the instructional agent to determine the progress being made by the learner and/or to plan future instructional interventions. In some settings, it may be appropriate to hold a group discussion among the students for the purpose of helping students to focus on appropriate features of the program, recognizing that in such open-ended situations there may be a variety of things deserving the students' attention.

Encoding

Encoding is the process by which information is prepared so that it can be manipulated in short-term or working memory. In most instances, encoding involves the addition of personal

---

[1] For example, the student might believe that the earth is flat as a result of always attending to the level horizon. A conception of the earth as spherical might have been more likely if he or she had paid attention to the fact that as an object (e.g., a ship) approaches the horizon, it not only gets smaller, but the lower half of the object gradually disappears in a progressive manner (as if the image was being erased from the bottom up). Having once acquired an incorrect conception, it may be considerably more difficult to learn the appropriate one.

meaning to the new information, such as when we look at a visual display and encode what we see as a car. The same information can be encoded in a variety of different ways — e.g., the visual display might be encoded by another person, or by the same individual under slightly different conditions, as a van, a bus, a sedan, or a limousine. Obviously, the way in which information is encoded has important consequences for the way in which it is subsequently processed.

Although an argument can be made for combining attention and encoding into one function, they are kept separate here on the premise that a person can attend to something without necessarily encoding it. Even if the information is encoded, it may not be encoded in a manner consistent with achieving the desired instructional goal. For example, if the visual display in the preceding paragraph is encoded as a limousine, the schema that is elicited (rich occupants, special occasion, etc.) may lead to different inferences than would have been the case if the display had been encoded as a van or a car. Thus, concern for the way in which information is encoded (i.e., the way in which knowledge is represented) has important implications for the planning of meaningful learning experiences.

Comparison

A potentially meaningful body of knowledge — including those associated with relatively unstructured instructional experiences such as microworlds — contains a network of interrelated facts and concepts. In order to acquire this body of knowledge in a manner that involves understanding rather than rote memorization, the learner must compare these facts and concepts in a search for similarities and differences that permit the formation of those higher-order relationships that comprise understanding. In order to accomplish this goal, the learner must make comparisons among: (a) different aspects of the material presented by the instructional agent, (b) information in the instructional material or experience and information that is part of the learner's prior knowledge, and (c) various aspects of the learner's prior knowledge as that prior knowledge is modified to accommodate new information in the instructional event. The instructional agent can elicit such comparisons by asking the learner to compare two or more pieces of information or visual displays, and then indicate the similarities and differences that are observed. This type of comparison could be done with an open-ended format, or the learner could be presented with a series of possible similarities and differences and then asked to indicate those which are an accurate description of the items being compared. Although the latter procedure is more structured than some developers might prefer, it does have certain advantages with regard to assessment and providing the learner with feedback.

Hypothesis Generation

The active, constructive nature of meaningful learning requires the learner to generate various hypotheses as he or she seeks a more adequate understanding of the material being learned. These hypotheses, for instance, might concern a particular way of relating or interpreting certain facts and concepts — e.g., a person reading (learning from) this chapter might hypothesize that "One way in which a learning function can be utilized in an ITS is to write a production system for its implementation." Such hypotheses set the stage for seeking and interpreting feedback (another learning function) that can lead the learner to either retain the understanding that is implicit in the hypothesis or to discard it in favor of a more viable alternative. The hypotheses generated by the learner represent tentative meanings that he or she places on the instructional task, and the confirmation or disconfirmation of these tentative meanings is a critical part of the learning process. Hypothesis generation plays a central role in VanLehn's [56] theory of impasse-driven learning, and it has also been incorporated into several ITSs, including SHERLOCK and SMITHTOWN [28, 51].

The generation of appropriate hypotheses can be accomplished in various ways. With regard to the example in the preceding paragraph, for instance, the instructional agent might pose the following question to the learner (in this case, most likely by means of an insertion in the text, by a live teacher, or by a peer reading the same material): "Identify at least one way in which learning functions can be used in the development of an ITS." This function might also be initiated by the reader (learner) who wonders about the same issue. In both cases, of course, the learner must actually generate an appropriate response (hypothesis) in order for learning to be facilitated.

Repetition

Seldom, if ever, is understanding of a complex, potentially meaningful body of knowledge achieved from a single exposure. In a statement that may seem counterintuitive to some, repetition is as necessary for meaningful learning as it is for simple learning, although there are differences of the type of repetition that is effective. It takes time, and multiple exposures, to find meaningful ways of relating the various parts of a complex body of knowledge. However, the type of repetition in which one engages is very important, for repetition can lead to the rote memorization of isolated pieces of information if one merely repeats the same thing over and over. Meaningful learning requires repetition in different ways — e.g., different contexts and examples, alternate ways of looking at the information being acquired, etc. Thus, in order for repetition to lead to understanding, the repetition must encourage the acquisition of relationships and alternative perspectives.

Feedback

Learners engaged in meaningful learning are continually testing hypotheses about various relationships, the accuracy of various statements, and alternate ways of accomplishing the instructional task and its sub-goals. In order for the learner to determine if he or she is on the right track, feedback must be received on the accuracy and/or appropriateness of what was done — either overtly or covertly — in testing the hypothesis. Without adequate feedback, learning will flounder, the student may become lost, inappropriate behaviour may be practiced, and the learner may give up in frustration.

Various types of feedback serve various purposes. In some cases, for example, simply being informed that an action, judgment, or hypothesis is correct or incorrect may be sufficient. However, in many situations involving meaningful learning, accuracy feedback alone may be inadequate — the learner may need to know *why* his or her response was correct or incorrect in order for the feedback to be useful. In order to be effective (useful to the learner) the feedback that is obtained must be instructionally relevant, which means that it must be of a nature that assists the learner in using the feedback to assist in the learning process — e.g., explanatory feedback rather than accuracy feedback when the learner does not understand why an action was incorrect. Although there is less empirical evidence than one might think regarding feedback in meaningful learning, several excellent discussions of ways in which feedback can be employed in the development of ICSs are available [17, 45].

Evaluation

Simply receiving appropriate feedback is not sufficient; the learner must interpret and evaluate the feedback and determine how it can best be used in the learning process. For example, does the feedback make sense to the learner? Does the learner consider the source of the feedback to be reliable? (The learner, after all, receives feedback from many sources, and sometimes the sources provide contradictory feedback — e.g., an ITS, a textbook, and/or another student's explanation.) The learner must also decide if the feedback actually addresses the concern, question, or skill that he or she is currently trying to learn. Receiving feedback is not a passive activity in meaningful learning.

The evaluation function could be initiated, for example, in an ITS by basing a step in the program on the learner's *evaluation* of feedback provided by the preceding step. The instructional agent could also ask the student to specify the extent to which certain information is useful for achieving a particular instructional goal; such an evaluation could be utilized in either an open-ended or a didactic computer learning environment. The learner could initiate this function by explicitly making judgements about the usefulness or relevance of reactions to his or her actions.

Monitoring

It has already been noted that meaningful learning is self-regulatory, and an effective learner keeps track of the progress being made toward achieving the instructional goal. The learner needs to be aware of what he or she does and does not know about the topic or skill being learned, the kind of additional information that is needed to understand a particular point, contradictory statements, etc. These types of metacognitive activities are discussed at greater length in the chapters by Derry and Dillenbourg.

Combination, Integration, Synthesis

As information is acquired, the more-or-less isolated pieces must be combined in ways that permit the learner to integrate and synthesize information from several sources. Meaningful learning, as already noted, involves a complex network of interrelated concepts, facts, and procedures. Consequently, the learner must engage in mental activities that serve to organize and integrate this material in meaningful ways.

One way in which the instructional agent can initiate this function is by the use of a device that demonstrates how the material might be organized — e.g., a matrix. The matrix could be presented in either a completed form or with only the rows and columns labeled and a request for the learner to fill in the cells. Graphics also provide a useful way of depicting the underlying structure of a topic. One way in which the learner can initiate this function is to consciously look for and try to articulate various higher-order relationships.

The Design of ICSs for Student Learning

A number of issues arise when one begins considering exactly how the principles of learning discussed in the two preceding sections can be incorporated into the design of instructional computing systems. It is far easier for us to focus on what we (developers and programmers) must do than it is to focus on what the learner needs to do, but the latter is of primary importance if our ICS is to be instructionally valid.

The situation is further complicated by the multiplistic nature of instructional computing. Clearly, not all instructional computing is the same. Computer-assisted instruction (CAI), intelligent tutoring systems, microworlds, databases, simulations, tutorials, utilities, and educational tools are among the different types of ICSs that can be readily identified. In addition, there are two fundamentally different approaches to instructional computing. On the one hand, there is the top-down, didactic approach evident in traditional CAI, complete with pre-defined objectives. On the other hand, there is the inductive, learning-by-discovery approach evident in many microworlds.

It is fruitless to argue which type of ICS or which approach is best, for each is best for accomplishing a different purpose. For example, didactic instruction is most appropriate for that aspect of instruction in which students need to acquire factual knowledge in a minimal amount of time. Exploration and discovery learning, on the other hand, are most appropriate for those situations in which the goal is to have students learn how to apply knowledge, develop higher-order relationships, and/or develop proficiency as independent learners.

The development of an ICS should be based on our best understanding of how students learn and the psychological processes that need to be engaged if learning is to occur. The learning functions and principles discussed in the preceding sections are applicable across a wide range of computer learning environments. The manner in which they operate varies greatly across this range, but their relevance remains constant. Prior to discussing two fundamentally different ways in which student learning can be utilized in developing ICSs, it may be helpful to consider some of the unique advantages of using computers for instruction. Since these characteristics represent the advantages of using computers rather than a different mode of instruction, an effort should be made to capitalize on these advantages whenever possible.

Advantages of Using Computers for Instruction

Much of the early instructional software was criticized for being little more than electronic page turners. Even today, when there are numerous examples of ICSs with extremely high instructional validity, it is easy to get caught up in the excitement of new hardware and to forget about the advantages and limitations of using computers (or any other instructional mode, including a live teacher) for instructional purposes. For those of us who tend to take computers for granted, it may be worthwhile to consider some of the capabilities of computers that provide strong advantages with regard to their use for instructional purposes. It might be healthy for developers of instructional software to continue asking themselves the following question: "What can computers do that books (which are cheaper and easier to carry around), or any other form of instruction (TV, videotape, etc.), cannot do just as effectively?" The answers to that question, along with the principles of learning discussed earlier, should provide a list of strengths on which the developer can capitalize. The following list provides several ways in which computers can be used to advantage in delivering instruction, and it is likely that others could be added to the list.

Visual displays and graphics. Computers have the capability to present various kinds of dynamic examples that would not be possible if the instructional agent had to depend on a chalkboard, diagrams, and/or handouts, etc. For example, objects can be rotated so that they can be viewed from various perspectives, chemical reactions can be stopped in mid-stream to observe the changes in slow motion, and plots or objects can be presented so that the learner can see the effect that different parameters have on the object or process in question (spreadsheets provide a useful analogy). Two caveats concerning visual displays are worth mentioning. First, we should remember that static diagrams and pictures are just as easily presented in books or by means of an overhead projector; careful consideration should be given to the rationale for using a large number of static diagrams in an ICS. Second, the visual display should be relevant to the instructional content of the program. I have seen many impressive (from a visual point of view) graphic presentations that had nothing, or very little, to do with the substantive material that the student was supposed to be learning. Such irrelevant presentations can distract the learner from the learning task and actually lead to a decrement in learning.

Feedback and record keeping. Computers are able to provide a wide range of immediate feedback to students on the adequacy and accuracy of their responses. In addition, they are able to keep a record of students' responses, the material to which they were exposed, and the feedback they received. Although in a linear or non-intelligent system, the latter two sources of data may be determined from the program, in an ITS such information is neither pre-determined nor automatically retrievable. Since all three sources of data can be useful to both the teacher and the student in monitoring the learning process, some provision should be made for making this information available for inspection after a particular lesson has been completed. However, since in many cases the raw data may be too extensive to interpret easily, some thought should be given as to how it can be summarized in a manner that is useful for the teacher and/or the learner, remembering that merely reporting the number of correct or incorrect answers is not very informative to either.

Exploration. A variety of computer learning environments from microworlds to an exploratorium permit students to explore and investigate various options, as well as offering an opportunity to experiment with the consequences of various actions. In the process, there are many opportunities for them to set their own goals for learning, generate relevant hypotheses, and receive feedback.[2] In some cases, ICSs provide opportunities for students to explore phenomena that would be impossible for them to explore without the simulation capability of computers; in other cases, computers merely facilitate the explorations that students theoretically could do on their own (e.g., by means of independent work in a library or laboratory). Although open-ended explorations are extremely valuable, it is my belief that the educational benefit of such experiences is greatly enhanced if they are accompanied by appropriate instructional intervention and structuring — e.g., discussions with the teacher and/or peers regarding such things as: (a) those features of the learning activity to which students might attend; (b) observations made by various students; and (c) what students feel they learned from engaging in the experience.

One-on-one individualization. Instructional computing systems are able to provide the kind of individualized instruction that is seldom possible in a normal educational environment. At least theoretically, the ICS can tailor the presentation to the prior knowledge of the individual, as well as to any learning strategy differences and personal preferences that might be appropriate. Without computers, such individualization is available only with highly skilled tutors. Even with computers, however, effective individualization of instruction is not easy to accomplish, for clearly more is involved than mere pacing of the curriculum or providing a smorgasbord of alternatives from which the learner can choose.

Networking. Students have long worked together on projects and assignments, although the encouragement of such cooperation has only recently become wide spread in standard classrooms. Computers offer a variety of networking capabilities, both within the local setting (classroom and school building) and, via telecommunications, with students, teachers, and other individuals throughout the world. The use of networking by ICSs provides an opportunity, especially when the networks stretch beyond the local level, that is totally new to education.

Direct manipulation and interaction. Use of computers in the instructional process can provide opportunities for the student to manipulate various objects and phenomenon in ways that frequently would not be possible with conventional instruction. In addition, ICSs are

---

[2] Students, however, do not always take advantage of these opportunities, either because they are not aware of them when they occur or do not know how to take advantage of them. More frequently than many people would like to acknowledge, students need both instruction and practice in order to make these experiences beneficial.

capable of engaging students in the dynamic, interactive exchanges suggested by most cognitive models of learning.

Access to common databases. Computers are able to search for and process information in multiple and idiosyncratic ways from a wide variety of databases that are rapidly becoming available. In some cases, conventional and already easily accessible databases such as encyclopedias — now available on CD ROM disks — can be searched far more effectively (not only more quickly, but also in ways that are not possible with a standard encyclopedia, e.g., with multiple key words). In other cases, databases that are less accessible, such as past issues of the *New York Times* and *Washington Post*, can be accessed by any student with telecommunication capabilities. Other databases — e.g., the complete collection of the National Gallery, with all accompanying information, currently available on interactive videodisc — are extremely difficult, if not impossible, for most people to access without the use of an ICS.

Focussing on specific parts of the material. Various aspects of the material being learned can easily be highlighted or magnified for special purposes in ways that might be difficult or impossible without the aid of a computer. For example, in a program concerned with art history, a particular part of several paintings could be magnified in order to compare how artists from two different schools use detail, coloring, or texture. In a similar manner, various parts of a diagram could be highlighted in different ways depending on factors such as the learner's past history, the number of times the diagram, or a similar one, had been presented, and so forth. Although such highlighting and focussing could be accomplished with conventional instruction, it would clearly be more difficult, if feasible at all.

Ways of Incorporating Learning Principles in ICSs

In developing an instructionally valid ICS, the system must be designed in a manner that elicits those psychological processes in the learner that will result in his or her acquisition of the desired instructional goal. The learning functions discussed earlier represent the processes that must be engaged in the learner, but the big question is how this task can be accomplished in a reasonable manner, taking into account those advantages of using computers just discussed. Before discussing the instructional design process, it may be helpful to examine the two ways in which principles of learning can be incorporated into an ICS: first, by writing explicit computation rules in the program itself; and second, by designing the presentation in a manner consistent with the principles.

Explicit implementation. Although it is not difficult to write production systems for most of the learning functions outlined earlier, the real challenge comes from how one might incorporate them into the overall architecture of a system. One example of how this might be accomplished is afforded by Barbara Wasson's [6] dissertation research on the Content Planner component of the SCENT-3 system developed at the University of Saskatchewan by McCalla and Greer [33]. The SCENT-3 architecture contains an Instructional Planner component consisting of a Content Planner and a Delivery Planner. The Content Planner devises a content plan that specifies the concept on which the system should focus during the next instructional interaction with the student. This content plan is then passed to the Delivery Planner which plans the actual instructional actions that will help the learner to engage in appropriate learning activities.

Each node in the content plan consists of an operator, a modifier, and a content. The content is the concept selected as the focal point of the instructional interaction, the modifier indicates the type of learning (fact, analysis, synthesis) appropriate for the concept in this lesson, and the operator specifies the reason for including the content in the plan — e.g., **focus** (put in context), **review** (go back over already acquired material in the belief that the concept is already known to the student) and **achieve** (plan to have the student learn a concept for the first time). It is with the operators that the learning functions can aid in providing more specific content plans for the Delivery Planner to use in planning specific learning situations for the student.

For example, the type of expectation that needs to be established is likely to vary, depending on the specific operator and modifier involved. Thus, if a student is to be presented a concept for the first time and the desired instructional goal involves learning factual information about the concept [operator = **achieve**; modifier = **fact**], then it may be desirable for the student to expect that he or she will be receiving information about a concept that has not been introduced previously and that only the acquisition of factual information will be assessed. However, if the ITS decides that an apparent misconception held by the student needs to be corrected and that he or she should conduct an analysis of the similarities and differences between the correct and incorrect conceptions [operator = **remediate**; modifier = **analysis**], then the student should be led to understand that the next series of interactions are directed toward eliminating the apparent misconception and that he or she will be expected to analyze the two concepts. Thus, a computational specification for the latter instance might set the top-level goal to [remediate analysis x] and the subgoal to [set expectations type b analysis x ...].

When the Delivery Planner encounters this node in the content plan during the process of planning the specific instructional actions that will be carried out by the system, decisions will be made as to the best way of initiating the appropriate type of expectations. For example, in the case of remediating a misconception, alternatives might include: (a) the presentation of a schematic or visual representation of the two concepts; (b) a matrix or diagram, perhaps presented initially in an incomplete form, of the similarities and differences between the misconception and the appropriate conception; or (c) a verbal statement on how misconceptions in general can be overcome. The architecture and operation of the Delivery Planner component of SCENT-3 remain to be worked out, and additional psychological research is needed to guide the decision making process, but hopefully this extended example will serve to show one way in which the various learning functions can be incorporated into an ITS.

Implicit implementation. In addition to the writing of specific computational rules, the various learning functions can be incorporated into an ICSs by the way in which various activities are carried out or the way in which displays are presented. Eliciting motivation, for example, is often a by-product of the way things are done, as in the case of WEST described earlier, rather than a result of specific computational rules in the program. Similarly, organizational processes may be elicited by the location of items in the visual display, and although a computational rule specifies where the items are placed on the screen, the psychological impact depends far more on the specific locations selected by the developer than the production system in which the rule resides. The development of an instructionally effective ICS must take into account this implicit use of learning principles.

The Instructional Design Process

There is extensive literature on instructional design [40, 42]. Unfortunately, much of it is based on behavioristic and receptive views of learning and a didactic view of teaching [48]. The present approach to instructional design (outlined in Table 2) is based on the cognitive theories of learning discussed earlier in this chapter. Although it is not inconsistent with traditional models of instructional design, the present approach is somewhat broader and more flexible. Although there is a certain logic to the sequence in which the steps are listed, in practice there can be considerable recursiveness as the activities associated with one step raise issues associated with other steps. Such recursiveness is a healthy part of the design process.

Identify Purpose and/or Goals

The first step in designing an instructional system is to identify the instructional goals that you hope to accomplish. Although general statements such as, "To teach quadratic equations" or

- Identify Purpose and/or Goals
- Consider the Audience/User
- Specify Instructional Procedures
    - Present the *knowledge* that is to be acquired
    - *Motivate* the learner
    - Engage those psychological *processes* necessary for learning to occur
- Assess Learner's Knowledge and Understanding
- Provide for Alternate Instruction
- Field Test with Real Students and Make Changes as Necessary

Table 2: The Instructional Design Process

"To teach students how to think logically" tend to be thought of first, such goals are of little value except for purposes of general planning. This type of statement has two main difficulties with regard to instructional design: it does not provide sufficient detail for implementing an instructional unit, and it focusses on the goal and activities of the instructional agent (i.e., teaching) rather than on the goal and activities of the student (i.e., learning). The specification and use of pre-defined objectives provide one way — but only one way — of addressing these difficulties, and their use involves both advantages and disadvantages [50]. Serious limitations exist with regard to the way in which instructional objectives have traditionally been used — most notably the top-down, teacher dominated approach to learning and the difficulty involved in specifying precise statements for higher level cognitive goals such as those involved in reasoning. However, many of the strong advocates against the use of instructional objectives fail to realize that the implementation of any but the most open and free instructional environment involves a fairly clear idea of what students are expected to accomplish, even if it is only, "I'll know it when I see it." The difference is that in the latter case the instructional goals are implicit, and it is more difficult to debate their relevance and communicate them to students.

Several things are involved in identifying the instructional goals and purpose of a program. One might begin by asking questions such as: "What would I like the student to be capable of doing at the completion of this instructional experience?" and "How will I, and the student, recognize whether or not these goals have been achieved?" With the responses to these questions in mind, the next step would be to carry out a cognitive task analysis of the desired student outcome, which should include an analysis of what is considered to be competent performance on the task [e.g., 10, 11, 24]. This task analysis would seek to identify the key components, sub-tasks, and prerequisites of the desired performance, as well as the relationship between the program and the way in which the learning experience fits into the curriculum.

Consideration of Audience/User

Wide ranges exist in the students for whom instructional computing systems are designed, and no one would expect, for instance, the same program to be ideally suited for both primary and university students. "Know your audience" has long been good advise for entertainers, speakers and teachers, and it is also good advice for developers of ICSs. It is extremely easy for one to assume too much about the student audiences for whom ICSs are developed. Even students who appear quite similar to the casual observer (e.g., 7th graders) possess characteristics and exhibit differences that influence the extent to which a particular instructional program is effective.

Some of the student characteristics that should be taken into account when developing an ICS include: (a) the prior knowledge, both formal and informal, of the target population of students who are likely to be using the program, including common misconceptions that they are likely to have; (b) relevant affective and motivational characteristics of students that are likely to affect their reaction to the program, including concerns such as their likes and dislikes for the topic being presented, personal interests they might have, and overall motivational level; and (c) the strategies that the target students are likely to use to process information and ways in which the students are likely to think. Some of this information can be drawn from the psychological literature, but developers also need to find ways of diagnosing relevant student characteristics and determining the range of knowledge that the students might exhibit.

Instructional Procedures

After instructional goals are established and consideration is given to the target audience, the next major concern is the way in which the instructional materials will be presented to the learner. This concern involves three separate but interrelated factors: (a) presenting the content necessary for the learner to achieve the desired instructional goal; (b) ensuring that the students are sufficiently motivated to participate meaningfully in the instructional activity; and (c) engaging those psychological processes in the student that are responsible for learning.

Presenting the content. Obviously, information relevant to the instructional goal must be presented. This information can be related to the desired outcome in one of two ways. First, the relationship can be a direct one in that the instructional goal, or some part of it, requires the student to learn the presented material in the form in which it is presented — e.g., that Russia is the largest producer of oil in the world, that quadratic equations are solved in a particular way, or that a particular work of literature or art is usually interpreted in a particular way. At other times, however, the student is not expected to learn the material itself. Rather, the information must be used by the student as a means of learning something else, perhaps through inference. This indirect relationship is especially evident in microworlds, but it also can occur in more didactic situations, especially when higher order thinking and problem solving are involved. With both direct and indirect relationships, a variety of curricular issues are involved — e.g., issues such as prerequisites and sequence must be considered [30].

Motivating the learner. In developing an instructional system, some attention must be paid to ensuring that the learner is appropriately motivated, although this factor is ignored in many theories of instructional design. As noted earlier in this chapter, the mere fact that students are working with computers rather than another instructional medium does not automatically guarantee that they will be motivated. The relationship between the development of appropriate expectations and student motivation has also been noted. In one of the few attempts to incorporate motivational concerns into the instructional design process, Keller [25] identifies four basic categories of motivational conditions that must be addressed. *Interest* is concerned with the extent to which the learner's curiosity is aroused and sustained; *relevance* refers to the extent to which the learner perceives that the instruction is linked to one or more of his or her important needs; *expectancy* refers to the learner's perceived likelihood of being successful and the extent to which that success is under his or her control; and *satisfaction* is concerned with the combination of extrinsic rewards and intrinsic motivation, and the extent to which they are compatible with learner's anticipations. Among the motivational techniques suggested by Gage and Berliner [19], the following (in addition to those discussed in the section on expectations) appear to have relevance for designing ICSs: (a) capitalize on the arousal value of suspense, discovery, curiosity, and exploration, (b) occasionally do the unexpected, (c) whet the appetite, (d) use familiar material for examples, (e) use unique and unexpected contexts when applying concepts and principles, (f) make students use what they have previously learned, and (g) use simulations and games.

Engaging learning processes. Knowledge building issues such as those discussed in the first paragraph often receive more attention in the development of ICSs than do concerns for the manner in which the learner is likely to process the information, even though the latter is equally important in determining what the student actually learns. As noted in the section on learning functions, various psychological processes need to be elicited in the learner in order for him or her to achieve the desired goals. A number of specific methods for accomplishing this task have been discussed in earlier sections of this chapter, and many other possibilities exist. The system, of course, must also be able to provide feedback to the learner on the adequacy of the responses that he or she makes in interacting with the system, a concern that is closely related with the concern for assessment addressed in the next section.

Assessing Learner's Knowledge and Understanding

The instructional process does not end with the presentation of material to be learned or a relevant instructional experience. Ways must be devised to assess the learner's performance (i.e., knowledge and understanding) as the learning process evolves. Such assessment serves two purposes: first, information obtained from the assessment can be used by the system to make decisions regarding the content and the process associated with the instructional experience provided. Second, the information can be fed back to the learner so that he or she is aware of the progress being made toward achieving the instructional goal. As noted previously, however, this feedback must be presented to the learner in a form that he or she will find useful for guiding the learning process.

Care must be taken that the items or tasks presented to the learner for purposes of assessment are consistent with the instructional outcome being assessed. Thus, if the instructional goal involves understanding rather than simple recall, the task that the learner is asked to perform must require a demonstration of understanding rather than recall in order to be answered correctly. A variety of test-question formats can be used to assess understanding, and several sets of criteria can aid in constructing appropriate items. For example, the characteristics associated with the concept of understanding discussed in the section on meaningful learning (i.e., paraphrasing, summarizing, answering questions, etc.) as well as the better known Bloom's taxonomy of educational objectives, can be used in this regard [5, 26].

Other concerns also need to be taken into account, including a variety of new assessment procedures and a growing concern for affective as well as cognitive aspects of instruction [53]. Instructional computing systems provide opportunities for assessment based on complete records of the learning episodes, and many new ideas are being discussed with regard to the fine-grain assessment of these records [27, 57]. In assessing student performance, concern should be given to the context of the educational system in which the assessment is being conducted [18].

Provide for Alternate Instruction

As the instructional program continues, information is received from the assessment component on the progress the learner is making toward achieving the instructional goal. If the student is not making reasonable progress, then additional instruction is indicated. However, simply having the learner repeat the same instructional program that he or she has just completed is seldom effective; after all, the first exposure has already proven unsuccessful [30]. Thus, the additional instruction must be different from the original in some meaningful way. Perhaps presenting the material from a different perspective would be helpful to the student, or using examples from a different context or source, or using a verbal rather than a visual display (or visa versa).

Alternate forms of instruction should also be available to accommodate various types of individual differences among learners. Although the search for reliable aptitude-treatment-interactions (ATIs, in which one type of student learns best with one type of instruction while a different type of student learns best with a different type of instruction) has been elusive, there is some evidence to support certain types of ATIs [15, 52]. For example, low-ability students tend to learn better when instructional support and structure are provided; high-ability students, on the other hand, tend to learn better when left to their own resources (i.e., little or no instructional support is provided) [52].

Field Test with Real Students and Make Changes as Necessary

Instructional computing systems are designed for the purpose of helping students to learn. Consequently, the instructional design process must include field testing with students from the actual target population for which the system is intended. Students often respond in a very different way from teachers and developers to an instructional presentation, and information on how students respond during all phases of a lesson is critical for the development of effective instructional software. This information should not merely include an end-of-unit achievement test, even though such tests provide useful information on how well students are learning from the current version of the instructional program, especially when compared to pre-test scores, scores obtained with an earlier version of the current program, and/or learning with other forms of instruction.

In addition, a range of information should be obtained on a variety of factors such as the extent to which the learners understand the requirements of the learning task and the perceived clarity of information being presented. This type of information can be extremely useful in modifying the way things are currently being done. For example, after many years of going over tests with students in my classes, I continue to be amazed by what must be acknowledged as legitimate ambiguities in certain items, items that in some cases have been used "successfully" for several years. Although these ambiguous items are small in number, they nevertheless are ambiguities that never would have become apparent without the students' input. Perceptions and perspectives of teachers/developers and students are different in ways that have important implications for the effective delivery of instruction. Thus, the design process is not complete until the field testing has been satisfactorily completed.

Conclusions

The impact of instructional computing will be wide spread, for it will change the way in which we learn and the way in which education is conducted. This change, however, is likely to be far more gradual than some pundits would like us to believe, but it will come. During the next decade, the computational power of our machines will increase substantially, but the fundamental challenge for the field does not reside in the capacity of the hardware. The fundamental challenge resides in our understanding of how that power can be best used for instructional purposes.

If instructional computing systems are to be educationally valid, they must be based on our best understanding of how students learn from instruction. This chapter has discussed some of the ways in which current psychological theories of teaching and learning are relevant to the development of effective ICSs. But the teaching-learning process is complex, and the instructional design process is not always straightforward. In many cases, principles of teaching and learning can be incorporated into an ICS by the writing of explicit computational rules. At other times, however, the principles are reflected in the way something is performed (e.g., the manner in which the display is arranged) — that is, the principles reside in the way the rules are implemented rather than in the rules themselves.

Given this complexity, it may be asking too much to expect that sufficient expertise will reside within a single individual, that is, to expect a developer to be an expert in both computational science and instructional psychology. One way of ensuring that the full expertise of both fields is brought to bear on the development of an ICS is to encourage more team efforts in which computational scientists and instructional psychologists work together on developmental projects. It may even be advisable to expand the team by adding other individuals with relevant expertise (e.g., teachers who will be using the final product).

Another relevant issue has to do with the way students learn from computers. The way in which we learn depends on the technology at hand (e.g., stories, lectures, textbooks). As the nature of the task changes, the way in which we learn also changes. Several hundred years ago, for example, stained glass windows were used to tell stories, teach lessons, and convey information. Prior to the invention of the printing press, people typically learned by listening to sermons, lectures, and stories. The advent of printed materials required a new set of intellectual skills that moved us from oral to printed-word modes of learning. Books put different demands on the learner and required new ways of processing information. Computers are likely to do the same, although it is too early to know the exact way in which this new set of learning skills will differ from current ones. Learning theories will certainly evolve as these new skills become more evident, although older skills (e.g., listening and reading) are likely to remain important in their own right.

A number of problems will be encountered as we face the challenge of developing effective ICSs. Among the problems likely to arise are the following issues associated with concerns addressed in this chapter:

1. How can we tell if students are learning anything worthwhile from a particular computer-based experience? What are some viable ways of assessing the extent to which the learner has achieved both intermediate and terminal goals? [Note: More than "number correct" is needed.]
2. What kind of computer learning experiences are best suited for different types of instructional outcomes and/or situations?
3. How can we help students to manage the learning process in the face of so much information? — e.g., establish priorities, decide what information to obtain next, etc.
4. How can affective and emotional considerations (including issues such as self-efficacy, relevance to student's life, interest in social relevance of topic, etc.) be incorporated into an ICS?
5. What is the role of instructional computing with regard to other forms of instruction, including a live teacher?
6. How can instructional computing take the learning needs of students into account? — e.g., the ability to take notes on-line.

The manner in which these and similar issues are resolved will determine the value of instructional computing for years to come.

Acknowledgements

The author wishes to thank Susanne Lajoie for her helpful comments on an earlier draft of this chapter. The author also wishes to gratefully acknowledge the collaboration of Barbara Wasson in the writing of the section, *Ways of Incorporating Learning Principles in ICSs*.

References

1. Anderson, J. R.: Skill acquisition: Compilation of weak-method problem solutions. *Psychological Review*, 94, pp. 192-210 (1987)
2. Anderson, L. M., Brubaker, N. L., Alleman-Brooks, J., & Duffy, G. G.: A qualitative study of seatwork in first-grade classrooms. *Elementary School Journal*, 86, pp. 123-140 (1985)
3. Anderson, R. C., Shirey, L. L., Wilson, P. T., & Fielding, L. G.: Interestingness of children's reading material. In: *Aptitude, learning, and instruction (Vol. 3): Conative and affective process analysis* (R. E. Snow, & M. J. Farr, eds.). Hillsdale, NJ: Lawrence Erlbaum Associates 1987
4. Bereiter, C.: The role of an educational learning theory: Explaining difficult learning. In: *Toward a unified approach to learning as a multi-source phenomenon* (W. J. McKeachie, chair). Symposium conducted at the meeting of the American Educational Research Association, San Francisco, March 1989
5. Bloom, B. S.(ed.): *Taxonomy of educational objectives, Handbook I. Cognitive domain.* New York: Longmans, Green 1956
6. Brecht (Wasson), B. J.: Determining the focus of instruction: Content planning for intelligent tutoring systems. Unpublished doctoral dissertation, University of Saskatchewan, Saskatoon 1990
7. Brown, J. S.: Toward a new epistemology for learning. In: *Intelligent tutoring systems at the crossroads of AI and education* (C. Frasson, & J. Gauthier, eds.). Norwood, NJ: Ablex 1990
8. Brown, J. S., Collins, A., & Duguid P.: Situated cognition and the culture of learning. *Educational Researcher*, 18, pp. 32-42 (1989)
9. Burton, R. R., & Brown, J. S.: An investigation of computer coaching for informal learning activities. In: *Intelligent tutoring systems* (D. Sleeman, & J. S. Brown, eds.). Orlando, FL: Academic Press 1978
10. Carpenter, T. P., Moser, J. M., & Romberg, T. A. (eds.): *Addition and subtraction: A cognitive perspective.* Hillsdale, NJ: Lawrence Erlbaum Associates 1982
11. Champagne, A. B., Klopfer, L. E., & Gunstone, R. F.: Cognitive research and the design of science instruction. *Educational Psychologist*, 17, pp. 31-53 (1982)
12. Collins, A., & Brown, J. S.: The computer as a tool for learning through reflection. In: *Learning issues for intelligent tutoring systems* (H. Mandl, & A. Lesgold, eds.). New York: Springer-Verlag 1988
13. Collins, A., Brown, J. S., & Newman, S. E.: Cognitive apprenticeship: Teaching the crafts of reading, writing, and mathematics. In: *Knowing, learning, and instruction: Essays in honor of Robert Glaser* (L. B. Resnick, ed.). Hillsdale, NJ: Lawrence Erlbaum Associates 1989
14. Corno, L.: Teaching and self-regulated learning. In: *Talks to teachers* (D. C. Berliner, & B. V. Rosenshine, eds.). New York: Random House 1987
15. Cronbach, L. J., & Snow, R. E.: *Aptitudes and instructional methods.* New York: Irvington 1977
16. Fischer, G.: Enhancing incremental learning processes with knowledge-based systems. In: *Learning issues for intelligent tutoring systems* (H. Mandl, & A. Lesgold, eds.). New York: Springer-Verlag 1988
17. Fischer, P. M., & Mandl, H.: Improvement of the acquisition of knowledge by informing feedback. In: *Learning issues for intelligent tutoring systems* (H. Mandl, & A. Lesgold, eds.). New York: Springer-Verlag 1988
18. Frederiksen, J. R., & Collins, A.: A systems approach to educational testing. *Educational Researcher*, 18, pp. 27-32 (1989)
19. Gage, N. L., & Berliner, D. C.: *Educational psychology.* 4th ed. Dallas: Houghton Mifflin 1988
20. Gagné, R. M.: *The conditions of learning.* New York: Holt, Rinehart and Winston 1965
21. Gilbert, J. K., Watts, D. M., & Osborne, R. J.: Eliciting student views using an interview-about-instances technique. In: *Cognitive structure and conceptual change* (L. H. T. West, & A. L. Pines, eds.). New York: Academic Press 1985
22. Glaser, R.: The reemergence of learning theory within instructional research. *American Psychologist*, 45, pp. 29-39 (1990)
23. Gott, S. P.: Apprenticeship instruction for real-world tasks: The coordination of procedures, mental models, and strategies. In: *Review of research in education*, 15 (E. Z. Rothkopf, ed.). Washington, DC: American Educational Research Association 1988
24. Greeno, J. G.: Some examples of cognitive task analysis with instructional implications. In: *Aptitude, learning, and instruction: Vol. 2. Cognitive process analyses of learning and problem solving* (R. E. Snow, P.A. Federico, & W. E. Montague, eds.). Hillsdale, NJ: Lawrence Erlbaum Associates 1980.
25. Keller, J. M.: Motivational design of instruction. In: *Instructional-design theories and models: An overview of their current status* (C. M. Reigeluth, ed.). Hillsdale, NJ: Lawrence Erlbaum Associates 1983

26. Kintsch, W.: Comprehension and memory of text. In: *Handbook of learning and cognitive processes: Vol. 6. Linguistic functions in cognitive theory* (W. K. Estes, ed.). Hillsdale, NJ: Lawrence Erlbaum Associates 1978
27. Kyllonen, P. C., & Shute, V. J.: A taxonomy of learning skills. In: *Learning and individual differences* (P. L. Ackerman, R. J. Sternberg, & R. Glaser, eds.). New York: Freeman 1989
28. Lajoie, S. P., & Lesgold, A.: Apprenticeship training in the workplace: Computer-coached practice environment as a new form of apprenticeship. *Machine-Mediated Learning*, 3, pp. 7-28 (1989)
29. Lepper, M. R., & Chabay, R. W.: Socializing the intelligent tutor: Bringing empathy to computer tutors. In: *Learning issues for intelligent tutoring systems* (H. Mandl, & A. Lesgold, eds.). New York: Springer-Verlag 1988
30. Lesgold, A.: Toward a theory of curriculum for use in designing intelligent instructional systems. In: *Learning issues for intelligent tutoring systems* (H. Mandl, & A. Lesgold, eds.). New York: Springer-Verlag 1988
31. Mandl, H., & Lesgold, A. (eds.): *Learning issues for intelligent tutoring systems*. New York: Springer-Verlag 1988
32. Markman, E. M.: Comprehension monitoring. In: *Children's oral communication skills* (W. P. Dickson, ed.). New York: Academic Press 1981
33. McCalla, G. I., Greer, J. E., & the SCENT Research Team: SCENT-3: An architecture for intelligent advising in problem solving domains. In: *Intelligent tutoring systems: At the crossroads of artificial intelligence and education* (C. Frasson, & G. Gauthier, eds.). Norwood, NJ: Ablex 1990
34. McClintock, R.: The place of study in a world of instruction. *Teachers College Record*, 73, pp. 161-205 (1971)
35. McCombs, B. L., & Whisler, J. S.: The role of affective variables in autonomous learning. *Educational Psychologist*, 24, pp. 277-306 (1989)
36. Naveh-Benjamin, M., McKeachie, W. J., & Lin, Y.: Two types of text anxious students. *Journal of Educational Psychology*, 79, pp. 131-136 (1987)
37. Palincsar, A. S.: Less charted waters. *Educational Researcher*, 18, 4, pp. 5-7 (1989)
38. Paris, S. G.: Fusing skill and will: The integration of cognitive and motivational psychology. Paper presented at the meeting of the American Educational Research Association, New Orleans, April 1988
39. Perkins, D. N., & Simmons, R.: Patterns of misunderstanding: An integrative model for science, math, and programming. *Review of Educational Research*, 58, pp. 303-326 (1988)
40. Reigeluth, C. M. (ed.): *Instructional-design theories and models: An overview of their current status*. Hillsdale, NJ: Lawrence Erlbaum Associates 1983
41. Resnick, L.: Learning in school and out. *Educational Researcher*, 16, 9, pp. 13-20 (1988)
42. Roblyer, M. D.: Fundamental problems and principles of designing effective courseware. In: *Instructional designs for microcomputer courseware* (D. H. Jonassen, ed.). Hillsdale, NJ: Lawrence Erlbaum Associates 1988
43. Rohwer, W. D., Jr.: An invitation to a developmental psychology of studying. In: *Advances in applied developmental psychology* (F. J. Morrison, C. A. Lord, & D. P. Keating, eds.). New York: Academic Press 1984
44. Rohwer, W. D., Jr.: An invitation to an educational psychology of studying. *Educational Psychologist*, 19, pp. 1-14 (1984)
45. Schimmel, B. J.: Providing meaningful feedback in courseware. In: *Instructional designs for microcomputer courseware* (D. H. Jonassen, ed.). Hillsdale, NJ: Lawrence Erlbaum Associates 1988
46. Shuell, T. J.: Cognitive conceptions of learning. *Review of Educational Research*, 56, pp. 411-436 (1986)
47. Shuell, T. J.: The role of the student in learning from instruction. *Contemporary Educational Psychology*, 13, pp. 276-295 (1988)
48. Shuell, T. J.: Learning theory and instructional design: Engaging the learning in meaningful ways. In: *Recent directions in cognitive instructional design theory*. In: Symposium conducted at the meeting of the American Educational Research Association (H. F. O'Neil, chair). Boston, April 1990
49. Shuell, T. J.: Teaching and learning as problem solving. *Theory into Practice*, 29, pp. 102-108 (1990)
50. Shuell, T. J., & Lee, C. Z.: *Learning and instruction*. Monterey, CA: Brooks/Cole 1976
51. Shute, V. J., & Glaser, R.: A large-scale evaluation of an intelligent discovery world: Smithtown. *Interactive Learning Environments*, 1, pp. 51-77 (1990)
52. Snow, R. E.: Research on aptitude for learning: A progress report. In: *Review of research in education*, 4 (L. S. Shulman, ed.). Itasca, IL: F. E. Peacock 1977
53. Snow, R. E.: Toward assessment of cognitive and conative structures in learning. *Educational Researcher*, 18, pp. 8-14 (1989)
54. Tobias, S.: Anxiety research in educational psychology. *Journal of Educational Psychology*, 71, pp. 573-582 (1979)

55. Tobias, S.: Another look at research on the adaptation of instruction to student characteristics. *Educational Psychologist*, 24, pp. 213-227 (1989)
56. VanLehn, K.: Toward a theory of impasse-driven learning. In: *Learning issues for intelligent tutoring systems* (H. Mandl, & A. Lesgold, eds.). New York: Springer-Verlag 1988
57. Wenger, E.: *Artificial intelligence and tutoring systems.* Los Altos, CA: Morgan Kaufmann 1987
58. Wineburg, S. S.: Remembrance of theories past. *Educational Researcher*, 18, 4, pp. 7-10 (1989)

Artificial Instruction: A Method for Relating Learning Theory to Instructional Design

Stellan Ohlsson

Learning Research and Development Center, University of Pittsburgh, Pittsburgh, PA, USA

Abstract: In the past, research on learning has been linked to instruction by the derivation of general principles of instructional design from learning theories. But such design principles are often difficult to apply to particular instructional issues. A new method for relating research on learning to instructional design is proposed. Different ways of teaching a particular topic can be evaluated by teaching that topic to a simulation model of learning, and recording the complexity of the resulting learning processes. An application of this method to a traditional problem in mathematics education suggests that conceptual instruction in arithmetic causes more cognitive strain than mechanical instruction, contrary to a widely held belief in the mathematics education community. The advantages and disadvantages of the general method are discussed.

Keywords: arithmetic, augmenting, computer simulation, instructional design, learning theory, regrouping, subtraction, understanding.

On the Relation Between Learning Theory and Instruction

Instruction is an artifact, a social practice deliberately designed to achieve a particular purpose. A theory of instruction is therefore a *prescriptive* theory. The task of such a theory is to state principles that constrain search through the space of instructional designs [30]. A theory of learning, on the other hand, is a *descriptive* theory. The task of a learning theory is to state principles that accurately describe the mechanisms of cognitive change. Instructional theory and learning theory are distinct intellectual enterprises, just as agriculture and botany, medicine and physiology, engineering and physics are distinct enterprises [10, 12].

As these analogies suggest, the enterprises of instruction and learning, although distinct, are closely related. Physical therapies that ignore the chemistry and physiology of the human body are likely to do the patient more damage than good; machines that violate the laws of

NATO ASI Series, Vol. F 85
Adaptive Learning Environments
Edited by M. Jones and P. H. Winne

physics cannot work. Similarly, instructional designs that are not in accord with the mechanisms of cognitive change are unlikely to facilitate learning.

The notion that a theory of instruction should be informed by a theory of learning is hardly controversial when stated abstractly. Glaser traces this idea back to both John Dewey and Edward L. Thorndike [10], but there are many recent advocates [13, 32, 34, 35]. But how, specifically, are the two enterprises supposed to interact? How can instructional designs be informed by principles of learning? The traditional method for applying learning theory to instructional questions is to derive general principles of instruction from general principles of learning. The application of the derived principles to the design of instruction in a particular topic is left to the designer. The first systematic application of this method was launched by the behaviourists. Principles of stimulus-response relations and reinforcement gave rise to instructional principles that emphasized behavioural objectives and maximally efficient reinforcement schedules [11]. The application of piagetian research to instructional questions has taken a similar form. The principle that equilibrium requires a balance between assimilation and accommodation has given rise to training programs that deliberately induce disequilibrium in order to accelerate cognitive change [22]. David Ausubel's theory of learning as successive elaboration gave rise to Reigeluth's theory of instructional design [32]. In each approach, general principles of instruction are derived from general principles of learning, but the application of those design principles to particular instructional topics is based on intuition, common sense, and seat-of-the-pants judgement.

Modern cognitive psychology, based on information processing concepts, has surpassed earlier approaches with respect to the power of its theories, and with respect to the depth and the detail of its descriptions of cognitive processes. But its application to instructional questions has so far taken the same old form. General principles of instructional design are derived from general principles of learning. The application of those principles to particular instructional designs is left to the designer. For example, the principles of the ACT* theory [1] have given rise to several instructional principles, including the idea that one should teach the goal tree for cognitive skills [2]. This principle is surely correct, but its application to a particular instructional topic is nevertheless problematic. How is this principle to be applied, for example, in the teaching of arithmetic? Should one teach the entire goal tree for subtraction with regrouping to all students, even to very young students? Are there no situations in which the complexity of the goal tree might be an obstacle to learning? Should the entire goal tree be taught at once, or should one introduce it component by component? If so, how should the components be sequenced? The general principle does not, by itself, answer instructional questions of this detailed sort.

This chapter explores a different approach to the interaction between the theory of learning and the theory of instruction. Instead of deriving *general* principles of instruction from a learning theory, this approach exploits the fact that information processing theories of learning can be embodied in runnable simulation models to answer *particular* instructional questions. A common and important type of instructional problem — perhaps the only type — is to decide between alternative ways of teaching a particular topic. Problems of this type can be solved, I suggest, by teaching the relevant topic to a simulation model of learning. To compare two ways of teaching a particular topic, we teach that topic to the learning model in both ways, and we measure the computational complexity of the learning processes induced in the two cases. If the simulation model expends less computational work to learn under one form of instruction than under another, then it predicts that the former is preferable to the latter. The main purpose of this chapter is to present an application of this method to a traditional issue in arithmetic instruction.

The method of teachable simulation models has three prerequisites. First, it requires a *runnable* model. So-called information processing models that consist of labelled boxes with arrows of varying thickness going in and out of them are of no help; nor are computer models with such shaky implementation that they can barely produce a single demonstration run without breaking; nor are programs that only embody *some* of the assumptions of the underlying theory (while the other assumptions are embodied in some other program). The method of teachable simulation models requires a robust, integrated computer model that can be run on a variety of inputs. Second, the method requires that the simulation model is capable of *learning*. A performance model is not enough. Third, the learning mechanisms of the model must be such that their inputs can be interpreted as *instruction*. A model of learning by doing is not enough; the method requires a model of learning from declarative messages that originate in an outside source. The HS model described below satisfies these three prerequisites.

The particular instructional question investigated in this chapter concerns the teaching of arithmetic. The question of how to teach an arithmetic skill like subtraction has been approached in different ways by different generations of researchers. An earlier generation focussed on the question of which subtraction algorithm is easier for children to learn. Large scale empirical research programs were launched to answer this question [5, 6]. The answer was, briefly summarized, that the method of regrouping (or "decomposition") is easier to learn than the method of augmentation (or "equal addition"), at least when subtraction is taught conceptually (as opposed to mechanically). I show in this chapter that the method of teachable simulation models implies a different answer to this question.

The current generation of researchers in mathematics education focusses on the contrast between rote and insightful learning of arithmetic algorithms. They strive to find methods that facilitate school children's acquisition of the conceptual rationale for arithmetic algorithms, in the hope that conceptual understanding will eliminate errors, improve retention, and facilitate transfer to unfamiliar problems [15]. The method of teachable simulation models leads me to a rather contrary answer to this question.

In summary, the present chapter has both a methodological and a substantive purpose. I propose a general method that exploits the fact that information processing theories of learning can be embodied in runnable simulation models to answer particular instructional questions. The method is introduced in the context of a particular application. The application is not merely a demonstration of the method. The specific conclusions reached have important implications for instruction in arithmetic.

Regrouping versus Augmenting

There are several mathematically correct algorithms for computing the difference between two multi-digit integers. Educational researchers at the beginning of this century asked whether one of these algorithms is easier to learn than the others, a very reasonable question. In the *regrouping* algorithm non-canonical columns, i.e., columns in which the minuend digit is smaller than the subtrahend digit, are dealt with by incrementing the relevant minuend digit with one place-value unit. To keep the value of the minuend constant, this change in the minuend is compensated by decrementing the first non-zero minuend digit with a higher place value than the incremented digit. In the *augmenting* algorithm non-canonical columns are also dealt with by incrementing the minuend digit, but in this case the change in the minuend is compensated by *incrementing* the *subtrahend* digit with the next higher place value. (Strictly speaking, the entities which are incremented and decremented are the *numbers* which the digits refer to. Since no ambiguity results, I use the somewhat inaccurate locution "decrementing a digit" instead of the accurate but tedious "decrementing the number a particular digit refers to")

Which Algorithm is Easier?

The regrouping and augmenting algorithms build on different mathematical ideas. The regrouping algorithm is based on *the associative law:*

$$(a + b) + c = a + (b + c)$$

The associative law implies that the value of the minuend remains constant through the regrouping operation. (A complete derivation of the regrouping algorithm from first principles is available in [25].) The augmenting algorithm, on the other hand, is based on *the constant difference law:*

$$a - b = (a + k) - (b + k)$$

This law implies that the difference between the minuend and the subtrahend remains constant through the augmenting operation. (A more detailed discussion of the rationale for the augmenting algorithm is available in [8].) Since the two algorithms build on different mathematical ideas, it is entirely plausible that one of them is easier to learn and/or to execute than the other.

Large-scale classroom studies were performed in the early decades of this century in an effort to settle this issue empirically. William Brownell concluded: "Even a cursory survey of the ... experimental results ... reveals the impossibility of deciding simply and finally between D (the regrouping method) and EA (the equal addition method) as the better procedure for teaching 'borrowing'" [5, p. 169]. Augmenting was found to be easier than regrouping more often than the other way around, but the observed difference was small in magnitude. Brownell argued that the results were only in favor of augmenting when subtraction was taught as a mechanical performance. If subtraction was taught conceptually, he claimed, the results favored regrouping [5, 6]. Brownell's argument was widely accepted and politically instrumental in settling the issue in favor of teaching the regrouping method in American schools. Educators in other nations were not equally convinced, and the augmenting method is still taught in some European schools.

The empirical studies did not clearly distinguish between performance and learning. They confused the question *which algorithm is easier to use*? with the question *which algorithm is easier to learn*? One reason for the lack of separation of these two questions is that pure measures of learning are hard to come by. We can only observe by recording performances, so most empirical measures will confound the two questions. In the context of a simulation model, the two questions can be cleanly separated. This section investigates which algorithm is easier to use, while the next section investigates which algorithm is easier to learn.

In information processing terminology, the question of which algorithm is easier to use can be reformulated as follows: What is the relation between the cognitive complexity of the mental procedure corresponding to the regrouping algorithm and the cognitive complexity of the procedure corresponding to the augmenting algorithm? This question can be answered by implementing the two algorithms as psychologically plausible simulation models, running those models, and measuring their relative complexity.

Simulating Regrouping and Augmenting

The hypothesis that cognitive skills (mental procedures) are encoded as production systems was first proposed by Allen Newell and Herbert A. Simon [23], and has been adopted by a number of researchers [1, 18, 19]. According to the production system hypothesis, cognitive skills are encoded in sets of *production rules*, where each production rule has the general form

Goal + Situation --> Action.

The symbol "Goal" stands for a specification of a desired situation, "Situation" stands for a description of the relevant features of the current situation, and "Action" refers to something the person knows how to do. The intended interpretation of such a rule is that when the person has the specified goal, and he or she is in a situation that fits the situation description, then he or she will consider the specified action. A collection of interrelated production rules is a *production system*. Each cognitive skill is hypothesized to correspond to a production system.

A production system *architecture* is a program that can interpret a production system. In this context, to interpret means to (a) decide which production rules (in a particular production system) are satisfied in the current situation, (b) select one or more rules to be evoked, and (c) execute the actions of the evoked rules. Each pass through the three steps (a)-(c) is one production system *cycle*, or operating cycle. The number of cycles required to complete a pass through the production system is one of the measures of cognitive complexity used in this chapter.

The satisfied rules are identified by matching the situation against the so-called working memory, a data base which contains the system's information about the current state of affairs, and by matching the goal against the system's current goal. If both components match, the rule is satisfied and is therefore a candidate for being evoked. Selecting which rules to evoke is sometimes called *conflict resolution* [21]. A typical conflict resolution scheme is to select those rules that match against the most recent information in working memory. Execution of the primitive actions must involve calls on motor programs that control the muscles of the relevant limbs, e.g., the finger muscles for the action of writing a digit, but production system theories do not have much to say about this aspect of human cognition.

The HS architecture is a relatively standard production system architecture. It has a single working memory which contains information about both the current state of affairs, and the systems' current goal(s). All available rules are matched against working memory in each operating cycle. There is no conflict resolution. Every satisfied rule is evoked. There is no complexity limitation on the left-hand side of the rules, but the right-hand side (the action part) is limited to a single action. The system continues to match and evoke rules until either there are no satisfied rules, or the current problem is solved. Detailed descriptions of the HS architecture are available in [28, 29].

In order to simulate subtraction with regrouping, the HS system was extended with a (simulated) task display and a (simulated) visual-motor interface consisting of an eye and a hand. The *task display* is a data structure in the computer which contains the same information as a piece of paper with a subtraction problem written on it. Technically speaking, the task display is a two-dimensional array of digits. (I am assuming that the subtraction problem is written in vertical format.) Information about the task display enters into the working memory of the HS system through a simulated *eye*, a program module which can only access one digit at a time. When the simulated eye "looks" at a digit, information about that digit is entered into working memory. In order to gather information about some other digit, the eye has to be moved. The eye can move left, right, up, and down. Eye movements are distinct computational steps, so control of visual attention is encoded in production rules. The model can alter the external task display only through the use of a simulated *hand*. The hand can cross out an existing digit and write a digit in a blank space. These two primitive actions count as distinct computational steps, so the hand is also controlled by production rules. In short, the model simulates subtraction at the level of individual eye movements and individual writing actions, a very fine grained level of analysis compared to most simulation models.

HS was also equipped with a long-term memory for number facts, e.g., 8 - 7 = 1. Retrieval of number facts was simulated with a function which returns the (correct) answer to any query about the relations between two numbers. HS does not simulate the probabilistic nature of memory retrieval, nor the existence of incorrect number facts. Like attention allocation and writing, memory retrieval is a distinct computational step which is controlled by production rules.

The HS models of regrouping and augmenting consist of 38 and 35 production rules, respectively. The numbers of different rules in different categories are shown in Table 1. The distribution of rules over visual steps (i.e., move the eye), motor steps (i.e., write, cross out, and say the answer), cognitive steps (i.e., the creation and revising of working memory expressions), and memory steps (i.e., retrievals from long-term memory) is approximately the same for both models. The details of the rules themselves are not important for present purposes. Examples of complete production rules are available in [8].

In order to estimate the cognitive complexity of the two subtraction algorithms, the two simulation models were run on a subtraction test consisting of 66 subtraction problems with varying number of columns, varying number of non-canonical columns, and varying number of *blocking zeroes*. A blocking zero is immediately to the left of a non-canonical column or another blocking zero.) The number of production system cycles required by each model to complete each problem was recorded. In addition, each cycle was classified with respect to the type of rule that was evoked in that cycle.

Rule type	Regrouping	Augmenting
Visual	4	3
Motor	11	11
Write & cross out	6	6
Say answer	5	5
Cognitive	20	17
Create expressions	11	12
Revise expressions	9	5
Memory	3	4
All rules	38	35

Table 1: The distribution of production rules in two canonicalization algorithms

The results are shown in Figure 1. The figure shows the cognitive complexity of the regrouping and augmenting algorithms on eleven different problem types. Problem types 1-4 have two, three, four, or five canonical columns, respectively, but no non-canonical columns. The number of cycles required to complete such problems is the same for both models. Problem types 5-8 have one, two, three, or five non-canonical columns, respectively. The regrouping model requires more steps to handle each such column than the augmenting model. The difference is small in magnitude. The difference is located entirely in the visual-motor interface, i.e., the regrouping algorithm requires more cycles because it involves more complicated attention allocation.

Problem types 9, 10, and 11 have one, two, or three blocking zeroes, respectively. The regrouping model has a slight advantage on these problem types. The reason is that once a set of columns has been traversed by the regrouping procedure, no further regrouping of those columns is needed. The augmenting algorithm, on the other hand, has to augment every column with zero as the subtrahend digit and a non-zero minuend digit. Consequently, if there are

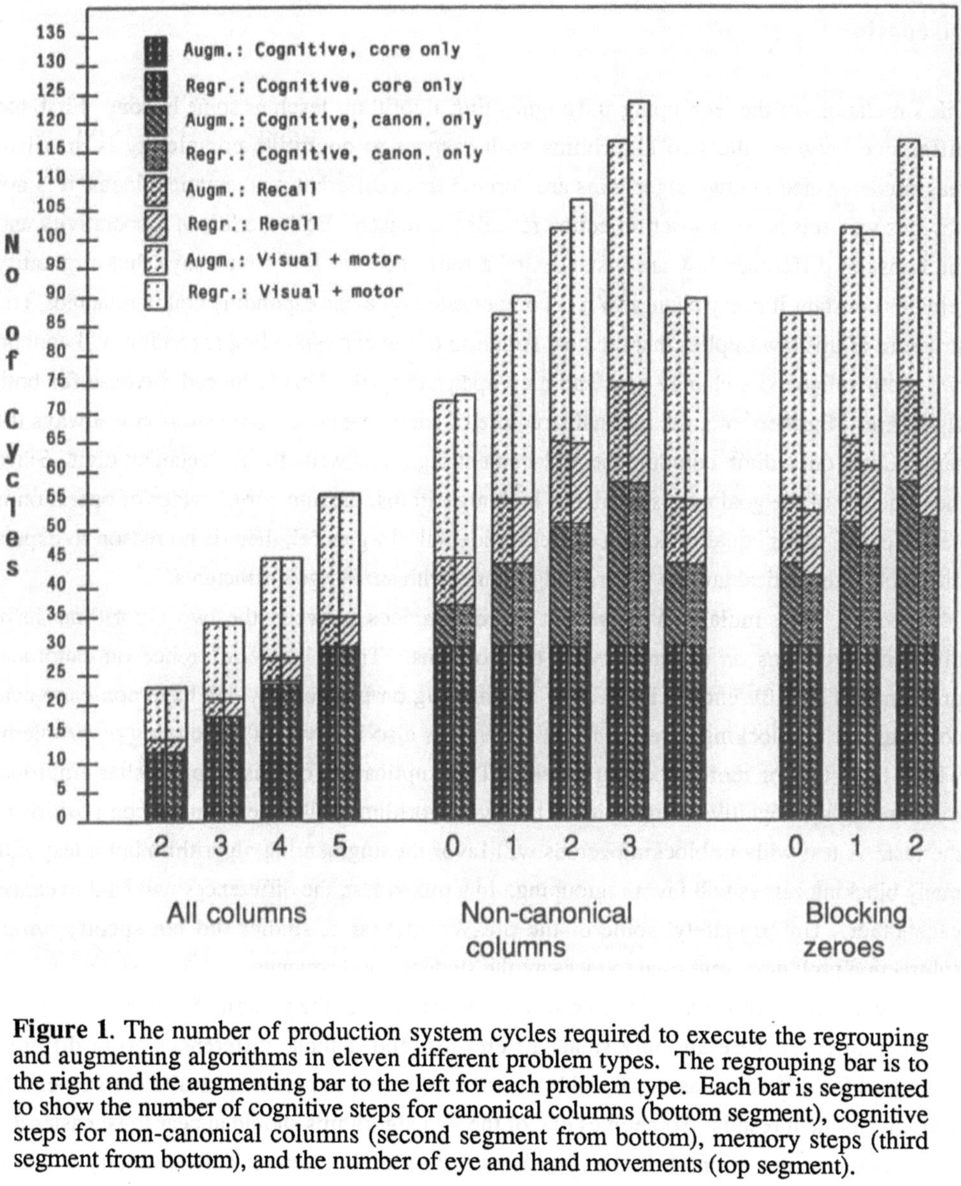

Figure 1. The number of production system cycles required to execute the regrouping and augmenting algorithms in eleven different problem types. The regrouping bar is to the right and the augmenting bar to the left for each problem type. Each bar is segmented to show the number of cognitive steps for canonical columns (bottom segment), cognitive steps for non-canonical columns (second segment from bottom), memory steps (third segment from bottom), and the number of eye and hand movements (top segment).

several blocking zeroes in a problem, the regrouping algorithm completes that problem in slightly fewer operating cycles than the augmenting algorithm. Once again, the difference is small in magnitude. A more extensive discussion of these results is available in [8].

Discussion

The simulations of the regrouping and augmenting algorithms teach us some lessons. First, the difference between the two algorithms with respect to cognitive complexity is small in magnitude. Since the two algorithms are derived from different mathematical ideas, it is not obvious why this is so. Closer reflection reveals the reason. Both the law of associativity and the constant difference law are instances of a more general law which says that a quantity remains constant if every change in it is compensated by a corresponding counterchange. The structure of this law implies that the goal structure of the corresponding algorithm will contain two main subgoals: a change goal and a compensate goal. This is indeed the case for both algorithms. Furthermore, the internal structure of each change or compensation is always the same: Cross out a digit, compute the replacement digit, and write the replacement digit. Since the structure of the goal tree is similar in both algorithms, the number of cycles of operation is nearly equal. This equality is, in a sense, accidental. In general, there is no reason to expect different mathematical laws to generate algorithms with similar goal structures.

Second, the simulations show that the differences between the two algorithms have different directions on different types of problems. There is no difference on canonical problems. The difference is in favor of augmenting on problems which have non-canonical columns but no blocking zeroes. The difference is also in favor of regrouping on problems which have two or more blocking zeroes. The implication of this result is that empirical measures of the cognitive complexity of the two algorithms will depend on the composition of the test. A test without blocking zeroes will favor the augmenting algorithm, but a test with many blocking zeroes will favor regrouping. In a mixed test, the differences will tend to cancel each other. Unfortunately, some of the pre-World War II studies did not specify which subtraction problems were used to measure the students' performance.

The outcomes of the simulation runs are consistent with the pattern of empirical results in the literature. If there are only small differences, and if those differences go in different directions for different classes of problems, then we would expect empirical measurements to give inconsistent results. Sometimes one of the two algorithms should appear to be easier due either to the composition of the test problems or to sampling error. This is exactly what the literature shows [5, 6].

These simulations imply that it does not matter which algorithm is taught. Regrouping and augmenting are equally complicated; the differences in cognitive complexity are too small to be of pedagogical significance. This conclusion is consistent with the fact that both algorithms are, in fact, taught in different school systems, without noticable higher degree of success in one system than in the other. However, the study summarized in this section (and reported in more detail in [8]) only concerned the *execution* of the two algorithms. The two algorithms are equally complex to use, once learned. But Brownell's argument was that regrouping is easier to learn than augmenting, at least if subtraction is taught conceptually. We therefore need to investigate the cognitive complexity of the *construction* (as opposed to execution) of the two algorithms. In addition, we need to compare the cognitive complexity of the construction under both conceptual and mechanical instruction.

Conceptual versus Mechanical Instruction

As mathematics educators deepen their analysis of mathematical cognition, they become more and more concerned with the question of conceptual understanding [15]. This concern is partly fuelled by research into childrens' mathematical errors. Catalogues of error patterns have been compiled for a number of mathematical tasks, including subtraction [4, 38, 39, 41] and fractions [9, 14, 17, 27, 31, 36, 37]. Most of the error patterns described in these catalogues are senseless; they have no discernable relation to the correct mathematical operations. To observe children making senseless mistakes is a frustrating experience, and it is impossible not to believe that if children only understood what they were doing, they would not make those mistakes. Following this line of reasoning, mathematics educators have tried to design conceptually-based instruction in arithmetic.

Does Conceptual Understanding Help?

The purpose of many instructional interventions in arithmetic is to show that if children are taught the conceptual rationale for the arithmetic algorithms, they will have less difficulty in learning those algorithms, and their performance will be less error prone and more flexible in response to changing task demands [15]. Unfortunately, this enterprise has not been spectacularly successful.

A training study by Resnick and Omansson can serve as an example [33]. Children with faulty subtraction performance were taught the conceptual rationale of the regrouping algorithm with the help of Diene's blocks. The instruction was designed to force children to map back and forth between blocks and numbers. The children first performed a step with the blocks, and then performed the same step with the symbols. At the end of the instruction, several of the children could explain the correct subtraction procedure. When they were given subtraction problems to perform, they nevertheless made errors. As a second example, Ohlsson, Bee, and Zeller taught children how to add fractions with an interactive computer tool that enabled children to switch back and forth between graphical and numerical representations of fractional quantities [27]. A change in one representation was automatically mirrored by the corresponding change in the other representation. A detailed analysis of the children's performance on the pre- and posttests revealed that they could map back and forth between the fraction symbol x/y and concrete representations of fractional quantities. All of them nevertheless committed the standard error of adding fractions by adding both numerators and denominators on the posttest. In both of these studies, instruction that was carefully designed to make the meaning of the mathematical operations evident failed to prevent or cure senseless errors.

These empirical failures focus attention on the lack of theoretical analysis of conceptual understanding in the context of arithmetic. What is meant by conceptual understanding, and what is its (supposed) function in procedural learning? How does conceptual instruction interact with the construction of a mental procedure? Why should we believe that knowledge of the rationale of an arithmetic procedure facilitates the learning of that procedure? In spite of the recent emphasis on conceptual understanding in arithmetic instruction, little effort has been spent in answering these questions.

My approach to these questions is to extend the HS architecture with a learning mechanism that enables the model to learn procedures on the basis of instruction. The instruction is modelled as a set of declarative knowledge units that the user gives to the system. Such a learning mechanism enables us to *teach* the model how to do subtraction. We supply the system with a set of declarative knowledge units which correspond to the instructions a teacher would give a student, and the system learns by converting those knowledge units into a cognitive skill, i.e., into production rules. By giving the system *different* sets of declarative knowledge units, we can simulate the effects of *different* ways of teaching subtraction. In particular, we can compare conceptual instruction with mechanical instruction.

Making HS Teachable

In a production system architecture, a *learning mechanism* is any process that can revise existing production rules or generate new ones. When a new rule is added to a production system, the behaviour of the system changes. The new rule will control behaviour in those situations in which it matches working memory. Since the new rule is different from previous rules, the system's behaviour will be different. The fact that the behavior changes is the main reason to regard the generation of new rules as a simulation of (procedural) learning.

A number of simulation systems model procedural learning as the construction of new production rules (cf., [1, 3, 16, 18, 19, 24, 39]). These models simulate learning by doing, i.e., they model the effects of *practice*. In spite of their differences, they all instantiate the same abstract theory. The first principle of this abstract theory is that humans have access to one or more weak problem solving mechanisms (analogy, hill climbing, planning, search, etc.) which can generate task oriented behaviour on unfamiliar problems. The second principle is that information about each problem solving activity — the reasons for taking it, the desirability of the outcome, the temporal order of the steps, and so on — is stored in long-term memory. The third principle of the abstract theory is that the learning mechanisms construct new rules through some form of induction over the individual steps. For example, the SAGE system described by Langley carries out forward search and stores steps in which a particular action had good outcomes, as well as steps in which that action had bad outcomes [20]. The system learns by identifying one or more situation features that discriminate between the two classes of situations, and it constructs a new rule by incorporating those features into the rule that controls that action. Different models of learning by doing differ with respect to which weak methods they postulate, which information they assume is stored in memory, and which induction procedure they use, but they all instantiate the three abstract principles stated above.

Simulation models that instantiate the abstract theory of learning by doing are quite successful in modelling the effects of practice. But models of practice are not sufficient for present purposes. There is nothing in such systems that corresponds to instruction, i.e., to a set of messages that originate outside the system and which are used to construct new procedural knowledge. A learning mechanism which is to simulate learning from instruction must take declarative knowledge units among its inputs.

In the HS system, general world knowledge, including knowledge imparted by instruction, is assumed to consist of *constraints* on cognitive processes. For example, the laws of the number system impose constraints on arithmetic operations. Unless an addition procedure yields the same result for (a + b) + c as for a + (b + c), i.e., unless it satisfies the constraint imposed by the associative law, it is not a correct addition procedure. The notion of general knowledge as constraints is not limited to arithmetic, or, indeed, to mathematics. For example, the laws of conservation of energy, mass, and momentum are examples of natural science principles which are naturally cast as constraints. Traffic laws are good examples of constraints in everyday life. I do not claim that all general knowledge can be formulated as constraints, only that constraints are one important form of knowledge, a form, moreover, which is particularly relevant to arithmetic. In the HS system, constraints are encoded in knowledge elements which are distinct from both working memory elements and from production rules.

An incorrect or incomplete arithmetic procedure typically leads to results that *violate* one or more of the relevant constraints. For example, an incorrect or incomplete regrouping procedure might violate the constraint that the value of the subtrahend is to remain constant over regrouping. The basic idea behind the HS system is that a constraint violation contains information about how to revise the faulty procedure so that similar constraint violations are avoided in the future. In each operating cycle, the system matches all available constraints against the current state of affairs. If a constraint is satisfied, no action is taken. If one or more constraints are violated, the learning mechanism is triggered. This corresponds to having a tutor who watches the process of problem solving and provides instruction when needed. (The HS system is given all the constraints at the beginning of the simulation run, rather than single constraints — instructions — at select points during problem solving. Since the system effectively does not "see" a constraint until it is violated, this difference from real tutoring is less significant than it first appears.) The learning mechanism analyzes the constraint violation, and revises the faulty rule accordingly. The technical details of the learning mechanism are not important for present purposes. A detailed description of the HS learning mechanism is available in [28, 29].

Since learning happens when the behaviour of the system causes a constraint violation, there must be some initial rules which can generate behaviour. HS must be supplied with at least one initial rule for each problem solving operator. In the simulation runs reported in this chapter, the initial rules are minimal, i.e., their condition sides contain only the applicability conditions for the relevant action. These incomplete rules generate almost random behaviour. Each action is considered in every situation in which its applicability conditions are satisfied. The probability of causing a constraint violation is high. The system detects the violation, revises the faulty rule, and then starts over on the problem. The cycle of trying to solve the problem, detecting a violation, revising the faulty rule, and starting over continues until the problem can be solved without any constraint violations. This is a reasonable first approximation model of learning to solve problems under tutelage.

In summary, the HS system encodes declarative knowledge, including instructions, as constraints on behaviour. In arithmetic, the effect of faulty or incomplete procedural knowledge is typically to generate results that violate the constraints imposed by the laws of numbers. HS learns by analyzing a constraint violation, and revising the rule that caused the violation in such a way that similar constraint violations are avoided in the future. This capability makes HS *teachable*. To teach HS a particular procedure, the user supplies the system with an initial set of (incomplete) rules and the constraints that define the correct procedure. Each constraint corresponds to an instruction. The system tries to solve problems, makes mistakes, and learns from the instructions it has been given. If the instructions are complete enough, the system will eventually arrive at the correct procedure.

Teaching HS Subtraction

The HS system was taught both the regrouping and the augmenting algorithms for subtraction, and both algorithms were taught in two different ways, corresponding to conceptual and mechanical instruction. This subsection describes the inputs to the four simulation experiments, and the next subsection describes the results.

What does it mean to do subtraction procedurally, as a mechanical skill? A person who does subtraction mechanically is not thinking about the mathematical objects — the numbers — symbolized by the digits in the problem display, nor about the mathematical relations between those numbers. For example, he/she does not think about the fact that the "3" in the numeral "32" denotes the number 30. Instead, he/she thinks about the digits themselves. He or she performs crossing out and writing actions on the physical display (i.e., the paper) without considering the mathematical meaning of those actions.

Consistent with this interpretation of what it means to do subtraction mechanically, HS was supplied with a representation of a subtraction problem that was isomorphic to the information available in a standard problem display (vertical format). The representation contained information about which digits occurred in which spatial arrangement, but little else. In particular, there was no representation of the place values of the different digits, nor of the current value of either the subtrahend or the minuend. In this representation, a subtraction problem appears as two strings of digits. The representations for the regrouping and the augmenting algorithms were very similar.

If the learner thinks of a subtraction problem in terms of physical operations on the digits in the problem display, he or she cannot benefit from conceptual instruction. For example, instructions that mention the place value of a particular digit can have no impact on a learner who has not internally represented that place value. There is nothing for such an instruction to relate to. The constraints we supplied to HS in the mechanical case were shallow and superficial. They were not derived from the laws of the number system, and they did not mention the conceptual or mathematical meaning of the operations involved.

What does it mean to do subtraction conceptually? The learner who does subtraction conceptually thinks about the numbers symbolized by the digits in the problem display, and he/she is aware of the mathematical interpretation of the actions performed on that display. Consistent with this view, the HS representation for conceptual learning was very different from the HS representation for mechanical learning. In the conceptual representation, a subtraction problem is encoded at the top level as a difference between two numbers. The subtrahend and the minuend are both associated with particular additive decompositions, i.e., sets of numbers that add to those numbers. The elements of the additive decompositions are associated with a face value and a place value. In the conceptual representation, the distinction between numbers and digits is explicit, and the face values of the additive components are associated with the digits in the problem display. The operations of crossing out and writing digits correspond to internal, mental operations on the numbers symbolized by those digits.

The representations for the regrouping and augmenting algorithms were once again very similar.

In addition to the representation of the problem and the constraints, HS must also be given some initial procedural knowledge. Without initial rules HS cannot generate behaviour, and so cannot discover constraint violations. In the simulation runs presented in this subsection, HS was *given* the correct procedure for *canonical* subtraction problems, i.e., problems in which the minuend digit is larger than the subtrahend digit in every column. The system *learned* to solve *non*-canonical problems, i.e., problems for which the minuend digit is larger than the subtrahend digit in at least one column. In common parlance, the system learned to "borrow." I shall refer to this process as *canonicalization*, since the purpose of "borrowing" is to bring a non-canonical problem into canonical form. In summary, the system learned two different canonicalization methods, regrouping and augmenting, with two different representations of each method.

In each training run the system tries to solve its current problem. Since the rules for canonical problems cannot handle non-canonical problems, the system commits mistakes. The mistakes are identified by the constraints, and the system applies its learning mechanism to revise the rules. It then starts over. Eventually it learns to solve the problem correctly. If the system is given a second training problem, it may or may not solve that problem correctly. It depends on the relation between the training problems. If it fails to solve the second training problem correctly, it revises its procedure further. In the simulation runs reported below, the system was given successive training problems until it arrived at the correct subtraction procedure. The number of training problems required varied between two and four, depending on condition. The correctness of the learned procedure was verified by running it on the 66 item subtraction test described earlier in this chapter.

Computational Results

Table 2 shows the amount of computational work required to learn to canonicalize in each of the four conditions, summed over all training problems in each condition. It contains several interesting effects. First, the regrouping models require more learning to handle columns with blocking zeroes than columns without blocking zeroes. The augmenting models, on the other hand, are not affected by blocking zeroes. Second, regrouping is computationally more expensive than augmenting. The only exception is that if we disregard blocking zeroes, then regrouping is easier to learn than augmenting *with a mechanical representation*. Third, conceptually based learning is more complex than mechanical learning for both regrouping and augmenting. Also, the difference between the conceptual and the mechanical representations is larger in the case of regrouping than in the case of augmenting. The conceptual regrouping model required 2.3 times as many cycles as the mechanical one, while the conceptual augmenting model required 1.3 times as many cycles as its mechanical counterpart. Finally, it makes no difference whether we measure the computational complexity by the number of cycles or by the number of search states visited during learning. All effects mentioned here occur in both variables.

	Type of representation			
	Conceptual		Mechanical	
Algorithm learned	States	Cycles	States	Cycles
Regrouping				
No blocking zeroes	968	940	464	449
Blocking zeroes	1843	1815	828	794
Augmenting				
No blocking zeroes	889	862	689	687
Blocking zeroes	889	862	689	687

Table 2: The amount of computation required by the HS model to learn to canonicalize under four different conditions, measured both in terms of the number of search states visited and the number of production system cycles required

It is, of course, possible to question the psychological relevance of both the number of production system cycles and the number of search states visited. Both measures are heavily dependent on the theoretical assumptions behind the simulation model. If the human learner is not doing a search, or if human cognition is not a production system architecture, there might be no relation between these measures and measures of cognitive work in humans. In addition, both measures depend on the particular implementation of the four simulation models.

But the complexity of the four learning processes can also be measured in terms of the number of learning events and the number of rules learned. A learning event is an event in which the system discovers a constraint violation, and revises its current rule set. A learning event might lead to the construction of one or more new rules. The number of learning events required is not primarily a function of the theoretical assumptions behind the models or of the implementation details. It is a measure of how many "things" there are to learn before the correct procedure has been acquired; it is primarily a function of the logic of the learning task.

Table 3 shows the amount of learning required to master regrouping and augmenting, measured in terms of the number of learning events as well as the number of new rules learned. All the effects observed in Table 2 are reproduced in Table 3: regrouping is more complex to learn than augmenting (except for problems without blocking zeroes, in the mechanical representation), the conceptual versions require more learning than their mechanical counterparts, and the difference between the conceptual and the mechanical versions is larger in the case of regrouping than in the case of augmenting. All effects appear with both measures. The main difference between Tables 2 and 3 is the distance between the conceptual and the mechanical representations. Both the absolute and the relative values of the effects are smaller in Table 3.

	Type of representation			
	Conceptual		Mechanical	
Algorithm learned	Events	Rules	Events	Rules
Regrouping				
No blocking zeroes	23	35	16	23
Blocking zeroes	32	50	24	32
Augmenting				
No blocking zeroes	20	29	18	24
Blocking zeroes	20	29	18	24

Table 3: The amount of learning required by the HS model to learn to canonicalize under four different conditions, measured both in terms of the number of learning events required and the number of new rules created

Table 4 shows yet another way to measure the outcome of the simulation experiments. Instead of measuring the amount of *learning*, Table 4 measures the amount of *instruction* needed to teach the HS model the two subtraction algorithms. The amount of instruction is measured in terms of how many constraints — instructions — we had to provide HS with in order to bring it up to correct performance. All the relevant effects from the other tables are reproduced in this variable. Regrouping requires more constraints than augmenting, and the difference is larger in the conceptual than in the mechanical case.

	Type of representation			
	Conceptual		Mechanical	
Algorithm learned	Constraints	Problems	Constraints	Problems
Regrouping	31	4	21	4
Augmenting	25	2	20	5

Table 4: The amount of instruction required by the HS model to learn to canonicalize under four different conditions, measured both in terms of the number of constraints (instructions) required and the number of training problems needed

The amount of instruction can also be measured in terms of the number of training problems needed to bring the model up to correct performance. This measure shows a different pattern; with respect to regrouping, the number of training problems is the same for both conceptual and mechanical representations. Augmenting requires one more training problem than regrouping in the mechanical representation. Finally, to learn augmenting with the conceptual representation requires only two training problems, the lowest of the four measures. This is the only case where the conceptual representation has an advantage. The number of training problems is a coarse measure of the complexity of the learning processes involved, and this result carries little weight against the consistent pattern across the five other measures.

Discussion of Substantive Conclusions

The results from the learning runs imply, briefly put, that regrouping is more difficult than augmenting, and that learning subtraction conceptually is more difficult than learning it mechanically. Since these results go against current wisdom in the mathematics education community, it is natural to ask what confidence we can place in them. The simulation model that produced these results might not be an accurate model of human learning. There is the possibility that the production system hypothesis is wrong. Also, the particular learning mechanism implemented in HS might not correspond to any type of learning that humans do.

In either case, we would have to admit that HS does not simulate human performance or learning. The relevance of the computational results to instruction is then doubtful.

Another possibility which would lessen the relevance of the computational results is that the production system hypothesis is correct, but HS is the wrong implementation of it. Simulation models are always underdetermined by the theories they embody [26]. There is always the possibility that the computational results depend upon this or that technical detail of the implementation. It would clearly be capricious to base instruction on results which depend on programming style.

Although both of these objections to computer simulations are valid in principle, I believe that the particular computational results reported here are principled. The effects in Tables 2 through 4 are not caused by this or that exotic feature of the implementation of HS, but by the fact that the gap between principles and procedures in arithmetic is wide, much wider than the intuitions of mathematically literate people suggest. To support this claim, I will discuss three aspects of that gap: the role of spatio-temporal relations, the function of expediency in algorithm design, and the importance of attention allocation.

The role of spatio-temporal relations. Equality relations between quantities are timeless and without spatial interpretation. For example, the associative law:

$$(a + b) + c = a + (b + c)$$

states that the sum of any two numbers x and c, where x is the sum of any two numbers a and b, is equal to the sum of the two numbers a and y, where y is the sum of b and c. The law does not say anything about spatial locations or directions. The fact that the law has a left-to-right linear structure is a property of the paper medium. If the law was encoded as a list-structure in a computer, the individual symbols might be distributed in a very different spatial pattern, but the law would have the same meaning. Neither does the law speak about temporal order. The addition operations mentioned in the law are not related through relations such as *before* and *after*; and concepts like *first, next*, and *last* have no role in the understanding of the law. The laws of the number system express equality relations abstracted from time and space.

The control of action, on the other hand, is all about spatio-temporal relations. The main function of an algorithm or a problem solving procedure is to order primitive actions in time, to regulate which action is to be done before or after which other action. Furthermore, the actions, to the extent that they are motor actions, have to be performed at some particular location in space, on some particular object. If a digit is to be crossed out, the spatial coordinates for that object must be known. If the right action is performed in the wrong spatial location, an error is likely to result. To learn a cognitive skill is to acquire a structure for the spatio-temporal control of action.

If the mathematical structure — the set of laws that constitutes the rationale for a particular algorithm — ignores time and space, and if the cognitive skill involved in executing that algorithm is a structure for spatio-temporal organization, it follows that the mathematical structure does not fully determine the skill. One cannot derive that *this* action has to be performed before *that* action from mathematical laws which do not speak about temporal relations; one cannot direct an action to *this* spatial location rather than *that* with the help of laws which do not speak about space. Information about time and space has to be added to the mathematical principles in order to control action. Knowledge about the mathematical rationale for an algorithm is not sufficient for the construction of the algorithm.

The role of expediency in algorithm design. The belief that mathematical principles determine mathematical action ignores the role of expediency in the design of the place value algorithms. Why, for example, do we solve place value problems by processing the columns in order from lower to higher place values? There is no *mathematical* reason for this rule. It is equally correct to begin subtracting to the left, i.e., with the highest place value column, and work towards the right, i.e., towards columns with lower place values. Unlike the standard procedure, this alternate procedure, although mathematically correct, requires that the already processed columns have to be processed again every time the minuend is regrouped. Beginning with the lowest place value column saves work; it is a choice dictated by expediency, not by correctness. Indeed, there is no mathematical reason to regroup in the first place. It is possible to perform subtraction by processing each column independently of the others, recording negative results when appropriate, and then combine the column results into the final answer. The decision to regroup is dictated by economy considerations, not by mathematical principles.

The place value algorithms evolved over a long period of time as efficient means of performing calculations. The main reason to adhere to those algorithms is that they save work, as compared to other, mathematically equally correct procedures. But there is no relation between the mathematical theory of place value and the expediency of the algorithms that build on it. One cannot derive that *this* way of doing subtraction is more efficient than *that* way from the laws of the number system. The shape of these algorithms is not determined by the underlying mathematical principles, so understanding those principles contributes little to the learning of the algorithms. Any aspect of a procedure which is grounded in expediency rather than in mathematical concepts and relations will appear arbitrary and incomprehensible regardless of how well the conceptual rationale for that procedure is understood.

School children cannot be aware of the expediency of the place value algorithms. In order to realize how economical they are, one must have something to compare them to. Since children are taught the efficient algorithms, they have no experience of *less* efficient ways of doing calculations. Also, since children are not doing calculations for a living, they have no interest in expediency.

The importance of attention allocation. One of the most robust findings of cognitive psychology is that there are severe limits on how much information can be kept in working memory at any one point in time. This limitation is simulated in the HS system by letting working memory elements decay as time passes. The main consequence of this limitation is that the control of attention is a central issue in all action, including mathematical action. If you cannot keep all information in the problem display in your head simultaneously, then you have to access it sequentially, by moving your eye over it in a carefully controlled manner. *To learn subtraction is to learn where to look.* Obviously, mathematical principles have nothing to say about this aspect of mathematical action. No matter how well one understands the concept of place value, one still has to figure out where to look at each moment during subtraction.

Summary. There are at least three principled reasons to believe in a wide derivational gap between mathematical principles and mathematical action. First, mathematical principles ignore questions of space and time, while a cognitive procedure is a structure for the spatio-temporal control of action. Second, mathematical principles ignore the cost of computing a result, while the standard place value algorithms are designed for maximum expediency. Children cannot understand those features of place value algorithms which are designed with expediency in mind, because they have no experience of the less expedient alternatives, and, unlike the professional calculators who developed the algorithms, children have no particular interest in economy. Third, the limited capacity of human working memory implies that all task information cannot be kept active at all times. Consequently, any cognitive skill must specify how attention is to be allocated over the task information. But mathematical principles have nothing to say about the allocation of attention.

If the gap between mathematical principles and mathematical action is as wide as the above discussion suggests, then how is an understanding of the mathematical concepts and principles underlying a particular algorithm supposed to facilitate the construction of the cognitive skill? This question has not been clearly answered by any current theory of mathematical cognition, and I suggest that no answer exists. The gap between mathematical knowledge and mathematical action *is* difficult to bridge. That is why it took two millennia to develop the place value algorithms, and that is why school children make mistakes even after they have grasped the rationale of an algorithm.

The fact that the derivational distance between mathematical principles and mathematical action is large does not in and of itself explain why the HS model needs to compute more in the case of a conceptual representation than in the case of a mechanical representation. Granted that the derivational distance is large, we still need an explanation for why it is *larger* in one case than in the other. The explanation is simple: There is more work involved in updating and processing a rich representation than an impoverished one. There are more relations to keep track of, and, therefore, more operations to perform. Each of those operations has to be controlled by some procedural rule; hence, there are more rules to learn, or more complicated conditions for the rules. The same must be true of humans: updating and maintaining a richer mental representation must require more cognitive work.

Because the gap between the mathematical principles and the mathematical procedures is so wide, I believe that any reasonable simulation model of knowledge-based acquisition of an arithmetic procedure will reproduce the results reported here. The reader who disbelieves this is urged to prove me wrong by developing a simulation model that can learn subtraction both conceptually and mechanically, and which expends less computation in the former case than in the latter.

According to the results reported here, William Brownell could not have been more wrong. Regrouping is more difficult to learn than augmenting. In particular, regrouping in a conceptually rich representation is more difficult to learn than regrouping done mechanically, and the disadvantage of the conceptually rich representation as compared to the mechanical case is much larger for regrouping than for augmenting. These results directly contradict Brownell's conclusion that regrouping is easier than augmenting, particularly when taught conceptually [5, 6].

At first glance, this contradiction seems devastating for the model. After all, Brownell's conclusion was based on empirical observations, and in the case of a contradiction between theory and data, it is the theory that must go. However, unlike simulation studies, empirical studies cannot differentiate between learning and performance, between the amount of cognitive work needed to learn an algorithm and the amount of cognitive work needed to execute it, once learned. The only way to measure the cost of learning is to observe performance, so any empirical measure will necessarily confound the two. As the reader might recall, the simulation of performance in the first study reported in this chapter did produce results which fit the empirical data rather well. It is reasonable to interpret those data as measures of the cognitive cost of executing the algorithms rather than of the cognitive cost of learning them. We then have a good fit between the theory and the data themselves, but no support for Brownell's interpretation of the data.

The result that conceptual instruction requires more computational work than mechanical instruction is comforting to the researcher who desperately wants to know why well-intended, carefully planned and skillfully executed instructional interventions that aim to impart conceptual understanding do not succeed in producing correct performance [27, 33]. But it is less comforting to the educator or teacher who is responsible for designing efficient instruction. The simulation results imply that it is a mistake to expect conceptual understanding to facilitate procedural learning. Instead, the results indicate that conceptually based instruction will be more costly in terms of time and effort than mechanical instruction. The relation between the conceptual rationale of an arithmetic procedure and the procedure is an instructional topic in its own right, a topic, moreover, which is complicated and therefore requires time and effort on the part of both instructor and student. Instead of being a tool for teaching the same old arithmetic, conceptually based instruction in arithmetic constitutes a higher pedagogical ambition, as compared to mechanical instruction.

It is easy to feel sympathy with this higher ambition. Obviously one would want students to grasp the rationale behind the arithmetic algorithms. The present discussion is not meant to imply that conceptual instruction in arithmetic is wrong or undesirable. What is wrong is the expectation that such instruction can be digested more easily and with less effort than mechanical instruction.

Conceptually based instruction in arithmetic might need to revisit the idea of a spiral curriculum [7, pp. 52-54]: teach the algorithms with a small amount of conceptual interpretation at an early age, teach them again with a deeper presentation of the conceptual rationale when the students have acquired more mathematical knowledge, and so on. The topic could be visited as many as four or five times between third grade and college, each visit probing deeper into the conceptual rationale, until the students are able to carry out a relatively tight derivation of the algorithms (see [25]). To the best of my knowledge, no large scale empirical evaluation of such a spiral curriculum for arithmetic has yet been done.

Evaluation of the General Method

The specific conclusions about arithmetic instruction presented in this chapter are controversial and unlikely to be accepted without a debate. Such a debate would be welcome. But the controversial nature of the *domain-specific conclusions* should not be allowed to obscure the fact that the present study also contributes a *general method* with a potentially greater impact.

The main method of traditional educational research is well exemplified by the studies conducted in order to choose between the regrouping and augmenting algorithms: to determine the relative advantage of an instructional design A as compared to an alternative design B, teach one set of students with design A and a second set of students with design B, and compare the outcomes. This empirical method is laborious and time consuming. In addition, it is rarely successful in settling the instructional issue at hand. Measures of instructional outcomes are so imprecise and coarse that a negative outcome is unconvincing. Opponents of the hypothesis favored by the author of such a study can always feel justified in questioning whether the measures used were sensitive enough to register even quite significant effects. On the other hand, a positive effect is equally unconvincing. An observed effect cannot be ascribed to the instructional intervention with any certainty because it is almost impossible to achieve control over all the determinants of an instructional outcome. Empirical comparisons between alternative instructional designs carry little intellectual authority, regardless of outcome.

Teachable simulation models enable an alternative method for investigating instructional questions. Instead of teaching the relevant instructional topic in different ways to different groups of students, we can teach it in different ways to a model of learning, if that model takes the form of a robust, runnable simulation. The simulation runs provide us with measures of the amount of computational work required to learn the target topic under different modes of instruction. A significantly lower value for mode A than for its rival B constitutes a prediction that A is the preferred way of teaching the target topic.

Using this method, an instructional designer can invent a new approach to a particular topic, use it to teach that topic to the model, and have a preliminary outcome, all in a matter of days. Preparing the inputs (the initial procedural knowledge and the instructions) to a teachable simulation model is not a trivial task, but it is measured in hours or days, rather than in months or years. Such rapid turnaround between an instructional idea and its evaluation has the potential to facilitate search through the space of instructional designs [30]. Many different designs can be tried out and compared at a relatively low cost and in a relatively short time.

A teachable simulation model can also help identify fruitless questions and inappropriate techniques. Consider once again the large scale classroom studies of the pre-World War II era that attempted to settle the controversy between regrouping and augmenting empirically. My simulation results show that there is no reason to expect any differences between regrouping and augmenting on measures of performance. The two algorithms are nearly equal in cognitive complexity, once learned. Hence, trying to measure the difficulty of the two algorithms by measuring performance is not a useful endeavor. The differences between the algorithms only affect the amount of cognitive work required to learn the algorithms. But pure empirical measures of learning are hard to come by. One possibility is to count the number of learning events per unit time as revealed by think-aloud protocols, a measure hardly ever used in learning research (see [40] for an exception). No such measure was employed in the pre-World War II studies that compared regrouping and augmenting. Those studies could not, in principle, resolve the issue they were addressing because they were approaching it with the wrong tools. Theoretical clarification is a necessary prerequisite for meaningful data collection in instructional science as in other sciences. Implementing and using a teachable simulation model is one way to achieve such clarification.

A second traditional approach to instructional design, over and above empirical comparisons between alternative teaching methods, is to base particular decisions on general design principles, which, in turn, are derived in some more or less intuitive way from a learning theory. The debate about how to teach subtraction could conceivably be decided by the application of such a principle. For example, we could apply the principle of successive elaborations: a topic should be taught by first presenting a kernel idea, an epitome, which is then successively elaborated [32]. But this principle does not discriminate between the different ways of teaching subtraction. Both regrouping and augmenting can be taught by first presenting the basic idea of the algorithm, and then elaborating on it. As a second example, consider the principle, proposed by Anderson, Boyle, Farrell, and Reiser, that one should teach the goal hierarchy of the target skill [2]. Once again, this principle does not discriminate between alternative subtraction algorithms. As a last example, a colleague of mine suggested that one should prefer regrouping over augmenting on the principle that teaching should facilitate future learning, and the regrouping operation is more generally useful than the augmenting operation. But it is unclear in what sense the law of associativity is more generally useful than the constant difference law; both seem equally necessary for continued study in mathematics. In short, the disadvantage of using general design principles as mediators between theories of learning and instructional designs is that the application of those design principles is seldom straightforward.

The method of teachable simulation models links learning theory to instructional design in a different way. The method brings learning theory to bear on particular issues, without mediation by general design principles. For example, the simulation runs presented in this chapter tell us that augmenting is easier to learn than regrouping, and that the advantage of augmenting is increased with conceptually based instruction. The simulation runs resolve the particular issue of regrouping versus augmenting, but they do not suggest any principle of arithmetic instruction, let alone any general design principle. The principles of learning embedded in the model are applied directly to the instructional issue at hand. Whether this is, in general, a better way to proceed than via general design principles cannot be determined here. The two different ways of linking learning theory to instructional design are not incompatible. A mixture of both approaches will probably prove most advantageous.

Testing instructional designs by trying them out on a simulation model seems to presuppose that we have accurate simulation models. There are three answers to this objection. First, the lack of accuracy of today's models and theories is a temporary disadvantage. As research into human learning progresses, we will be able to construct more and more accurate theories. It is desirable to have a method which allows us to channel increased theoretical understanding into improved instructional designs. The dependence on the accuracy of our learning theory is not only a bug, it is also a feature. Second, the extent to which particular computational results depend upon the accuracy of the model is a matter for debate. In the preceding section, I argued that the results reported in this chapter are consequences of deep features of arithmetic and hence, are relatively independent of the particulars of the HS model. (It is clear how to provide evidence for or against claims of this kind. A claim about independence of results from a particular model is supported if the results can be reproduced with a different model.) Third, a theory need not be entirely accurate to be useful. Even approximate theories can often supply information that improves upon common sense and rules of thumb.

Answering questions through theoretical calculations goes against the grain in a discipline that was shaped in the heydays of the peculiar brand of empiricism advocated by the logical positivists. It is therefore useful to look up from our local concerns and observe that the ratio of theoretical calculation to empirical observation tends to grow as scientific disciplines mature. Once upon a time, geometers measured angles in order to decide whether a triangle was a right triangle or not. By the time Euclid wrote his great treatise, geometry was already a purely theoretical discipline in which answers to questions were derived from first principles. Mechanics went through a similar development. Brahe and Galileo needed observations, but since the "rational mechanics" of the 19th century, questions like how much force it takes to lift a particular payload into orbit are answered by calculation, not by observation. If it were necessary to send up hundreds of rockets with different payloads and different thrusts in order to decide the issue empirically, space travel could never have gotten off the ground. In short, to observe is to confess ignorance; it is what scientists do when they have little or no theoretical understanding. As a science matures, calculations replace (some) empirical measurements. There is every reason to expect instructional science to develop similarly. The present chapter is but a small step in that direction.

Acknowledgements

The research reported in this chapter is supported by grant No. N00014-89-J-1681 from the Cognitive Science Program of the Office of Naval Research, and an institutional grant for the Center for the Study of Learning from the Office of Educational Research and Improvement, US Ministry of Education.

References

1. Anderson, J. R.: *The architecture of cognition..* Cambridge, MA: Harvard University Press 1983
2. Anderson, J. R., Boyle, C. F., Farrell, R., & Reiser, B. J.: Cognitive principles in the design of computer tutors. In: *Modelling Cognition* (P. Morris, ed.). New York, NY: Wiley 1987
3. Anzai, Y., & Simon, H. A.: The theory of learning by doing. *Psychological Review*, 86, pp. 124-140 (1979)
4. Brown, J. S., & Burton, R. R.: Diagnostic models for procedural bugs in basic mathematical skills. *Cognitive Science*, 2, pp. 155-192 (1978)
5. Brownell, W. A.: An experiment on "borrowing" in third-grade arithmetic. *Journal of Educational Research*, 41, pp. 161-263 (1947)
6. Brownell, W. A., & Moser, H. E.: *Meaningful vs. mechanical learning: A study in Grade III subtraction.* Durham, NC: Duke University Press 1949
7. Bruner, J. S.: *The process of education.* New York, NY: Vintage Books 1960
8. Ernst, A. M., & Ohlsson, S.: *The cognitive complexity of the regrouping and augmenting algorithms for subtraction: A theoretical analysis.* Technical Report No. KUL-89-06. Pittsburgh, PA: University of Pittsburgh 1989
9. Evertz, R.: *A production system account of children's errors in fraction subtraction.* Technical Report No. CAL 28. Milton Keynes, UK: The Open University 1982
10. Glaser, R.: Components of a theory of instruction: Toward a science of design. *Review of Educational Research*, 46, pp. 1-24 (1976)
11. Glaser, R.: The contributions of B. F. Skinner to education and some counterinfluences. In: *Impact of research on education: Some case studies* (P. Suppes, ed.). Washington, D.C.: National Academy of Education 1978
12. Glaser, R.: Instructional psychology: Past, present, and future. *American Psychologist*, 37, pp. 292-305 (1982)
13. Greeno, J. G.: Some examples of cognitive task analyses with instructional implications. In *Aptitude, learning, and instruction. Volume 2: Cognitive process analyses of learning and problem solving* (R. E. Snow, P. A. Federico, & W. E. Montague, eds.). Hillsdale, NJ: Lawrence Erlbaum Associates 1980
14. Haseman, K.: Die Beschreibung von Schulerfehlern mit kognitionstheoretischen Modellen. *Der Mathematikunterricht*, 31, pp. 6-15 (1985)
15. Hiebert, J. (Ed.): *Conceptual and procedural knowledge: The case of mathematics.* Hillsdale, NJ: Lawrence Erlbaum Associates 1986
16. Hollan, J. H., Holyoak, K. J., Nisbett, R. E., & Thagard, P. R.: *Induction: Processes of inference, learning, and discovery.* Cambridge, MA: MIT Press 1986
17. Hunting, R. P.: Alan: A case study of knowledge of units and performance with fractions. *Journal for Research in Mathematics Education*, 14, pp. 182-197 (1983)
18. Klahr, D., Langley, P., & Neches, R. (Eds.): *Production system models of learning and development.* Cambridge, MA: MIT Press 1987
19. Laird, J., Rosenbloom, P., & Newell, A.: *Universal subgoaling and chunking: The automatic generation and learning of goal hierarchies.* Boston, MA: Kluwer 1986
20. Langley, P.: A general theory of discrimination learning. In: *Production system models of learning and development* (D. Klahr, P. Langley, & R. Neches, eds.). Cambridge, MA: MIT Press 1987
21. McDermott, J., & Forgy, C.: Production system conflict resolution strategies. In: *Pattern-directed inference systems* (D. A. Waterman, & F. Hayes-Roth, eds.). New York, NY: Academic Press 1978
22. Murray, F. B., Ames, G. J, & Botvin, G. J.: Acquisition of conservation through cognitive dissonance. *Journal of Educational Psychology*, 69, pp. 519-527 (1977)
23. Newell, A., & Simon, H. A.: *Human problem solving.* Englewood Cliffs, NJ: Prentice-Hall 1972
24. Ohlsson, S.: Transfer of training in procedural learning: A matter of conjectures and refutations? In: *Computational models of learning* (L. Bolc, ed.). Berlin, West Germany: Springer-Verlag 1987
25. Ohlsson, S.: *The conceptual basis for subtraction with regrouping: A mathematical analysis.* Technical Report No. KUL-02-88. Pittsburgh, PA: University of Pittsburgh 1988
26. Ohlsson, S.: Computer simulation and its impact on educational research and practice. *International Journal of Educational Research*, 12, pp. 5-34 (1988)
27. Ohlsson, S., Bee, N. V., & Zeller, P. A.: *Empirical evaluation of a computer-based environment for fractions.* Technical Report No. KUL-89-07. Pittsburgh, PA: University of Pittsburgh 1989
28. Ohlsson, S., & Rees, E.: Adaptive search through constraint violations. *Journal of Experimental and Theoretical Artificial Intelligence* (in press)

29. Ohlsson, S., & Rees, E.: The function of conceptual understanding in the learning of arithmetic procedures. *Cognition & Instruction.* (in press)
30. Pirolli, P. L., & Greeno, J. G.: The problem space of instructional design. In: *Intelligent tutoring systems: Lessons learned* (J. Psotka, L. D. Massey, & S. A. Mutter, eds.). Hillsdale, NJ: Lawrence Erlbaum Associates 1988
31. Post, T. R., Wachsmuth, I., Lesh, R., & Behr, M. J.: Order and equivalence of rational numbers: A cognitive analysis. *Journal for Research in Mathematics Education,* 16, pp. 18-36 (1985)
32. Reigeluth, C, M., & Stein, F. S.: The elaboration theory of instruction. In: *Instructional-design theories and models: An overview of their current status* (C. M. Reigeluth, ed.). Hillsdale, NJ: Lawrence Erlbaum Associates 1983
33. Resnick, L. B., & Omanson, S. F.: Learning to understand arithmetic. In: *Advances in instructional psychology* (R. Glaser, ed.). Hillsdale, NJ: Lawrence Erlbaum Associates 1987
34. Scandura, J. M.: *Problem solving. A structural/process approach with instructional implications.* New York, NY: Academic Press 1977
35. Shuell, T. J.: Cognitive conceptions of learning. *Review of Educational Research,* 56, pp. 411-436 (1986)
36. Smith, J.: *Learning rational numbers.* Unpublished doctorial dissertation, School of Education, University of California at Berkeley 1990
37. Tatsuoka, K. K.: *Analysis of errors in fraction addition and subtraction problems.* Technical Report, Urbana-Champaign, IL: University of Illinois January 1984
38. VanLehn, K.: Bugs are not enough: Empirical studies of bugs, impasses and repairs in procedural skills. *Journal of Mathematical Behavior,* 3, pp. 3-71 (1982)
39. VanLehn, K.: *Mind bugs: The origins of procedural misconceptions.* Cambridge, MA: MIT Press 1990
40. VanLehn, K.: Rule acquisition events in the discovery of problem solving strategies. *Cognitive Science* (in press)
41. Young, R. M., & O'Shea, T.: Errors in children's subtraction. *Cognitive Science,* 5, pp. 153-177 (1981)

Part 2

Representing Curriculum and Designing Instructional Tasks

Representing Curriculum and Designing Instructional Tasks

Jim Greer[1] and Ellen Mandinach[2]

[1]ARIES Laboratory, Department of Computational Science, University of Saskatchewan, Saskatoon, Canada
[2]Educational Testing Service, Princeton, NJ, USA

The issue of curriculum in computer-based instruction further illustrates how attempts to computationalize educational actions lead to a better understanding and a more scientific analysis of education itself. Curriculum design, the process of selecting and sequencing material that constitutes a program of study for the learner, was once considered to be an art. Instructional scientists have been making the process of curriculum design more explicit and have specified a variety of principles and rules to guide the selection and sequencing of activities for the learner. Those interested in automating instruction further force this explicit analysis of curriculum. In fact, in order to truly individualize instruction in a computer-based learning environment, the computer system must be able to reason about the curriculum, understand the implications of a particular curriculum plan, and must be able to dynamically redesign the curriculum to meet the individual's learning needs.

In most kinds of education, including school learning, a curriculum consists of a prerequisite map of the content domain, learning objectives with specific achievement levels, possible educational activities, and often a set of testing and evaluation materials. These curricula typically are externally imposed. In addition, another phase of curricular design is carried out by the teacher. This consists of tuning the imposed curriculum to be consistent with the needs of the individual learner. The process of individualizing the curriculum might involve changing the sequence of content, changing the learning objectives, or changing the desired achievement levels. It might involve adding additional objectives, perhaps from a related content area or from the affective domain, or perhaps adding subtle objectives aimed at attitudinal change (sometimes termed the "hidden curriculum"). In fact, almost every element of the curriculum may be subject to change by the teacher, with changes ranging from minor adjustments to radical alterations. This demonstrates two distinct phases of curriculum design, the first resulting in the generic curriculum, designed by a subject area specialist for a content domain with a stereotypical learner in mind; and the second resulting in the individualized curriculum, designed by the classroom teacher and adjusted, hopefully, for the individual learner's needs. In typical classroom situations this approach to implementing the curriculum is common.

NATO ASI Series, Vol. F 85
Adaptive Learning Environments
Edited by M. Jones and P. H. Winne

If a computer system is charged with the responsibility of curriculum design for an individual learner, then it must possess the knowledge and ability to make informed curricular decisions suited to the particular domain of instruction, the learning goals, the instructional style or philosophy, and the characteristics and state of the individual learner. Without individualization, a system would suffer the same criticisms levelled against early forms of computer-assisted instruction, i.e., that of an inflexible, lock-step approach to presenting a generic curriculum. Individualizing the curriculum for a particular learner is a knowledge intensive activity. Since much of the generic curriculum is subject to change during the process of individualizing the curriculum, the two traditional levels of curriculum design perhaps should not be so distinct. It may be argued that the knowledge required for realizing an individualized curriculum for a specific learner subsumes much of the knowledge needed for designing the generic curriculum for a subject domain. The two-phased design of the generic and then the individualized curriculum might not be the best division of tasks in a computer-based learning system. This points out the need for re-examining curriculum design issues in artificial intelligence-based learning environments.

In an attempt to synthesize a new view of curriculum consistent with the requirements and capabilities of computer-based learning environments, this section presents two papers. Gordon McCalla describes curriculum from the computational perspective, describing intelligent tutoring projects that have explicitly dealt with issues of curriculum planning. He describes curriculum as an emergent phenomenon, arising from the goals of the learner and system, as well as from the knowledge that the system possesses about the content domain and about the learner. McCalla's description of curriculum seems to refer to the individualized curriculum described above, while the issue of the static curriculum seems to be implicitly (or sometimes explicitly) present in the system's knowledge about the domain. J. R. Hartley, on the other hand, seems to focus on the static curriculum, describing curriculum as something that emerges from the semantic linkages in the content domain. He takes a more traditional education perspective, distinguishing curriculum from instruction, where instructional planning is thought of as individualizing the curriculum for the current situation.

The two papers in this section both claim that curriculum in a computer-based learning environment is best modelled using artificial intelligence planning techniques. The curriculum planning process uses a variety of knowledge sources including the content domain, the learning goals, the instructional method or instructional philosophy, and the model of the individual learner. This planning process produces a set of instructional actions (sometimes called teaching operators), which if applied would most likely achieve the learning goals. The planning necessary for generic and individualized curricular design can be accomplished using similar artificial intelligence-based computational algorithms, but they vary in terms of the relative emphasis placed on the various knowledge sources used.

Planning is a very active area of research in artificial intelligence. Although most of the research efforts in planning have focussed on robot motion planning, route planning, and discourse planning, many of the techniques that have been developed in these domains readily apply to curriculum planning. A wide variety of planning paradigms have emerged over the past ten years. Most of them find their roots in the STRIPS planning system of Sacerdoti [7]. Blackboard planning using multiple knowledge sources and opportunistic plan revision was popularized by Hayes-Roth [3]. More recent work has focussed on dynamic planning, reactive planning, case-based planning, and multi-agent planning. Allen, Hendler, and Tate [1] recently edited a collection of papers surveying various planning methods. Many of these planning approaches seem to hold promise for various activities within intelligent tutoring systems, and particularly for curriculum planning. For example, Peachey and McCalla [6] investigated dynamic course planning; blackboard-based instructional planning has been used by Macmillan and Sleeman [4], and by Murray [5]; and reactive planning has been used by Wasson [2] for individualized content planning. Wasson [2] also provides an excellent survey of AI-based planning as it applies to curriculum planning in intelligent tutoring systems.

A curriculum planner must make its decision based on many complex and relatively uncertain knowledge sources. Both papers in this section describe a variety of attempts to automatically plan curricula. Of course, actually constructing a comprehensive curriculum planner is extremely difficult and many compromises are made. The apparent naivety of many of the early systems attests to the subtlety and difficulty of this planning task.

References

1. Allen, J. , Hendler, J , and Tate, A. (eds.): *Readings in Planning*. Morgan Kaufmann 1990
2. Brecht (Wasson), B. J.: Planning the Content of Instruction. PhD. Thesis, University of Saskatchewan, Saskatoon, Canada, (Also available as Research Report 90-4, ARIES Laboratory, Department of Computational Science, University of Saskatchewan) 1990
3. Hayes-Roth, B.: A blackboard architecture for control. *Artificial Intelligence*, 26, pp. 251-321 (1985)
4. Macmillan, S.A. & Sleeman, D.H.: An architecture for a self-improving instructional planner for intelligent tutoring systems. *Computational Intelligence*, 3, 1, pp. 17-27 (1987)
5. Murray, W.R.: A blackboard-based dynamic instructional planner. Proceedings of the 8th National Conference on Artificial Intelligence, Boston, MA, pp 434-441 (1990)
6. Peachey, D. R. & McCalla, G. I.: Using planning techniques in intelligent tutoring systems. *International Journal of Man Machine Studies*, 24, pp. 77-88 (1986)
7. Sacerdoti, E. D.: *A Structure for Plans and Behavior*. New York: Elsevier 1977

The Search for Adaptability, Flexibility, and Individualization: Approaches to Curriculum in Intelligent Tutoring Systems

Gordon I. McCalla

ARIES Laboratory, Department of Computational Science, University of Saskatchewan, Saskatoon, Canada

Abstract: Curriculum is a pervasive concern in education, but is barely an issue in intelligent tutoring system (ITS) research. This is because most intelligent tutoring systems are restricted to working in a tightly constrained domain, and thus have little need for subject organization at the macro level of curriculum. Nevertheless, there is a small, but interesting, line of research in ITS that has explored issues of direct concern to curriculum. This research has led to the idea of curriculum as an emergent phenomenon, created dynamically in response to student needs, to requirements of the subject matter, and to pedagogical goals. Such a curriculum is adaptable to a changing environment, flexible in instructional goals, and individualized to the student. This paper traces the evolution of the notion of curriculum in intelligent tutoring systems, in order to show how and why the current idea of curriculum came about, and to demonstrate its power. Along the way, particular systems are used to illustrate interesting aspects of ITS curriculum and to give concrete foundation to the discussion.

Keywords: intelligent tutoring systems, curriculum, instructional planning.

Introduction

Curriculum issues have been central to education. In actual classroom practice, the curriculum is the stellar object around which most teaching activities orbit. Teachers are encouraged to organize their classes according to a curriculum which guides their decision making throughout. Although the border is often fuzzy, curriculum can be distinguished from pedagogy: pedagogy involves actual teaching decisions made locally; curriculum involves global decisions as to how to organize material. A standard definition is given by Halff [23]: curriculum is "the selection and sequencing of material for purposes of instruction."

NATO ASI Series, Vol. F 85
Adaptive Learning Environments
Edited by M. Jones and P. H. Winne

Curriculum issues have not been central to researchers concerned with building intelligent tutoring systems (ITSs), that is, systems constructed using artificial intelligence techniques. Instead, the focus of most ITS research has been on representing the knowledge students are to learn, understanding student behaviour, and providing a challenging and stimulating learning environment for students. The problems inherent in doing these things are so immense that most ITSs must drastically constrain their domain of applicability. In such narrow, focussed domains there is no need for an overall organization of material, hence no need for curriculum. Moreover, most ITS research is aimed at giving students individual control over their own learning; curriculum is viewed as necessitating strong tutor control, anathema to the idea of student initiative.

Nevertheless, there is a small, but significant line of ITS research with curriculum as a central focus. In this research the notion of curriculum evolves from one quite compatible with Halff's definition to one where the supposedly irreconcilable goals of overall organization and individualization can mutually co-exist. In this new definition, curriculum is not an overall order imposed on a course of material, but is an emergent phenomenon that arises through the interaction of current pedagogical goals, student goals, and the system's knowledge of the domain and the student. Often the results of this interaction are expressed as an instructional plan that can be used by the system to guide its pedagogical decision making. This plan can change as circumstances change. In a real sense, curriculum is computed "on the fly" and is correspondingly individualized to a particular student's needs, adaptable as circumstances change, and flexible as to what pedagogical goals should be pursued.

In this paper I will trace the evolution of the ITS notion of curriculum towards the ideals of individualization, adaptability, and flexibility. I will start with some necessary background, first by outlining various approaches to the application of artificial intelligence to education. Then, features of a typical one-on-one intelligent tutoring system will be discussed, with particular emphasis on the need for the system itself to understand its own subject. With this background, a brief historical tour will be taken through the development of the ITS notion of curriculum, with particular attention being paid, naturally enough, to work in which I have been involved! Finally, important trends in ITS-based curriculum development will be discussed.

Before proceeding to a more detailed description of ITS curriculum issues, I should point out that there is a body of work applying artificial intelligence techniques (and other techniques) to the construction of design aids for human curriculum developers. This includes work such as that of Wipond and Jones [50], Merrill's ISD system [36], and the IDE system [42]. The aim of this work is to construct an interactive and supportive environment that human teachers can use as they develop curricula for courses (either automated or not). While interesting in its own right, work on creating design aids for human curriculum developers does not deal with the creation of a curriculum for a computing system itself to use. My concern in this paper is with internalized curriculum, that is, curriculum internal to the system and useable by the system.

Intelligent Tutoring Systems

Intelligent tutoring systems can be roughly divided into three categories: discovery learning systems, coaching or helping systems, and one-on-one tutoring systems. Discovery learning systems provide students with a challenging and interesting environment which they can explore, learning relevant concepts and honing their problem solving abilities as a by-product of these explorations. Examples of such discovery learning systems are legion, and include Logo [39], the Alternate Reality Kit [45], LEPUS [19], and BOXER [14]. The system itself makes no commitment to any particular exploration path. Curriculum must be imposed externally, if it is imposed at all. Because of the innovative nature of most of these environments, new notions of curriculum can arise. For example Abelson and diSessa [1] suggest a philosophy of "increasingly complex microworlds" to be used with Logo. In this philosophy, students are encouraged to incrementally build increasingly complex environments on top of each other, using the lower-level environment as a tool to aid in the construction of the higher-level environment. Despite their potential for stimulating new kinds of curriculum, discovery learning systems will not be further discussed here since they do not illustrate the internalized notion of curriculum that is the central focus of this paper.

Coaching systems provide "behind the scenes" advice to students as they explore an environment. For example, the EUROHELP system [49] provides help to students learning how to use the Unix mail system. Other coaching systems include such systems as COACH [18], the first SCENT prototype [33], the LISP Critic [17] and GIL [41], all of which provide advice to students learning LISP. The STEAMER system [25] is halfway between a discovery environment and a coaching system. As in a discovery environment, STEAMER provides a rich simulation (of a complex steam boiler system) which students can inspect at many levels of detail and from many perspectives; the coaching happens surreptitiously in the kinds of "dynamic graphical explanations" provided to the student using the system. By its very nature, coaching involves responding to a student's needs. A coaching system is thus essentially reactive. The concept of curriculum is not central in most coaching systems, although various pedagogical strategies can be utilized in reacting to the student's needs.

The third kind of intelligent tutoring system engages in one-on-one tutoring. Systems in this category can actually follow a teaching strategy aimed at increasing the student's understanding of the domain. In contrast to discovery learning environments, this strategy can be internalized. In contrast to coaching systems, this strategy can lead the one-on-one tutor to be proactive as well as reactive. Thus, BIP [2, 47] has a teaching strategy for moving students through a course on the programming language BASIC, TAPS [13] helps students learn how to solve arithmetic word problems by tracking their progress through a course of material, and Murray's tutor [37] has a set of lesson plans used to guide students towards an understanding of how to maintain a large navy gun.

One-on-one tutoring systems often share with coaching systems a desire for students to have as much control as possible. Thus, the boundary between coaching and one-on-one tutoring systems isn't sharp. SCENT-3 [34], for example, is an architecture that incorporates an explicit role for instruction in the general context of an advising system. Elsom-Cook [15] discusses the idea of guided discovery tutoring where the tutoring system can choose tutoring options along a continuum ranging from total tutor control, through mixed initiative, to total student initiative. Nevertheless, most one-on-one tutoring systems have at least the option of taking control, and must have, implicitly or explicitly, something like a curriculum which guides them on these occasions. Thus, it is mostly in one-on-one tutors where notions related to curriculum have arisen, and it is such tutors which will form the central focus of the rest of this paper.

Knowledge-Based Instruction

One of the central features of an intelligent tutoring system is that it understands its subject domain. It does this by representing the domain knowledge in some sort of representation formalism that it can manipulate. A variety of formalisms have been used in various tutoring systems: semantic networks (e.g., SCHOLAR [9]), frames (e.g., Proust [26]), procedures (e.g., SOPHIE [8]), production rules (e.g., GUIDON [12]), qualitative models (e.g., QUEST [48]), etc. These representation formalisms seem quite different on the surface, but at a conceptual level they bear considerable resemblance to each other. From the perspective of curriculum, the important things are that the system itself has access to the domain knowledge and that the formalism imposes structure on that knowledge.

Another component of a typical one-on-one intelligent tutoring system is responsible for implementing the system's tutoring strategy. It must decide what instructional activities to engage in. The tutoring strategy can take advantage of the structure the knowledge representation formalism imposes on the domain knowledge. Thus, a semantic network representation scheme may influence the design of the tutoring strategy to disseminate information along generalization or aggregation dimensions, moving from specializations to generalizations, or moving from parts to wholes, or vice versa. Whatever information it uses, the tutoring strategy component is responsible for deciding how to sequence knowledge in order to achieve the instructional goals of the tutoring system, and is responsible for selecting a particular instructional activity relevant in the current context.

In addition to the knowledge base and the tutoring strategy component, there is still a third important component that a tutoring system must have: the student model. The student model represents the system's perspectives on the student's state of knowledge and the student's attitudes. The student model is used to modify the kind of instruction the system undertakes according to the individual needs of the particular student being tutored.

Curriculum in an intelligent tutoring system can now be more precisely defined. Curriculum is an emergent phenomenon arising from the interaction of all three components. The structure of the knowledge base helps to structure the curriculum, the student model helps to individualize it, and the tutoring strategy decides how to select and sequence the knowledge based on the system's instructional goals. A definition of the ITS notion of curriculum might be that *"curriculum is the selection and sequencing of knowledge for the purposes of achieving instructional goals appropriate to the current context and the individual being tutored"*. Compare this to Halff's definition above: the ITS definition emphasizes knowledge rather than material, the individual rather than some generic student, the current context rather than a timeless unvarying approach. This is precisely the kind of shift in perspective towards individualization, adaptability, and flexibility that was mentioned above as being typical of intelligent tutoring systems.

The Evolution of Curriculum in Computer-Based Instruction

In this section, representative systems in the evolution of the notion of curriculum will be discussed. For each system, characteristics of the three important components (knowledge base, student model, and tutoring strategy) will be presented, and lessons for ITS curriculum research will be drawn.

Traditional Computer Assisted Instruction: Rigid Control

The earliest automated teaching systems were not imbued with artificial intelligence. Typically, such traditional computer assisted instruction (CAI) systems (reviewed in [11]) represent information about their domain in frames (not to be confused with the AI variety). This information is not in a form that can be analyzed by the system itself; instead, it is stored in canned phrases that can be presented to the student when appropriate. Also in a frame can be a test or other evaluation mechanism to be used when deciding whether or not students have understood the concepts presented to them. The test score is essentially the student model. The tutoring strategy involves explicitly branching to an appropriate subsequent frame, based on how well a student may have done on the current frame's test. The branching can be either forward to more sophisticated concepts or, if there are misconceptions to be overcome, backward to remedial frames .

In a traditional CAI system designed around this architecture, curriculum is essentially a control path through the frames, with the particular sequence of frames depending on how an individual student performs on each frame's test. Curriculum is a fairly central notion in traditional CAI in that complete courses are usually represented, and the sequencing and selection issues are thus critical to their design. Unfortunately, the need to explicitly predict control paths makes such systems rigid. The diagnosis is not subtle; not only is the evaluation of the student usually made in overt tests, but that evaluation ignores many dimensions of student understanding and misunderstanding. Finally, the fact that the information in the frames is unexaminable by the system itself means that the system in a real sense does not know the subject it is teaching, and thus cannot ever make "on the spot" decisions or understand the implications of its own actions. All of these drawbacks mean that, while curriculum is central, it is not a particularly individualized, adaptable, or flexible kind of curriculum. It shares much with programmed learning approaches.

When regarding traditional CAI approaches, early researchers in ITS knew that improving the various components of a tutoring system would necessitate a limitation of the domain. The problems of building a knowledge-based tutor were so hard that complete courses could not be built. Once the domain of the systems was reduced, knowledge representation and diagnosis issues took precedence over pedagogical and curriculum issues. In fact, it is only relatively recently that curriculum and pedagogical issues have become more fashionable in ITS. Thus, the early false lesson that ITS research should not be focussed on curriculum issues has finally been overcome.

SCHOLAR: Using the Structure of the Knowledge Base

Generally conceded to be the first intelligent tutoring system, SCHOLAR [9] helped students learn about South American geography. SCHOLAR pioneered a couple of important ITS ideas, most importantly representing domain knowledge in a form that the system itself could manipulate (thus giving the system a limited ability to understand its own subject). In particular, SCHOLAR's geographic knowledge is stored in semantic networks allowing the system to move about along various links connecting related concepts. A kind of student modelling is accomplished as well by keeping track of each concept the student has referenced during dialogue between student and system. This represents an early version of the "overlay" concept of student modelling, where the student's knowledge is deemed to be a subset of the expert's. SCHOLAR's tutoring strategies are extremely primitive, and essentially involve making a random selection among concepts that are relevant (i.e., near in the semantic network) to concepts in which the student has shown recent interest in the dialogue.

From the perspective of curriculum issues, SCHOLAR is important because it shows how the structure of the domain knowledge can affect the selection of the next topic. The path the system follows through the knowledge base is not preordained by explicitly specified control paths through this knowledge; instead, the system can move about freely among related concepts as it seems relevant to do so in interaction with the student. Of course, SCHOLAR's pedagogical strategies in using this knowledge base are fairly unsophisticated, and the knowledge base itself is quite restricted in the kinds of knowledge it is able to represent. Nevertheless, SCHOLAR represents an important first step towards achieving the kind of flexible curriculum which is the thrust of ITS curriculum design. SCHOLAR also illustrates the narrowing of domain so favoured in most ITS research — the range of topics covered in SCHOLAR is extremely limited, although the techniques might more readily generalize to other domains than is the case for many ITS approaches.

BIP: Skill-Based Task Sequencing for Large Courses

The BIP [2, 47] tutors are an exception to the rule that ITSs are designed only for a microcosmic world. BIP-I and BIP-II are tutoring systems that teach a complete introduction to the BASIC programming language. Built as much on principles of traditional computer assisted instruction as they are on ITS principles, the BIP tutors represent their knowledge in a curriculum information network (CIN) which shows how techniques, skills, and tasks relate to one another. One such CIN for part of BIP-I's knowledge of BASIC is shown in Figure 1, and illustrates how a particular task (e.g., writing a program to print a string) can exercise particular skills (e.g., printing string literals) and particular programming techniques (e.g., writing out single values).

In BIP-II, skills are further broken down into a semantic network such as that shown in Figure 2. The "C" (component) and "K" (kind-of) links represent standard "part-of" and "isa" semantic network relationships; "D" represents the idea of mutual dependency and "H" (harder than) shows increasing difficulty among concepts. As in SCHOLAR, the BIP tutors have access to knowledge about their subject that is much more amenable to examination and manipulation by the system itself than in traditional CAI.

The BIP tutors also have student modelling capabilities based on the overlay idea. Skills that the student is deemed to have mastered are so marked in the CIN. The tutoring strategy is then to find appropriate follow-up skills to current skills on the fringe of the student's understanding. Links in the semantic network can be used to choose these follow-up skills, in particular "dependency" and "harder than" links. Then, appropriate tasks that exercise these skills can be chosen. It is also possible in BIP to move up or down "component" and "kind-of" links in order to focus on particular sub-skills or generalize concepts.

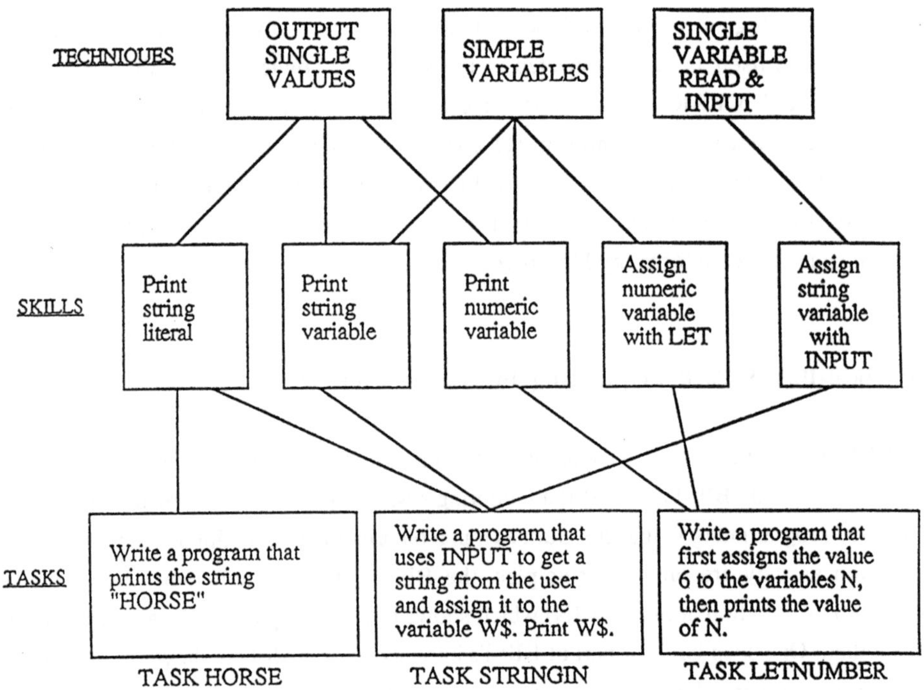

Figure 1: Part of the Curriculum Information Network in BIP-I (originally in [2], from [46], p. 109)

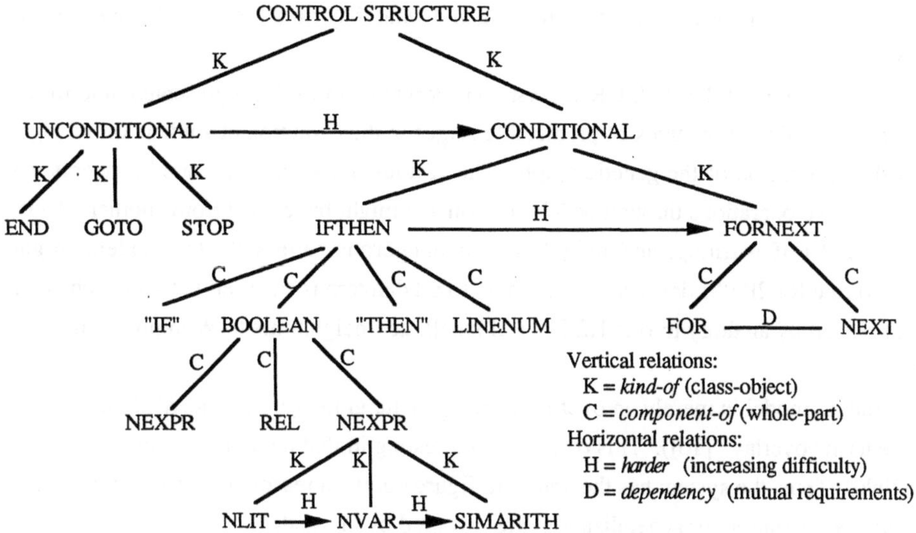

Figure 2: Portion of BIP-II Semantic Network (originally in [47], from [46] p. 111)

The BIP systems are most notable for their emphasis on full courses. This emphasis has led to a central role for curriculum, most unusual in ITS. The notion that tasks are the relevant things for the student to be working on, and that they can be sequenced appropriately by mapping from the curriculum is also original to BIP. Moreover, this task sequence is not preplanned as in traditional CAI but can be dynamically generated as the student-tutor interaction proceeds. It is not until many years later in work such as that of McArthur, Stasz, Hotta, Peter, and Burdorf [30] that skill-based task sequencing again has such an explicit role.

WUSOR-III: The Genetic Graph

The WUSOR-III system [20] provides a marked contrast to the BIP systems in two ways. First, its domain is a small microworld, namely a gaming environment where students "Hunt the Wumpus" as they wander through a simulated cave. Second, it is a coaching, not a teaching system: students are provided with hints, as needed, to get them around obstacles and to help them learn relevant rules that are useful in playing the game. These differences suggest a much more prominent role for students in determining their own paths through the knowledge to be learned, and a much less prominent role for the system. Increased student control, in turn, leads to a need to structure the knowledge in ways that the system can use in order to tell how students have come to their current understanding and what they might reasonably be expected to do next.

Thus, at the centre of the WUSOR-III system is domain knowledge represented in terms of a genetic graph, which keeps track of predictable stages in the evolution of student knowledge. Figure 3 shows a region of the genetic graph. The various links connect related concepts via possible cognitive operations through which one concept might be learned from another. Thus, from rule R2.2 ("if warning, add neighbours to dangerous cave set") the student might specialize to rule R2.2P ("if draft, add neighbours to pit dangerous cave set") from which he or she might reason by analogy to rule R2.2W ("if smell, add neighbours to Wumpus dangerous cave set").

The student model is merely an overlay on the genetic graph (in fact the WUSOR project coined the term "overlay" [10]). This overlay is interesting in that not only are nodes overlaid, but also links. Thus, the system has the ability to figure out what reasoning strategies (analogy, refinement, specialization, or generalization) are favoured by the student.

The tutoring (i.e., coaching) strategy in WUSOR-III is to identify fringe nodes known to the student, and then to use genetic relationships from these fringe nodes to suggest where coaching might help. Explanations can be generated to encourage the student to make a cognitive leap to the next concept; in fact, there is an explanation possible for each such next concept for each fringe node in the genetic graph. Figure 4 shows possible explanations depending on the genetic link connecting the nodes. The choice of which explanation to give depends on the kinds of reasoning favoured by the student in the past. For example, students who favour reasoning by analogy can have new concepts explained that way. Because there are often many possible paths to a node in the graph, quite different sequences of explanations can be given to each student while still covering all the concepts in the graph.

Curriculum in WUSOR-III is thus an interaction between the student model and the genetic graph. It is a somewhat strange notion of curriculum, however, since the system does not impose its will on the student. The curriculum is dynamically generated as needed to help the student. This is the first system discussed where the flexibility and adaptability to student needs have been so obvious. Curriculum in student-centered situations must be adaptive and flexible. It is also the first, and heretofore almost the only, system to explore curriculum in terms of evolution of student knowledge (although follow-up work by Wasson and Jones [7] shows how the genetic graph can be used in other domains such as ballet).

The AND/OR Graph: Making Control Implicit

At a time when most research in ITS was focussed on microworlds and issues not related in a direct way to curriculum, McCalla, Peachey and Ward (MPW [35]) were exploring how

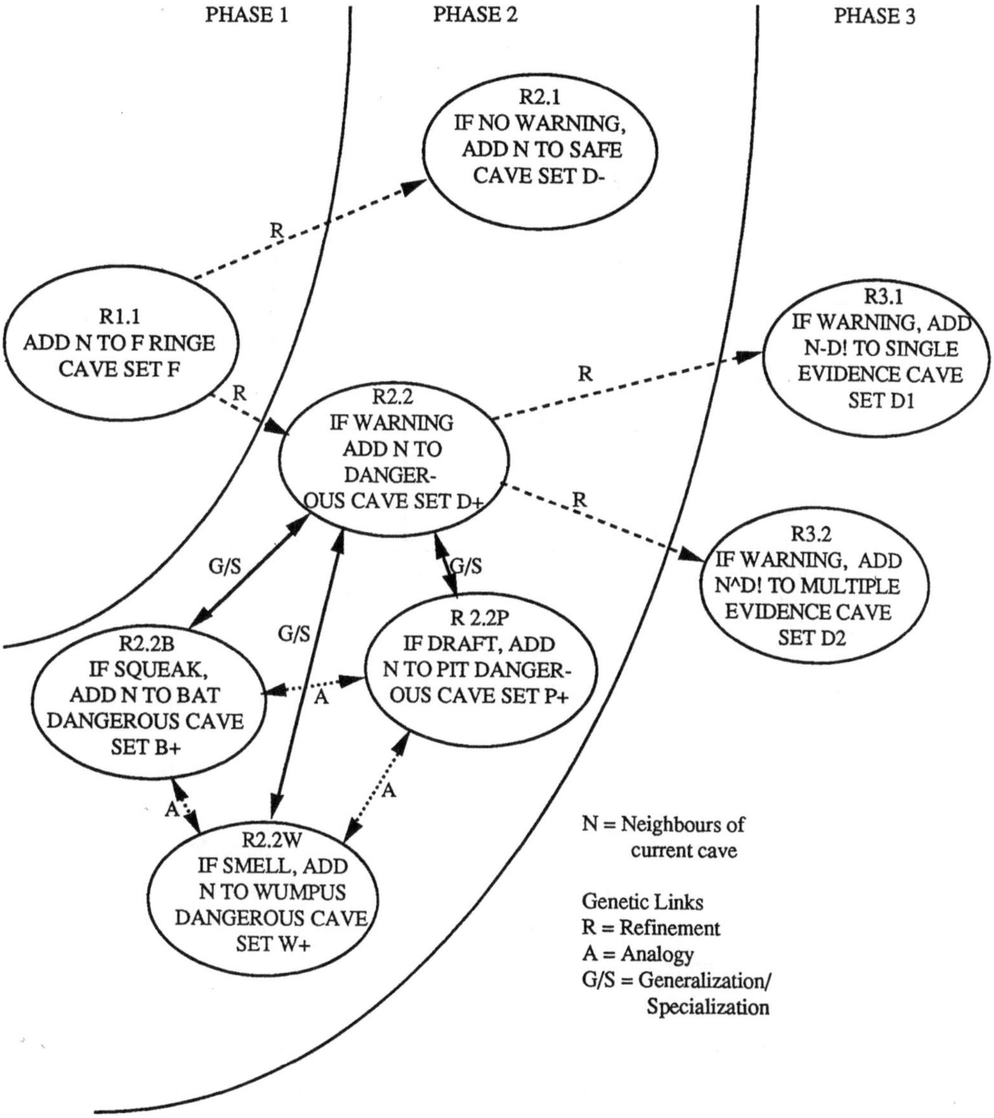

Figure 3: A Region of the Genetic Graph (from [20], p. 57)

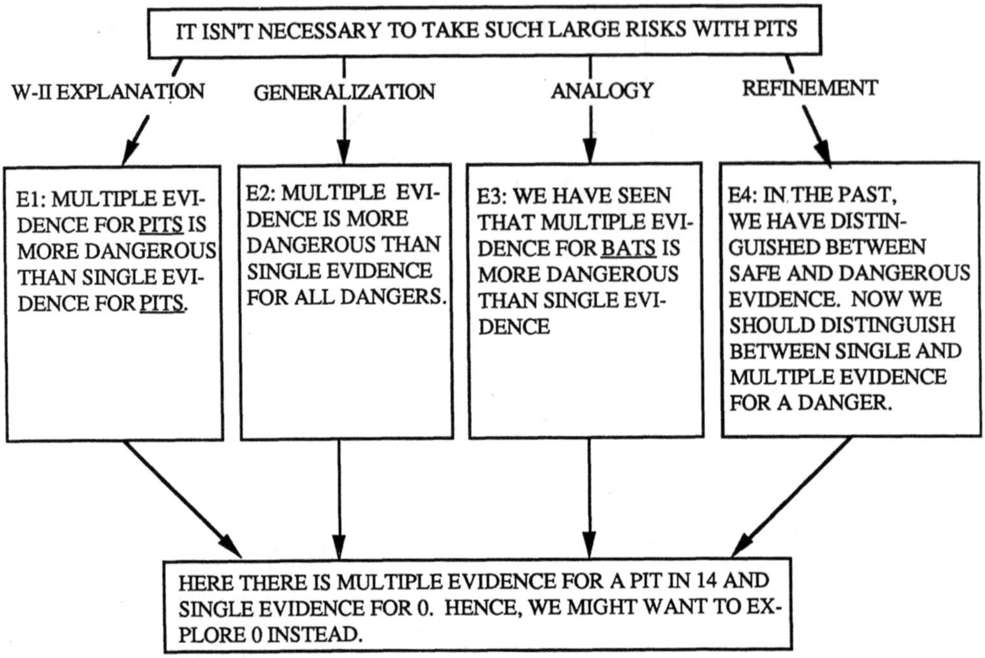

Figure 4: Variations on an Explanation in WUSOR-III (from [20], p. 66)

artificial intelligence techniques could be used to help structure large courses. Curriculum issues are central in this research. Key to the MPW approach is the use of a standard AND/OR course graph, four examples of which are shown in Figure 5. The nodes in these graphs are concepts to be learned by the student, in this case concepts in the programming language LISP. Links in these graphs are prerequisite links, so that in sub-graph 1 "basic function calling notation" has as its prerequisite "data structures." If an arc connects the links, then all of the nodes are prerequisites (they are ANDed); for example in sub-graph 3 both "CAR recursion" and "CDR recursion" are prerequisites for "CAR/CDR recursion." If no arc connects the links, then any of the descendent nodes can be prerequisites (they are ORed); for example, either of the two conjunctions of concepts shown in sub-graph 1 can be prerequisites for "lambda-expressions." The resulting AND/OR graph allows an entire course to be represented in terms of its prerequisite structure. The course graph is more complex than this, however. Recognizing the granularity of knowledge, any node in the AND/OR graph can be broken down into a sub-graph of finer grained concepts which together constitute the superconcept. In Figure 5, the "basics of LISP" node in sub-graph 4 expands into sub-graph 1, the "recursion" node there expands into sub-graph 2, and the "types of recursion" node there expands into sub-graph 3.

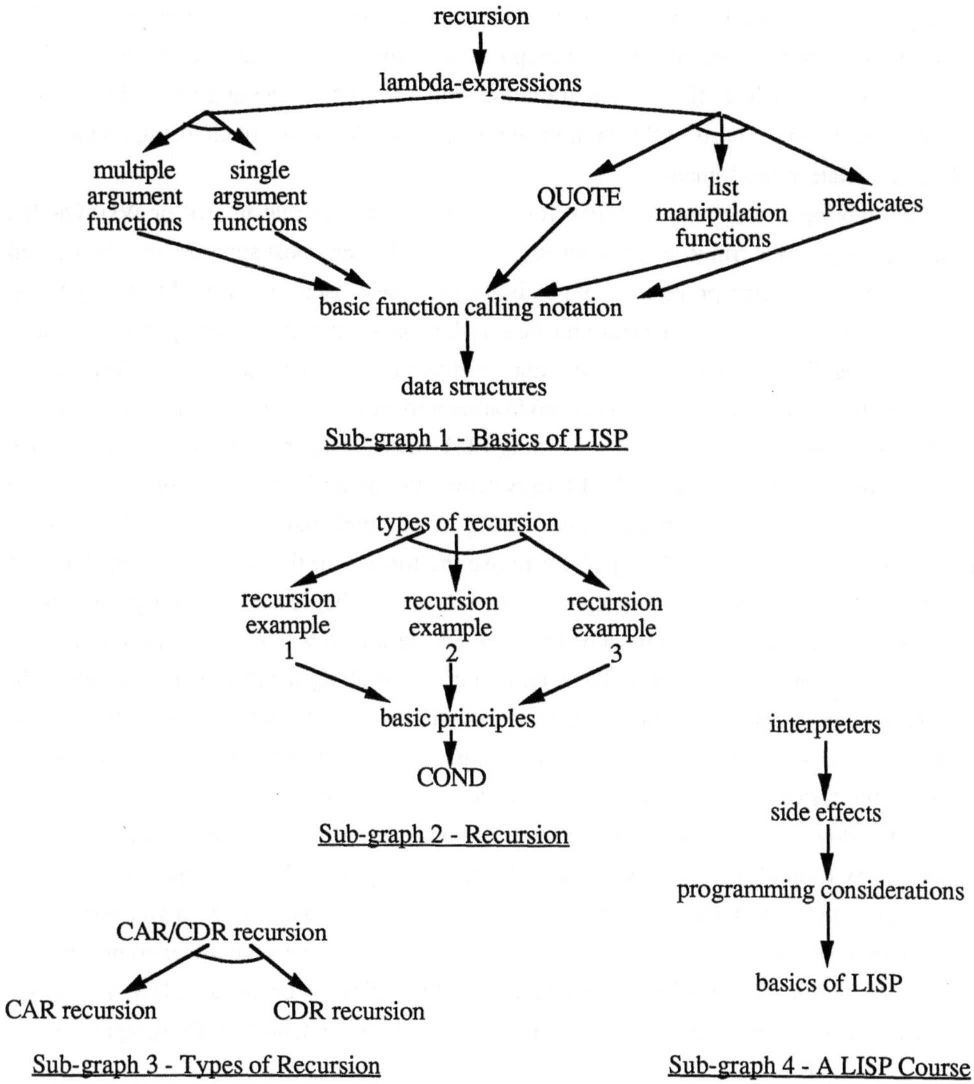

Figure 5: Segments of an AND/OR Course Graph (from [35], p. 87)

The student model in this nested AND/OR graph is a standard overlay, indicating which concepts are known or unknown to the student. Markers indicating known and unknown concepts can propagate through levels of nesting, and along prerequisite links in order to compute a fringe of known nodes beyond which lie concepts unknown to the student. At a given level of detail, AND/OR semantics allows the fringe to be automatically computed through prerequisite links since a node is unknown if any of its AND prerequisites is unknown, and if all of its OR prerequisites are unknown. There are various possibilities as to how this propagation can move up through the nested levels: a super node could be deemed unknown if a majority of the nodes in its sub-concept graph are unknown, or if the last prerequisite node is unknown, or if certain critical nodes are unknown. The knowledge engineer who builds a tutoring system on the basis of this architecture is left with the choice of choosing propagation rules appropriate to the domain.

The tutoring strategy in the MPW formalism is similar to that in BIP or WUSOR-III. Nodes just beyond the fringe are the concepts which are the next most appropriate to be learned by the student. An appropriate level of detail must also be chosen. The actual teaching of any such concept is done by procedures attached to the concept's node. These procedures have arbitrary capabilities, ranging from emulating traditional CAI "blurb and test" styles through providing the student with a discovery environment to explore. An experiment in using the MPW formalism in the creation of a working LISP tutor (unreported in [35]) resulted in the construction of a fairly traditional CAI-like system: tutor-controlled presentation of material in prestored natural language blurbs, and testing of comprehension using standard testing methodologies. Although it is expedient to use the formalism this way, the many kinds of flexibility available to the system designer mean that such rigidity is not a necessary outcome.

Although the course graph must be prespecified, the way in which it is used is adaptable to individual students, and flexible. Thus, curriculum is similarly adaptable and flexible. The course designer has the capability to experiment with different teaching styles and to integrate them easily, to try out different decisions as to what level of detail to present various concepts (or to let the system itself decide). A major advantage of the formalism is that the semantics of AND/OR allows the course designer to totally avoid issues of what concept to teach next; the fringe at any level of detail can be computed automatically by a global interpreter. Control is thus implicit in the AND/OR semantics, and does not require the knowledge engineer to wire in explicit branches beforehand, as is done in traditional CAI. Perhaps the major contribution of this research is the reaffirmation that standard AI technologies can be useful in ITS, in this case, the idea that an AND/OR graph can help in organizing curriculum, both for the designer and for the system itself.

Dynamic Planning of Instruction

Building on the lessons of the MPW formalism, Peachey and McCalla [40] were led to investigate ways of avoiding the need to prespecify the course graph. To this end, the robot planning approach of STRIPS [16] was adapted to the needs of instruction, the first appearance of the idea of instructional planning. In the Peachey and McCalla formalism, STRIPS-style planning operators are used not to represent robot actions, but to represent teaching actions for each unit (lesson) in the course. Each of these teaching operators has capabilities similar to the concepts in the AND/OR graph formalism: each operator is fully responsible for providing the student with a learning environment of some sort for the concept it represents. Additionally, associated with each teaching operator are prerequisites describing the conditions under which the teaching operator is relevant, and expected post conditions if the teaching operator succeeds. These prerequisite and post conditions are specified as logical propositions.

The student model is also specified as logical propositions indicating concepts the student knows or concepts which are misconceptions. These do not constitute an overlay on the units of the course, however, since any information can be in a proposition, not just information related to a unit. Moreover, the ability to represent misconceptions is different from the traditional notion of overlay.

The tutoring strategy is a standard STRIPS-style planning algorithm. Starting with some goals as to what target concepts the student should eventually know, this planning algorithm is able to reason backwards through expected post conditions and prerequisite conditions to get a sequence of teaching actions that will take the student from his or her current state of knowledge as specified in the student model through to an understanding of the target concepts. All possible action sequences are generated, resulting in a plan graph representing a curriculum individualized to a particular student's state of knowledge. Some simple plans are shown in Figure 6, where the boxes represent the teaching operators and the circles represent the predicted result of the teaching operators. As a plan is executed, the student model may change or misconceptions may arise which block certain learning paths. Alternative paths can then be chosen. If all paths are blocked, the system can dynamically create a new instructional plan that takes into account the new student model.

Curriculum in this formalism is a dynamic instructional plan, created from the teaching operators and individualized according to the student model. A plan-based approach allows the curriculum to be tailored to the student, to be adaptable as circumstances change, and to be flexible through having multiple paths created in the plan. This work is also further evidence of the value of applying standard AI techniques to the design of intelligent tutoring systems.

A Generic Curriculum Architecture

In a series of experiments at the Learning Research and Development Center at the University of Pittsburgh, Alan Lesgold and his colleagues have explored the idea of curriculum. One result was the creation of the conceptual architecture for a curriculum-centered intelligent tutoring system shown in Figure 7. This architecture forms the underpinnings for an electronics tutor called MHO [28]. The architecture proposes that domain knowledge, pedagogical goals and

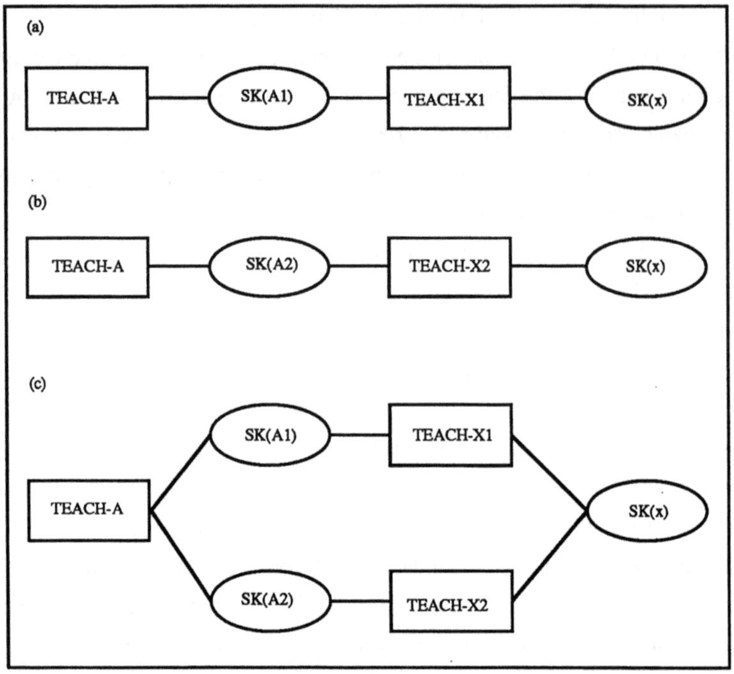

Figure 6: Simple Plans (from [40], taken from [5] p. 91)

metacognitive skills be structured in three layers: knowledge layer, curriculum layer, and aptitude layer. The knowledge layer contains the system's domain knowledge, complete with knowledge links such as part/whole, isa, etc. The curriculum layer contains goals and subgoals which organize the knowledge layer according to various pedagogical perspectives. Different perspectives can impose entirely different organizations on the knowledge in the knowledge layer, thus allowing multiple viewpoints on the knowledge. The third layer contains various meta-cognitive reasoning skills. These are associated with various pedagogical goals, the achievement of which might exercise these meta-cognitive abilities. In MHO, there is a fourth treatment layer (parallel to the curriculum layer) interconnected to the knowledge layer that is used to generate various tasks that test domain knowledge exercised by the tasks (this is similar to the relationship between tasks and skills in the BIP curriculum information network).

The entire architecture is distributed over an object-oriented representation; the layers don't actually exist separately but are instead implicit in links between various objects. Thus, a given object might have conceptual links, curricular links, links to tasks, links to procedures for diagnosing a student's knowledge or testing that knowledge, etc. Student modelling is simply an overlay on these objects; each object has a slot indicating the level of student mastery of the concept represented by the object. Since some of the objects are at the metacognitive level,

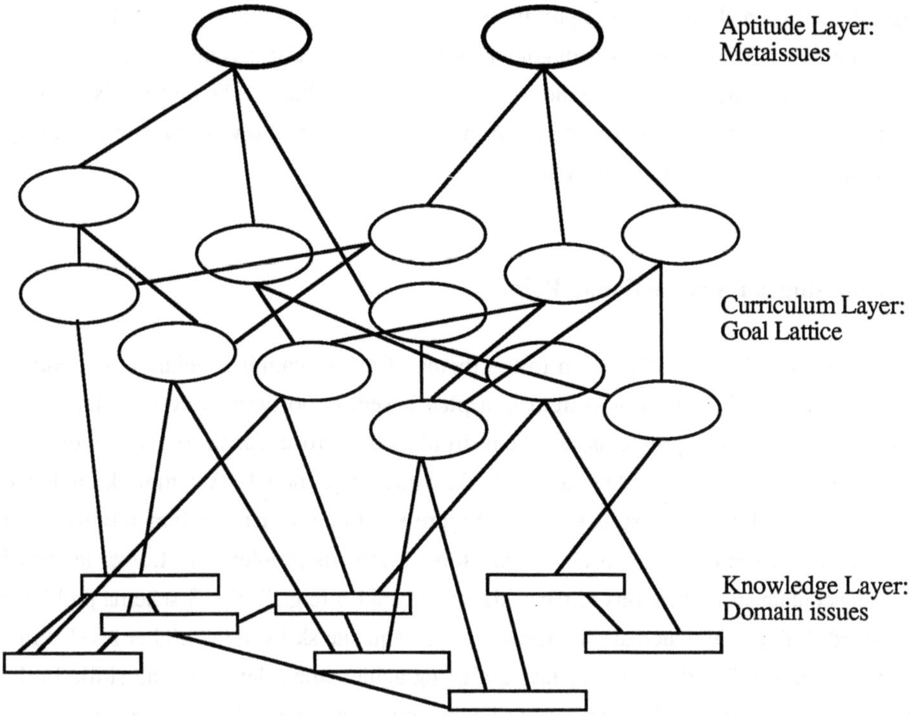

Figure 7: Layered Curriculum Representation (originally in [27], taken from [46] p. 148)

some at the pedagogical level, and some at the knowledge level, the student model can keep track of students' learning preferences as well as their knowledge of the domain.

The curriculum architecture allows for many different teaching styles. The one used by MHO involves the generation of tasks that are appropriate to the system's pedagogical goals, to the student's current frontier of knowledge, and to the student's meta-cognitive abilities. Equally important, however, is the generation of a task that makes the diagnosis of student understanding easier. Often this involves carrying out explicit tests of student capabilities. In fact, Lesgold calls the approach "steering testing" since the student is steered using relevant tests towards an understanding of the domain. The close integration of the need to test the student and the need to advance their knowledge may well pay pedagogical dividends. Knowledge must be exercised to be learned. This idea is supported by the success of mastery learning which similarly reinforces learning through testing and achieves a one standard deviation improvement over regular classroom teaching (see [4]).

The curriculum architecture proposed here shows the value of organizing knowledge with an eye to curriculum issues. Particularly interesting is the ability to represent multiple pedagogical perspectives, and the possibility of bringing metacognitive factors to bear on pedagogical decision making. Also important is the close interconnection between testing and learning. This synergy not only has pedagogical advantages, but also has the added advantage of making diagnosis easier, thus easing the student modelling problem. The idea of distributing knowledge over many objects improves system modularity which allows enhanced flexibility both at the design level and within the system.

TAPS: Choosing an Instructional Point

Derry, Hawkes, and Ziegler [13] return to the theme of using planning techniques to aid in instruction. Their TAPS tutoring system is a plan-based, opportunistic system that helps students solve algebra word problems. At the heart of their approach, as in so many intelligent tutoring systems, is their knowledge base, called a knowledge model. A sample knowledge model for word problem expertise is shown in Figure 8. Higher order problem solving skills are expressed at the top of the hierarchy (e.g., "solve 3-schema problems"). Lower levels of the hierarchy contain specializations of these higher level skills (e.g., "solve 3-schema problems using forward chaining"), which are interpreted as prerequisite skills to the higher level skills. The student model in TAPS is an overlay, assigning achievement levels to the skills in the knowledge model. Three qualitative levels of achievement are possible: non-master, novice-master, and expert.

The TAPS tutoring strategy starts by choosing an instructional point, i.e., a skill appropriate for the student to learn and an achievement level for that skill. This is done using the semantics of the prerequisite relationship and the order of the achievement levels. Briefly, higher level skills are not chosen without adequate prerequisites; higher levels of achievement are not required before lower levels have been achieved. The propagation of these rules is done bottom-up through the knowledge model in a fashion somewhat similar to the discovery of the fringe in the AND/OR graph of McCalla, Peachey and Ward. Once an instructional point has been chosen, the next task is to call in a lesson planner to build a plan to accomplish the goal of having the student achieve the instructional point. This plan is a sequence of tasks for the student to work on. As the student works on the tasks, his or her performance is monitored. Hopefully, the student achieves the required level of performance in the chosen skill, but the system has capabilities to recognize both opportunistic achievement of other skills and failure to achieve the required skill or other skills. In any case, the student model is updated appropriately and, upon completion of the lesson, the cycle can begin again with the selection of a new instructional point.

Curriculum in TAPS is once again a function of planning heuristics, knowledge base and student model. The most interesting aspect of TAPS for curriculum is the explicit notion of

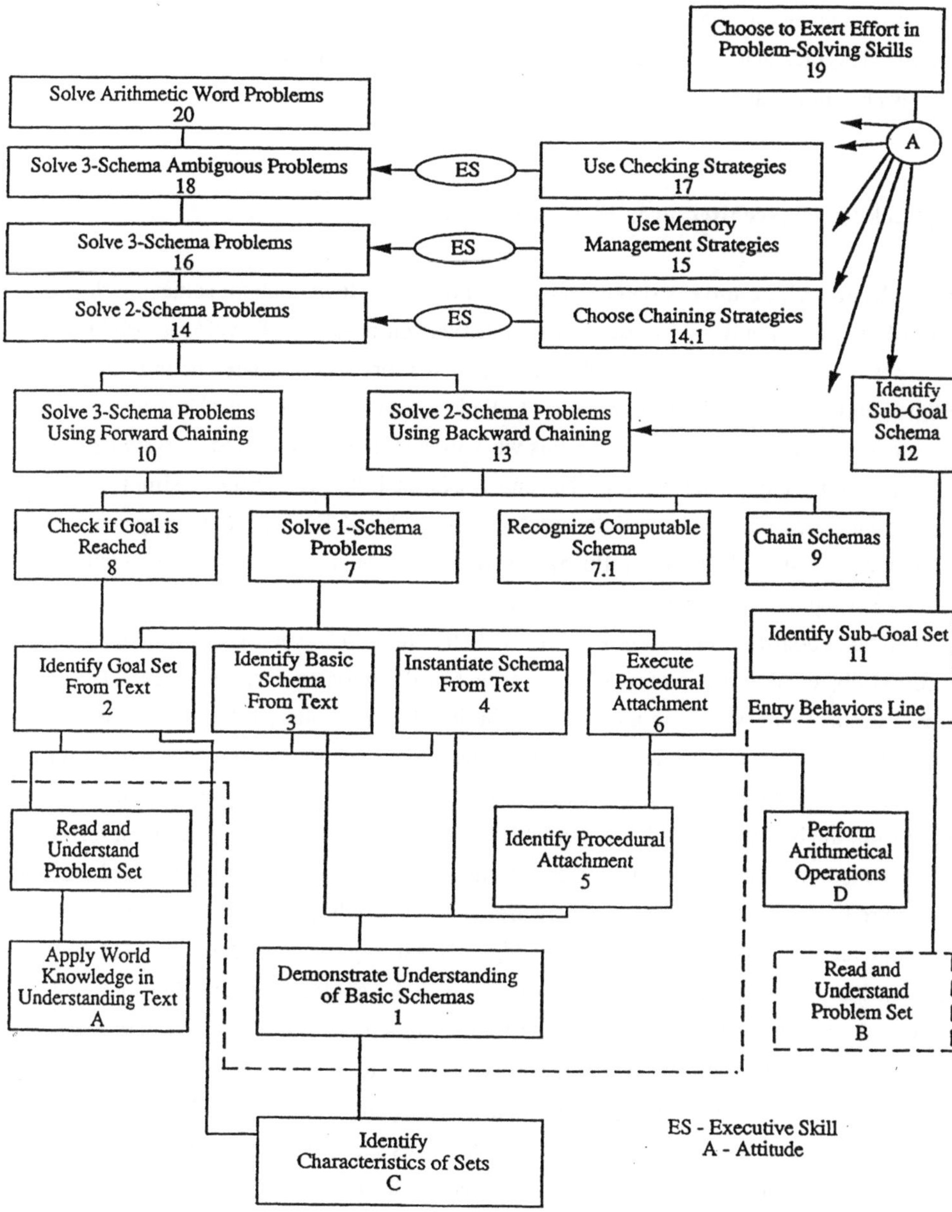

Figure 8: A Knowledge Model in TAPS (adapted from [13])

instructional point, expressed in terms of both a skill to be learned and an achievement level for that skill. The fact that a curriculum-based approach is also relevant for a relatively small domain is also illuminating.

The Blackboard Architecture: Flexibility in Control

The blackboard architecture is a standard artificial intelligence technique for achieving flexibility in control in systems built out of many quasi-independent modules. Developed originally for use in speech understanding, the blackboard idea has more recently been adapted for use in intelligent tutoring. Macmillan and Sleeman [29] pioneered the use of a blackboard architecture in instruction. Murray [37] has built on this work in his tutoring system to help students learn how to maintain a large navy gun. Ng and McCalla [38] investigate a simpler kind of blackboard architecture that is used during diagnosis in the SCENT-1 advising system. I will use Murray's BB1-based system to illustrate how the blackboard idea can aid the flexibility of curriculum design in intelligent tutoring systems.

In a blackboard system, knowledge is distributed in a set of knowledge sources, procedural objects that are experts in some aspect of the tutoring system. These knowledge sources communicate with one another only indirectly, via a shared data structure called a blackboard. Essentially, a knowledge source needing information posts a request on the blackboard. Any knowledge source capable of responding to that request can pick up the request from the blackboard and, after suitable computation, can post the required information on the blackboard. Murray's system uses a particular blackboard architecture called the BB1 architecture [24]. In this architecture there are two main kinds of blackboard: one for domain knowledge and the other for control knowledge. In Murray's system the domain knowledge blackboard is used by knowledge sources relating to the subject matter being tutored (e.g., "motivate the lower hoist assembly"). It constitutes the domain knowledge of the system. The control blackboard is used by knowledge sources relating to instructional planning itself (e.g., "suspend current instructional plan"). The instructional plan is kept on this blackboard. There are a number of other blackboards that Murray introduces specifically for instructional planning purposes, including a skeletal plan blackboard, used in the creation of instructional plans, and a curriculum/overlay blackboard where the student model is kept. The student model is essentially an overlay on domain knowledge. Figure 9 shows these blackboards and the general control cycle used in carrying out instructional actions.

The tutoring strategy is extremely dynamic, but essentially takes part in three phases: plan lesson objectives, select a tutorial strategy, and execute the instructional plan. During lesson planning, topics are refined and sequenced and a current topic is selected (e.g., "introduce topic"). The lesson plan is created from stored skeletal plans and is not individualized to the student (Murray hopes to make this more dynamic in future versions of the instructional planner). The second phase, selecting a tutorial strategy, involves finding an appropriate presentation and assessment strategy for the current topic. The combination of the lesson plan and the presentation plan constitutes the system's full instructional plan, which is stored on the control blackboard. During the third phase, plan execution, any number of knowledge sources may think they are relevant (in the vernacular they may "want to fire"). For example, if the student is investigating the lower hoist assembly, then knowledge sources relating to this may want to fire.

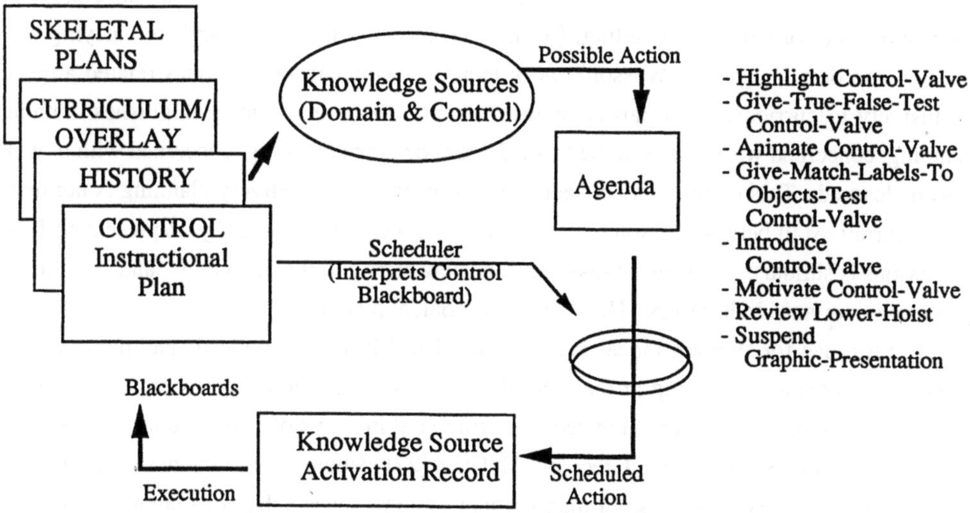

Figure 9: Blackboard Control Cycle (originally in [37], from [5] p. 97)

All such knowledge sources are put on an agenda where a scheduler, after consulting the instructional plan, decides which is the most relevant. For example, if the current plan objective is "introduce topic", then the "introduce lower hoist assembly" knowledge source would be more relevant than other knowledge sources pertaining to the lower hoist assembly like "review lower hoist." Dynamic changes in student behaviour can result in new knowledge sources feeling they are relevant, and can result in changed instructional actions or even the creation of new instructional plans. This is particularly true if the student shows initiative and asks for a change in direction (such student requests are dealt with by a discourse strategy planner).

Curriculum in a blackboard system is truly dynamic: it emerges from the interaction of many independent knowledge sources and changes as the tutorial interaction proceeds. Murray's system, although still somewhat crude, illustrates that the flexibility this provides is both attainable and useful. The central role that Murray sees for the instructional plan as an arbiter among competing knowledge sources also suggests the importance of curriculum issues to ITS. Finally, the use of a blackboard architecture in instructional systems is yet another example of how standard AI methodologies can find a new and often fascinating manifestation in the tutoring world.

PEPE: Reactive Planning of Content

Wasson [5, 6] discusses the instructional planning component of the SCENT-3 [34] LISP advising system. Taking advantage of the other components of the SCENT-3 architecture that are responsible for student modelling, for interacting with the student, and for carrying out shallow and deep diagnosis, Wasson's work is able to concentrate on issues related almost exclusively to curriculum, in particular instructional planning. She distinguishes content planning, concerned with what is to be learned, from delivery planning, concerned with how it is to be learned. This distinction between content planning and delivery planning is not new (e.g., Murray's split between lesson planning and selecting a tutorial strategy to present each of the lessons is similar). However, Wasson brings new clarity to the distinction, and it assumes a central importance in her work. Her focus is on content planning.

The test bed for Wasson's ideas is a system called PEPE (pronounced "pay pay") which actually does content planning in the LISP domain. Domain knowledge is represented in a content knowledge base, where knowledge is structured in terms of two granularity relations, noted in her work ISA and POF. Greer and McCalla [22] elaborate the subtleties of this notion of granularity and its usefulness in instructional systems, especially for diagnosis. To the granularity relations, Wasson adds prerequisite information. This is useful, as has been seen in other systems, for sequencing instructional actions. Figure 10 shows a portion of a knowledge base for the LISP concept of recursion. It is important to note that there is nothing unique about LISP: the content knowledge base can represent any knowledge to be learned by the student. A particularly intriguing possibility (unexplored by Wasson) is to construct a content knowledge base for various problem solving skills, thereby allowing metacognitive skills to be explicitly dealt with by an intelligent tutoring system.

The student model in PEPE is a set of propositions describing the system's perception of the student's current knowledge about concepts in the content knowledge base. There are four different predicates: SK (the student knows the concept), ~SK (the student doesn't know the concept), ?SK (it is questionable whether the student knows the concept), and MC (the student has some misconception about the concept). In addition, Wasson has adapted from Bloom [3] the idea that there are various kinds of knowing. She boils Bloom's categories down to three that are particularly useful in the LISP domain: fact (e.g., the student knows the definition of recursion), analysis (e.g., the student knows how to analyze what recursive programs do), and synthesis (e.g., the student knows how to create recursive programs). Such levels of knowing are attached within a predicate to each concept as a modifier. Thus, if it is questionable whether the student knows how to synthesize the concept of recursion, the predicate ?SK(s, recursion) would be added to the student model. The student model in PEPE is a particularly sophisticated overlay model, not on domain expertise *per se*, but on ways of understanding and misunderstanding domain expertise.

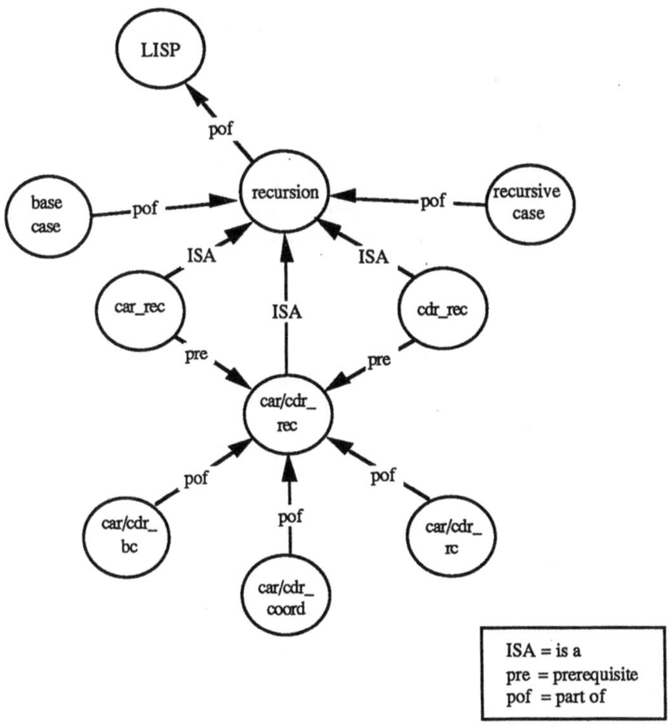

Figure 10: A Portion of a Content Knowledge Base in PEPE (from [5], p. 132)

PEPE's tutoring strategy is managed by a set of production rules. These rules make use of the content knowledge base, the student model, as well as the student history and plan history, to carry out content planning. There are three stages in content planning: finding the instructional goal, generating a content plan, and monitoring the execution of that plan. Each of these phases is managed by its own set of rules, summarized in Figure 11. Goal generation rules are used to choose both a content and a modifier for that content to serve as the instructional point. A sample goal generation rule is "achieve fact before analysis." Plan generation rules then create a content plan by elaborating the instructional point and adding operators such as achieve, review, findout, remediate. These operators fall somewhere between regular teaching operators and Shuell's student-centered learning functions [44]. A sample plan generation rule is "if planning to achieve the analysis of some content x, then focus on

GOAL GENERATION

- Goal Prerequisite Rules
- Subgoal Generation Rules
- Subgoal Selection Rules
  - Meta-Rules
  - Concept Prerequisite Rules
  - Pedagogical Preference Rules

PLAN GENERATION

- Operator Assignment Rules
- Modifier Assignment Rules
- Content Assignment Rules
- Plan Subnodes Generation Rules

PLAN MONITORING

- Blocked Goal Rules
- Adapting Plan Rules

Figure 11: Types of Pedagogical Planning Rules (from [5], p. 137)

the analysis of x and findout what the student has learned about x." An example of a content plan is shown in Figure 12. After the content plan is created, it is passed to a delivery planner that figures out how to actually carry out the plan. As the instructional interaction proceeds, the content planner must monitor the plan looking for changes to the student model, blocked learning paths, etc. This process is undertaken by plan monitoring rules such as "if SK(m,x) appears in the student model for some content x, then plan nodes dealing with x can be removed." Such rules allow dynamic replanning to occur as situations change. Control rules such as "use goal prerequisite rules before subgoal generation rules" are used to help impose order on rule firings.

PEPE can implement a variety of instructional styles. The particular style favoured by Wasson is general concepts before specific concepts, prerequisite concepts first, fact before analysis before synthesis. By changing just a few rules, however, this style can be altered to reflect a different teaching style where, for example, specific concepts might be presented to the student before general concepts, or synthesis before analysis. The ability to easily plug in new teaching styles makes the PEPE approach highly adaptable to different needs.

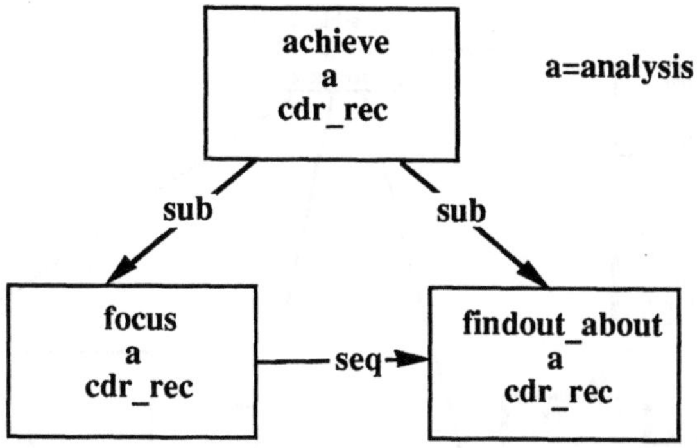

Figure 12: A Small Content Plan (from [5], p. 130)

For a given student at a given point in time, PEPE's planning rules could be run to generate a complete explicit plan that would form the curriculum for that student at that time, based on the assumption that the student will learn each concept in the order presented. Such a plan is shown in Figure 13. Unfortunately, this plan will be relevant only if the student actually follows the predicted learning path set out for him or her in the plan. Individualized instructional interactions are normally far too dynamic for this to occur. Thus, in PEPE, only the small subpart of the plan, shown in bold in the figure, will actually be generated. The rest of the plan is implicit. If things go as expected, the entire explicit plan will incrementally be generated. If not, then a new plan that takes into account the changed circumstances, will be devised. The generation of an implicit plan makes the planner efficient, while at the same time being justified by the extreme dynamism of instruction.

Curriculum in PEPE is thus an implicit content plan, generated dynamically from domain knowledge, student model, student history, and plan history. PEPE makes many contributions to curriculum issues. The distinction between content and delivery clarifies the role of curriculum as a content role. Also interesting is the idea that curriculum need only be implicit; a complete curriculum need not be explicitly generated. Computational precision is given to two ideas originating in educational research, including levels of knowing attached as modifiers to content in the curriculum and operators that are used to represent desired instructional actions at each step. Moreover, PEPE has the ability to straightforwardly represent a variety of teaching styles, each of which would result in quite different curricula being generated. Overall, the PEPE architecture is perhaps the best example so far of an adaptable, flexible, individualized approach to curriculum.

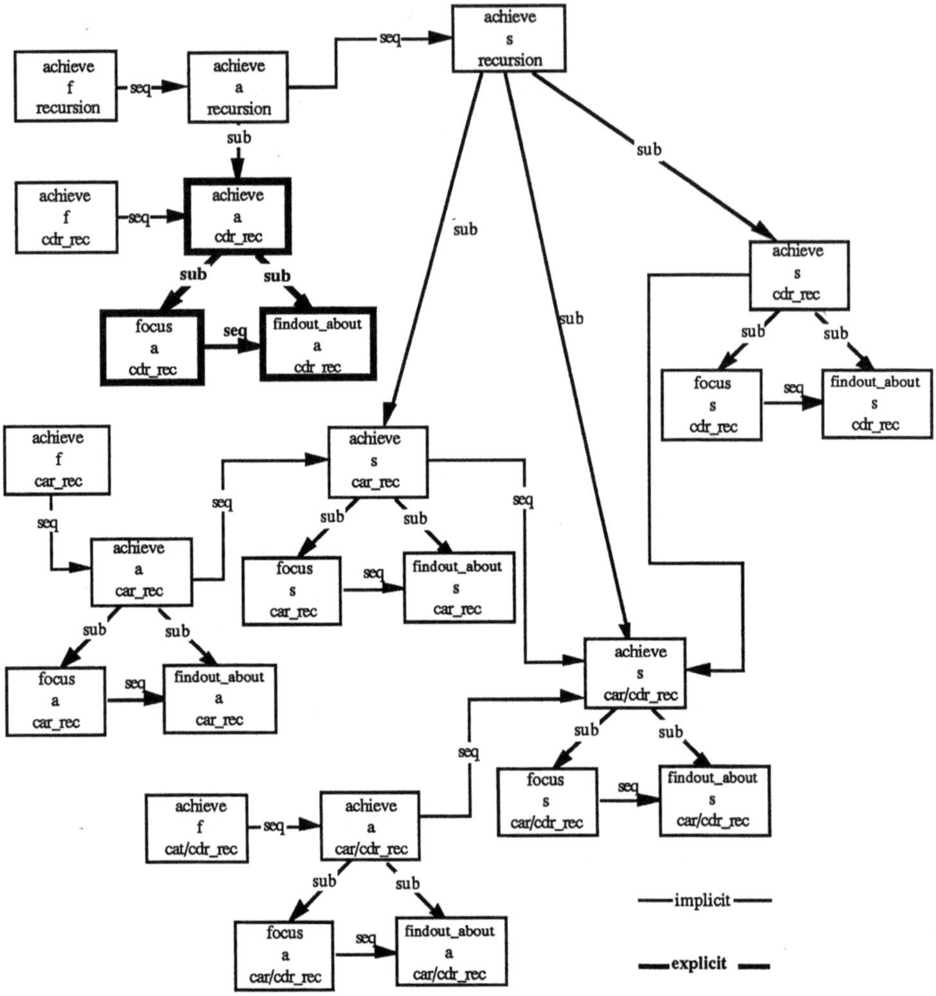

Figure 13: Implicit Versus Explicit Planning (from [5], p. 197]

Trends in Curriculum for Intelligent Tutoring Systems

As ITS research has progressed over the years, curriculum issues have taken on enhanced importance. Curriculum has evolved from being something externally imposed by the designer of the tutoring system, to something that the system itself can access and manipulate. Rigid course graphs have given way to flexible knowledge bases. Prespecified and predictable control paths have been supplanted by instructional plans dynamically created by the system according to the individual needs of the student, and changed as these needs change.

There are a number of trends affecting curriculum that are emerging from research in ITS. As mentioned throughout the paper, the trend is towards individualization of the curriculum to the student, flexibility of control during "execution" of the curriculum, and adaptability of the curriculum to context, i.e., the ability to change the curriculum as circumstances change. Other trends include an increasing realism of domains and goals; the domains are no longer toy domains, the goals are becoming broad and multi-dimensional. There is integration of different aspects of tutoring with curriculum, especially student modelling, pedagogy, and domain knowledge representation. The lesson is that curriculum cannot be isolated from other aspects of the tutoring process, but arises from interactions among a number of system components. Important dimensions affecting curriculum are being clarified, including: the difference between content and delivery; notions of implicit versus explicit planning; different kinds of knowing by the student and about the student; the idea of multiple pedagogical perspectives and instructional goals; the existence of various student achievement levels; and the specification of different relationships interconnecting domain knowledge, most importantly prerequisite, generalization, and aggregation. In recent ITS research, there seems to be increased fidelity of computational approaches to what we know about human domain knowledge representations, about actual student learning, and about real teacher behaviour. The trend is towards research that is better informed than in the past by ideas from other disciplines (especially education, artificial intelligence and cognitive science) and to methodologies that involve gathering experimental evidence for claims made. Transference of ideas among these related disciplines should increase, to the mutual benefit of all of them.

A number of questions arise, as well. Student modelling is crucial to the modern notion of curriculum, but is it possible? Are there end runs around problems in diagnosis and tracking student knowledge? How can curriculum methodologies still work with an inaccurate student model? Papers by Self [43], and McCalla [31, 32] shed some light on the hard problems of student modelling and provide some general ideas about how such problems might be overcome.

How important is individualization? It is a major goal in ITS generally, including work involving curriculum, but is it really necessary? Can the two sigma gain in instructional effectiveness, which Bloom claims can be achieved through individualization [4], be gained through the use of clever canonical plans instead? Or is individualization better attained through discovery environments and total student control? No easy answer to these questions is possible. However, it does seem that good human teachers have an incredible ability to help students to avoid pitfalls and achieve enhanced understanding. It seems important to continue to investigate how human teachers achieve their success in such individualized interactions.

Building one-on-one tutoring systems is an excellent way of exploring this question at a computationally precise level.

Is it possible to do the vast amount of knowledge engineering that the evolving notion of curriculum will require? It seems clear that in any sizeable ITS, it will be a huge job to specify the domain knowledge base, the student model, and the tutoring strategies out of which curriculum emerges. This becomes even worse when multiple perspectives are taken on the knowledge, when a student's possible genetic learning paths are represented, and when multi-dimensional notions of teaching and knowing are modelled. Again, this is not a trivial problem, but ideas such as blackboard control and object-oriented design make it much easier to modularize the design process. Moreover, as general AI research into knowledge representation, reasoning, planning, etc. progresses, it should become possible to build bigger systems based on sounder principles adapted from mainstream artificial intelligence.

The NATO Advanced Research Institute, out of which this paper emerged, was an attempt to bridge "the abyss" between instructional science and computer science. It has been a promising start, but there remain serious gulfs separating the various perspectives. It is a good question whether mutual understanding and synergistic interaction will eventually come to pass. Work such as that of Lesgold and Wasson begins to show how ideas from education can be merged into ITS. The synergy is starting to happen. In fact, curriculum may be just the arena to continue to explore how to bridge the abyss. Thoroughly understood by educators, curriculum is now beginning to become significant in the design of intelligent instructional systems as these systems tackle larger subject domains. Ideas from education about curriculum should increasingly be incorporated into intelligent tutoring systems. In return, the individualized, adaptable, and flexible approach to curriculum being explored by ITS researchers should feed back interesting ideas to education. ITS should thereby gain theoretical justification, education should gain computational precision, and both should gain in representational power and in their ability to deal with real problems in learning and teaching.

Acknowledgements

I would like to thank my students and colleagues over the years for their contributions to my research. In particular, my ideas on curriculum have been influenced greatly by the work of Barb Wasson, Darwyn Peachey, and Blake Ward, and discussions with Jim Greer and Marlene Jones. I would also like to express my appreciation to all of my fellow participants at the NATO Advanced Research Institute in Calgary in July of 1990. It was a stimulating two weeks, and your various opinions on the issues of ITS have affected my thinking in many ways. Thanks to the organizers, Marlene Jones and Phil Winne, for arranging the Institute and to NATO for funding my trip. I think the Big Rock brewing company is also owed something! I acknowledge the ongoing financial support of the Natural Sciences and Engineering Research Council of Canada for my research. Permission by the following publishers to reproduce figures is gratefully acknowledged: Academic Press for Figures 1, 3, 4, and 6; Association for Computing Machinery for Figure 2; IOS Press for Figure 9.

References

1. Abelson, H., & diSessa, A.: *Turtle geometry: The computer as a medium for exploring mathematics.* Cambridge, MA: MIT Press 1980
2. Barr, A., Beard, M., & Atkinson, R.C.: The computer as a tutorial laboratory: The Stanford BIP project. *International Journal of Man-Machine Studies*, 8, pp. 567-596 (1976)
3. Bloom, B.S.: *Taxonomy of educational objectives, Handbook I: Cognitive domain.* New York: David McKay 1956
4. Bloom, B.S.: The 2-sigma problem: The search for methods of group instruction as effective as one-to-one tutoring. *Educational Researcher*, June/July, pp. 4-16 (1984)
5. Brecht (Wasson), B.J.: Determining the focus of instruction: content planning for intelligent tutoring systems. Ph.D. thesis, Department of Computational Science, University of Saskatchewan, Saskatoon 1990
6. Brecht (Wasson), B.J., McCalla, G.I., Greer, J.E., & Jones, M.L.: Planning the content of instruction. Proceedings of 4th International Conference on Artificial Intelligence and Education, pp. 32-41, Amsterdam 1989
7. Brecht (Wasson), B.J., & Jones, M.L.: Student models: The genetic graph approach. *International Journal of Man-Machine Studies*, 28, pp. 483-504 (1988)
8. Brown, J.S., Burton, R.R., & deKleer, J.: Pedagogical, natural language, and knowledge engineering techniques in SOPHIE I, II, and III. In: *Intelligent Tutoring Systems* (D.H. Sleeman, & J.S. Brown, eds.). London: Academic Press 1982
9. Carbonell, J.R.: AI in CAI: An artificial intelligence approach to computer-assisted instruction. *IEEE Transactions on Man-Machine Systems*, 11, 4, pp. 190-202 (1970)
10. Carr, B., & Goldstein, I.P.: Overlays: A theory of modeling for computer-aided instruction. MIT AI Lab. Memo 406, Cambridge, MA 1977
11. Chambers, J.A., & Sprecher, J.W.: Computer assisted instruction: Current trends and critical issues. *Communications of the ACM*, 23, 6, pp. 332-342 (1980)
12. Clancey, W.J.: *Knowledge-based tutoring: the GUIDON program.* Cambridge, MA: MIT Press 1987
13. Derry, S.J., Hawkes, L.W., & Ziegler, U.: A plan-based opportunistic architecture for intelligent tutoring. Proceedings of the International Conference on Intelligent Tutoring Systems (ITS '88), pp. 116-123, Montreal 1988
14. diSessa, A., & Abelson, H.: BOXER: A constructible computational medium. *Communications of the ACM*, 29, 9 (1986)
15. Elsom-Cook, M.T.(ed.): *Guided discovery tutoring: A framework for ICAI research.* London: Paul Chapman 1990
16. Fikes, R.E., & Nilsson, N.J.: STRIPS: A new approach to the application of theorem proving to problem solving. *Artificial Intelligence*, 2, pp. 189-208 (1971)
17. Fischer, G.: A critic for LISP. Abstracts of the Third International Conference on Artificial Intelligence and Education, p. 26, Pittsburgh 1987
18. Gentner, D.: COACH: A tutor based on active schemas. *Computational Intelligence*, 2, 2, pp. 108-116 (1986)

19. Goforth, D., & McCalla, G.I.: LEPUS: A language to support student learning in non-mathematical domains. *AEDS Journal*, 17, pp. 14-29, 1984
20. Goldstein, I.P.: The genetic graph: A representation for the evolution of procedural knowledge. In: *Intelligent Tutoring Systems* (D.H. Sleeman, & J.S. Brown, eds.). London: Academic Press 1982
21. Greer, J.E., & McCalla, G.I.: A computational framework for granularity and its application to educational diagnosis. Proceedings of 11th International Joint Conference on artificial intelligence, pp. 477-482, Detroit 1989
22. Greer, J.E., Mark, M.A., & McCalla, G.I.: Incorporating granularity-based recognition into SCENT. Proceedings of 4th International Conference on artificial intelligence and education, pp. 107-115, Amsterdam 1989
23. Halff, H.M.: Curriculum and instruction in automated tutors. In: *Foundations of intelligent tutoring systems* (M.C. Polson, & J.J. Richardson, eds.). Hillsdale, NJ: Lawrence Erlbaum Associates 1988
24. Hayes-Roth, B.: A blackboard architecture for control. *Artificial Intelligence*, 26, 3, pp. 251-321 (1985)
25. Hollan, J.D., Hutchins, E.L., & Weitzman, L.: STEAMER: An interactive inspectable simulation-based training system. *AI Magazine*, 5, 2, pp. 15-27 (1984)
26. Johnson, W.L., & Soloway, E.M.: PROUST: An automatic debugger for Pascal programs. *Byte*, 10, 4, pp. 179-190 (1985)
27. Lesgold, A.M.: Toward a theory of curriculum for use in designing intelligent instructional systems. In: *Learning issues for intelligent tutoring systems* (H. Mandl, & A.M. Lesgold, eds.). New York: Springer-Verlag 1988
28. Lesgold, A.M., Bonar, J.G., Ivill, J.M., & Bowen, A.: An intelligent tutoring system for electronics troubleshooting: DC-circuit understanding. In: *Knowing and learning: issues for the cognitive psychology of instruction* (L.B. Resnick, ed.). Hillsdale, NJ: Lawrence Erlbaum Associates 1987 (as reported in Wenger)
29. Macmillan, S.A., & Sleeman, D.H.: An architecture for a self-improving instructional planner for intelligent tutoring systems. *Computational Intelligence*, 3, pp. 17-27 (1987)
30. McArthur, D., Stasz, C., Hotta, J., Peter, O., & Burdorf, C.: Skill-oriented sequencing in an intelligent tutor for basic algebra. *Instructional Science*, 17, pp. 281-307 (1978)
31. McCalla, G.I.: Some issues for guided discovery tutoring research: Granularity-based reasoning, student model maintenance, and pedagogical planning. NATO Advanced Research Workshop on Guided Discovery Tutoring, Tuscany, Italy 1989
32. McCalla, G.I.: The centrality of student modelling to intelligent tutoring. NATO Advanced Research Workshop on Intelligent Tutoring Systems, Sintra, Portugal 1990
33. McCalla, G.I., Bunt, R.B., & Harms, J.J.: The design of the SCENT automated advisor. *Computational Intelligence*, 2, 2, pp. 76-92 (1986)
34. McCalla, G.I., Greer, J.E., & the SCENT Research Team: SCENT-3: An architecture for intelligent advising in problem-solving domains. In: *Intelligent tutoring systems: at the crossroads of artificial intelligence and education* (C. Frasson, & G. Gauthier, eds.). Norwood, NJ: Ablex 1990
35. McCalla, G.I., Peachey, D.R., & Ward, B.: An architecture for the design of large scale intelligent teaching systems. Proceedings of 4th National Conference of the Canadian Society for Computational Studies of Intelligence, pp. 85-91, Saskatoon 1982
36. Merrill, M.D.: The new component design theory: Instructional design for courseware authoring. *Instructional Science*, 16, pp. 19-34 (1987)
37. Murray, W.R.: Control for intelligent tutoring systems: A blackboard-based dynamic instructional planner. Proceedings of the 4th International Conference on Artificial Intelligence and Education, pp. 150-168, Amsterdam 1989
38. Ng, T.H., & McCalla, G.I.: A plan-based approach to blackboard control in an intelligent tutoring system. International Computer Science Conference on AI Theory and Practice '88, pp. 39-45, Hong Kong 1988
39. Papert, S.: *Mindstorms: children, computers, and powerful ideas.* New York: Basic Books 1980
40. Peachey, D.R., & McCalla, G.I.: Using planning techniques in intelligent tutoring systems. *International Journal of Man-Machine Studies*, 24, pp. 77-98 (1986)
41. Reiser, B.J., Friedmann, P., Kimberg, D.Y., & Ranney, M.: Constructing explanations from problem solving rules to guide the planning of programs. Proceedings of International Conference on Intelligent Tutoring Systems (ITS '88), pp. 222-229, Montreal 1988
42. Russell, D.M.: IDE: The interpreter. In: *Intelligent tutoring systems: Lessons learned* (J. Psotka, L.D. Massey, & S.A. Mutter, eds.). Hillsdale, NJ: Lawrence Erlbaum Associates 1988
43. Self, J.A.: Bypassing the intractable problem of student modelling. In: *Intelligent tutoring systems: At the crossroads of artificial intelligence and education* (C. Frasson, & G. Gauthier, eds.). Norwood, NJ: Ablex 1990

44. Shuell, T.: Designing instructional computing systems for meaningful learning. In: *Foundations and frontiers in instructional computing systems* (P.H. Winne, & M.L. Jones, eds.). Berlin: Springer-Verlag 1991
45. Smith, R.: The alternate reality kit: An animated environment for creating interactive simulations. Proceedings of IEEE Workshop on Visual Languages, pp. 99-106, Dallas 1986
46. Wenger, E.: *Artificial intelligence and tutoring systems.* California: Morgan Kaufmann 1987
47. Wescourt, K, Beard, M.. & Gould, L.: Knowledge-based adaptive curriculum sequencing for CAI: Application of a network representation. Proceedings of the National ACM Conference, pp. 234-240, Seattle, 1977
48. White, B.Y., & Frederickson, J.R.: Intelligent tutoring systems based upon qualitative model evolution. Proceedings of 5th AAAI Conference, pp. 313-319, Philadelphia 1986
49. Winkels, R., & Breuker, J.: Discourse planning in intelligent help systems. In: *Intelligent tutoring systems: At the crossroads of artificial intelligence and education* (C. Frasson, & G. Gauthier, eds.). Norwood, NJ: Ablex 1990
50. Wipond, K., & Jones, M.: Curriculum and knowledge representation in a knowledge-based system for curriculum development. Proceedings of International Conference on Intelligent Tutoring Systems (ITS '88), pp. 312-319, Montreal 1988

The Curriculum and Instructional Tasks: Goals, Strategies, and Tactics for Interactive Learning

J. Roger Hartley

Computer Based Learning Unit, University of Leeds, Leeds, England

Abstract: Recent curriculum debates reflect an increasing interest in the content of what is taught in the classroom. Teachers are expected to apply their pedagogy to the arrangement and support of this content so that learners can acquire new knowledge in ways that suit and utilize their prior experience and preferred learning styles. These teacher-learner considerations influence both the type and sequence of curriculum goals, and the strategic design of instructional tasks as well as their on-going tactical management. Building interactive learning systems to achieve such functions requires a semantically rich representation of domain content at the level of topics (for study planning) and of their associated procedures and concepts (for constructing task interactions). Examples are taken from knowledge-based instructional planners, and from on-line help systems where the learner has curriculum and some instructional control. This experience argues that a common pool of pragmatic/semantic links can service both topic-goal decision-making, and the content of task interactions, and that dialogue-game theory may provide a useful framework for strategic and tactical control.

Introduction: Shifting Interest to the Curriculum

In recent years, particularly in the UK, there has been sharper discussion about the school curriculum — about what should be taught in the classroom. This questioning of the content of instruction is partly a response to the increasing and changing roles of technology in society but, more importantly, to a perceived lowering of performance standards, particularly in the basics of language, mathematics and science. The argument is that with an agreed curricula in a corpus of school subjects, priorities can be made clear, attainment standards set and achievements monitored. Thus, the function of the curriculum is not only to accommodate change but to serve as an instrument of control.

NATO ASI Series, Vol. F 85
Adaptive Learning Environments
Edited by M. Jones and P. H. Winne

It is not the intention here to contribute to the debate about the UK National Curriculum (see, for example, [36]). However, it is worth noting that, in the main, educational researchers have not concentrated on the content of what is taught in the classroom nor how pedagogical knowledge is employed to bring such content, with its conceptual difficulties, within the comprehension of students [17]. There are exceptions, for example in mathematics, but most studies have tended to be more concerned with patterns of classroom interactions without direct emphasis on the curriculum domain in which they are placed. In some contrast, this paper will attempt to show, for computer assisted learning, that it is the semantic richness of the curriculum domain representation which directly influences the planning of study goals, the strategic design of instructional tasks, as well as their tactical management with learners.

By way of introduction it is worthwhile commenting briefly on the UK National Curriculum which is organized as conventional school subjects. In Science, the content is focussed on topic domains or themes including, for example, Processes of Life, Genetics and Evolution, Types and Uses of Materials, Earth and Atmosphere, Electricity and Magnetism, and Information Transfer. Within these topics, attainment targets or objectives are placed and grouped into four main components including Knowledge and Understanding, and Exploration and Investigatory Skills. Programmes of Study have then to be devised so that, through their instructional tasks, students are enabled to reach the attainment targets at different levels commensurate with their age and experience. The curriculum scheme is summarized in Figure 1.

A basic principle of the Science Curriculum is that the programs of study and the attainment targets can be made adaptive yet coherent by developing "levels" of knowledge and skill. For example, in "Science for ages 5-16" (published in 1988 by the Department of Education and Science) under the topic "Types and uses of materials" the program of study for ages five to seven includes the objectives "children should collect, handle and look for similarities and differences in a variety of everyday materials, natural and manufactured, including rocks, air, and water. They should work with and change some of these materials by simple processes such as heating and cooling, squashing, bending...." For the ages seven to eleven, this has been extended to "work with a wider range of everyday materials, exploring their origins, using them in construction, and investigating properties such as mass, volume, strength, hardness, flexibility, compressibility, and solubility. They should measure some of these properties...."

These study outlines are sharpened by statements of attainment, reflecting in their "levels" the changing nature of the instructional tasks required to achieve these goals.

For example, (level 2, 5-7 age group), children should "be able to recognize important similarities and differences, such as hardness, flexibility and transparency in materials" and "be able to group materials according to their characteristics..." and "know that heating and cooling materials can cause them to melt or solidify." At the 7-11 age band (level 4), the list of

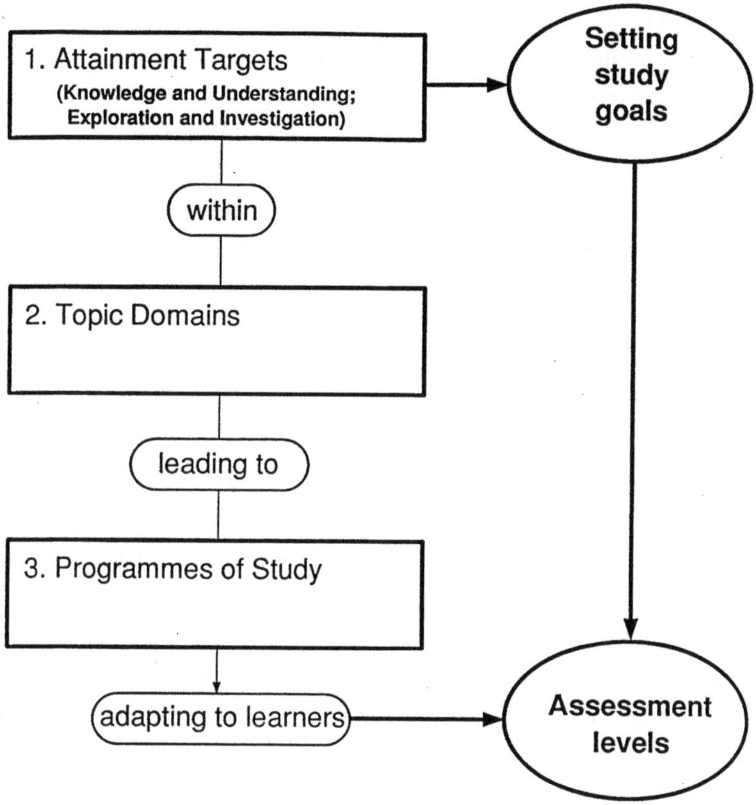

Figure 1: Curriculum Components

properties of materials has increased, measurement is introduced, more formal terms — such as change of state are apparent. Also, there is an elaboration of knowledge, for instance "know that when materials change their state there is no change in the substance of which they are made."

The curriculum framework is being supported by commissioned teams of teachers and educationists producing study and assessment materials, to ensure that objectives, study content, and performance appraisal are coordinated. Nonetheless, teachers have flexibility in sequencing their class study plans and in designing instructional tasks to suit preferences and local conditions. Classroom instruction has to employ much tactical adaptation and re-planning and, from experience, teachers are able to bring support and illustration to deal with particular conceptual difficulties, and to maintain motivation of their students. In short, the curriculum, covering a large subject domain, becomes an interpretation of content by teachers which is developed, expressed and adapted to the experience and progress of their students. These characteristics were also noted in a small experimental study of university teachers of Applied

Statistics [2]. There was wide agreement on the actual topics which they considered should form a curriculum for descriptive statistics, and in the topics they grouped to form segments of that curriculum. However, there was considerable variation in the size and preferred teaching sequence of these segments, and in the preferred order of their constituent topics. Teachers used notions of "prerequisite" and "part-of" in explaining these groupings and sequencing decisions. However, it was very clear that they felt well able to produce tasks and develop a coherent framework to suit a variety of curriculum study plans.

Educational Study Advisers

Having outlined some features of the curriculum schemes which practising teachers encounter in their day-to-day work, it is interesting to compare computer based learning, and so-called intelligent teaching systems, that have attempted to construct adaptive curricula to suit particular styles of learning. There is general agreement in such research that the curriculum can be viewed as a series of study goals, defining the learning, and arranged in an organized sequence so that understanding is developed in a systematic manner. In this regard note that the statements of science attainment, outlined above, can be analyzed into the "topic-objects" of their knowledge domain. For example, in "types and uses of materials" these "materials" are specialized into classes with their attributes (physical properties) and state-changes, such as melting in response to heat, leading to a semantic network of topics that represents conceptual knowledge of that domain. The attainment skills to be acquired, e.g., classifying, measuring, and comparing, overlay the domain objects to produce an associated task space that organizes the procedural knowledge requirements of the curriculum (see [11] and [32] for a discussion of technique). Hence, the design of a study plan is the ordered navigation of these semantic networks to produce a linear work-sequence of goals to suit the student, and this plan has to be readily re-structured depending on progress.

Much of the work on the design of computer based educational planners has been influenced by Peachey and McCalla [24]. In brief, teaching materials are considered to be operators that can produce learning objectives (i.e., a knowledge state-change in the student) provided that certain prior knowledge requirements are met. Hence, given the final-state knowledge description, the set of operators can be matched to them, and those successful will set up their own prior requirements as sub-objectives. This chaining process can be repeated until all pre-conditions have been met (or no successful solution found). Any operator-sequence meeting these requirements is judged to be a satisfactory plan, but other criteria could be introduced to place successful plans in a preferred order. This conception of educational planning emphasizes, as do teachers, instructional tasks (the operators) and assumes that they can be designed to deliver the objectives of a curriculum to the intended student group. The planner also checks and arranges the prior knowledge requirements. Of course, in practice the success of an operator cannot be guaranteed, but failure would expose further information of the students' knowledge or deficiencies, and these data could then be inserted for re-planning.

However, such schemes are simplistic in that they produce a linear traversal of operator-goals to reach a prime goal, and techniques of covering a curriculum of semantically related goals in some convenient or optimal manner are not directly addressed. The Excalibur project in its ECCLES program [27] moves some way in this direction; it analyzes the knowledge requirements of test questions representing the objectives, and then assembles them in an ordering which takes account of the related knowledge held by the student.

More conventional work in computer based learning (CBL) using pre-stored materials has experimented with learner controlled systems that aim to provide sufficient topic information to allow students themselves to arrange the sequence of study goals. Even if these decisions are not always satisfactory, it is argued that the exercise of having the student consider and decide on study plans and reflect on progress is useful, even necessary for "learning how to learn." Perhaps the best known and documented project has been TICCIT [18, 19] where the curriculum was represented as a topic network at different levels of detail. Chosen topic nodes at the detailed level then allowed access to styles of on-line teaching and testing materials. However, the associations between nodes were only represented as unlabelled arcs so the semantic nature of these relations was not exposed. Further, the planning advice provided for students was minimal, effectively only providing performance checks against (pre-stored) requirements of a study region.

The systems discussed so far have only taken into account the prior domain knowledge of students when considering planning decisions. This was too simplistic for Pask who noted that in open learning situations students had preferred styles of working with materials. Pask [21, 22] maintained he could distinguish different types of organizational or cognitive styles, originally named serialists and holists. The former preferred to study a limited number of issues in sequence, establishing these links before moving on to use these elements in assembling other closely related topics. In contrast, holists tended to set a wider focus, opening up more topics in a learning episode and hence working with a more complex organizational scheme. Pask did not consider one style inferior to another; his argument and data showed these were learning preferences but if teaching styles ran counter to them, learning gains were reduced. Consequently, different arrangements of study goals are needed for these types of students, and since learners are not always aware of their own study styles, Pask noted the need for "conversation" to help in this decision making. In a prototype system, CASTE [23] dealing with Applied Statistics, the topic network was overlaid with a measure of the student's "knowledge strength" set against each topic. As students knew more of the domain, they were permitted to involve more topic nodes in their plans (i.e., prior knowledge was used adaptively to designate an appropriate study range).

Work at Leeds [1, 2] has also considered a wider range of student attributes in building computer based curriculum planners, using techniques that take greater advantage of the semantic links between topics. Although generic in design, a first application area was Applied Statistics, concentrating on descriptions of statistical distributions and including correlation and regression. A topic network representing the domain was produced, a small portion of which is shown in Figure 2.

Each of the node topics represents a teaching issue which will attract learning materials to achieve its curriculum goals. Hence, the Concept of Central Tendency and the purposes and desirable properties of such measures (e.g., stability, representativeness) can be discussed independently of the specialized measures (i.e., mean, median and mode) themselves. Indeed, such conceptual knowledge is some of the "glue" which binds the measures into an association (see Lesgold, [15] for a discussion of this point and its relevance in constructing views of a curriculum topic domain). Thus, Central Tendency can serve as an organizing introduction to Mean, Median, Mode and/or can be used subsequently to make comparisons and contrasts between the measures. Teachers are well able to perceive and use such organizations, and computer based planners should be able to demonstrate similar flexibility.

In general, the attainments linked to each topic can emphasize *conceptual, procedural* or *operational* knowledge. For example, the concept of arithmetic mean has attributes (e.g., member of the class of central tendency measures, applies to interval data, has a zero sum for its data deviations, is sensitive to extreme values) and there are standard procedures for its calculation. Indeed, the concept definition and attributes, and the methods of its calculation and interpretation are interlinked, and the [C-P] goal labels on the topics of Figure 2 reinforce this. Operational knowledge, though, is defined to be the application of conceptual/procedural knowledge in *context*, typically where more than one approach or decision can be taken. For example, deciding which measure of central tendency is the most appropriate summary measure in a given context might not be straight-forward, with advantages/disadvantages having to be resolved, and even some data transformation techniques considered. Consequently all conceptual and procedural knowledge requirements of a topic (and its specialized or constituent subtopics) should be fulfilled before operational knowledge becomes an active objective.

The topic space is set out as a lattice but the arcs form two types, those which show the analysis of topics, and those that indicate cross-requisites. Thus, arcs showing class membership (type-of) and components (part-of) belong to the first category, and the "contained-in" and "applies-to" arcs, to the second. The contained-in relation between mean and standard deviation suggests it is more convenient to deal with the mean-topic first, as a prerequisite, but the applies-to arc shows interval data is an initial condition for the mean to be calculated, and

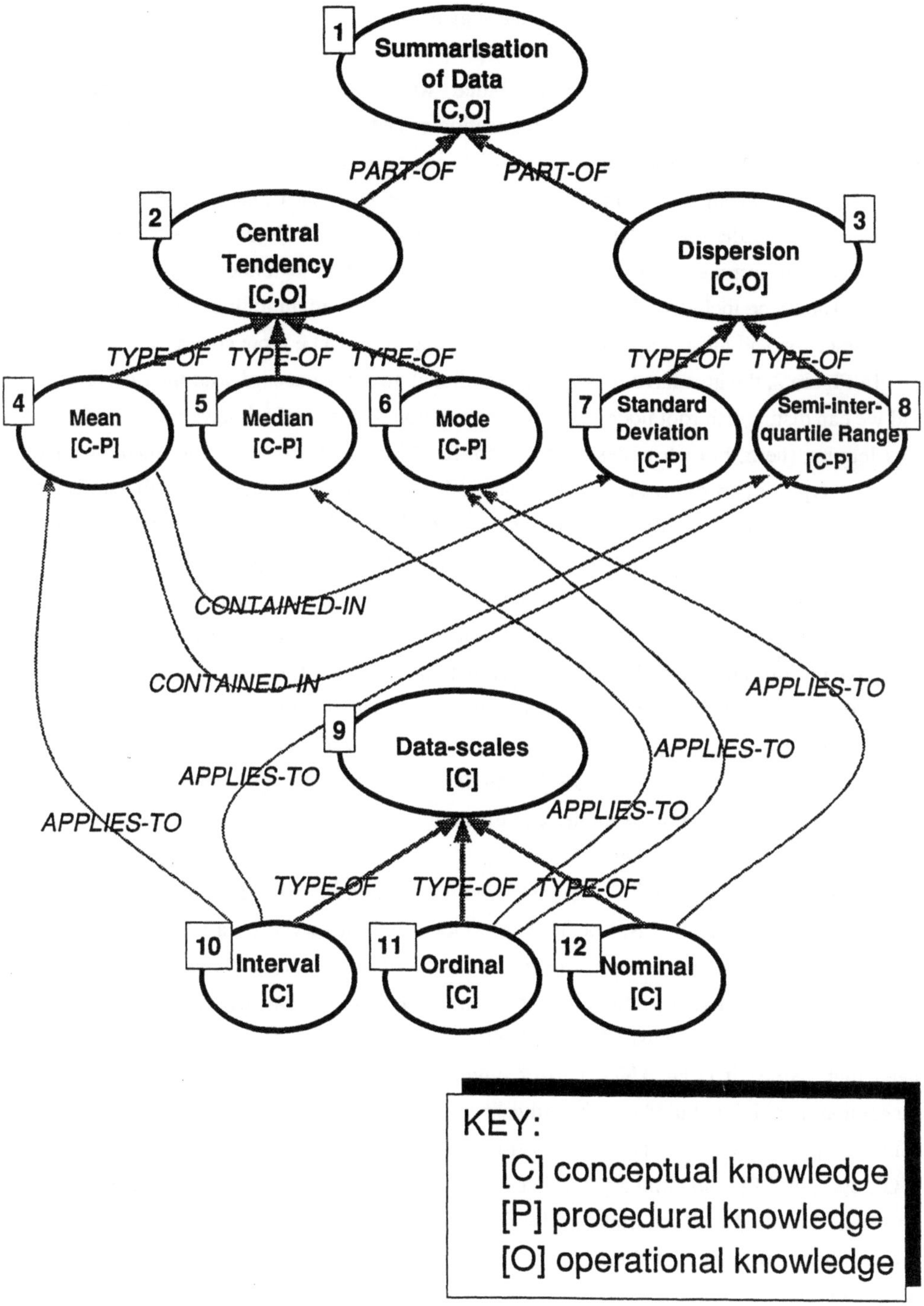

Figure 2: A topic network for a part of Descriptive Statistics

while not strictly a precedence condition, the suggestion is that topics connected by such an arc should be studied in close sequence.

When the cross-requisite arcs are faded, we are left with a set of type-of, part-of hierarchies, in Figure 2 those using Summarization of Data, and Data Scales as foci. The type-of arc indicates specialization. For example, in the case of central tendency measures, this specialization is according to the types of data scales concerned, essentially forming OR-junctions at the header nodes. The component arcs indicate an AND-junction since to fulfill the requirement of summarizing a data distribution, both a central tendency *and* a dispersion measure should be included. The general point is that these semantic links suggest constraints on the selection and linear sequencing of topics so that they can be more coherent.

In Figure 2, the arcs have been given directional arrows to accord with their descriptions, and we can distinguish root nodes (e.g., summarization of data), which have no type-of/part-of arcs leaving them, branch nodes, and bottom-level leaf nodes (e.g., mean, median, mode) where no type-of/part-of arcs enter. The root nodes, and the subtopics they entail, can be used to partition the domain into study regions, and within each region the topic graph can be navigated in variety of plausible ways, each producing a linear sequence of nodes to form a study plan. The rules governing these selections have been set out [2] and cover sequencing of objectives (e.g., all conceptual-procedural objectives entailed by an operational knowledge objective must be completed before it is activated), as well as top-down analysis versus bottom-up synthesis, breadth-first spanning versus depth-first specialization, and rules which regulate the focus of study. These rules, which determine the main types of study plan, take account of constraints introduced by AND-OR junctions, and the cross-requisites, contained-in and applies-to. Two contrasting examples can illustrate how the prototype program searches these relations and constructs its plans.

Suppose the Study Advisor program (which is written in SMALLTALK and is being re-implemented in Common Lisp) decides the student is best served by a holistic type of plan which sets a prime focus on topic 1 (Summarization of Data) and activates rules regulating a depth-first, top-down navigation of the topic space. The concept knowledge objective (C) is set at topic 1 since the pre-requisite Knowledge (C-P) conditions for the (O) objective have not yet been met. Since it is an AND (part-of junction), both measures of central tendency and dispersion must be included and the Advisor will continually try to meet this condition. The following partial-plan candidates are constructed down (depth-first) each root-leaf track, namely 1[C], 2[C], 4[C-P]; and similarly 1,2,5; 1,2,6; 1,3,7; and 1,3,8. The contained-in requirement between Mean (topic 4) and Standard Deviation (topic 7) backing up to the Central Tendency, Dispersion level leads to a shuffling, giving order preference to 1,2,4, and 5 and 6, over the 1,3,7 candidate.

The proximity condition of the applies-to links attaches topics 10[C], 11[C], 12[C] to each of the candidates. At this point the AND condition can be met since both Central Tendency (e.g., Mean) and Dispersion (e.g., Standard Deviation) specialize into common types of data (e.g., Interval data). So do Median and Semi Interquartile Range. Hence, the study plans form teaching loops, e.g., 1[C], 2[C], 4[C-P], 10[C], 1[C-Remind], 3[C], 7[C], 10[C-Remind]. Similarly for the 1,2,5,11,1,3,8, Loop, and the remaining 1,2,6,12 topics.

What is the preferred order for these study sequences? This decision can rest on the previous knowledge strengths of students (either following a policy of playing to strength or supporting weakness — see Hobbs [13] for a discussion of this issue). Alternatively, a domain-dependent link called "transform" can be introduced which notes the fact that a set of interval data can be placed in ordinal form which, in turn, can be put into classes. The current prototype has such a link and thus gives order precedence to the Mean and Standard Deviation Loop.

When the above study loops are completed, the knowledge prerequisites of node 9 (Data scales) are immediately met; this topic is given active status and the synthesizing approach of the study plan then becomes apparent. Completion of 9[C] satisfies the Operational knowledge pre-requisites for topics 2 and 3. Topic 2[O] takes precedence following the sequence established previously, and when 3[O] has been completed, the prime focus node (topic 1[O]) becomes activated and the study plan for this curriculum region is finished.

Thus, the suggested plan takes as its unit the topic loops uniting the two components of the focus node — Central Tendency and Dispersion Measures. Note the approach follows an organizing but analytic phase (depth-first, top-down) set at the conceptual level using the study loops that take seven topics to complete. Operational knowledge objectives are then used to summarize and integrate these sequences.

However, other plausible study schemes can employ different navigational rules. For example, suppose the prime focus set on topic 1 was devolved to the organizing branch nodes 2 (Central Tendency) and 3 (Dispersion) and that a bottom-up breadth-first scheme was followed. Using the same precedence and prerequisite arguments noted previously, the study plan would be topic 4[C-P], Mean, then 10[C], Interval data, followed by 5,11; and 6,12. The pre-conditions for 9 (Data scales) are now met so this node is activated allowing the C and O objectives to be set on the first devolved focus topic 2 (Central Tendency). In a similar manner, the objectives of topic 3 can be met leading to a final synthesis under Summarization of data.

This study plan is more serial in character, establishing the properties of the mean in terms of its data scales, completing the same for median and mode before comparing them under measures of central tendency. Dispersion follows in a similar manner before being united under the root node, topic 1. Note that, although topic objectives may be the same as other plans (e.g., C-P knowledge objectives for the Mean), in this scheme the immediate focus of study, and the direction of semantic links to other topics changes between plans. The current Advisor program is able to select and fill-out prestored templates that point out these features when describing the plan. They note the study focus, and the semantic link, as well as the type of objective of the topic, and the requirements of the AND-OR junctions [2].

By giving prominence to the Depth-first/Breadth-first, Top-down/Bottom-up and study focus rules, the Advisor is able to produce coherent plans which have different characteristics. Depth-first follows a narrowing, specialized approach, whereas Breadth-first exposes a wider range of topic nodes earlier in the work plan. Top-down navigation allows general components (topics) to be analyzed and act as organizers, whereas bottom-up schemes delay the synthesis of the knowledge topics. The use of a study focus, set at root node or devolved, controls the length and span of the study elements, i.e., the number of topic nodes they contain [2, p. 157].

The Advisor program has to decide how these study plans will suit particular types of learners, or act as a guide to their preferences. Four main student characteristics have been considered in this decision-making. First, background knowledge of the domain (e.g., mathematics experience) as well as topic knowledge which allows support-strength, support-weakness policies to be followed; second, preferred organizational style following serialist/holist categories; third, confidence in ability to learn about the topic/study region; and fourth, the relative time donated for study. These measures are collected on-line, as self-report questionnaires, and the Advisor program has rules for making its suggested allocations. Briefly, where confidence is low, study span is reduced by using devolved focus rules. Additionally, bottom-up navigation is preferred when relative time is low since these schemes delay the synthesis of topics so that there is less re-visiting of inter-related nodes. Serialists are considered to prefer a devolved focus, depth-first approach whereas the holist, following breadth- first schemes, will receive a wider range of concepts during the initial stages of the study plan.

Instructional Tasks: The Strategies for Achieving Curriculum Goals

The design of instructional tasks represents the strategy by which curriculum (topic) goals will be achieved and are synonymous with the "operators" noted in the Peachey and McCalla [24] planning programs. Perhaps because of the influence of (pre-stored) computer based learning emphasizing the authority of instructional systems, task descriptions in these applications tend to concentrate on the functions of the teacher. For example, Van Marcke [34] sees instructional tasks as "the building blocks of an instruction process. They embody recognizable activities of a tutor, such as teaching, selecting a topic, introducing a topic, describing concepts...." Instructional methods then become the mechanisms to "realize a particular instructional task." A similar orientation is taken by Russell et al. [29].

Research from Intelligent Teaching Systems (ITSs) often takes a more cognitive and learner-based view so that acquiring knowledge is "not so much a process of assimilation as of generating new directions to acquire new concepts" and instructional tasks are "methods of operating in an environment for the learner ... to express what they think, try out hypotheses, engage in reflective abstraction ... and look at problems from different viewpoints" [3].

Hence, it is recognized that instructional tasks represent some formalization of teaching-learning interactions that vary in the types of educational "moves" they permit or encourage, and in the locus of control between teacher and student. The instructional tasks and materials used with the Statistical Study Advisor discussed previously make this distinction, with types of learning moving from directed to investigatory, to which attach conceptual, procedural, and operational knowledge objectives (see Figure 3). The Advisor is able to suggest these different types of tasks/materials to suit learning styles and preferences by referencing a materials description database.

Objectives	Types of learning materials and tasks
[Student appraisal]	On-line tests and diagnostic items Self-report questionnaires Personal interviews
Conceptual knowledge	(i) Exposition/illustration through lectures and seminars. Textbooks; on-line tutorial material (ii) [Investigatory]; associated illustrations using MINITAB
Procedural knowledge	(i) On-line practice materials. Example classes and worksheet exercises (ii) [Investigatory]; on-line use of MINITAB as a programming language for statistical calculations
Operational knowledge	(i) On-line problem-solving support systems (ii) [Investigatory]; MINITAB-based problem projects using prepared data set(s) or those generated by students

Figure 3: Instructional Tasks and Learning Objectives

Hence the specification of an instructional task should include: 1) the learning goal, 2) a representation of the content domain, and instructional supporting materials which are available for the tasks, and 3) the types of interactions which are permitted during the performance of the tasks.

The content domain making up the topic objective can be analyzed as a propositional structure using the semantic arc-node techniques noted previously. For example, the conceptual-procedural objective of the arithmetic mean could produce 1) is-a class membership of measure of central tendency, 2) has-purpose to give a representative (summary) measure for such data, 3) applies-to interval data, 4) is-obtained-by <calculation procedure>, and 5) has-qualities deviation data sum to zero, takes account of all values, and is sensitive to extreme values. This framework will have to be supported and supplemented so that the teacher or teaching system can provide, for example, tests, questions, expositions, illustrations, analogies, diagnosis of errors and feedback, explanations, advice, challenges, summaries and previews. These are some of the educational moves that may be required by the functional roles of the teacher, and correspondingly, the student. Shuell [30] discusses such functions, initiated by teacher and learner, and notes the variety of actions which can allow them to be fulfilled. The actions chosen, and their tactical management through the conventions of turn-taking or intervention depend on the types of learning interactions which are being designed, and which have to be serviced by the instructional tasks.

It is useful to distinguish five main types of interactions in which teacher and student cooperate to achieve particular learning goals. These interactions differ in how and when initiatives are taken by participants. In *exposition*, the teacher expert is transmitting knowledge, providing illustrations and asking questions to check understanding. Students are permitted or encouraged to ask questions when clarification is needed. Teacher demonstrations also fit into this exposition category. For *tutorial* interactions, though teacher directed, the emphasis shifts to diagnosis and correction following students' task responses. Test-teaching falls into this class and so does socratic instruction [6] where the teacher delivers "correction" by posing counter-examples that require the student to modify assertions if an inconsistency is to be avoided.

Tait [31], in devising his authoring tools, has provided a specification language (and supporting software) for tutorial interactions. A task module is composed of a series of presentation frames that hold the interaction moves. These frames have information panels containing type of content (e.g., questions, notes, definitions, responses, feedback, with rules that control their display time/sequences and their placing on the screen). Once this generic specification has been made, and the particular content provided, an interactive run-time version is prepared automatically by the computer. Building a library of such presentation frames allows them to be selected and combined, with given content, to form a customized variety of task interactions.

A third type of interaction, not well researched, is that of *debate* in which knowledge is interchanged by partners. The aim is to change or discount the arguments of the other by exposing inconsistencies, logical shortcomings or overgeneralization. Moore [20] has studied such dialogues between students and between students and teacher on such contentious topics as pollution, control of pets, and capital punishment. Other classes of interaction where the emphasis is placed on the students' work are *simulation/help systems* and *construction/problem solving*. In the former, the student can take the initiative and seek advice and explanation, but the teacher also can intervene opportunistically to comment on performance, improve plans, and correct misconceptions. In problem solving and composition, the learners develop material from their own viewpoints, and the teacher usually examines and criticizes the completed performances from those perspectives.

The EUROHELP Experience

A good example of the specification of instructional tasks, and their interactions, within an on-line Help system is provided by the EUROHELP project [4]. This was a collaborative project funded under the CEC ESPRIT Programme with the aim of providing intelligent on-line assistance for users of information processing systems (IPSs) such as editors, spreadsheets, and electronic mail. In fact, the most thoroughly worked and evaluated Help example was for UNIX-Mail. This domain was represented by a series of knowledge spaces, with the curriculum being shown as a task hierarchy ranging from high level classes of tasks, e.g., creating, deleting, sending, managing mail, to low-level interaction tasks whose methods referenced the UNIX-Mail commands and mail objects. Descriptive information about these commands and mail objects was set out as semantic hierarchies and networks and, through browsers, was available for question asking. The conception of the Help system is set out in Figure 4.

In EUROHELP, although a planned teaching sequence could be imposed by the system on the task hierarchy, users can determine their own task curriculum. As a consequence, EUROHELP has to provide its assistance opportunistically in ways which take account of the user's working contexts, and which consolidate and extend their current understanding of the functioning of the IPS. This cooperation is achieved by allowing both the Help system and student to take initiatives that control their interactions. EUROHELP, when monitoring the users' actions with the IPS, can intervene (i.e., Active Help mode) to correct detected errors, or repair misconceptions, or to point out inefficiencies in method-plans. If the commands or procedures that would improve a method are within didactic range (determined by genetic graph measures [37]) then EUROHELP will intervene and extend student knowledge through its coaching. For their part, students can ask questions (i.e., Passive Help). Since users have to work out method plans, translate these into IPS system language, and interpret the IPS response to these instructions, the questions of Enablement (how-to-do tasks), Elaboration (of the properties of system objects and commands), Evaluation (of what-happened), and Comparison (similarities/differences to what is known or experienced) are needed to provide help and explanation.

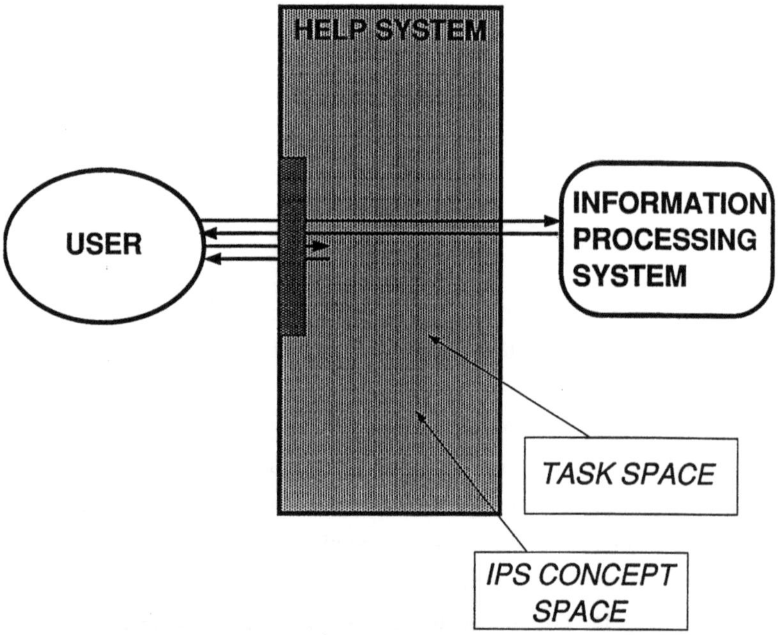

HELP SYSTEM FUNCTIONS

(i) Response Intepretation
(ii) Active Help: [Intervention]
Coach out errors
Repair misconceptions
Improve inefficient plans
(iii)Passive Help:
Answer questions:
Explain and expand knowledge

Figure 4: The conceptualization of Help

The material for supporting these "moves" of the student and Help system, i.e., the content of the coaching and question-answers, is derived from the knowledge representation of the task space, the IPS concept space, and the emulation model of the IPS. For example, if a student requests to be told about a command, e.g., the delete command, the answer may contain (i) descriptives: defining the command, placing its class membership, and describing its effects; (ii) imperatives: giving instructions on how to use the command; (iii) explanatives: explaining how the command effects are caused or achieved; (iv) comparatives: referencing other similar or contrasting commands; and (v) elaboratives: providing information on how the command and its arguments are amended or enhanced to deal with other situations.

To allow the provision of such descriptions, the domain representation must contain formalized semantic links that enable the Help system to search and select the propositional content. Other pragmatic relations organize these propositions into answer schemas. In its research, the EUROHELP project developed a set of rhetorical predicates, extending the work of Lehnert [14] and McKeown [16], for describing these relations and for maintaining coherence. A brief synopsis is given (Figure 5) but see [10, 26, 33] for detailed and formalized accounts.

The predicate set was developed from experimental studies (using the VI editing system) which examined the passive help comments human experts gave to users when both were connected on-line. A small example (see Figure 6) illustrates how the comments were analyzed under the predicate scheme, showing both the clausal and organizational predicate levels.

The strategies for organizing the predicate content are represented as answer-plans (e.g., Instruct/Inform/Explain) which activate their predicates and identify the way one proposition is coordinated or subordinated to another. Figure 7 shows a filled-in schema for a description of the "delete" command. In practice, the activated predicates seek and collect information from the domain representation, the schema prepares an organized/sequenced propositional structure which is passed to an utterance generator that prepares well-formed text [10, 33]. The EUROHELP system, recently evaluated, is written in Common Lisp running on SUN workstations.

Note that the predicate relations have to be so "knowledgeable" that the correct data can be retrieved from the domain representation. For example, the Mail-System has no direct understanding of the purpose of a command — the system operates as instructed by the key presses it receives. The purpose of a command has to be interpreted by the predicate as the task, lowest in the hierarchy, to which it attaches as a method plan; it enables that goal to be achieved, e.g., erasing a message. Note also that the answer generation takes account of the prior knowledge of the user about the topic in question. Thus, in Figure 7 the user's knowledge is not strong, so specific information and an example are given through the "replacement" and "representative" predicates. Since "message-spec" is a sub-topic that occurs

- *ELABORATE*
    - **Membership** A definitional kind of link of the form "is a member of the class of," where one object, action, state or state-change, is defined in relationship to another.
        - Form: <a> is a <b>
        - e.g., "dd is a command."
    - **Attribution** Links an object, action, state or state-change, to its properties.
        - Form: <a> takes <parameter <b>>
        - e.g., "The yank command takes double quotes."
    - **Constituency** Consists of :
        - **Representative** Example
        - **Replacement** Concrete expression replacing generic one.
- *COMPARE AND CONTRAST*
    - **Differentiate** Organize similarities and differences
    - **Difference** Collect differences
    - **Similarity** Collect similarities
    - **Equivalence** x is the same as y
- *EXPLAIN*
- **Cause-consequence** The cause-consequence relation links some object, action, state or state-change where one concept is the cause of the other.
    - Form: <a> consequence <b>
    - consequence <a> because <b>
    - e.g., "Typing Y causes the line to be yanked into a buffer."
    - or, "You yanked the line into a buffer because you typed Y."
- **Condition-consequence** This relates some state-change to some object, action, state or state-change in a causal way; it is an enablement relation i.e., it states a precondition for the outcome but the relationship is not obligatory; the causal relation is more temporal than physical.
    - Form: when <a> then <b>
    - e.g., "When you are in insert mode, you type text."
    - Form: if <a> then enable <b>
    - e.g., "If you move into command mode, then you can use dd."
    - Form: before <a>, <b>
    - e.g., "Before using the dd command, leave insert mode."
- *DIRECT*
    - **Goal orientation** Problem solution, organize instrument achievement
    - **Instrument achievement** x by doing y
- *ORGANIZE*
    - **Collection** Group propositions together
    - **Additive** x and y before z is possible
    - **Adversative** x but not y
    - **Setting trajectory** Time and/or place (first, then, next)
- Thus the predicates are divided into classes, including causal, elaborative, comparative, and organizational. The causal predicates are those which present an argument, that is, they link premises and conclusions, conditions and consequences, cause and effect, and therefore have a logical (though not formally logical) sequence. Elaborative predicates, on the other hand, relate attributes of concepts; they deal with class membership and the relationship between the parts of a concept and the whole concept.

Figure 5: Rhetorical and Semantic Predicates

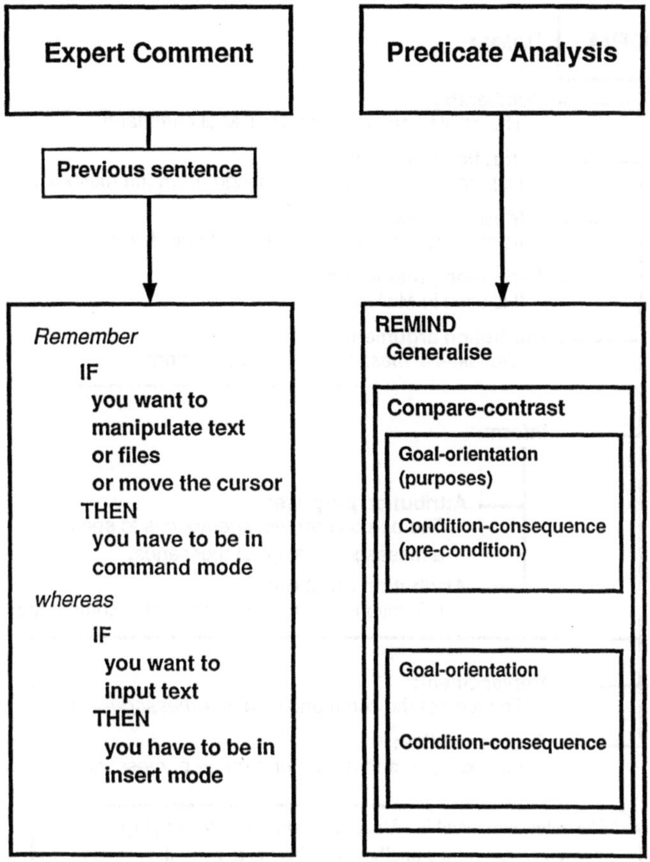

Figure 6: A predicate structure of an expert's comment

in the developing answer and about which the student's knowledge is weak, a sub-frame schema is activated and its contents placed appropriately in the answer sequence. As the user's knowledge about "delete" increases, the answer schema alters its tactics, dropping the old and well-known content and introducing comparisons to other commands to consolidate and extend understanding.

The general point is that decision-making is required to form curriculum plans, to design study tasks that will achieve these goals, and to decide the content and organization of "moves" that constitute task interactions. At all these levels, the decision-making is dependent on the quality of the semantic relations which make up the descriptions of the curriculum task and concept knowledge, for planning in these knowledge spaces involves search, selection, and organization, i.e., the same operations are involved though at different levels. The argument is that a relatively small number of semantic links can produce both flexible curriculum plans and

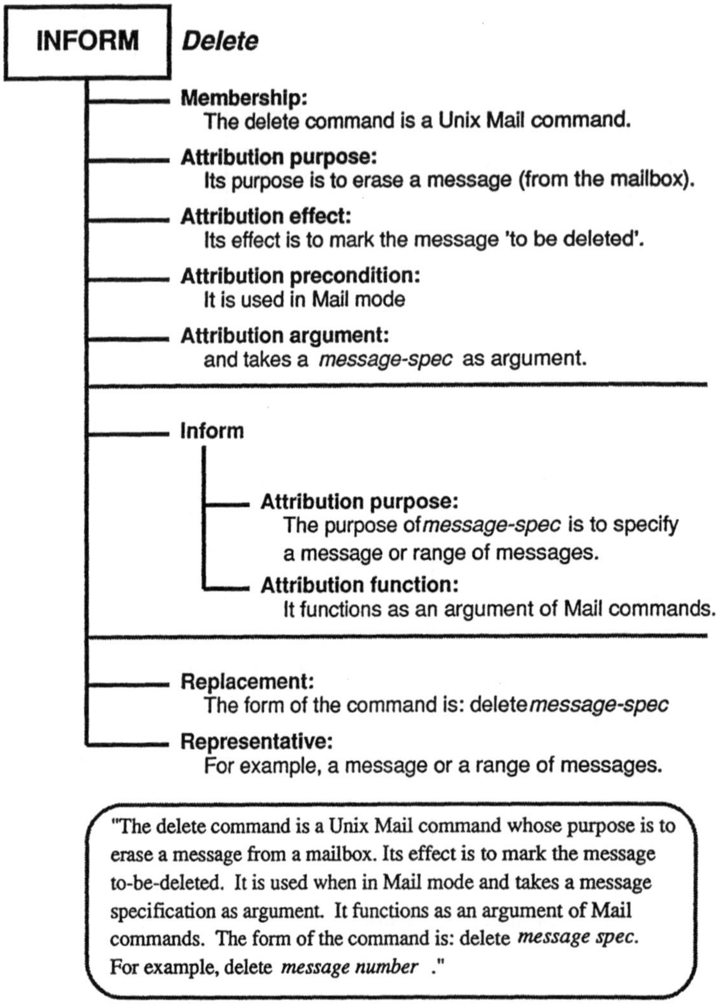

Figure 7: Sub-topic Expansion for an Inform Answer Schema

task interactions with adaptive content. The organization is achieved through navigation rules for sequencing (through types of curriculum plans or answer schemas) and by organizational predicates i.e., connectives (or comments in the case of study plans) which show the coordination of one element to the next. Although the curriculum planner described earlier arrives at its suggestions non-interactively on the basis of data held about the student, and the EUROHELP system allows users to determine their own curriculum sequences, the educational process usually benefits from discussion between those involved in the decisions.

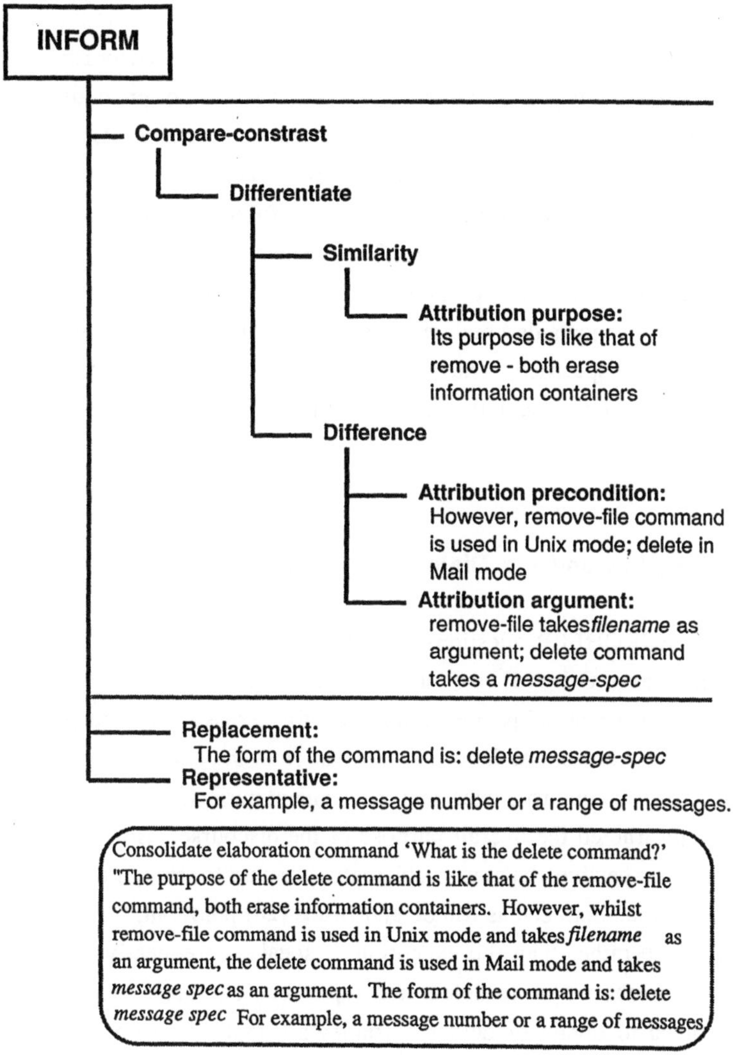

Figure 8: Comparing and Contrasting in a Consolidation Answer

Hence, in the instructional task specification, it is suggested that the functional "moves" undertaken by participants, and rules for intervention or turn taking, should form part of that task description.

Five participative modes of instruction, varying in locus of control, were identified earlier and, for one of them, the Help system mode, active and passive components have served as an example of (limited) coöperation. However, the EUROHELP experimental studies featuring human experts [11, 26] provided interesting data. For example, in approximately half of their questions, users included additional information about their intentions or knowledge of the topic. More to the point, following answers given by the expert, some type of follow-up ensued. Sometimes this was for further information of terms introduced, or for a more detailed explanation. Occasionally, it was to challenge the answer in terms of previous information (or their understanding of it), or the resulting consequences with the IPS. Also, questions were sometimes put in the form of suggestions that requested a commitment from the expert, e.g., can I...?. Although EUROHELP permits and encourages follow-up questions, it was clear that its interaction rules were somewhat restrictive. The problem is to find some formalism which is computationally tractable, but which permits a more varied range of initiatives from the user. Our suggestion is to move towards a dialogue-based "game" framework [5] in which functional roles for participants are specified. The consequences for the status of locutions forming the discourse are made explicit through the dialogue "rules," which also govern turn-taking and commitment.

Strategies and Tactics under a Dialogue Framework

In designing the EUROHELP question-answering system, we were initially very much influenced by the ideas of Grice [8] who maintained that determining the intention of the agent providing an utterance was of prime importance for assessing its meaning and answer requirements. Hence, the work of Grosz [9] was also relevant, since she broke discourse into segments on the basis of linguistic cues, and the segment purposes, with those of their linked segments, then constructed the overall purpose of the discourse. However, as she admits, "viewed from this perspective, the most problematic structure for recognition is the intentional one." Indeed, in human dialogue as Ringle and Bruce [28] point out, "conversational failure seems to be the rule rather than the exception ... speakers frequently misunderstand one another, but are somehow able to detect and repair one another's errors." Similarly, for instruction we need to obtain or devise a framework that will more easily expose (and categorize) patterns of intent or strategies in student/teacher interactions. At Leeds, Pilkington [25] has made some progress in studying socratic and tutorial types of dialogue.

A further difficulty in maintaining the focus in human discourse, apart from "red herrings" and tautologies [7], is a lack of common commitment, i.e., each participant tends to follow their own line of argument without due consideration of the other's contributions [20]. It is on overcoming this conversational mismanagement that dialogue-game theory might make a contribution [7] and, with modification, be applicable across the broad categories of interaction discussed previously.

The arrangement of a dialogue-game format can be represented as in Figure 9 with the computer instructional system acting as one participant, or with human participants communicating through linked keyboards to a common display screen.

Each statement (or performance) from a participant (its type can be coded) is entered on the locution board, but each agent has a commitment store to which are transferred those statements (or performances) he has made, and the statements of his partner which he has not challenged. In the basic Mackenzie (DC) game (well discussed by [35]), participants can ask questions requiring a commitment (e.g., "Is-it-the-case-that-p?").

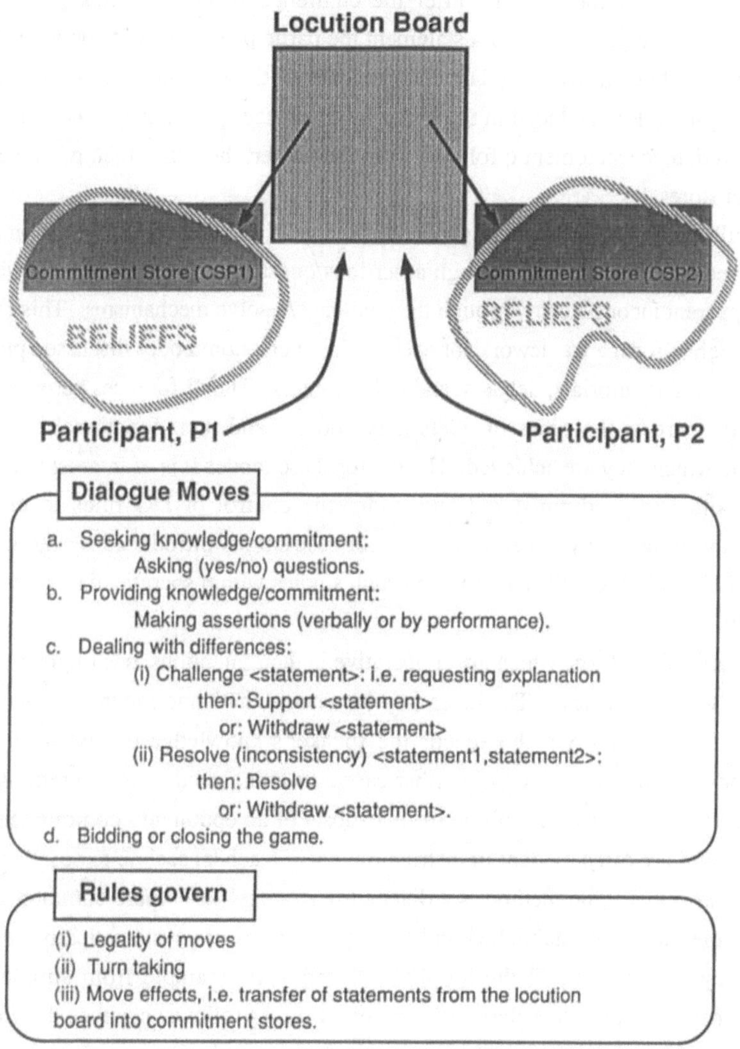

Figure 9: Dialogue Game Interactions

Within instructional contexts, if information is needed on some factual matter, for instance, then the game would be temporarily suspended while this data is obtained. Assertions/statements are made (which can be "performances" or truth-functional compounds of statements) and challenges, why-is-it-supposed-that-p? Resolutions demands, resolve-whether-p-q, and withdrawals, no- commitment-to-p, complete the basic move types. A limited number of rules govern the legality of moves, e.g., after the challenge why-p? the next event must be a withdrawal, a resolution demand, or a statement the participant believes supports p and will not be challenged. Other moves regulate the contents of the commitment stores (e.g., after a challenge why-p?). P is included in the hearer's but not the speaker's commitment store. If an unchallenged defence statement q follows from the hearer, then "if q then p" is placed in both commitment stores.

Hopefully, this short exposition gives the flavour of DG theory. It thrives on participants making or seeking commitment through assertions/questions, and then dealing with a lack of clarity or apparent inconsistency through the challenge/resolve mechanisms. This conception is general enough to form a framework for each of the interaction modes discussed previously but particularly socratic tutorials, debates, and help systems. The differences between these types of interactions are in the types of goals they address and their functional moves, i.e., the strategies by which they are achieved. Hence, for these modes it is of interest to examine such discourse both freely administered and under the control of DG rules to uncover these strategies, and to note any apparent benefits or restrictions introduced by the game format. Pilkington [25] and Moore [20] are making such studies within socratic dialogues and debates, respectively.

In educational contexts, which are cooperative in their intentions, one might enquire when a participant "wins" or "loses"! The latter may be when a challenge cannot be answered, i.e., an assertion has been made which exceeds the speaker's knowledge to sustain it, or when an inconsistency cannot be resolved. In either case a teaching need is uncovered. A win can be awarded if a thesis is shown to follow from a subset of an opponent's commitment store [12]. Such techniques are often evident in instruction where teachers seek to expose inconsistencies in students' working. One method is a distancing strategy [25] where common ground, well away from the thesis, is established and then connections are systematically made until the inconsistency is exposed and the loophole closed. An example from simple arithmetic, provided for illustration rather than realism, might run as follows: suppose the child made an assertion 5+2=10; the teacher might challenge and try to obtain an explanation, or take the initiative and set up a "distance" statement to which the child would agree, e.g., 5=>1+1+1+1+1, then 2=>1+1 and so on, leading to a total of 7 and an inconsistency. The teacher may also probe 5x2=>10, again leading to inconsistency or explanation. Which strategy is followed will depend in part on whether the teacher considers the performance a specific mistake, merely requiring feedback, a confusion between the + and x operators, and/or a mis-parsing of the task as "what total equals five sets of two?"

Other realistic and more complex strategies are evident in the socratic instructional dialogue discussed by Collins [6] where the intention is to stimulate the learner to reason, and both generalize from instances and apply principles to specific cases. For example, in the geographic dialogue, the tutor asks if Newfoundland or Montana is likely to have the coldest winter temperatures. On choosing the former, the student is challenged, giving, by way of support, the (correct) fact that Newfoundland is further North. The teacher then invites commitment to the general principle of further north means colder in winter, before producing the correct fact that Montana is colder in winter and requesting the student to resolve this inconsistency. Collins has examined socratic dialogues in a variety of knowledge domains and, from his analyses, has identified a series of rules governing these interactions. Pilkington [25] has adapted these rules to suit a dialogue-game format and, with Hintze, has provided examples from medicine, specifically a causal model of heart functions/malfunctions.[1]

Thus far, work on DG theory has concentrated largely on competitive debate and procedural contexts have been ignored, though some suggestions have been put forward by Girle [7]. The notions of "dialogue games" seem to provide an interesting framework for representing, planning, and controlling educational interactions in ways which permit initiatives from the student but in a restricted form that is more computationally tractable. This should interest workers in Cognitive Science/Artificial Intelligence and if, in the debate with instructional designers, they take up the challenges and resolve inconsistencies, a useful cooperative dialogue-game should result. This will bring particular benefits both to the quality of on-line instructional systems and to the students they are designed to serve.

References

1. Arshad, F.N.: Knowledge based learning advisors. Proceedings of the Sixth International Conference on Technology and Education, Vol. 1, pp. 213-217, Orlando, FL 1989
2. Arshad, F.N.: The design of knowledge based advisors for learning. Unpublished Ph.D. thesis. University of Leeds, UK 1990
3. Boder, A., & Cavallo, D.: An epistemological approach to intelligent tutoring systems. *Intelligent tutoring media.*, 1, 1, pp. 23-29 (1990)
4. Breuker, J. (ed).: EUROHELP: Final report. CEC ESPRIT Programme, Brussels 1990
5. Carlson, L.: *Dialogue games: An approach to discourse analysis.* Reidel 1983
6. Collins, A.: Processes in acquiring knowledge. In: *Schooling and the acquisition of knowledge* (R.C.

---

[1] This work has been funded by the CEC DELTA Project TOSKA concerned with authoring requirements for such computer based schemas, and under the NAT*LAB Project with techniques of user-modelling to maintain such dialogue.

Anderson, R.J. Spiro. & W.E. Montague, eds.). Hillsdale NJ: Lawrence Erlbaum Associates 1977
7. Girle, R.A.: Dialogue and discourse. In: *Proceedings of CAL conference in tertiary education* (G. Bishop, & W. van Lint, eds.). University of Adelaide, Australia 1986
8. Grice, H.P.: Logic and conversation. In: *Syntax and semantics: 3 speech acts* (P. Cole, & J.L. Morgan, eds.). Academic Press 1975
9. Grosz, B.: *Discourse structure and intentions.* Stanford University Press 1985
10. Hartley, J.R., & Smith, M.J.: Question answering and explanation giving in on-line help systems. In: *Artificial intelligence and human learning* (J.A. Self, ed.). Chapman and Hall 1988
11. Hartley, J.R., Pilkington, R., Tait, K., & Tattersall, C.: Question interpretation and answering. In: *EUROHELP: Final report* (J. Breuker, ed.). CEC ESPRIT Programme, Brussels 1990
12. Hintikka, J., & Saarinen, E.: Information seeking dialogues: Some of their logical properties. In: *Studia logica*, 38 (1979)
13. Hobbs, D.J.: Design of a knowledge based educational advisor. *Programmed learning and educational technology*, 25, 4, pp. 294-298 (1988)
14. Lehnert, W.: *The process of question answering.* Hillsdale, NJ: Lawrence Erlbaum Associates 1978
15. Lesgold, A.: Towards a theory of curriculum for use in designing intelligent instructional systems. In: *Learning issues for use in designing intelligent tutoring systems* (H. Mandl, & A. Lesgold, eds.). New York: Springer-Verlag 1988
16. McKeown, K.: *Text generation.* Cambridge University Press 1985
17. McNamara, D.: The national curriculum: An agenda for research. *British Educational Research Journal.*, 16, 3, pp. 225-235 (1990)
18. Merrill, M.D.: Premises, propositions and the search underlying the design of a learner controlled computer assisted instruction system: A summary of the TICCIT system. Working Paper No.4, Instructional Sciences Division, Brigham Young University 1973
19. Merrill, M.D.: Learner control in computer based learning. *Computers and Education*, 4, pp. 77-95 (1980)
20. Moore, D.: A companion of DC and unconstrained dialogue. Internal Report, Computer Based Learning Unit, University of Leeds & Leeds Polytechnic. 1990
21. Pask, G.: Styles and strategies of learning. *British Journal of Educational Psychology*, 46, pp. 128-148 (1976a)
22. Pask, G.: Conversational techniques in the study and practices of education. *British Journal of Educational Psychology*, 46, pp. 12-25 (1976b)
23. Pask, G., & Scott, B.C.E.: CASTE: A system for exhibiting learning strategies and regulating uncertainties. *International Journal of Man-Machine Studies*, 5, pp. 17-52 (1973)
24. Peachey, D.R., & McCalla, G.: Using planning techniques in intelligent tutoring systems. *International Journal of Man-Machine Studies*, 24, pp. 77-98 (1986)
25. Pilkington, R.M.: Dialogue game theory. Internal Report, Computer Based Learning Unit, University of Leeds 1990
26. Pilkington, R.M., Tattersall, C., & Hartley, J.R.: Instructional dialogue management. Technical Report, ESPRIT P-280 ULE-ICL/EUROHELP/050, Computer Based Learning Unit, University of Leeds 1988
27. Richards, T., & Webb, G.I.: Topic structuring in ECCLES: A simplified CAL authoring methodology. Technical Report 9, La Trobe University, Bundoora, Victoria, Australia
28. Ringle, M.H., & Bruce, B.C.: Conversation failure. In: *Strategies for natural language processing* (W.E. Lehnert, & M.H. Ringle, eds.). Hillsdale, NJ: Lawrence Erlbaum Associates 1982
29. Russell, D.M., Burton, R.R., Jordan, D.S., Jensen, A., Rogers, R.A., & Cohen, J.R.: Creating instruction with IDE: Tools for instructional designers. *Intelligent Tutoring Media*, 1, 1, pp. 3-16 (1990)
30. Shuell, T.J.: The role of the student in learning from instruction. *Contemporary Educational Psychology*, 13, pp. 276-295 (1988)
31. Tait, K.: The building of a computer based teaching system. *Computers and Education*, 1, 1, pp. 15-19 (1984)
32. Tait, K.: Task-space design: electronic mail applications. Technical Report ULE-ICL/EUROHELP/044, Computer Based Learning Unit, University of Leeds 1988
33. Tattersall, C.: Question answering and explanation in on-line help systems: A knowledge based approach. Unpublished Ph.D. thesis, University of Leeds 1990
34. Van Marcke, K.: A Generic tutoring environment. DIDA*EL Technical Report, 89-19-02 (1990)
35. Walton, D.N.: *Logical dialogue games and fallacies.* Lanham University Press of America 1984
36. White, J.: Two national curricula — Baker's and Stalin's: Towards a liberal alternative. *British Journal of Educational Studies*, 36, 3, pp. 218-231 (1988)
37. Winkles, R., Sandberg, J., & Breuker, J.: The coach. In: *EUROHELP: Final Report* (J. Breuker, ed.). CEC ESPRIT Programme, Brussels 1990

Part 3

Environments to Support Learning

Environments to Support Learning

Jim Greer[1] and Ellen Mandinach[2]

[1] ARIES Laboratory, Department of Computational Science, University of Saskatchewan, Saskatoon, Canada
[2] Educational Testing Service, Princeton, NJ, USA

Much of the work in computer-based learning has underestimated the role of the learner as an active participant in the midst of some learning activity. The papers in this section by Elliot Soloway et al. and by W. Patrick Dickson et al. take the view that learning and doing are inextricably intertwined; that the learner must be actively engaged in constructing his or her own knowledge; and that adaptive learning environments must support this knowledge construction activity. This view, sometimes termed *situated learning,* is espoused by Seeley Brown [3] among others.

Soloway is well known in the Intelligent Tutoring System (ITS) community for his influential work on Proust [6]. Despite the apparent success of Proust, at the NATO Institute, Soloway claimed that his earlier work, aimed primarily at building the "box" (the computer system), was misguided. He explained that when Proust was placed in the classroom, its clever and subtle diagnosis and advice went mostly unnoticed, being overwhelmed by surface issues and classroom considerations never dreamt of in the original system design. The conclusion that he drew is that work on one-on-one intelligent tutoring systems is not productive in the short-term. He claims that the issues of student modelling and individualization of curriculum and advice are “level 16 problems,” that is, problems that require long term study and offer little potential for immediate payback.

Soloway's paper in this volume focusses on domains in which the goal of the student is to design some kind of artifact. These domains might be more clearly defined as those in which problem-solving and synthesis-level student activities are dominant. Soloway attempts to construct two important distinctions: between learning to design and doing design, and between the process of design and the product of the design (i.e., the artifact). He points out that computer-based support facilities for learning design versus doing design seem to have different characteristics. Support for learning design should make the process *explicit*, should impose relatively *tight* process and product constraints on the learner, and should be *proactive* in leading the learner through appropriate processes to a “good” product. Support for doing design, on the other hand, should leave the process *implicit*, should be *loose* in its constraints on the user, and *reactive* in assisting the user only if requested.

Six interactive learning environments, each at a different stage of development, are used to illustrate various design support issues. The interaction of learning/doing with tight/loose

NATO ASI Series, Vol. F 85
Adaptive Learning Environments
Edited by M. Jones and P. H. Winne

process support is exemplified by the GPCeditor, MediaText, and SODA. The GPCeditor, an extension of Proust to guide the construction of Pascal programs, is presented as providing tight process constraints, and hence is more suitable for learning than for ultimately doing design. At the other extreme, MediaText offers loose constraints and hence is a flexible tool for doing multimedia compositions, but it seems less suitable for learning principles of the design process. SODA, an extension of the GPCeditor, attempts to offer adaptable levels of support, ranging from tight constraints during learning to loosening constraints during doing. Although no evaluation of SODA has been done to date, the argument is made that adaptability in process constraints will lead to a suitable learning and doing environment.

The interaction of learning/doing with explicit/implicit process support is exemplified by the Statics Calculator, IByD, and Emile. The Statics Calculator provides a single mental-model level representation for the construction of solutions to statics problems. As such, it leaves other mental-model representations implicit, and although it is useful for doing statics problems, it does not support learning the process. IByD, on the other hand, presents a variety of explicit representations that student teachers must consider as they construct lesson plans. This system is purported to lead to learning suitable instructional planning processes and developing better instructional plans. Emile, a Hypercard programming environment, allows adaptability over multiple representations, thus allowing both explicit and implicit representational support, and, as such, is hypothesized to be suitable for both learning and doing.

In summary, this complex argument boils down to three observations. Tighter constraints on the learner may be suitable during *learning* but not during *doing*. Explicit multiple representations may be unnecessary during *doing* but not during *learning*. Adaptability in constraints on the learner and in the number of explicit representations may offer the best of both worlds.

Soloway raises interesting issues with respect to adaptability, degree of learner control, and explicit representation of mental models. Considerable ITS research has been carried out in each of these areas. Adaptability has been a cornerstone issue in all of ITS research. Learner control has been studied by many ITS researchers including Collins [4], Elsom-Cook [5] and others. Intermediate representations consistent with students' mental models appear in much of the modern work in ITS, such as the Bridge Tutor [2], GIL [8], Angle [7], and Petal [1]. Soloway's observations emphasize the need to grapple with the issues of adaptability in learner control, finding an appropriate level of scaffolding for the learner, and moving among various explicit mental-model level representations and more implicit representations.

The Dickson paper describes a project that attempts to introduce exploratory environments, such as those found in interactive museums, into classroom settings. The project is unlike any of the other work represented in this volume. Rather than focus specifically on knowledge based approaches to the development of adaptive learning environments, Dickson et al. eschew the notion that they are in the software development business. Their goal is not so much to create exploratory environments as it is to develop "a conceptual framework for thinking about exploration in education." The relevance of this project in the context of the other chapters in this volume perhaps can be found in the fact that the MicroExploratorium implements technology in the form of a multimedia learning environment, not an intelligent tutoring system.

Unlike many other projects whose goals are to build systems that enhance the knowledge-base in computer science and artificial intelligence and that fail to specify instructional theories, the Dickson work approaches system development from the perspective of theory. The basis of the work is a specific pedagogical theory, namely exploration. The authors' objective is to transform exploratory activities, which have been used extensively in interactive science museum settings, into classroom learning environments. Consistent with their stated goals, Dickson et al. provide very little in the way of software design description. The importance of this work is not found in the development of a technology-based system for exploration; rather, the important implications to be drawn from the MicroExploratorium concern how the system is used as a framework for exploratory learning in the classroom.

The authors state that they sought to bring museum-like learning into typical classrooms. They further acknowledged that little rigorous evaluation was conducted on the implementation of the system. Evaluation in this instance takes on two roles. The first type of evaluation concerns design of the system and is relatively straightforward. The second form is evaluation of system use. This is more problematic. There is something fundamentally naive about the placement of a single system into a classroom of 25 fifth grade students. It is particularly troublesome when the system is based on the theoretical notion that students learn effectively through exploratory activities. There are some basic assumptions about this method of instruction, in conjunction with the use of technology, that can create chaos and a managerial nightmare in the classroom. For example, such learning requires substantial time and hands-on experience. The issue here is how to organize classroom activities when a few students are interacting with the technology, the remainder are doing something else, and there is only one teacher to manage everything. There also is ambiguity about how such activity relates to other instructional tasks. The technology-based activities are often perceived as tasks totally separate from the mainstream of instruction, and therefore are to be viewed as non-academic, irrelevant, or for entertainment. There must be explicit ties to the existing curriculum for students to perceive the activities as educational. Such integration is difficult for teachers but can be made easier with forethought and planning in the system design phase.

A related issue is the introduction of technology with only one computer. The structure of the typical classroom works against this model. Even the model of the technology-based classroom with active engagement on the part of the students cannot work effectively with only one machine for 25 students. It is also unreasonable to expect success when teachers are not trained in system operation. Once you have a system, what do you do with it to make it an effective instructional tool? It takes training, time, effort, money, and hard work for teachers to become effective users of technology. The work of Dickson et al. highlights the need for developers to give serious thought to the constraints imposed by classroom settings during the design phase. These considerations often are too little too late when they occur during implementation. Such forethought may help to prevent the introduction of systems that are difficult to integrate into the curriculum and use effectively in classrooms. In this way, systems and their implementation will provide a valuable educational function and a forum for computer and instructional research.

Both of the papers in this section demonstrate a move away from one-on-one tutoring, preferring exploratory, situated learning environments. Since both Soloway and Dickson argue in favour of more situated adaptive learning environments and against the more traditional one-on-one intelligent tutoring systems (ITSs), a few comments in defense of ITSs seems to be in order. Those taking the strongly situated learning perspective seem to unanimously criticize ITSs for not considering issues related to learning in context or creating one's own knowledge. ITSs have been accused of taking a "knowledge transfer" or "funnel" approach — that of "open learner's mind and pour in the knowledge." The cognitive information processing models of psychology also seem to be simultaneously under attack by the same "strongly situated" forces. (In fact, the "strongly situated" criticisms seem to be also levelled against the philosophical foundations of AI and even against the Cartesian scientific tradition.) The comments presented here will be limited to criticisms against ITSs.

First, let us assume that ITSs are those computer-based adaptive learning environments where learning interactions resemble those between a tutor and an individual learner. The ITS, then, could take on any role a supportive tutor might employ. This ranges from lecturer to story teller, coach, museum guide, passive observer, facilitator, mentor, collaborator, or evaluator. With this view, it is difficult to claim that ITSs must be necessarily limited to funnel learning.

It seems that learning can be categorized into high and low levels. Low level learning, such as assembling facts, inducing concepts, or learning standard procedures seems to be equally achievable by various uninteresting means. Low level learning frequently occurs in spite of the instructional approach. Higher level learning, that of analysis, synthesis, or evaluation, is harder to achieve, and consequently is more interesting. ITS approaches to achieving this higher level learning do so by explicitly representing the domain knowledge in the system, modelling the learner's cognitive state, and facilitating learning by conducting some adaptive interaction with the learner. It may be argued that representing knowledge in the system or modelling the learner's cognitive state are mere fictions (for the most part ignoring the context in which the learner is subtly situated). Nevertheless, they prove to be useful fictions. Attributing cognitive states to the learner allows one to make simplifying assumptions that make teaching possible. Education research has shown that teaching promotes learning, even high level learning, and that the greater the understanding the teacher has of the context in which the learning occurs, the more successful that learning will be. This raises the challenge to incorporate context into the interactions and the analysis of ITSs, not to abandon them.

Furthermore, if the ITS is a dead end, what does the situated perspective buy? If cognitive processes as we know them are oversimplified fiction, then the situated perspective makes learning opaque and unanalyzable (hearkening back to behaviourism). If, on the other hand, the situated perspective encourages us to provide CAD environments where the learner can experiment with the construction of artifacts (as Soloway claims) or rich exploratoria (as Dickson advocates), then why not capitalize on the facilities an ITS can offer in intelligently adapting the environment according to the needs of the learner? Perhaps these strongly situated criticisms of ITS reflect an American myth, rampant in the automobile industry, that rapidity of obsolescence is a measure of vitality of an area!

References

1. Bhuiyan, S.H., Greer, J.E., & McCalla, G.I.: Characterizing, rationalizing and reifying mental models of recursion. Proceedings of the 12th Annual Cognitive Science Conference, Chicago 1991
2. Bonar, J.G., & Cunningham, R.: Intelligent tutoring with intermediate representations. Proceedings of Intelligent Tutoring Systems, Montreal, Canada, pp. 25-32 (1988)
3. Brown, J. S.: Toward a new epistemology for learning. In: *Intelligent tutoring systems: At the crossroads of artificial intelligence and education* (C. Frasson & G. Gauthier , eds.). Norwood, NJ: Ablex 1990
4. Collins, A., Brown, J.S., & Newman, S.: Cognitive apprenticeship. In: *Cognition and instruction: Issues and agendas* (L. Resnick, ed.). Hillsdale, NJ: Lawrence Erlbaum Associates 1989
5. Elsom-Cook, M.: Guided discovery tutoring. *NATO Advanced Research Workshop on Guided Discovery Tutoring*, Tuscany, Italy 1989
6. Johnson, W. L., & Soloway, E.: PROUST: An automatic debugger for Pascal programs. *Byte*, 10, 4, pp. 179-190 (1985)
7. Koedinger, K.R., & Anderson, J.: Theoretical and empirical motivations for design of ANGLE: A new geometry learning environment. Proceedings AAAI Spring Symposium Series, Stanford University 1990
8. Reiser, B.J., Ranney, M., Lovett, M.C., & Kimberg, D.Y.: Facilitating students' reasoning with causal explanations and visual representations. Proceedings of the 4th International Conference on AI and Education, Amsterdam, Netherlands, pp. 228-235 (1990)

Exploratory Multi-media Environments

W. Patrick Dickson, Carrie Heeter, Mark Rosenberg, Pericles Gomes, and Itzik Artzi

College of Education, Michigan State University, East Lansing, MI, USA

Abstract: This chapter describes an on-going research and development project, funded by a grant from the W. K. Kellogg Foundation, that is attempting to bring insights from the design of exploratory environments in museums to bear upon the design of multimedia environments that can be integrated into classrooms. Features of exploratory environments observed in interactive museums are described, with the identification of features that can guide attempts at translating these environments into forms compatible with classroom constraints. Such an exploratorium differs from other applications of computer technology in being deliberately designed to invite exploration, evoke curiosity, and stimulate further exploration. We describe "rooms" that have been created in this computer-based "exploratorium" and the experience of testing these environments. The exploratory environment seeks to give children the feeling of freedom to run, roam, pause, poke, and play with images, ideas, and "objects" at their own pace and as they wish. The goal is to create an enclave in the corner of the classroom that allows children's imaginations to roam the universe.

Keywords: exploratory learning, interactive learning.

Introduction

The broadest context for this paper is the question of the role of exploration in education. Children spend a great portion of their waking hours in school classrooms. Occasionally, schools arrange field trips to visit other places that differ fundamentally from classrooms. Among the popular places to visit are science museums, broadly defined. In recent years, museums have become increasingly interactive and "hands on," with an increased emphasis on education for the public.

The enthusiasm and excitement shown by children in these settings is in marked contrast to the atmosphere in many classrooms, where children are frequently subdued, stationary,

NATO ASI Series, Vol. F 85
Adaptive Learning Environments
Edited by M. Jones and P. H. Winne

passive, and receptive. This contrast between the museum and classroom environment is potentially informative for the design of educational experiences.

The chapter begins with a description of exhibits found in interactive museums. We then contrast and compare a variety of educational settings in museums and classrooms in order to create a conceptual model for the elements of environmental design in interactive museum settings that are appropriate or adaptable within the constraints of classroom settings.

From this conceptual model, we describe some prototype activities derived from interactive activities in science museums that have been developed on a computer for use in the classroom. Among these types of activity are explorations of oneself, explorations of the physical world from outer space to the local community, as well as specific conceptual domains such as sound, music, fractals, and geometric shapes. The current embodiment of the computer-based "MicroExploratorium" consists of *hardware* (a Macintosh II computer equipped with color screen, a videodisc player, a CD-ROM player, a videotape player-recorder, a video camera and video digitizer, a sound digitizer, and printer), *software* (commercial and custom-produced videodiscs and software described later in this chapter) and, optionally, *a context* (the MicroExploratorium is sometimes housed in a portable, 6-foot diameter geodesic dome).

In summary, we conceive of the MicroExploratorium as a prototype for the museum on a desktop with abundant field trips at your fingertips.

Analogy to Museums

This project arose, as is often the case, from incidental observations. Over several years, Dickson and his children made many recreational visits to a variety of museums, zoos, and nature centers. Some readers may be unaware of two important trends among museums. First, during the past ten to twenty years, museums have given increased attention to the educative role of museums (as contrasted with their research and curatorial roles). A major influence in these changes were the Kellogg Projects in Museum Education directed by Arlon Elser [11]. Although education has always been a part of the mandate of museums, education has not been at center stage in many museums until recently. Second, a category of museums referred to variously as "children's museums," "science and technology museums," and "hands-on museums" has proliferated in recent years. Cleaver, in a guide to 225 such museums in the United States, says:

> What could be more fun than going to a hands-on museum? Fortunately, for families today, many museums are radically different from the museums of even fifteen or twenty years ago. A whole generation of children's museums, interactive science centers, nature centers, and hands-on discovery rooms has sprung up. Their mission is to bring things out from behind the red velvet ropes and the

> glass cases to be touched, handled, felt, explored, and experimented with.... Essentially, children's museums are learning playgrounds, full of choices that encourage visitors to pursue their interests as far as they want [1, p. 5].

Examples of such museums include the Exploratorium in San Francisco, the Ontario Science Center, and the Indianapolis Children's Museum. An excellent description of these museums from the point of view of environmental design can be found in the spring 1987 issue of *Children's Environments Quarterly*, edited by Gallagher and Dien [2], devoted to children's museums. If you have not visited such museums recently, preferably with some children, we would urge you to spend some time observing visitors in such interactive settings while reflecting on similarities and contrasts with other educational settings.

This type of museum has attracted attention in the educational community. Kornhaber, Krechevsky, and Gardner write, "Science, discovery, and children's museums offer a rich and powerful opportunity for children to draw upon the different forms of knowledge that are generally left unintegrated, treated in isolation from each other, or perhaps ignored in school. The materials in museums are in a sense already pretested for their appeal to children" [5, p. 191].

A central theme of our research is the deliberate attempt to take ideas from museum settings and find ways of incorporating them into classrooms in schools. In our view, these museums provide a rich testing ground for the design of environments for the purpose of engaging people's interest and engagement. During visits to many museums, Dickson photographed a variety of activities and exhibits. Although each museum was different, certain common themes and activities were found across the museums. Consider the contrast with classrooms. Children are legally required to be present in classrooms, but visiting museums is generally voluntary (with some parental encouragement). Activities in museums that are not interesting to visitors fail to "survive" and "replicate" across museums, while typical classroom activities are not subject to learner choice.

A complete presentation of the conceptual analysis of museum activities that we have carried out in this project is beyond the scope of this chapter. A few insights that have influenced the design of our computer-based MicroExploratorium will be described, however. For example, many exhibits in children's museums are interactive in the specific sense that children can "put themselves into" the exhibits. Examples of such exhibits include those in which children are able to freeze their shadows on a luminescent wall, record their faces with video cameras, or record their voices with sound recorders.

Extensions of these exhibits include the ability to manipulate aspects of oneself by transforming electronically the voice or image. Other exhibits encourage the hands-on construction of something three-dimensional, such as arches that trace the evolution of architectural design or geometric shapes from toothpicks and peas that invoke touch and other physical senses to stimulate learning and creativity. The attraction of creating something extends to activities such as drawing, writing, playing with musical instruments, and building with clay. Certain exhibits have their appeal in simulating experiences that otherwise would be impossible, dangerous, or impractical. For example, one can experience a simulation of the first landing on the moon at the Smithsonian Institute or, via a joystick and underwater videocamera, explore sea creatures at the Hewlett-Packard Aquarium in Monterey, California.

Exploration in science museums invites learning by implying an element of the unknown and possibilities of encountering something unexpected. In exploration, learners are navigating through unexplored territory of their own volition under their own control and with unknown consequences. The learner as explorer is an active seeker of experience.

Exhibits often focus on complex themes in physical sciences, mathematics, and social sciences, including such domains as light, sound, color, electricity, magnetism, mechanics, fractals, geometric expansion, emotions, optical illusions, ecology, and many others. In the museum settings, in contrast to school textbooks, these topics are usually presented in ways that invite hands-on interaction by visitors. Interactive technologies based on videodiscs and computers play an increasing role in the design of hands-on exhibits in museums.

Characteristics of Exploratory Environments

The exploratory environment seeks to give children the feeling of freedom to run, roam, pause, poke, and play with images, ideas, and "objects" at their own pace and as they wish. "Running" is a joyous, fast-paced movement that transports the explorer almost recklessly to a new place. "Roaming" implies a somewhat slower pace involving mulling and choosing without a specific destination in mind. "Pausing" allows for reflection and rest. "Poking" is almost a challenge — disturbing the peace of an object to see what it does. Exemplary museum objects should poke back. "Playing" suggests supposing, making believe, asking "what if," comraderie, and laughter. The MicroExploratorium attempts to enable explorers to move among these modes as well as move among the planets. The computer-based exploratorium is an attempt at creating an enclave in the corner of the classroom that allows children's imaginations to go exploring without leaving the classroom. The MicroExploratorium uses technology as a "medium for experiential learning" [6], but our goal is to design an environment that encourages a motivation to explore rather than create specific experiences with specific learnings in mind.

Motivation and Creativity

The approach taken in designing this exploratory environment differs from more common approaches in designing educational software. Priority is placed on creating intrinsically motivating experiences. None of the activities in the MicroExploratorium include feedback that behaviorists might design. There are no smiling faces or bells for "getting it right." Indeed, our environments do not have right answers, any more than there is a right answer to a trip to a zoo. Similarly, no specific content is targetted for learning. There is no scope and no sequence in this multimedia, hypermedia environment. This theoretical perspective on motivation is influenced by the work of Lepper and Malone [7] and Hatano [3], although our interest is not in instructional effectiveness.

In this environment, we take motivation and curiosity as the central educational objective, not as an issue for enabling the learning of something else. The approach has resonances with a recent paper by Sternberg and Laubart [14] in which they argue that "schools probably do at least as much to undermine creativity as to support it" (p. 614). Sternberg and Laubart emphasize the importance of motivation for creativity, and describe the importance of environmental contexts that "provide bases for lots of creative sparks" (p. 613). We believe that the kind of exploratory environments we are developing could stimulate more creative activities in classrooms.

Software design

The MicroExploratorium project brings together educators and software designers with a common purpose. The project benefitted from the expertise in the Michigan State University "Comm Tech Lab," which is directed by Heeter. Comm Tech Lab designers were part of Dickson's research team, working together with educational researchers to apply software design theories and techniques to create an exploratory desktop museum. The goal is the conception, prototyping, and testing of software components that embody the kinds of essential experiences identified in the preceding analysis of hands-on museums.

Metaphors in software design "have two distinct but related uses: as cognitive aids to users, and as aids to creativity for designers. Metaphors can help designers to use their own, often unconscious expectations to create new information links and mental structures." [10]. The organizing metaphor for the MicroExploratorium is a physical museum, to put designers and users in an appropriate frame of mind, as well as to use a metaphor with which classroom teachers could resonate.

A visit to the MicroExploratorium begins at the outer reaches of the universe. Visitors click their way in from outer space, zooming in on earth to a museum building. When they click on the door of the MicroExploratorium, the building opens up and reveals rooms containing exhibits that are "open" to visitors. (See Figure 1.)

Spatial metaphor

Field trips to a museum and visitors' exploration within museums have a spatial component. The use of a spatial metaphor for the organization of our computer-based museum is both natural and consistent with other lines of inquiry that suggest that spatial arrangement is one of the powerful modes for humans to organize information generally.

Humans do not, however, experience all of space in Cartesian coordinates. If we did, one might construct an exploratorium that allowed navigation by Cartesian coordinates. Explorations of the solar system do lend themselves to visualization in three-dimensional space; for example, the exploration of one's neighborhood and school seem to feel more like a two-dimensional surface (a map), and designing an exploration of the earth seems to lend itself to representation as the surface of sphere. Finally, the human body has a particular salience and topography that influences the design of a user interface for navigation.

The "field trip" is used as a metaphor for visiting a museum, collecting "specimens," bringing them back, naming them, and writing a story, poem, or report about them. Another class of activities popular with children in museums has to do with allowing children to capture or manipulate some aspect of themselves as in the shadow room where children can freeze their shadow on a luminescent wall. The computer exploratorium is equipped with a video camera and digitizer that will enable children to capture images of themselves or other people or objects in the classroom. They are able to zoom in on their eyes, collect images of parts of themselves, "edit" images of themselves, and merge pictures of themselves or their classmates with poems.

Exemplary Modules in the Museum

We will now describe some of the "rooms" open in the MicroExploratorium. At the outset, it is important to remind our readers that we view the project as one of developing a conceptual framework for thinking about exploration in education and not a software development project focussed on developing a marketable "package." We have concentrated on instantiating a user-interface for exploration and the design of a metaphor that enables us to integrate other existing hardware and software smoothly into this interface.

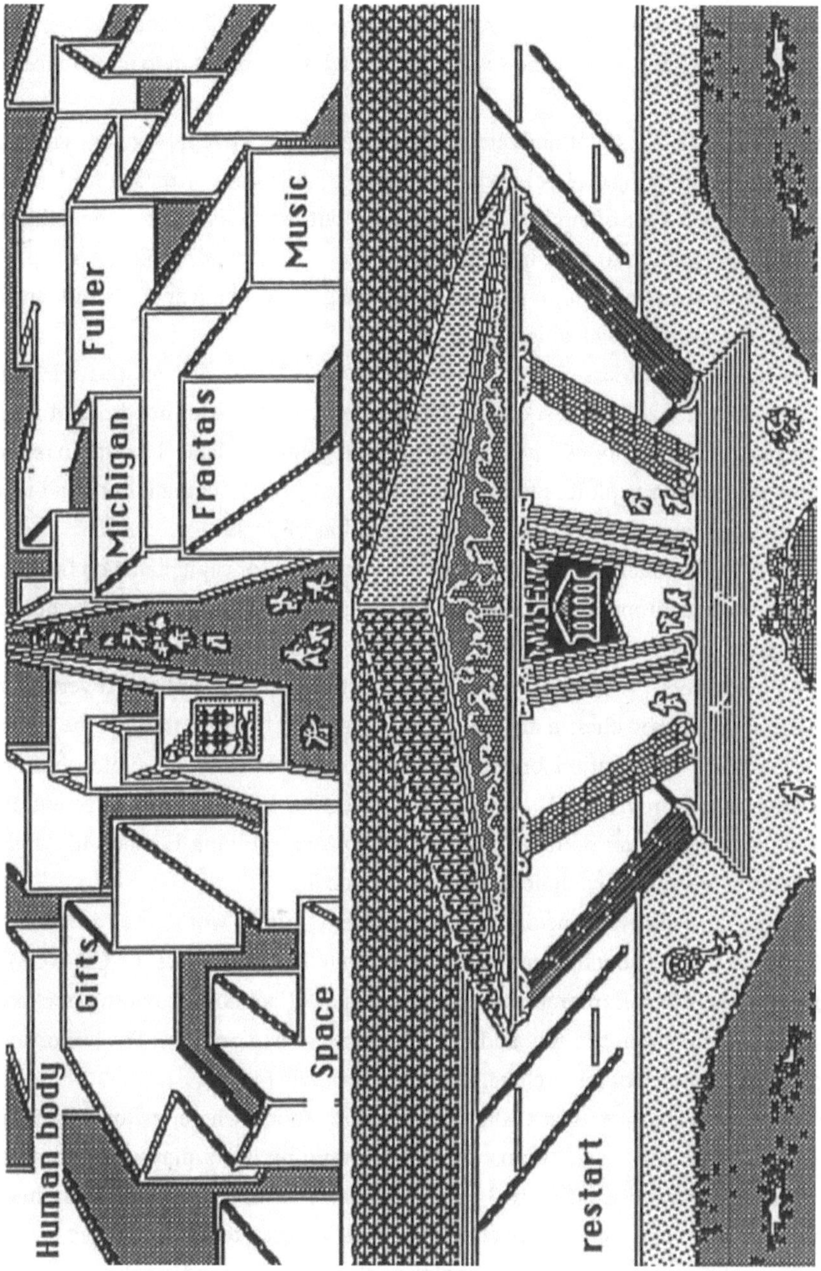

Figure 1: Entrance to the MicroExploratorium Museum on a Desktop

As visitors move the cursor across the rooms of the museum, exhibits that are open flash. A click opens the room. For example, the space room includes an invitation to explore the solar system (Figure 2).

Explorers click on buttons that activate sequences from the *Voyager Space* videodisc, zooming them across the surface of Miranda (a satellite of Neptune) or through the rings of Saturn or toward the red spot of Jupiter. Visitors can "put themselves into" the exhibit by adding their name and picture to a "ship's log" and writing "postcards" about their trip. The text on their postcards is imposed on top of the video image, taking advantage of the overlay capabilities of the Pioneer 4200 videodisc player.

Visitors may also explore Mars via the "*Mission to Mars!*" CD-ROM developed at Michigan State University by Heeter and her associates. *Mission to Mars!* includes hundreds of sounds, over 1,000 images, facts, animations, and quotations about going to Mars. The star map serves as the main index, allowing explorers to jump to a wide range of visual, auditory and textual information, providing room to roam, lots of choices and lots of depth.

The *Mission to Mars!* interface uses metaphor as a technique for capitalizing on familiarity. "Metaphors, if they are appropriate, are very quickly understood" [13, pp. 1-7]. The design of a screen can suggest "this is like a newspaper" or "this is like flying a space ship." *Mission to Mars!* uses two metaphors. A spaceship window, complete with forward and reverse levers, makes lever-like sounds when clicked and lets users navigate by "flying" through the program. A special "hyperspace" navigation button jumps the explorer randomly into some new, unknown location in the program. A "videophone" metaphor lets users dial different phone numbers to see and hear expert opinions about going to Mars. Flying is much like running through a museum ... visitors move quickly and it feels good.

Outside of school, learners, especially young learners, live in worlds rich in music and other sound. Inside school, sound is suppressed and limited. Throughout the CD-ROM and the other rooms in the MicroExploratorium are all manner of sounds, providing unexpected responses, sensory stimulation, and fun, adding to the sense of exploration. The use of sounds in hypermedia is a major area of research in the Comm Tech Lab [4].

A contrast to exploring outer space is the *Human Body* room, where visitors can click on the human ear and enter the music room. The music room invites a playful exploration of sounds and music in several ways (Figure 3). For example, visitors can click on an animal and a melody and hear the animal sing the selected song. Hearing such things as a sheep and a dog perform renditions of Three Blind Mice almost always elicits laughter and giggles from visitors. (We consider laugher, especially from grownups, as valuable evidence that the exploration is a good one.) Consistent with our goal of allowing visitors to "put themselves" into the activity, the music room also invites visitors to record their own sounds, which can then be used in renditions of existing songs. They manipulate aspects of themselves by playing back the sound

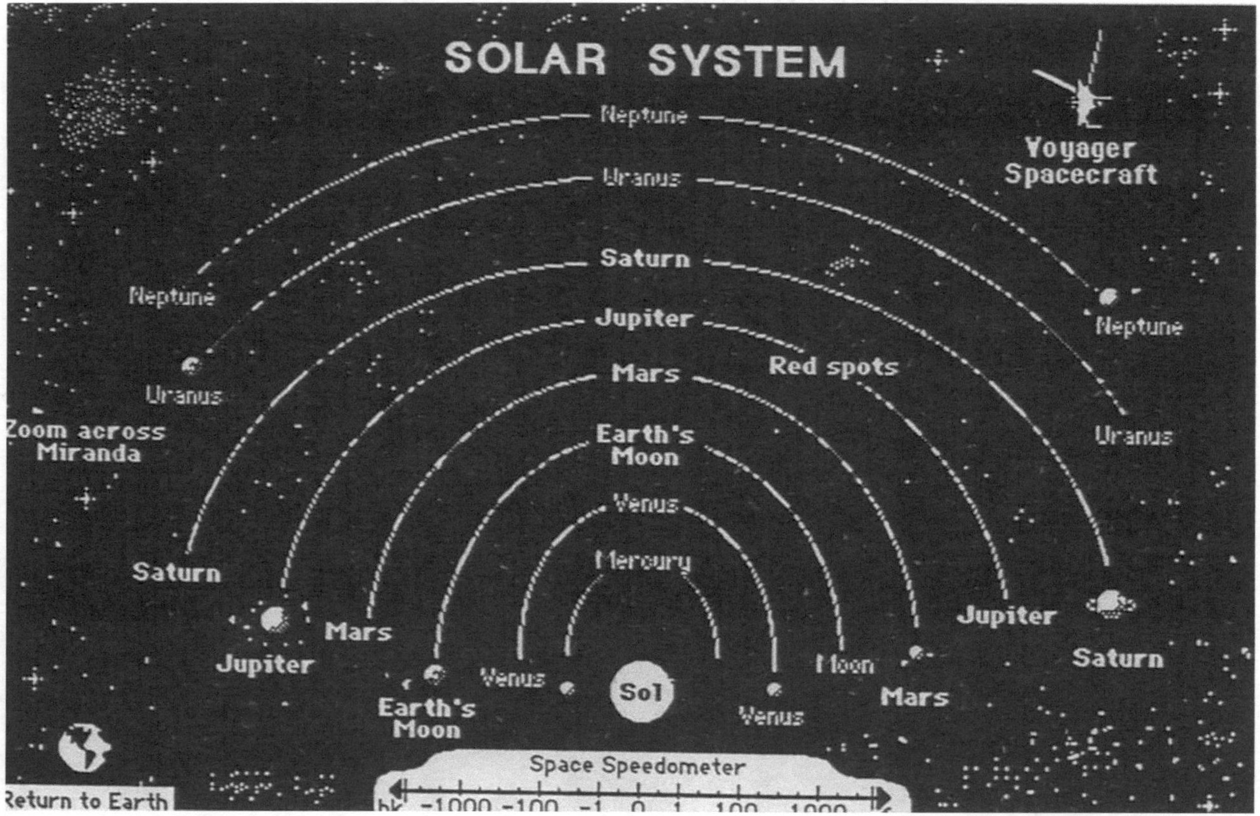

Figure 2: Home card for exploring the solar system

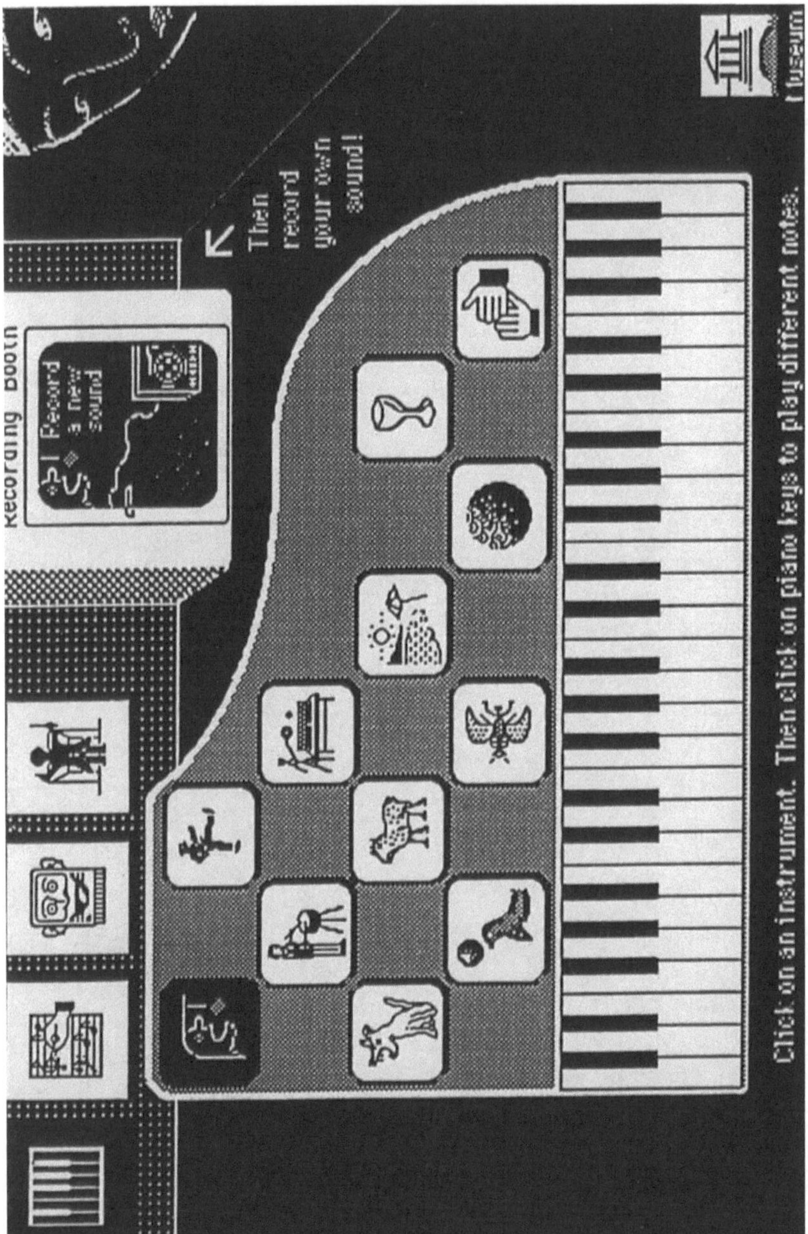

Figure 3: Keyboard in the music room of the MicroExploratorium

they made at different pitches by playing a special piano. The visitor can choose a sound they made or prerecorded sounds such as seals barking and then make up a melody on the keyboard by clicking the "ivories."

The MicroExploratorium also has a mathematics room, where the exhibit currently open is an exploration of fractals. This software allows visitors to draw fractal trees and to systematically or whimsically vary key parameters and see the changes in the fractal patterns generated. Fractals may be drawn in four windows, encouraging comparisons among different fractals. The environment attempts to make it irresistible to ask the question, "What if I do this?" and "What happens if we change that?" We experimented with a fractal card game, where players are dealt cards and win by making sets that match on some dimension.

A geometry room is designed around the work of Buckminster Fuller. This room illustrates several key features that we are seeking to integrate into our activities. Among other things, Fuller is famous for inventing the geodesic dome. (We have built a geodesic dome to house the MicroExploratorium.) His interest in structure and design arose from experiences in early childhood and may have been influenced by his impaired vision. The following quote is from an interview:

> My first objective structural experimenting occurred in my pre-eyeglass, blurred-vision, 1899 kindergarten. The teacher gave us equilength toothpicks and semidried peas. She told us to make structures — houses. All the other children, none of whom had eye trouble, put together rectilinear box houses. The peas were strong enough to act as angle-holding gussets. Not having visualized the rectilinearity around me, I used only my tactile sense. My finger muscles found that only the triangle had a natural shape-holding capability. I therefore felt my way into producing an octahedron-tetrahedron truss assembly. I, of course, knew naught of such names.
>
> I can remember the teacher, Miss Williams, asking other teachers to come and look at the strange structure I had produced. Fifty years later I heard from that teacher, who clearly remembered the strange event.... It was this experience which undoubtably started me off at fifteen to look for nature's own structural coordinate system.

This interview appeared as the Prologue to a biography of Alexander Graham Bell, who also explored the properties of the tetrahedron.

We include this lengthy quote because it exemplifies the recollection of early hands-on experiences that many creative people report having played a crucial role in their later work. Other examples include Seymour Papert's experience with gears that he recalls influencing his interest in mathematics and Frank Lloyd Wright's recollection of tactual explorations of wooden geometric shapes.

Visitors to our geometry room "ride" in a car designed by Fuller and hear a dialogue between Alexander Graham Bell and Fuller concerning the design of tetrahedral kits, which both of them explored independently. When visitors arrive at the geometry room, they can click on different geometric shapes, such as a tetrahedron or duodecahedron and see these Platonic shapes assembled. (The animations for this were done using Macromind Director.)

The Fuller exhibit ends with an encouragement to visitors to return to the "real" world and make something. Specifically, visitors are encouraged to try building some geometric shapes with toothpicks and peas, as well as experimenting with clay, marshmallows, and Q-tips. A handout allows visitors to cut out shapes and build a geodesic dome. These activities are consonant with Papert's [12] conception of "constructionism," which emphasizes the cognitive benefits of having the learner construct something external or at least shareable.

We give considerable thought to encouraging visitors to do follow-up activities to their experiences in the MicroExploratorium. This concept we refer to as "extensibility," that is, the likelihood that experiences will lead to further explorations of a topic, including such things as hands-on activities, seeking books to read, discussing the experiences with others, and choosing to watch related television programs. Drawing on the museum metaphor, we have created a gift shop where visitors can obtain recommendations for further readings or print off instructions for related experiments they can do at home (Figure 4).

Formative Evaluation

It would be misleading to claim that this project has conducted rigorous evaluation. The goal of the project is to develop a conceptual model for incorporating technology that encourages exploration into schools and other educational settings. Nevertheless, we have observed children using the MicroExploratorium in four different settings: a county fair, Exploration Days when 4-H youth visit the University campus, Impression 5 Museum, and, most extensively, in a fifth grade classroom in a local school.

What have we learned? First, the obvious: children are highly motivated by the rich exploratory world of the MicroExploratorium. In all settings, it has been necessary to set time limits on children's explorations in order to permit other children to have an opportunity. Second, also obvious: moving, setting up, and maintaining the hardware and software requires considerable effort.

In designing the MicroExploratorium, we have tried to find ways of encouraging children to extend their activities after they leave the MicroExploratorium. We tested the geometry room with elementary and middle school age visitors and found they spent ten or fifteen minutes building with toothpicks and peas after visiting the room. This duration of contact compares favorably with the common finding in museums and zoos that the average duration of visitor contact with exhibits is well under one minute.

Figure 4: MicroExploratorium gift shop to encourage follow-up activities

Our vision of placing a museum on a desktop in every classroom has been piloted during the past year in a single fifth grade classroom. We were fortunate to have the support and tolerance of a teacher who was willing to accommodate the MicroExploratorium in his room. The teacher's personal interests focussed more on children's writing and he used an Apple IIGS in his classroom for this work. During the course of the year, he began learning to use the Macintosh computer but he did not attempt to keep up with the continuing evolution of the MicroExploratorium, and indeed it would have been difficult to do so, as we designed, piloted, and modified new modules on a continuous basis.

The children worked alone or in pairs at the MicroExploratorium. A graduate student was in the classroom two or three days a week and introduced the children to the Macintosh environment.

Regulating access to the MicroExploratorium in a classroom setting proved difficult and we tried a variety of solutions. At the outset, we adopted a simple procedure that the teacher used for other activities. A child, or a pair of children, would begin using the MicroExploratorium and were expected to select the names of the children to have the next turn by drawing randomly names from a container on the teacher's desk. Although this worked to a degree, it was difficult to have children limit their time on the computer, causing other children to feel impatient. In addition, if children using the computer had a problem with the software, the teacher could not take time from his regular duties to come back and answer their questions.

In order to deal with both of these problems, we tried designating six children as "operators" and focussed on teaching them how to operate the system. An honor code for the operators was developed that emphasized their obligation to support other children assigned to them in using the computer. This approach seemed to work initially, but after a few weeks the "operators" began to monopolize more and more of the time available on the computer and began to assume a rather condescending attitude toward their classmates. We concluded that status differentials of this kind are dysfunctional if our goal is to create a community of users that encompasses the entire class.

Toward the end of the school year, we focussed on encouraging children's writing within the MicroExploratorium, trying to develop simplified writing environments that enabled children to select images from a videodisc and write stories about them. Our commitment to promoting writing came up against the limitations of children's typing speed. In a classroom of about 25 children who are in school about six hours a day for five days a week, an average child could have a maximum of about an hour a week if the computer were used continuously and no time were taken away for such things as lunch, recess, field trips, etc. In fact, the time available per child per week probably is about thirty minutes. Allowing for some browsing of the videodisc, thinking about what to say, hunting and pecking at about two to four words a minute, leads to children writing rather short pieces.

During the last month of the school year, the teacher felt the MicroExploratorium was distracting children from the many school assignments and tests that needed to be completed, so we removed the MicroExploratorium to the school library.

In summary, we consider this first year-long classroom test of the MicroExploratorium a somewhat qualified success. On the positive side, the children enjoyed it. They had an opportunity to experience first hand a multimedia writing environment that included experience with a videodisc, CD-ROM, HyperCard, and other technologies. They wrote, drew, published a newspaper, and explored the solar system. At the same time, we learned that it is difficult to set up and support such an environment in a classroom and articulate it with the vast demands on a teacher's time. Finally, we came to be much more aware of the difficulty in allocating scarce resources, both children's time and access time to technology.

Conclusions and Future Directions

Predicting the future of technology is relatively easy. Computers will increase in speed, memory capacity, power, ease of use, and integration of multimedia; the technologies will also decrease in size and cost; and software and other media will increase in quality and quantity. The technological power that will be available on a desktop in 1995 or 2000 will be extraordinary.

On the other hand, predicting the future of technology in education is extremely difficult. One educationally relevant prediction is certain: children and adults will continue to have only 24 hours per day. Therein lies the major challenge in attempting to envision uses of technology in education. Because technology can be used for a wide and growing set of purposes, advocates for each additional use or new software or hardware product describe exciting benefits for their applications. Our experience during the past year, however, has made us acutely aware of constraints on children's and teacher's time, as well as the further limitations on access to technology when the student-computer ratio is high.

The current state of affairs with regard to technology in education seems to us to be one of hundreds of concurrent natural experiments on every conceivable type of hardware, software, content, and configuration, from didactic software focussed on specific content to tools for writing and drawing to more open-ended exploratory worlds of the kind described here [8].

We believe the motivation to explore and skills of navigating through vast informational worlds are basic skills for the 21st century. We agree with Lepper and Gurtner [6, p. 170] that:

> In its ability to encourage active involvement and to provide immediate and graphic feedback, educational computing may provide one means of facilitating a transformation of the effects of

schooling from learning that is often forgotten as soon as the final exam has been taken to understanding that will remain even when specific facts and figures have long been forgotten.

But we would extend this to say that perhaps the most important outcome of education should be curiosity and a motivation to learn, coupled with comfort and skill in using new, powerful and rapidly changing technologies in the service of curiosity. It is toward this end that we are exploring the role of exploration in education.

Acknowledgements

This project was supported by a grant from the W. K. Kellogg Foundation to the first author. We would like to thank Arlon Elser for his support and encouragement, as well as Mr. Dennis Hayes for inviting us into his classroom.

References

1. Cleaver, J.: *Doing children's museums*. Charlotte, VT: Williamson Publishing 1988
2. Gallagher, J. M., & Dien, L.: Children's museums. *Children's Environments Quarterly*, 4, 1 (1987)
3. Hatano, G.: Social and motivational bases for mathematical understanding. In: *Children's mathematics* (G.B. Saxe & M. Gearhart, eds.). 1988
4. Heeter, C., & Gomes, P.: Next generation hypermedia: It's time for talking pictures. Unpublished manuscript. Michigan State University Communications Technology Laboratory 1991
5. Kornhaber, M., Krechevsky, M., & Gardner, H.: Engaging intelligence. *Educational Psychologist*, 25, 3&4, pp. 177-199 (1990)
6. Lepper, M. R., & Gurtner, J.: Children and computers: Approaching the twenty-first century. *American Psychologist*, 44, pp. 170-178 (1989)
7. Lepper, M. R., & Malone, T. W.: Intrinsic motivation and instructional effectiveness in computer-based education. In: *Aptitude, learning, and instruction: III. Conative and affective process analyses* (R. E. Snow & M. J. Farr, eds.). Hillsdale, NJ: Lawrence Erlbaum Associates 1987
8. Martin, L. M.: Introduction: Children and the electronic environment. *Children's Environment Quarterly*, 5, 4, pp. 2-3 (1988)
9. *Mission to Mars!* (CD-ROM) Designed by C. Heeter and P. Gomes. Comm Tech Lab, Michigan State University, East Lansing, MI 1990
10. Mountford, J.: Tools and techniques for creative design. In: *The art of human-computer interface design* (B. Laurel, ed.). Menlo Park, CA: Addison-Wesley 1990
11. Munley, M. E.: *Catalysts for change: The Kellogg projects in museum education.* Washington, DC: American Association of Museums 1986
12. Papert, S.: Introduction. In: *Constructionist learning: A 5th anniversary collection of papers reflecting research reports, projects in progress, and essays by the Epistemology and Learning Group* (I. Harel, ed.). Cambridge, MA: Massachusetts Institute of Technology Media Laboratory 1990
13. Rosendahl-Kreitman, K.: *User interface design.* Santa Clara, CA: Multimedia Computing Corporation 1990

14. Sternberg, R. J., & Laubart, T. I.: Creating creative minds. *Phi Delta Kappan*, 72, 8, pp. 608-614 (1991)
15. *Space Disc: Voyager Gallery: A HyperVideo Database* (Videodisc) Warren, NJ: Optical Data Corporation 1988

Technological Support for the Learning and Doing of Design

Elliot Soloway[1], Mark Guzdial[1], Kathy Brade[1], Luke Hohmann[1], Iris Tabak[1], Peri Weingrad[1], Phyllis Blumenfeld[2]

[1]Highly-Interactive Computing Environments (HiCE) Group, Department of EECS, University of Michigan, Ann Arbor, MI , USA

[2]School of Education, University of Michigan, Ann Arbor, MI, USA

Abstract: In this chapter, we explore the move from didactic instruction to a more constructivist, project-oriented learning model. At the heart of project-oriented learning is the notion that one learns through the process of constructing some type of artifact. The Highly-Interactive Computing Environments Group has been exploring technology that can support students as they engage in project-oriented learning as well as technology that can support teachers in making the transition to the new roles that such a project-oriented model entails. In this chapter we focus on the kinds of supports needed by students learning and doing design. The group has built and classroom tested a range of Computer-Aided Design (CAD) systems that were designed expressly to support students in both the learning and the doing of design in a variety of domains. In this chapter, we step back from the individual systems and identify key issues in the design of CAD systems to support project-oriented science curriculum.

Keywords: project-oriented curriculum, project-oriented learning, constructivist learning, Computer-Aided Design (CAD).

Introduction: Supporting Project-based Science via CAD

A transition is taking place in education: classrooms are moving from didactic instruction to a more constructivist, project-oriented learning model. For example, the Acid Rain Project, developed by TERC and the National Geographic Society [11], has students gather and analyze local water samples, and then, using telecommunications, share their findings with

NATO ASI Series, Vol. F 85
Adaptive Learning Environments
Edited by M. Jones and P. H. Winne

classes around the world. In the Acid Rain project, students are exposed to a variety of scientific concepts as well as how science relates to societal issues. Moreover, projects such as Acid Rain go further than traditional laboratory, hands-on experiments. That is, most classroom laboratory studies are attempts to verify an already known answer, as opposed to discovering information that is truly unknown. Uncovering information concerning water acidity in a particular local region is legitimate scientific inquiry, which is more engaging for the student.

The move to project-oriented curriculum reflects two more fundamental transitions: (1) in what kids need to know – from knowing "what" to knowing "how"; and (2) in the underlying model of learning – from a straight information processing model to a more situated model, in which interaction and context are given their due. There is growing recognition that students need to be life-long learners, that learning "how to learn" is critically important given the rapidity of change in our society. Moreover, learning is a social process; knowledge does not go directly from the mouths of the teacher into the students' heads. Instead, learning occurs during interactions between students, teachers, and the artifacts that students create.

At the heart of project-oriented learning is the notion that one learns through the process of constructing some type of artifact. For example, in the Acid Rain Project, students construct tables, charts, and reports to document their observations, and in the Solar House Project (another TERC and National Geographic Society project), students design a rudimentary solar house. There are some key characteristics that describe an artifact that is useful in project-oriented learning:

- the artifact is an externalization of the student's learning, providing an object to reflect upon [4];
- it is shareable, motivating the creation of the artifact [5]
- it is critiquable, motivating the quality of the artifact [7].

However, such constructive activity puts a severe strain on the traditional classroom. How does the teacher manage thirty odd kids all moving along at various rates, sharing their artifacts, and critiquing others' artifacts? While the didactic model works well in such a 1:30 situation, project-oriented curriculum presents a real challenge. How does the school day and curriculum adapt to include the design skills of analysis, synthesis, and debugging, necessary for constructing artifacts?

We are exploring technology that can support *students* as they engage in project-oriented learning, as well as technology that can support *teachers* in making the transition to the new roles that such a project-oriented model entails. In particular, we are developing computer-aided design (CAD) systems for students and teachers [10]. By definition, CAD systems attempt to support individuals and groups engaged in design, e.g., VLSI chip design, architectural design, and graphics art design. Currently, CAD systems only support a slice of the design process, e.g., circuit layout and drafting. However, as the field comes to better understand design, and as we shoot up the MIPS exponential curve of computer "zorch" (with industry predictions of 500 MIPS workstations in four years), we will see more and more of the design process supported by CAD systems. Coupling that amount of processing power with an understanding of how to support design, more computer resources can be spent on supporting students learning to design and supporting teachers managing these students. In this paper, we focus on the kinds of supports needed by students learning and doing design.

Over the last three years, the Highly Interactive Computing Environments (HiCE) research group at the University of Michigan has built and classroom tested (in both the high school and the university) a range of CAD systems that were designed expressly to support students in both the learning and the doing of design in a variety of domains.

- ***GPCeditor*** (GoalPlanCodeEditor) supports students learning to design software.
- ***MediaText*** supports students as they compose documents that include video, audio, graphics, animations, and other media, as well as text.
- ***Statics Calculator*** supports students developing free-body diagrams in mechanical engineering.
- ***IByD*** [3] (InstructionByDesign) supports students (teachers-in-training) learning unit and lesson design.

In this paper, then, we attempt to step back from the individual systems and identify key issues in the design of CAD systems to support project-oriented science curriculum. In particular, we focus here on a particular issue for educationally-oriented CAD systems: how do we provide support for both the *learning* and *doing* of design?

Building Educationally-Oriented CAD Systems Is Not Easy!

To help us in summarizing the key issues growing out of our system-building and classroom-testing experiences, we first present a model that attempts to characterize the basic dimensions of an educationally-oriented CAD system.

- ***Doing and learning:*** An electrical engineer uses a CAD system to do a task. In effect, a CAD system provides an infrastructure for accomplishing the desired task. In contrast, a student needs to learn how to do the task. Support for learning can be provided via

[3] Pronounced "ibid."

scaffolding, i.e., providing a set of mechanisms that enable a student to perform a task, but which fade away as the student becomes more expert.

- ***Process and product:*** There are steps that one takes in the creation of an artifact, i.e., a process. The artifact (product) can be characterized as a set of representations, e.g., a software artifact can be characterized in terms of its goals (specifications), plans (methods for realizing those specifications), and code (the actual program). A set of representations can also represent stages in the process.

These basic dimensions on which we describe these systems are coarse distinctions and certainly not opposites. In fact, we see learning and doing (and process and product) as being deeply interrelated. One learns to design as one designs, and better learning results in better doing. Similarly, a better process leads to a better product, and the representations used to describe the artifact can also be support for the process. Through articulation and reflection, we see the student learning in a doing environment, learning about process while producing product.

Nevertheless, the demands of learning and doing are decidedly different. A student spends more time learning than doing, while the expert spends a larger percentage of his/her time doing than learning. These designers need different kinds of support for their different activities. For example, the *doing* stages of process and product support are noted for being:

- ***implicit:*** not called to the user's attention,
- ***loose:*** permitting process strategies or orderings other than the one explicitly encouraged by the environment, and
- ***reactive:*** responding to the user's call, but not imposing itself on the user.

In contrast, the *learning* stages of process and product support are noted for being:

- ***explicit:*** to encourage the user's conscious reflection,
- ***tight:*** making control decisions for the student until the student has automatized the process, and
- ***proactive:*** acting for the user until the user understands and can choose when a support is required.

Given the divergent demands of learning and doing, building an effective CAD system is no mean feat!

In what follows, then, we present two examples of how our systems have attempted to cope with the issue of supporting both the doing and learning of design (Table 1). In the first example, we discuss the issue of tight versus loose process control; in the second example, we discuss the issue of explicit versus implicit design detail in the types of representations that need to be available. These are not totally separate issues. In the GPCeditor, for example, the tight control is realized in part through its explicit representations; and in IByD, the various representations are ordered to suggest a process.

Kind of Support	Learning	Doing	Outcome
Tight vs. Loose Process Support	GPCeditor's tight process support		Students develop surprisingly complex code in their first semester of use.
		MediaText's loose process support	Students quickly and easily develop multimedia compositions, but most lack sophistication.
	SODA's adaptable scaffolding provides support for both the novice and more advanced user by providing for flexible process support.		*In Development*
Explicit vs. Implicit Representational Support for Process and Product		Statics Calculator's single representation leaves artifact details implicit.	Students can solve problems far more easily and faster than with pencil and paper, but they want and need learning support.
	IByD's multiple representations requires explicit rationales and considerations.		Students using IByD demonstrate a systematic process and develop a well-reasoned product. But advanced users tire of the multiple representations.
	Emile's multiple representations with adaptable scaffolding and process review provides tools for managing and limiting the representations. The process review facility provides support for learning that can be effective even for experts.		*In Development*

Table 1: Technical Support for Learning and Doing in HiCE environments

In both examples, we will tie our analysis to student outcomes: what is the impact on student learning and performance of these various issues? In particular, we will use two types of outcomes:

- ***process:*** the degree of systematicity that students exhibit in carrying out a design, and the degree of generativity that students exhibit, i.e., to what extent can students transfer their understanding to situations in which there is no supporting CAD system.
- ***product***: the degree of thoroughness of the resultant artifact. Correctness is not a yea/nay type of decision; rather, it is one of degree.

We hasten to point out that by and large the evidence we use here will be qualitative in nature — telling anecdotes. However, we are currently in the process of analyzing a significant corpus of data on the use of two systems (GPCeditor and IByD). While the analyses are not complete, our clear sense is that the quantitative assessment is consistent with our more qualitative statements.

Example 1: The Impact on Student Outcomes of Tight versus Loose Process Control

The tradeoff of tight versus loose in the characteristics of learning and doing supports is especially clear when considering process control. How much should the environment direct and restrict the student's actions? For doing, the answer should be as little as possible, but for learning, the answer changes in relation to the kind and complexity of the process being learned.

The *GPCeditor* provides tight control over the student's design process. It attempts to provide students with support for key aspects of the planning phase of software design, identifying potentially useful modules ("decomposition"), and integrating those modules into a coherent system ("composition"). Written in some 15,000 lines of LISP, it runs on a Macintosh II equipped with a 19-inch monitor. The GPCeditor (and an associated curriculum designed expressly for the GPCeditor) has been in continuous use in an introductory programming class at Community High School, Ann Arbor, MI since Winter semester 1988-89[4].

[4] CHS is an alternative high school that students elect to attend. Students petitioned to get into this class. In concert with the principal and teacher, we chose students who represented differing backgrounds: subject matter (from art majors to math majors), gender, and race.

MediaText is a composition environment for the creation of multimedia documents; a user can associate a video clip, audio clip, animation, and other media clips to a piece of text (See Figure 3.) MediaText provides almost no process control. The environment contains a basic word processor for text composition, and a set of simple "media workshops" that allow the user to create, for example, a video clip (start frame, end frame) from a videodisc. Each clip appears as a clickable button (media *link*) whose icon represents the kind of media associated with that button. When a link is clicked on, the media clip plays. MediaText links can represent clips of graphics, single-frame animations, PICS animations, videodiscs, digitized sounds, and audio compact disc segments. In Hypertext fashion, MediaText also allows links to other documents, including to other applications. A presentation facility allows the user to automatically "write" a document presentation onto videotape using a standard VCR. MediaText was introduced in three classes at Community High School in the Fall semester, 1990.

How the GPCeditor Provides *Tight* Process Control

The GPCeditor was designed with a particular model of software design in mind. The top half of Figure 1 presents that model. This model requires defining what goals the designer has for the artifact, how the designer plans to realize that artifact, and in what way these plans are composed together to synthesize the artifact. Students using the GPCeditor are held to this process through tight control realized in the menu system and representations (bottom half of Figure 1) of the environment.

The GPCeditor requires students to explicitly deal with three levels of program description (Figure 2): *goals* (objectives that the final artifact must satisfy), *plans* (stereotypical techniques for achieving goals), and *code* (actual Pascal language constructs). A plan is made up of Pascal language statements, e.g., the GET-INPUT PLAN is made up of "writeln ('please input a number'); readln(input_variable);." At the lowest level of detail, a GPCeditor *plan* is a chunk of code, where each statement in the chunk works with the other statements to achieve a particular objective, e.g., asking the user to input a value, and then accepting that value. [6,9]. These goals and plans appear in three different representations: a linear list of goals and plans (upper left of Figure 2); a graphical representation of the goals and plans of the program (lower left of Figure 2); and the actual Pascal code corresponding to the program (upper right of Figure 2).

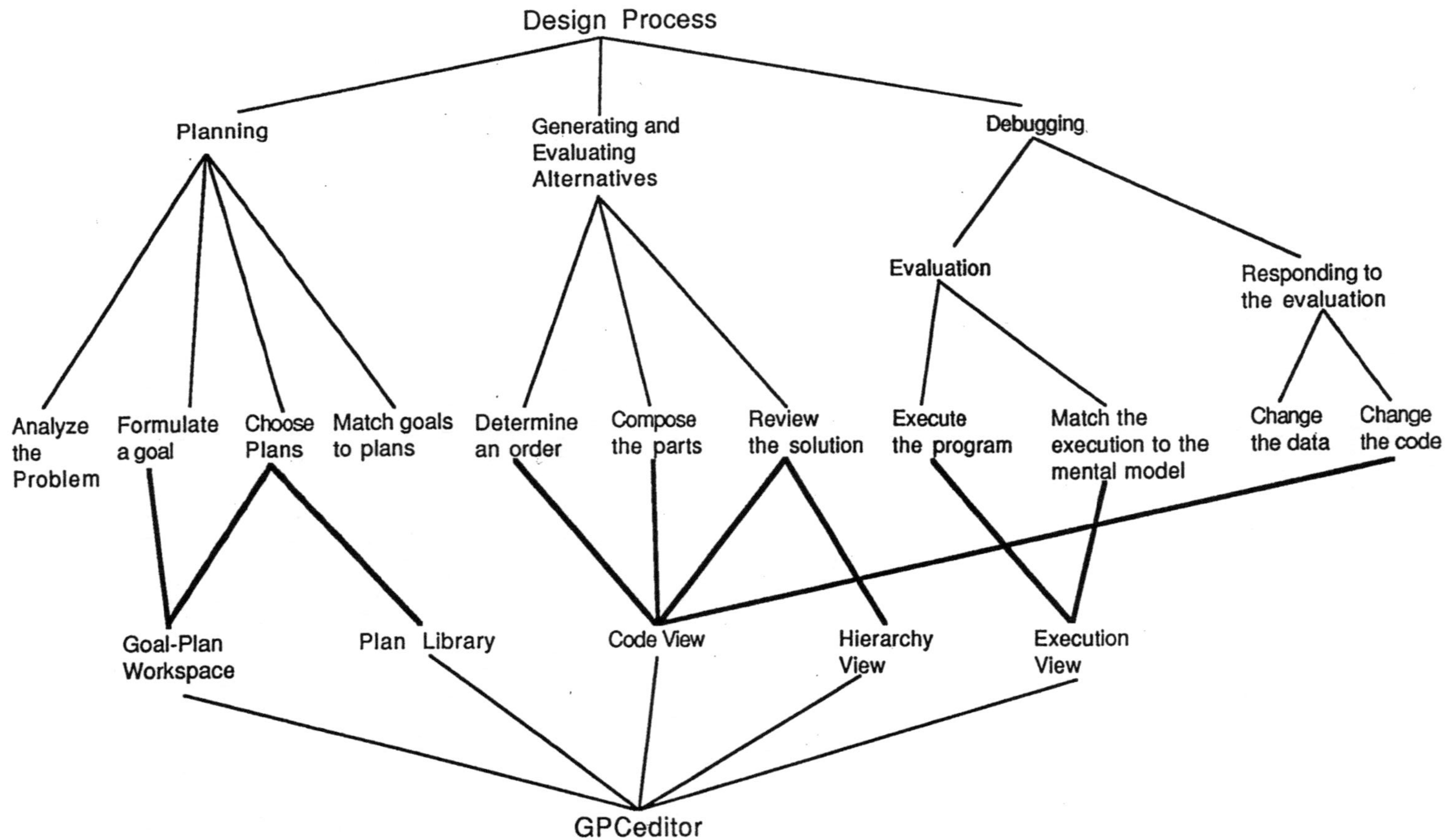

Figure 1: Software design process map to CPCeditor features

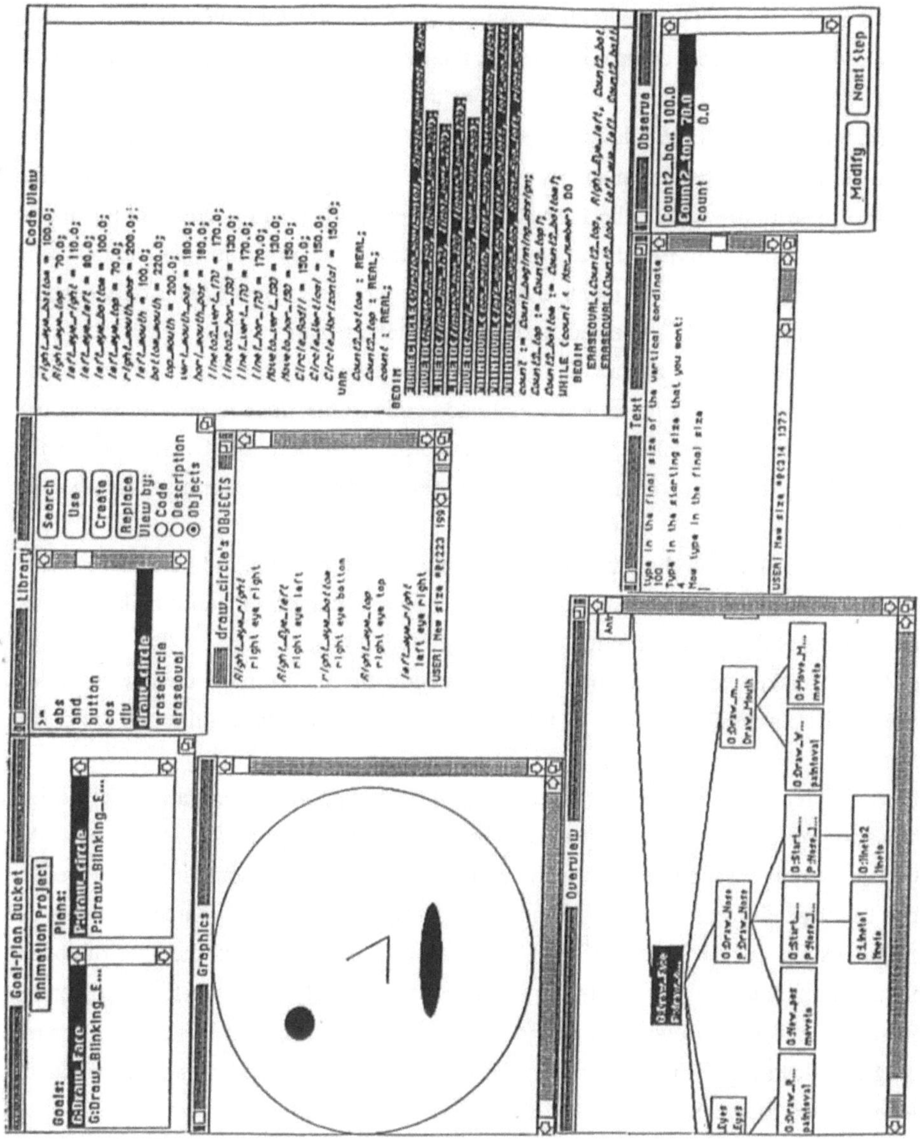

Figure 2: GPCeditor sample screenshot

Students are led through the design process (Figure 1), using these representations (shown in Figure 2), via tight process control realized in the menu system. The various activities of the student's design process appear as the names of the menus: first, the student *decomposes* the problem, then *composes* the solution, then finally *runs* the result. Explicitly, students are expected to define goals, and then plans for those goals, and then to compose those plans into the program. The items within the menus are enabled or disabled corresponding to the student's current design activity. For example, the menu item for creating a *New Goal* is always available in the Decompose menu, but the item for creating a *New Plan* is only enabled when a goal has been created, is selected, and has no matching plan.

Based on this description, we say that the GPCeditor provides *tight* control of the various stages in the design process; one cannot simply add code to the Code View, but rather one must first identify goals, then plans, and then put the pieces together. The GPCeditor can also be described using the other learning support characteristics. We can also say that the GPCeditor is:

- ***explicit:*** it makes explicit the various stages of the design process: the pull-down menus provide specific names for the activities (e.g., decompose, compose); and it makes explicit various aspects of the artifact through multiple representations.
- ***proactive:*** it makes some decisions for the student; the menu items change to reflect changes in the permissible actions, as the system is guiding the student through the design process.

These features of the GPCEditor are consistent with supporting the learning of design. One indication of this learning is that we see some generalizability of this learning to other Pascal programming environments. At the end of the semester, students in the GPCeditor class use Lightspeed Pascal in order for us to explore the question of whether students can write programs without the support of the GPCeditor. If we simply count the lines of code in the final program done by the students, we see that approximately 1/3 wrote final programs at the 850 statement level, 1/3 wrote final programs at the 250 statement level, and 1/3 wrote final programs at the 150 statement level. *Thus, 2/3rds of the class were able to produce a significantly sized program without the aid of the GPCeditor.* Moreover, by and large those programs did not exhibit "spaghetti code"; rather, these programs exhibited a highly modular structure.

While students wrote code directly in LightSpeed Pascal, they commented that they were definitely influenced by the GPCeditor experience. For example, one student noted that "I may not code in the GPC, but I think it," while another student commented that "I am seeing GPC in my mind when I write LightSpeed."

That said, *almost all* the students find the GPCeditor to be "too slow and tedious" when they are doing their assignments *towards the end of the semester*, while few make such comments at the beginning of the semester. The GPCeditor does not gracefully support students as they move to more of a *doing* mode from a *learning* mode. The scaffolding does not fall away; students must go through the same steps they did at the very beginning of the semester.

MediaText: *Loose* Control is Putting It Mildly

MediaText does not provide the tight process control that the GPCeditor does on the design process. Students can move between creating text, structuring their documents, and creating media links at any time. The environment responds to student demands and does not make suggestions or provide prompts to structure the design process. The design decisions behind the student's multimedia documents are left implicit, e.g., why choose a videodisc segment here? Why not an animation segment? What's the relation between this media link and the text next to it? Such an environment facilitates the *doing* of design, but not the *learning* of design.

We chose to support the doing of design with a simple metaphor for multimedia composition that required little learning to use. The design metaphor we have adopted for MediaText is that of annotation: use media to illustrate the points made in the text. The interface attempts to support that metaphor. One puts media buttons in the margin on the right hand side of a page of text (Figure 3). Students understood this structure easily and were soon creating multimedia compositions.

The lack of learning support for students doing multimedia composition has been clearly felt. At the beginning of the semester, students at Community High School created documents with two to four media links at best. At the end of the semester, a *few* highly motivated students were creating documents with upwards of 30 media links. We are currently in the process of analyzing the documents from the various classes, and assessing the degree to which students used the media types in ways that actually enhanced the text. While we have found instances where students did in fact capture an aspect of a topic through the use of a media button, this was far from universally true. When offered the opportunity to work in a less-structured version of MediaText, one in which media links could be placed within the text, students were not all in favor of it. This is not surprising since the less-structured version complicates the problem of composition. Now one is confronted with graphic design/layout issues. In unstructured multimedia composition, one has a canvas, not a piece of paper.

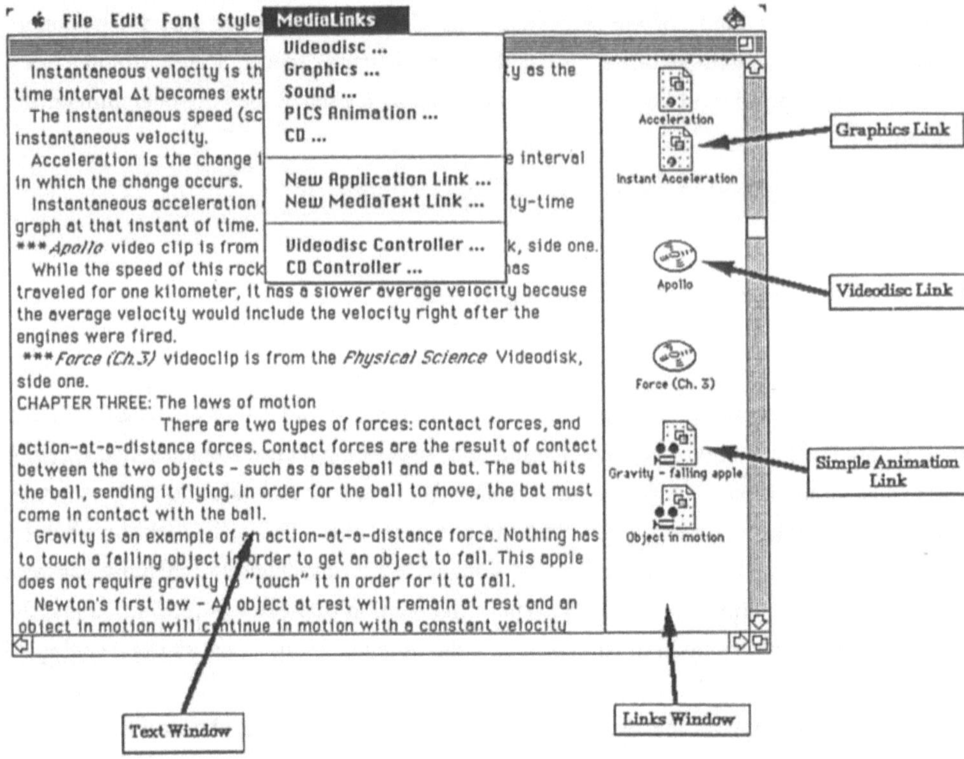

Figure 3: MediaText document featuring a text page with media links along the right margin

The fault for not providing more learning structure, however, lies not in our inability to provide a supportive computing environment, but in our ignorance of how to structure that environment. Of course, the key questions are these: What counts as a "good" multimedia document? What are the design considerations for using different media types effectively? How does one design in multimedia?

What *is* the spreadsheet for multimedia documents? The spreadsheet provides a clear metaphor for what to do with a two-dimensional grid. In software design, there are definite strategies for coping with complexity to produce a "good" design, e.g., modular, hierarchical composition. In contrast, pinning down specific guidelines and criteria for good writing (*without* multiple media types) is hard enough, and we have had several thousand years to come up with them. We cannot provide a structure to support multimedia composition until we understand its process, the problems, and the structures to provide learners [7].

Over the semester, the teachers (in physics and in composition) were able to provide structure for writing, e.g., "In a biography, make sure you describe the traits of the person," but they (as well as we) were at a loss on how to counsel students in using the various media types. Pea and colleagues at IRL had the same experience when they had students creating videotapes using a desktop video editing system. Pea found that he had to provide explicit strategies for how students should structure their video clips, e.g., when one is making an argument, one first presents the problem, etc.

Implications: What the Next Systems Should Look Like

We can summarize the above arguments. While the GPCeditor has good support for learning, it provides that support at only one level which does not extend to supporting doing. MediaText has a simple structure and good support for doing, but its lack of support for learning discourages some students from developing more sophisticated multimedia design. Emile and SODA, the successors to the GPCeditor, will have the ability to customize the design process. Briefly, the student will be able to change characteristics of SODA's support, e.g., as the student acquires more expertise, he or she can make SODA more streamlined, have it provide less assistance for learning, and have it provide more assistance for doing. In effect, customization is one way that SODA will realize the notion of "scaffold fading" [3].

SODA enhances the GPCeditor's support for both learning and doing with more extensive tools for the entire design process. Figure 4 presents the design process (seen for the GPCeditor in Figure 1) and how the features of SODA map on to it. SODA provides support for more breadth along the design process than GPCeditor. Managing this support is an explicit activity within SODA, in the same way that a designer explicitly chooses his/her tools for an activity.

The model of the design process, given in Figure 4, appears in SODA as an active "supporter" window. This is the student's toolbox. The student can call up the windows that support a process by simply clicking on the process' name. For example, clicking on "Analyze the Problem" will bring to the foreground the "Advice Library" and "PlanDraw." Similarly, by clicking on the name of a window, the processes which that window supports are activated, and any other windows associated with those processes are also called to the foreground.

There are two kinds of scaffolding customization that SODA permits:

- ***the student can change the associations between windows and processes.*** For example, a student may always want to run Proust before he/she executes his/her program (Figure 5). To achieve this, the student (1) clicks on the process "Review the Solution" in the Process/Windows Connection Window, then (2) drags to Proust. SODA creates a line

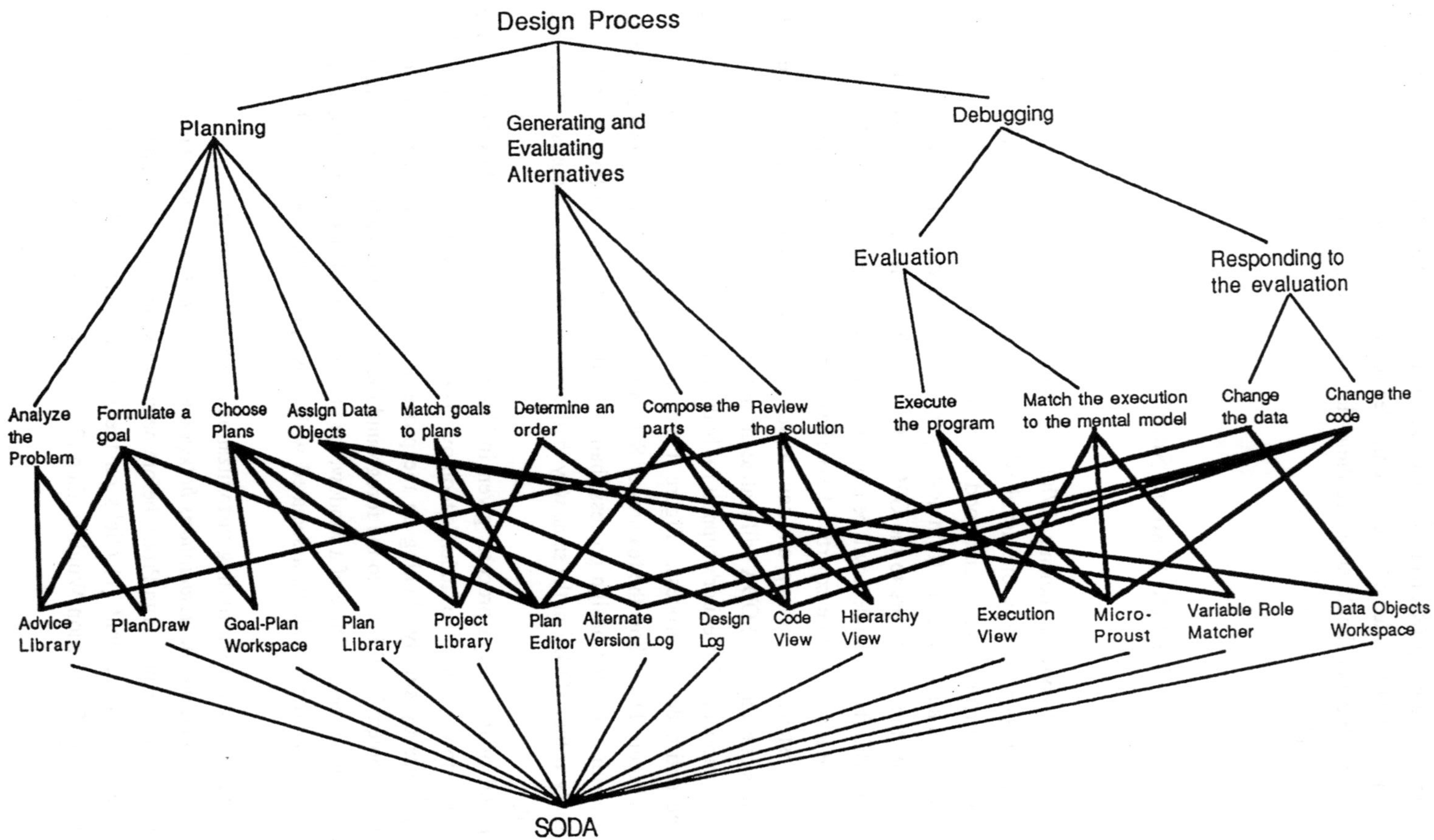

Figure 4: Software design process map to SODA features

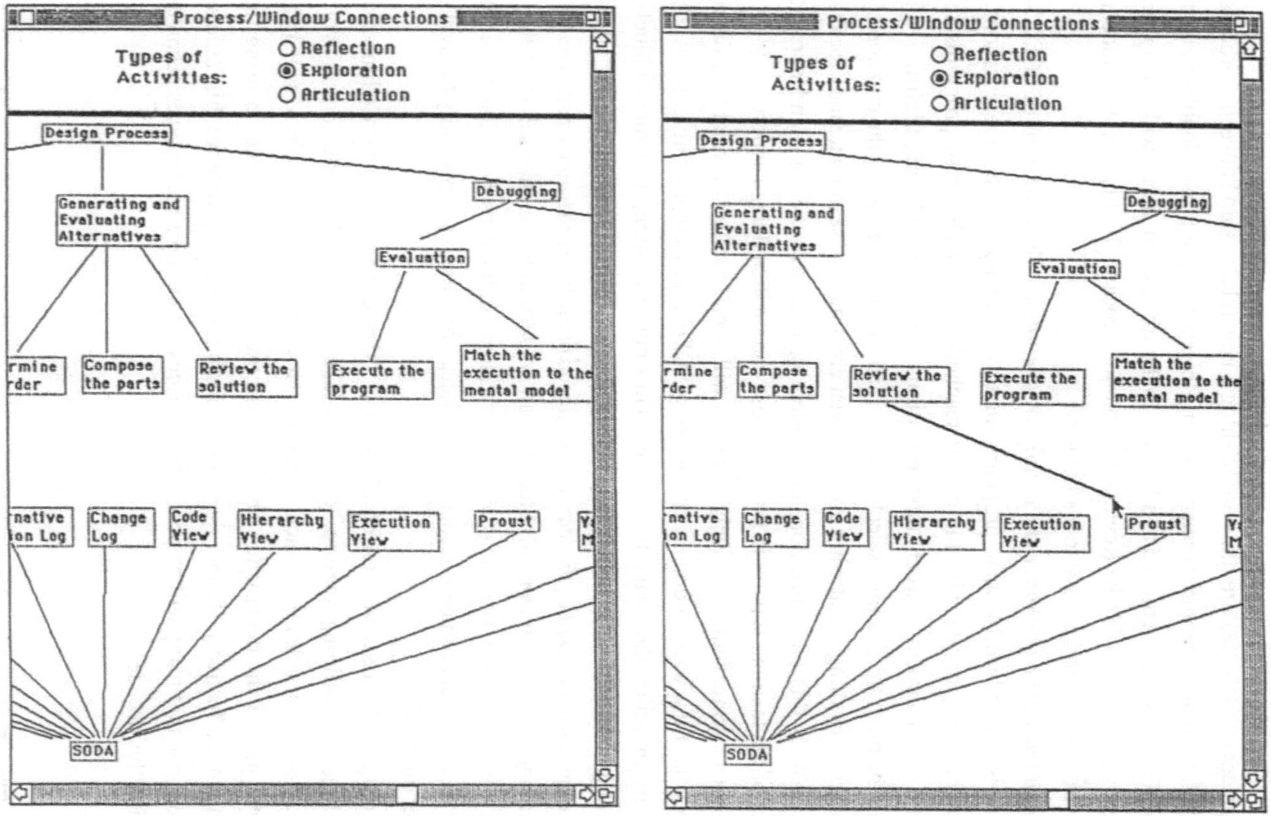

Figure 5: Adapting SODA's process scaffolding. The student clicks on the process stage "Review the Solution" and drags a line to the SODA feature, Proust.

between the process and the feature, thus establishing a new relationship between a process (Review the Solution) and a feature (Proust). When Review the Solution is double-clicked by the student, Proust will be activated and brought to the foreground, along with any other windows already associated with the Review the Solution process. In this way, the student makes the environment more reactive to his/her needs.

- ***the student (and teacher) can change the actions in a window.*** The behaviour of SODA's representations is determined by small programs underlying each of these representations. A student (perhaps in concert with his or her teacher) can change these programs to customize the environment. Such customizations might include highlighting all occurrences in the program of a plan selected in the Plan Library, permitting the creation of a plan without first awaiting a matching goal, or even creating new search methods for the Plan Library. With this customization, the student can remove the tight and explicit characteristics of the learning support in favor of loose and implicit doing support.

In order to use customization effectively, students will need to reflect on what they do in fact do, and on what they want to do. In customizing SODA, they are making explicit the pattern of activity in which they wish to engage. Thus customization, a feature uniquely expressible through computing technology, provides a mechanism for realizing important supportive techniques such as *enable the learner to make explicit his/her strategies* and *enable the learner to adapt his/her environment.* Students can do customization themselves, if they and the teacher wish. However, we also envision that customization activity will arise out of student-teacher discussions, or student-student discussions, providing an opportunity to invoke the social aspect of learning.

Correspondingly, the next version of MediaText cries out for more GPCeditor-like support. Adding an outlining feature, commonplace now in Macintosh-based word processors, provides a first level of such support. However, outlining might well help structure the text part of the document. The issue is how to support students in using the different media types effectively. Rather than putting forth speculation, we leave this issue as an open question, one that many will be pondering as access to multiple media types becomes ubiquitous during this decade.

Example 2: The Impact on Student Outcomes of Explicit versus Implicit Representations

Added representations in a CAD environment provide for more explicit relationships between components of the artifacts, rationales for these components, and stages of the design process.

Making these relationships, rationales, and stages explicit provides more opportunity for reflection and learning. With fewer representations, more of the product and process are left implicit, but the speed and ease of doing are improved. Thus the number and type of representations in the CAD environment is dependent on the tradeoff between supporting learning or supporting doing.

The *Statics Calculator* provides a single, active view for ease of doing statics design problems. It allows the student to draw a free-body diagram with icons representing bars, hinges, welds, and forces. From this schematic representation, the Statics Calculator solves the equations symbolically or numerically. This relieves students of tedious calculations in order to focus on the higher level issues like the designs of structures. The Statics Calculator has been used in an introductory statics course in the Mechanical Engineering Department at the University of Michigan.

Before entering a classroom, teachers must plan what to teach, how to teach it, and integrate knowledge about the subject matter, curriculum, classroom management, and much more. *InstructionByDesign* (IByD) is a software environment to aid novice teachers in this process of planning and integrating. It uses various views of the artifact being designed (a unit or lesson plan) to support learning this design process. IByD provides scaffolding for the organization, justification, and integration of the various elements of instruction (concepts, evaluation methods, classroom activities and so on). IByD was used in a semester course in Educational Psychology, in the School of Education at the University of Michigan.

One Active View Makes Design Implicit in the Statics Calculator

The Statics Calculator provides one active representation in which students create their free-body diagrams (Figure 6.) Within this canvas, the students create bars, connect them with hinges, select and modify these components, and call up operations to act upon the diagrams. Thus, all of the student's active engagement is centered on this one representation.

The Statics Calculator does provide additional representations which can lead to insight from different perspectives on the problems. For example, the student can select components of the free-body diagram (in the main representation) and get new representations that describe the forces on just these components, the moment equations on these components, and the interactions between these and other components (Figure 7). But these additional representations are not active. The student cannot manipulate anything in them, cannot use them to select elements of the free-body diagram, and cannot see changes to the free-body diagram updated in them.

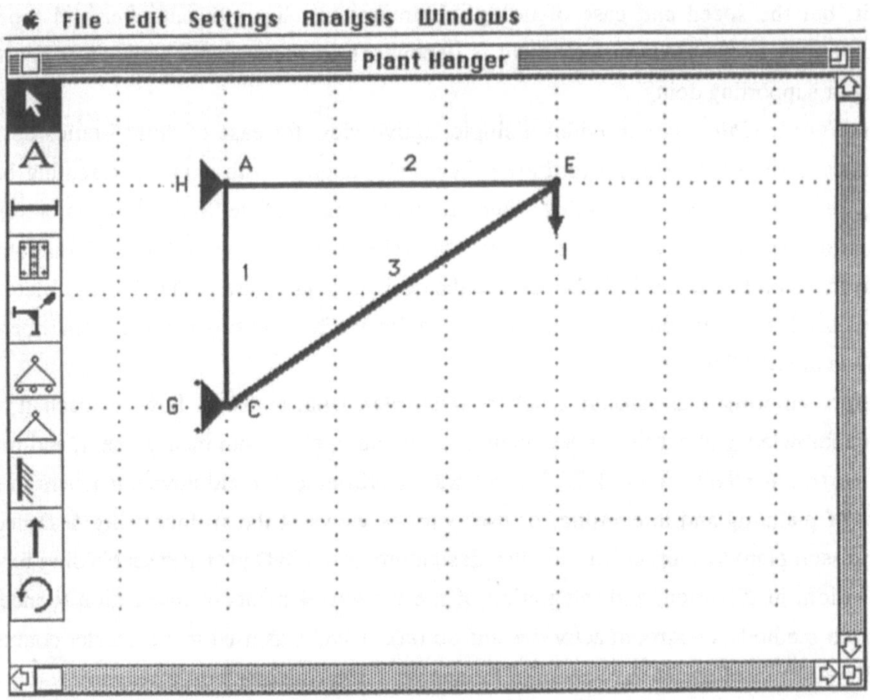

Figure 6: Statics Calculator basic active view

This single active view is the kind of support that is most appropriate for doing. When expert designers are in the midst of their design, they want tools that are flexible, unconstraining, and allow them to create structure out of the mess of constraints and possibilities that make up a design problem [8]. They don't want to deal with intrusive prompts and representations other than the one in which they are working. Designers want the tool they want, when they want it.

The Statics Calculator provides that sort of Spartan efficiency. All the tools needed for producing free-body diagrams are provided in connection with the one main representation. The environment allows essentially any design process, is only reactive to the designer's requests, and does not require explicit explanation of the design rationale.

Mechanical Engineering Students using the Statics Calculator have been favorably impressed with the support it provides for doing free-body diagrams. In particular, all of the students using the Statics Calculator reported on a survey that it provides excellent support for expert design skills, like exploring alternatives. The ease of use and speed of the system allow the designers to construct a design, evaluate it, and modify the design on the basis of that evaluation.

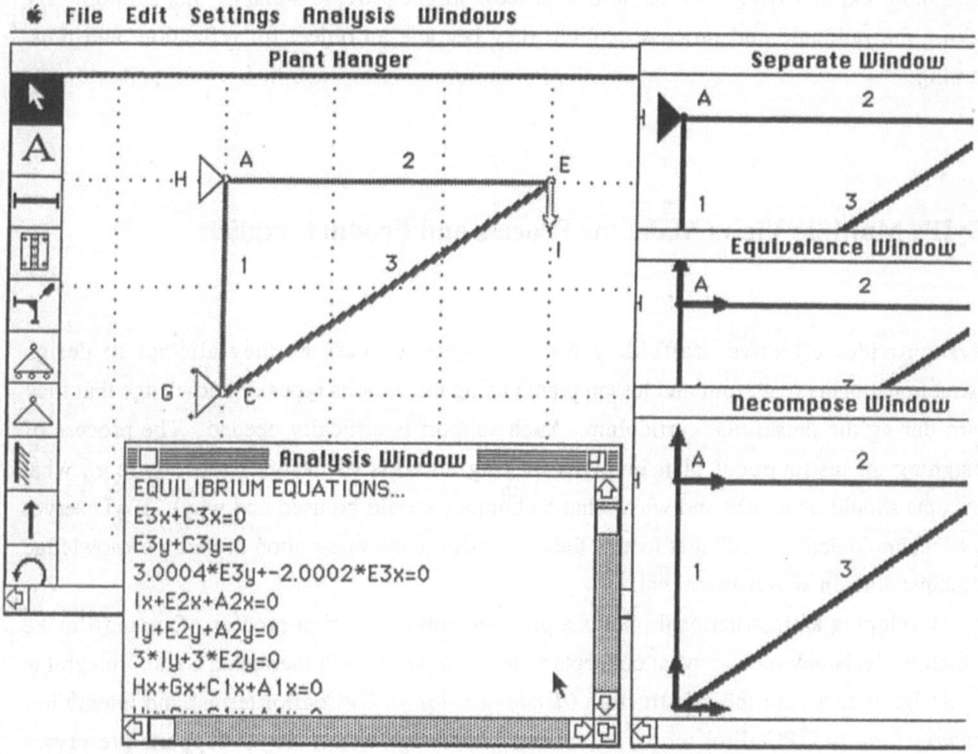

At the same time, the most common complaints about the environment centered around the lack of learning support. Students complained about the "lack of online help," and they explicitly requested "instructions as they worked," and "explanations/trouble-shooting help/instructions." Observations of students working with the Statics Calculator on the kind of problems that expert designers tackle indicate that students have no easier time with the real problems of design than they have without the Statics Calculator, difficulties such as transforming a real-life problem into an abstract representation and decomposing the elements of a complex structure.

Results on the quality of the students' artifacts are still being evaluated, but our clear sense is that the Statics Calculator makes the process of designing free-body diagrams easier to do. Students can build, evaluate, and manipulate their designs with an ease that paper and calculator solutions cannot approach. But these are still students, and they both need and want some support for the learning of the design process. Providing additional representations to make more explicit design rationale and process might provide some of this support. By making the rationale and process explicit, they become an object for reflection, and thus, learning.

IByD's Multiple Views Make the Process and Product Explicit

IByD provides effective scaffolding for preservice teachers as they attempt to design instructional plans (e.g., unit and lesson plans) using the various types of knowledge that they learn during the preservice curriculum. Such support is critically needed. The process of designing an instructional plan involves making all sorts of design decisions (e.g., what concepts should be taught and why, what techniques should be used and why). IByD serves as a "technological thread" that fosters the construction and integration of various knowledge domains: domain and instructional.

Developing an instructional plan is a problem-solving, design process. One must make numerous decisions such as what concepts to teach, how to teach them, and so on. Integral to the design process are the construction (*decomposition* in GPCeditor terms) and integration (*composition* in GPCeditor terms) of various knowledge bases. IByD supports preservice teachers learning those processes in the following ways:

- ***Constructing knowledge bases – personal libraries:*** Each preservice teacher has a permanent database that he/she constructs based on the material and experiences in the curriculum. There are libraries for *considerations* which contain detailed information about what should be taken into account when planning for all topics, such as developmental changes in cognition, features of effective instruction, e.g., how to provide clear explanations, and techniques for classroom management (Figure 8). There are also libraries for information such as possible student activities, teacher instructional strategies or examples, and evaluation activities, to use in covering specific content. IByD also supports a concept map representation.
- ***Integrating knowledge bases in planning:*** IByD supports the planning design process that facilitates the preservice teacher coming to integrate those knowledge bases in a productive, effective manner. In developing an instructional plan, the preservice teacher draws on these knowledge bases to identify objectives and strategies for teaching the content at hand. IByD supports this planning process. For example, in Figure 9, we see a student creating

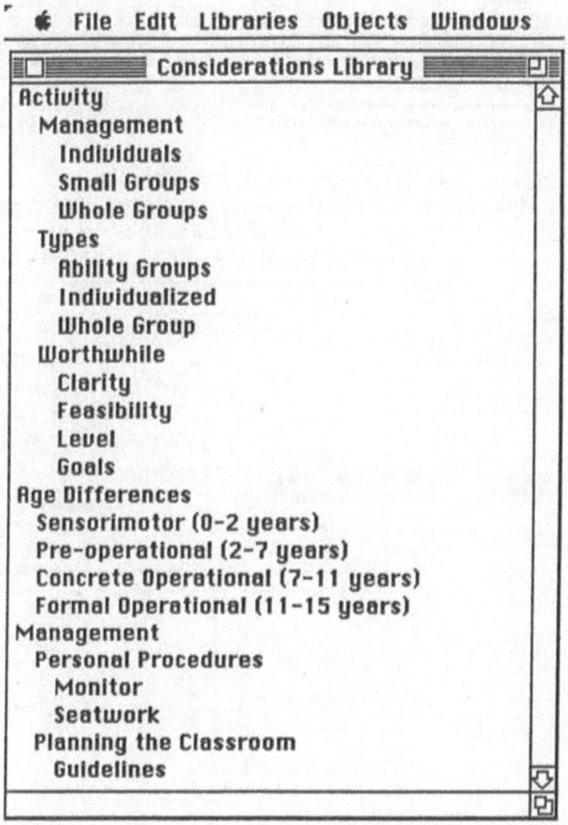

Figure 8: Sample IByD Considerations Library

the topmost step in a unit plan to teach about microorganisms. To create this plan, the student needs to integrate content information (microorganisms), pedagogical content knowledge (how to evaluate the student's learning), considerations for this activity, and rationales for these decisions.

IByD provides multiple, active representations to support this design process. Each representation not only provides a different view of the components of the developing artifact, but is also intimately tied to a particular stage of the design process (as are the representations of GPCeditor and SODA, as described in Figures 1 and 4). For example, the considerations library (Figure 8) must be created before these considerations can be addressed when selecting and developing an activity (Figure 9). Each of these representations is active: each requires action by the user; many require interactions with other components in the environment and in the artifact (e.g., the appearance of considerations when defining an activity); and they all draw together the various pieces of the design process.

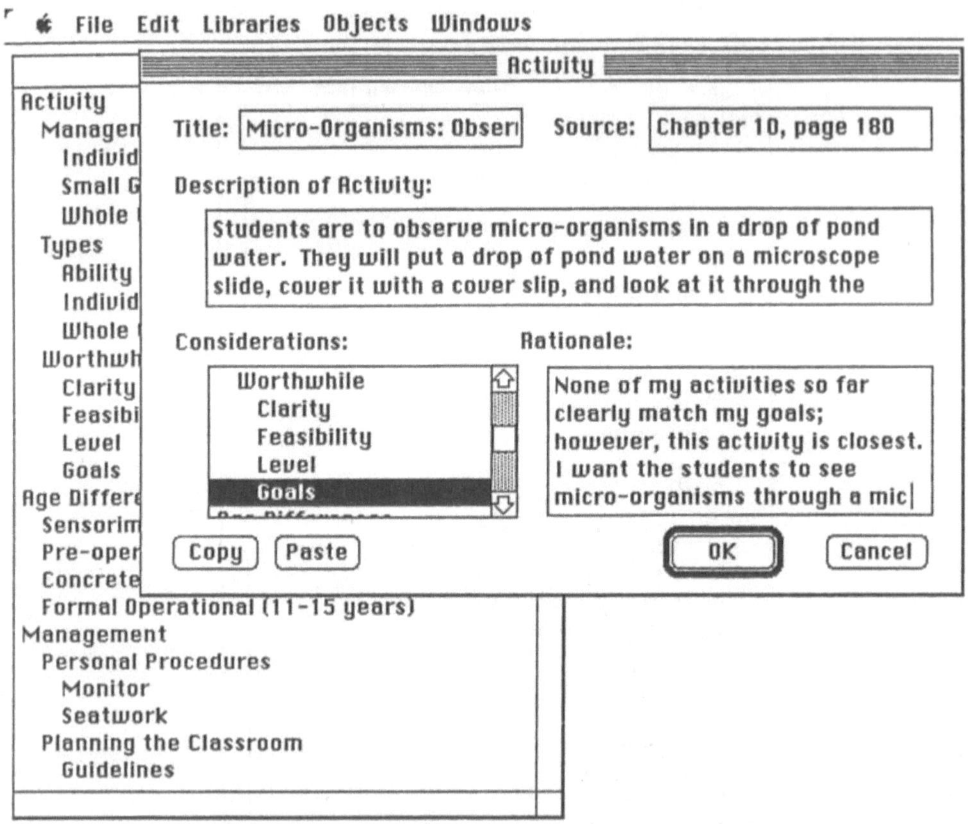

Figure 9: IByD Activities structured template with links to the Considerations Library

We have examined differences between the plans produced by preservice teachers who used IByD and those who did not. As anticipated, the plans of computer users were more explicit and more interconnected. IByD users were more likely to provide specific rationales for their decisions, e.g., they discussed many of the pros and cons that lead to their choice of activities where as students who worked with paper-and-pencil provided more global justifications. IByD users were also more specific about how the pieces of their plans were connected. IByD users had (1) a clear process, as defined by IByD, to follow in making decisions, (2) ready access to considerations libraries which contained relevant information for making decisions, and (3) scaffolded or structured templates (Figure 9) that required rationales for decisions.

By the end of the term, preservice teachers using IByD had adopted a "schema" for thinking about instructional decision making. They had internalized IByD's structure so that in thinking aloud and planning what they would do, they mentioned considerations and rationales, and they reflected on the pros and cons of their choices before typing anything on the computer. For example, when asked how her thinking had changed across the semester, an IByD user replied:

> Well, I guess for the first project [plan I did] you had to split up and only think about the goals and the concept maps first and then the activities that go with them....And now...even though right now I'm just doing the goal and concept map I'm still thinking about everything. I'm thinking about the evaluations. I kind of work on it together and not separately. I've already got notes for the evaluations, for what I think, so I won't forget everything by the time I get to it.

While IByD has clearly provided the support for learning that we hoped for, it is not clear if it provides enough support for doing. We have not tested IByD with in-service, expert teachers, but our feeling is that it would slow them down, without providing benefits to their planning process. To be a useful tool for doing as well, IByD would have to (1) provide a structure that has fewer learning supports and more doing supports and (2) provide a mechanism to support the continued learning that is the hallmark of expert designers.

Implications: What the Next Systems Should Look Like

Our arguments about the Statics Calculator and IByD suggest that the Statics Calculator needs better support for learning and that IByD needs better support for doing, especially by experts. The Statics Calculator's learning support might be enhanced with multiple representations tied to the design process — representations either of the entire artifact, as in the GPCeditor, or of components of the artifact, as in IByD. IByD's doing support might be enhanced in two ways: (1) a central, active representation of the entire artifact that draws together all the components (as in the Statics Calculator) and (2) a facility that provides the sort of reflection on the design process that experts can use to learn. Emile seeks to provide some of this support with a Design Activities View and a Process Review Facility.

Emile, like SODA, is an environment in which students learn software design, but in the domain of the Apple HyperCard programming language. Also like SODA, Emile provides an explicit, customizable representation of the design process that ties together the activities in the design process with the multiple representations of the environment (left side of Figure 10). Clicking on a stage in the list of design activities brings forward those representations that are linked to that design activity (right side of Figure 10). Students can customize these linkages to define which representations they wish to use, including specifying only single

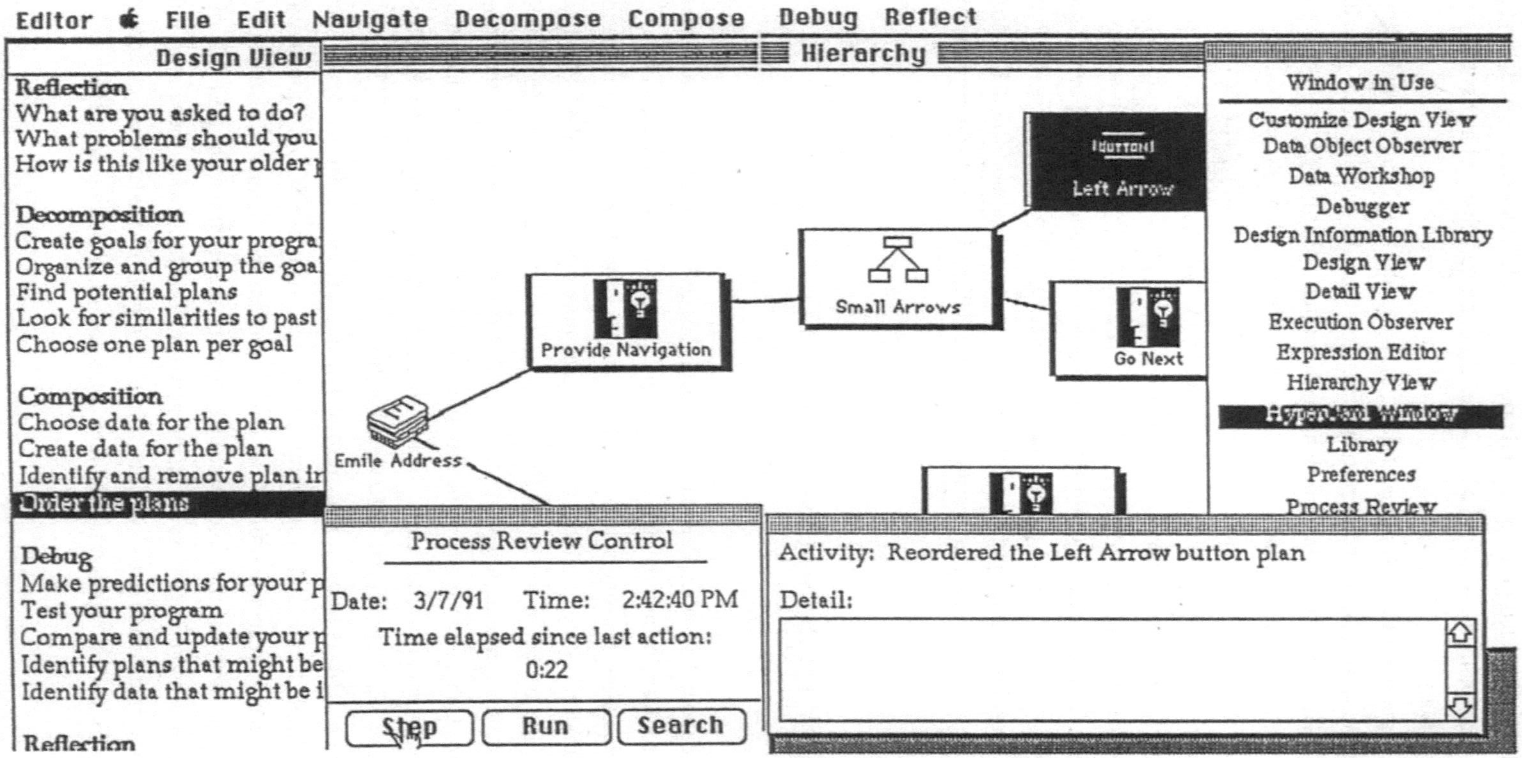

Figure 10: Emile's Process Review Facility

active views for certain activities. Thus, the Design Activities View acts as the unifying thread for the representations of Emile, providing both a guide as to when they should be used and a tool for managing their use.

The Design Activities View is also a cornerstone of the Process Review facility in Emile (Figure 10) which is used to replay a student's design process for him/her. By showing the student his/her own process, that design process becomes an object for explicit study. Using the controls in the Process Review Control palette (bottom of Figure 10), students can "play" their design activities on the Design Activities View and the Hierarchy View of Emile. Goals or plans that the students acted upon are highlighted in the Hierarchy View, the windows the students used become highlighted in the window list, and the design stages through which the student passed become highlighted in the Design Activities View. Students can jump forward or back in time to note when they used a particular representation and on what part of the program.

Reviewing their process with the Process Review Facility, students can get an understanding of how they design, where their problems are, and what tools they use. For example, they can see what areas of a design caused them the most problems by noting in what part of the Hierarchy View most of their activity occurred. They can see what their preferred tools are, as well as at what stages of the design process is. These observations can act as a guide to their customization of the linkages between the features and the design stages.

Student design processes, then, become an object for study: to review, reflect, and improve upon. This sort of meta-level view of design is a characteristic of expert level design, and we expect that such a tool will be useful in understanding one's doing of design and in learning how to be a better designer.

Concluding Remarks

In this paper, we have sketched how we are tackling the problem of providing computer-aided design (CAD) system support for students and teachers as they engage in constructing artifacts. We have focussed here on the serious problem of supporting both the learning *and* doing of design – we have pointed out the tension and demands of two types of activities, and we have described the position on each taken by various systems we have developed (and are developing). Besides the issues of tight versus loose process control and of explicit versus implicit representations, our systems explore a range of other issues:

- ***Process issues.*** What is the role of "critics" [2] that provide analysis and feedback about the students and teachers various products? We are no longer invested in the Intelligent Tutoring System (ITS) model. Underlying that model is the notion of information delivery – the tutor knows something that the student does not, and it is the goal of the tutor to transfer that something to the student. The ITS model does not differ qualitatively from the more traditional computer-assisted instruction (CAI) systems model of *instruction*. That said, the ITS world has developed interesting technology that can analyze student products and provide critiques. When used appropriately, such technology has a place in an interactive learning environment.

  How much of the entire analysis through design process should be supported in the computer? We are increasing the breadth of coverage of the design process in our various systems to explore how much can be supported in the computer. For example, in MediaText, we are adding the micro-computer-based lab tools (pressure, temperature sensors, etc.) developed by TERC. Thus, students can move from collecting data to analyzing and commenting on it in one consistent system. SODA will support more up-stream design activity as well as providing more structure for generating and evaluating alternatives — a key process during design.

- ***Product issues.*** Libraries are critically important representations: they capture expertise, they can be shared among the students, they provide structure for new design activity. Currently, libraries in our various systems are at best rudimentary lists of previously created entities. We need to add at least an order of magnitude more functionality to the indexing and search mechanisms in order to make the libraries more useful, more effective.

  While there are a range of representations in a system such as the GPCeditor, we have only just begun to explore the type of those representations (e.g., graphic, textual, sound). Given that a student might well have more than a dozen "windows" open on his/her large screen monitor, attention must be given to these representation issues.

We have addressed here key technological issues in bringing CAD systems to the classroom. We have ignored content and context issues — curriculum issues, teacher and administrator issues — the real stuff of classrooms! The omission of this topic from this paper reflects our initial naivete and hubris: the AI wisdom put the emphasis on the "box." What a rude awakening it was indeed, when classroom issues swamped whatever good the box might be able to contribute. For example, one day a student in the GPCeditor class at the high school came in wearing a swastika on the back of his shirt. The turmoil that this young man created was most significant. It took over a week for the class to settle back down to the class task! Similarly, it was difficult to use MediaText in the physics class in the high school because the mandated curriculum was quite rigid and demanding; students did not have sufficient time to explore an idea in any depth. If projects are to be integrated in the classroom, major changes must be made to curricula and to the ways in which curricula are developed and adopted. A fuller discussion of the non-technological issues will be dealt with in a future paper.

Collins [1] argues that technology will play a key role in transforming classrooms from a fact-driven model of learning, where the teacher is an information deliverer, to a constructivist model of learning, where the teacher is more a master and students are apprentices. In particular, there is no way that one teacher can be a master to 30 apprentices — a typical teacher/student ratio in public schools in the U.S. Technology will provide a supportive medium for the student to carry out his/her design activities. Technology off-loads some tasks from the teacher, but it in no way replaces the teacher. The means for making a significant improvement in education is at hand; the challenge is to realize the potential.

Acknowledgements

This research was supported by NSF Grant #MDR-9010362; Apple Computer; and The University of Michigan School of Education, Office of Instructional Technology, College of Engineering, Center for Research on Learning and Teaching, and the Undergraduate Initiatives Fund.

References

1. Collins, A., & Brown, J.S.: The computer as a tool for learning through reflection. BBN Technical Report #6457, Cambridge, MA: Bolt, Beranek, and Newman 1986
2. Fischer, G., & Lemke, A.C.: Construction kits and design environments: Steps toward human problem-domain communication. *Human-Computer Interaction,* 3, pp. 179-222 (1987)
3. Langer, J.A., & Applebee, A.N.: Reading and writing instruction: Toward a theory of teaching and learning. In: *Review of research in education* (E. Rothkopf, ed.). Vol. 13, Washington, D.C.: AERA 1986
4. Papert, S.: *Mindstorms: Children, computers and powerful ideas.* New York: Basic Books 1980
5. Papert, S.: Introduction. In: *Constructionist learning* (I. Harel, ed.). Cambridge, MA: MIT Media Lab 1990
6. Rich, C. : Inspection methods in programming. Technical Report AI-TR-604, Cambridge, MA: MIT AI Lab 1981
7. Scardamalia, M., & Bereiter, C.: Higher levels of agency for children in knowledge building: A challenge for the design of new knowledge media. *The Journal of the Learning Sciences,* 1, pp. 37-68 (1991)
8. Schön, D.A. : *Educating the reflective practitioner.* San Francisco: Jossey-Bass Publishers (1987)
9. Soloway, E.: Learning to program = Learning to construct mechanisms and explanations. *Communications of the ACM,* 29, pp. 850-858 (1986)

10. Soloway, E. : Quick, where do the computers go? *Communications of the ACM*, 34, pp. 29-33 (1991)
11. Tinker, R.F., & Papert, S.: Tools for science education. In: *1988 AETS yearbook: Information technology and science education* (J. D. Ellis, ed.). Association for the Education of Teachers in Science 1988

Part 4

Diagnosing Students' Learning and Adjusting Plans for Instruction

Diagnosing Students' Learning and Adjusting Plans for Instruction

Benedict du Boulay[1] & Peter Goodyear[2]

[1]School of Cognitive and Computing Sciences, University of Sussex, Falmer, Brighton, England
[2]Department of Educational Research, Lancaster University, Lancaster, England

The two papers in this section, by Diana Laurillard and by Beverly Park Woolf, nicely show up the interplay between two apparently very different approaches to the problem of student modelling. Laurillard grapples with human knowledge as expressed by students with its individuality, complexity, ambiguity, incoherence, sensitivity to context, and general slipperiness. Woolf robustly offers tools for capturing knowledge using all the technology that artificial intelligence can muster. For one, the issue is the difficulty of figuring out students' knowledge and beliefs on the evidence of what they say and do. For the other, the problem is more of constructing a coherent representation of some skill, essentially starting from a received view of the domain (though, viewing pedagogy as a domain, the difficulties of formalizing teachers' pedagogic theories are readily acknowledged). Crudely, Laurillard is concerned with how certain concepts actually are conceptualized by students, "how something is known", while Woolf is concerned with how concepts "ought to be" conceptualized, essentially "what" is to be known and "how" it should be taught.

Although Laurillard and Woolf start from different positions, the end points are markedly similar and each seems to offer the other some part of what she needs.

Laurillard takes the notion of a "student model" entirely seriously at its face value and argues that a true student model is not achievable: firstly, because AI/cognitive science cannot capture the full wealth and associations of any individual's knowledge and secondly, because that knowledge is, in principle, not entirely an invariant "thing" to be captured but is an emergent phenomenon of the interaction between the student and his or her environment (in its broadest sense). For example, how a student knows about Newton's Laws depends on the situation in which the student uses that knowledge. At Calgary, though not in this paper, Laurillard further argued that we cannot capture how students perceive, which necessarily affects what they believe and know and hence the models of that knowledge and belief.

Human and machine teachers need to make decisions about how best to teach the current student and this must depend, at least in part, on their beliefs about that student's current knowledge and belief. Laurillard offers phenomenographic methodology as a way of establishing how some topic, e.g., Newton's Third Law, can be known by students. Her methodology provides an "outcome space", i.e., a space of possible ways of knowing. From

NATO ASI Series, Vol. F 85
Adaptive Learning Environments
Edited by M. Jones and P. H. Winne

the perspective of someone working in the field of intelligent tutoring systems, an issue for the teacher (or the intelligent tutoring system) is to classify a given student (in order to best focus the teaching) and this is seen as largely equivalent to locating the student's conception in the outcome space. Laurillard would argue against the equivalence of classifying the student and locating that student's conception in outcome space because of her position on student modelling. The underlying difference would be the degree to which one believed that the classification reflected a relatively stable cognitive state as opposed to labelling a more transient and context-sensitive phenomenon.

The methodology makes use of carefully constructed questions which are systematically refined until the answers that they evoke can be reliably classified across different cohorts of target students. In the example given, various facets of Newton's Third Law are chosen and their underlying interactions laid open. This methodology ostensibly starts from the student and not from an expert's view of the domain, but the result, the outcome space, seems to us to be similar in many ways to, for example, the procedural network of the Buggy family of programs [2], the set of buggy student rules in the LISP Tutor [1] or the "MIS-KUs" — the misconceptions, erroneous facts and procedures from the TUPITS described by Woolf. In these other cases, the space of student misconceptions was derived from an extensive prior empirical analysis of students. It is doubtful whether the method used in the analysis was phenomenographic in nature, but it certainly had a similar cyclic feature in that the programs' failures to properly discriminate cases provoked further empirical detective work.

Laurillard stresses that her methodology guarantees the completeness of the outcome space. This is not guaranteed by the more ad hoc methods traditionally used by intelligent tutoring system builders — and is usually only approached via extensive testing and debugging of the system itself. That is, the editing cycle happens much later than in the phenomenographic method where, in a sense, it is part of the initial design. Indeed, Woolf explicitly acknowledges this in her paper. Of course, choice of a representation language for student modelling within an intelligent tutoring system limits the space of possible future adjustment in field testing to what is expressible in that language (unless the system is to be fundamentally reconceived). In principle, Laurillard's methodology does not force such early commitment.

The idea of an analysis starting from the student is not then so different from what is accepted, at least by some intelligent tutoring system builders. Why does Laurillard's analysis of the outcome space for Newton's Third Law, in particular, look so unexceptional in terms of intelligent tutoring systems? One reason is that the phenomenographic methodology has itself been applied to only a vary narrowly defined view of the Third Law, namely in terms of classroom-based descriptions derived from written materials. It is possible that the outcome space would be much larger (and messier) if it also included the students' physical responses to forces in the real world, for example, how they try to achieve certain effects in the world which implicitly depend on their view of the law. This would distinguish how they "know" their physics as physics students from how they "do" their physics as agents in the world.

The outcome space approach (and especially the claim about completeness) seems plausible in those situations where it can be justifiable to work with a single, canonical view of the subject matter or problem to be tackled and where the concepts involved are simple ones. Science educators often seem more prepared than those in other fields of education to make this leap. One can think of a concept sitting somewhere on a complexity line that has "red square" at one end and "glasnost" at the other. The "outcome space" approach really depends on an assumption that the concepts under investigation are nearer the "red square" end. One can spend a lot of time arguing that the concepts used in Science education are typically nearer to "red square" than are the concepts used by (say) Historians. But that misses an important point: the concepts *as experienced* by the learner are typically nearer the "glasnost" end. That is, concepts-being-learned are complicated by the mess of associations (helpful and unhelpful) activated in the learner's mind in the process of coming to understand them.

Laurillard suggests ways in which a diagnostic program might be set up to classify a student's conception within the outcome space for the Third Law. The program invites students to place arrows on diagrams and answer questions. There are two issues here. Classifying students' free text answers for such a narrow domain is on the limits of what is currently possible in natural language processing, if students can get some practice in learning how to express themselves to the given program [3]. But there are still likely to be uninterpretable answers. One way around this might be to offer a menu for students to choose from. But one problem here is that this changes the situation: the student is now attempting to discriminate between a set of given alternatives, rather than formulating their own view, and these two may not fall in the same outcome space. Related to this is the issue of whether "placing arrows on given diagrams" falls inside the same outcome space as "verbal descriptions of forces." This could, of course, be fixed by generating the outcome space using such diagrams and arrow placing in the first place.

The diagnostic dialogue has a second very important feature for Laurillard. This is that it can, in itself, be a form of teaching. In other words, the approach Laurillard describes is that the outcome space mapping exercise is part of, or is very closely coupled to, a subsequent tutoring system or teaching scheme construction process. The approach is saying, "Here's Newton's Third Law; here's how students can (mis)understand it; here's a tutor that will help them learn Newton's Third Law." But, as noted above, the outcome space revealed in this process will be different (in important ways) from the outcome space one might get if one had students working on problems which used the Third Law in conjunction with some other principles. The danger is that the outcome space might be so context/task dependent that it is not generalizable to other situations in which one might want to test or tutor things involving the Third Law.

Laurillard offers a sequence of snapshots of a student's interaction with a possible tutorial/diagnostic system. In the final snapshot the system confronts the student with an inconsistency in his or her reasoning, on the reasonably plausible educational assumption that the student will then attempt to deal with the inconsistency. This dialogue looks very like the "socratic" dialogues of traditional intelligent tutoring systems such as Why [4]. Never mind that the modelling of knowledge in Why was domain rather than student-based; the intertwining of diagnosis and teaching is very similar. So again, although Laurillard starts from a position outside classical intelligent tutoring systems, her end point will be familiar to those in the field.

Laurillard uses the above arguments to redraw the standard functional architecture of an intelligent tutoring system omitting the "student model" box. In some sense she is right, but all that has really happened is that the knowledge in the system which enables it to carry out its diagnostic-teaching strategy has been relabelled but has not disappeared: it is now hidden inside the diagnostic and teaching strategy boxes.

There are two issues on which to conclude Laurillard's section. How far might it be possible to automate the phenomenographic methodology itself, i.e., the production of the outcome space? This would be very hard at present since artificial intelligence, in general, and natural language processing, in particular, do not yet have the capability to analyze text with the requisite degree of finesse.

The second issue concerns the proper role of "intelligence" in an intelligent tutoring system. For Laurillard, the "intelligence" in a teaching system appears to be most usefully employed in the careful prior analysis of who and what is to be taught, culminating in intelligent design of what might, in fact, be an "unintelligent" teaching system or environment. Even if we adopt this view, it appears that the example of a diagrammatic diagnostic-teaching conversation offered in her paper could only be achieved by the use of artificial intelligence techniques. How else is the system to arrive at the conclusion that "...but you said for the law to hold, action and reaction must be equal and opposite...."

Woolf starts from the position that the field of intelligent tutoring systems already boasts some confirmed success stories but that more and better systems could be developed if specialized software engineering tools were available for their construction and testing. Not only would this increase the productivity of existing personnel, but, if the tools were provided with appropriate interfaces, would also enable educational researchers and cognitive scientists to make a more direct contribution. In her view, one of the reasons why the symbiosis between education, psychology and intelligent tutoring systems research has not been as fruitful as it might have been is due to the differing granularity of theories in the different fields. One of the effects of the provision of software tools by researchers in intelligent tutoring systems is that it forces users of the tools largely to adopt the tools' language and level of granularity, a level of granularity that can be applied directly in system building. It may be that parts of educational theory (e.g., motivation) are not amenable to this technology-driven coercion, but Laurillard's analysis shows that there is room for optimism. The flip side of providing tools is that the tool builders themselves will be influenced by the tool users into broadening their conception of the educational process.

Woolf acknowledges that student modelling is difficult but takes a more optimistic line about its eventual possibility than Laurillard. Both researchers argue for a style of interaction for intelligent tutoring systems that is more participative than the caricature of the "ideal," omniscient tutor. Woolf explicitly argues for the value of "guided discovery learning, coaching or coaxing and critiquing" as the way forward, a position not so different from Laurillard's diagnostic system (though arrived at by different routes).

One of the beneficial side-effects of producing software tools for the construction of intelligent tutoring systems is that the tools automatically provide a generic framework within which such systems can be developed. This reduces the effort involved for each new teaching system, but more importantly it helps to separate out the knowledge (domain, pedagogic, etc.) embedded in the system from other incidental issues. This, in principle, should help to move the field towards a more scientific analysis of learning and teaching (as advocated by [5]) from its current rather piecemeal accumulation of individual systems.

Three examples of software tools are briefly sketched together with instances of the pedagogic knowledge that can be (and has been) represented with them. The issue is not so much whether we agree with the instances but whether the tools are powerful enough to deal with the wide range of disagreement by educational researchers and cognitive scientists about what needs representing. These tools necessarily have certain educational assumptions hard-wired into them (e.g., see the space of activities in Woolf's second figure). Each tool tends to subdivide its field of application in some way and each tool provides, at bottom, a number of atomic entities which cannot themselves be further broken down and which provide the basic primitive expressivity of the tool's representation language.

It is an open question as to whether the debate between intelligent teaching system builders and educationalists should be addressing these built-in assumptions or whether the debate need only take place within the frame of reference defined by the tools themselves. Leaving the tool building process to the intelligent tutoring systems developers alone is an inefficient way of ensuring that we explore the space of potentially useful tools properly. In any case, working collaboratively with tools is a productive way of airing and articulating disagreements between educationalists and systems developers.

Apart from the possibility that Laurillard might be able to exploit one of the tools from Woolf's laboratory for her analysis, there are other points of contact between the two papers.

In Woolf's section on "A Computational Model of Explanation," she espouses a position about the individuality of how a learner knows a domain that is not so far from Laurillard's. Even if the theoretical underpinnings are different, they each end up offering us ways of getting to grips with the variability of students' relationships to the knowledge in a given domain, and underline the poverty of the view of a student (model) as simply a subset of the domain being taught.

References

1. Anderson, J.R., & Reiser, J.: The LISP tutor. *BYTE*, 10, p. 4 (1985)
2. Brown, J.S., & Burton, R.R.: Diagnostic Models for Procedural Bugs in Basic Mathematical Skills. *Cognitive Science*, 2, pp. 155-192 (1978)
3. Burton, R.R., & Brown, J.S.: Semantic Grammar: A Technique for Constructing Natural Language Interfaces to Instructional Systems. Bolt, Beranek and Newman Inc., Technical Report No. 3587, Cambridge, MA 1977
4. Collins, A., Warnock, E.H., Aiello, N., & Miller, M.L.: Reasoning from Incomplete Knowledge. In: *Representation and Understanding* (D. Bobrow & A. Collins, eds.). New York: Academic Press 1975
5. Self, J.: The Case for Formalising Student Models (and Intelligent Tutoring Systems generally). In: *Artificial Intelligence and Education* (D. Bierman, J. Breuker & J. Sandberg, eds.). Amsterdam: IOS 1989

Towards a Computational Model of Tutoring

Beverly Park Woolf

Department of Computer and Information Science, University of Massachusetts, Amherst, MA, USA

Abstract: This chapter addresses several issues around successful integration of instructional science and computer science. It addresses issues of building computational models of tutoring and incorporating instructional principles. The first barrier to overcome towards this integration is development of principled programs in which cognitive principles about learning and teaching are realized at a level of granularity consistent with building computational models. Such cognitive studies would facilitate fine-grained modelling of learning and teaching. The second barrier to overcome is the gap between the two disciplines, in terms of goals, motivations, literature, and even defining concepts. This situation suggests that a large effort should go into two areas: research on understanding basic principles behind learning and teaching, and the establishment of clearer lines of communication between instructional and computer scientists. This chapter addresses both these issues.

Keywords: knowledge-based tutoring, teaching and learning, artificial intelligence, computational design of tutors.

Integration of Instructional Science and Computer Science

This chapter addresses several issues around successful integration of instructional science and computer science. Combining the efforts of these two disciplines offers exciting possibilities for the scientific study of human learning and the building of powerful teaching systems; yet, as a research community we are only at the very beginning of asking whether such an integration is possible and of knowing how to develop one. This integration would move beyond the paradigm of either separate discipline and would create results more powerful than those obtainable separately or in combination. To assume that such an integration is impossible reflects a narrow perspective and a lack of learning from the recent history of science which has seen many "impossible" achievements become reality.

NATO ASI Series, Vol. F 85
Adaptive Learning Environments
Edited by M. Jones and P. H. Winne

This chapter describes conceptions about such an integration and addresses issues of building computational models of tutoring and incorporating instructional principles (e.g., low-level descriptions and analyses of learning and motivation). The first barrier to overcome towards this synthesis is development of principled programs in which cognitive principles about learning and teaching are realized at a level of granularity consistent with building computational models and these principles are integrated into computer systems. Such cognitive studies facilitate fine-grained modelling of learning and teaching and should ultimately provide the "zorch" that will make possible the building of powerful instructional systems. Other facets of advanced technology, e.g., multi-media or increased speed and power, including 200 MIPs (million instructions per second), will not significantly empower tutoring systems.

The second barrier to overcome is the gap between the two disciplines, in terms of goals, motivations, literature, and even defining concepts. Instructional scientists frequently work on issues and goals that are not addressed by computer scientists, and vice-versa. Instructional scientists do collaborate with computer programmers, but the latter are not typically versed in cutting-edge research developments in computer science. Computer scientists, on the other hand, do not strive to develop general design methodologies that will support participation of instructional designers in their efforts. Frequently, computer scientists build tutoring systems in collaboration with domain experts; however, they rarely collaborate with practicing instructional scientists in the design of these systems.

This situation suggests that a large effort should go into two areas: research on understanding basic principles behind learning and teaching, and the establishment of clearer lines of communication between instructional and computer scientists. This chapter addresses both these issues. The first issue discussed is the articulation of elements of cognitive principles for use in computational models. Cognitive modelling is directed at identifying computationally precise explanations of how cognition works, and, in this case, how, why, and when students learn. The true bottleneck in building powerful instructional systems today lies in our inability to fully understand and represent human learning and teaching processes.

The second issue discussed in this chapter is how computer scientists might clarify the process of building knowledge-based tutors so that instructional designers and others might collaborate in their design and implementation. Researchers in computer science have not generally developed their technology with an eye toward including teachers and instructional scientists. Yet, the experience of learning via a knowledge-based learning environment is so novel for both student and teacher that neither computer scientist nor instructional designer acting independently can foresee all the crucial learning and teaching issues that might arise when these systems are actually used. Gleaning insights, principles, and rules about teaching that will be encoded within knowledge-based tutors must originate from a rich synthesis of learning and instructional theories, insights from practising teachers, and on-line experimentation. Testbeds are needed for systematic integration of instructional design theory and advanced technology.

This chapter first examines some motivations for the development of knowledge-based systems and then describes salient success stories. Next, it looks at instructional research issues. Finally, it identifies contributions from researchers at the University of Massachusetts working to acquire, represent, and reason about tutoring knowledge.

Motivation for Building Knowledge-based Systems

Research into knowledge-based tutoring systems has created a great deal of interest on the part of academe, industry, and the military internationally. Tough educational problems, including outdated educational facilities, lack of public support for educational innovation, and in some cases inappropriate policies have left educators engaged in an uphill battle to reverse deficiencies in student learning and teacher training. Long distance learning, learning for the disabled, and a variety of non-traditional educational needs have spawned new educational research efforts.

Poor education in the United States has contributed to low-level entry abilities of industrial and military recruits and difficult retraining problems. Industry spends a tremendous amount on training. IBM, for instance, spends $900 million annually directed at training nearly 400,000 employees in 130 countries [5]. Industrial and military training is clearly faced with difficulties in the area of recruitment and selection of well prepared workers [10] and the military has, additionally, a two-year turnover problem for new recruits.

These and other problems have focussed attention on the possibilities offered by knowledge-based systems. The clear emergence of architectures for knowledge-based tutoring systems and positive training results has produced the feeling that progress is being made. Indeed, several systems have achieved the two-sigma effect [4], which is the same improvement in learning that results from one-on-one human tutoring over classroom tutoring. Several success stories have been described in which students using knowledge-based tutors learned knowledge and skills in one-third to one-half the time it took for a control group to learn the same material [17].

In one special case, students working with an Air Force electronics troubleshooting tutor for only twenty hours gained a proficiency equivalent to that of trainees with 40 months (almost four years) of on-the-job training [12]. In another example, students using a Lisp tutor at Carnegie-Mellon University [1] completed programming exercises in 30% less time than those receiving traditional classroom instruction and scored 43% higher on the final exam. In a third study, students using a microworld environment learned general scientific inquiry skills and principles of basic economics in one-half the time required by students in a classroom setting [18].

Given these results, one might ask why more intelligent tutors are not being used and why existing systems are not more effective. One reason relates to the lack of artificial intelligence development tools, such as shells and frameworks, similar to the shells used to rapidly build expert systems. Tools would facilitate large-scale development; a simple tool, such as a simulation tied to an expert system or to a lock-step tutor, might be a practical way for a designer to get started on a path of incremental design through feedback from the user. Some researchers suggest that a teacher should interact with a variety of tools, much as a conductor might orchestrate a suite of instruments.

Other reasons for the slow adoption of new systems include the need to reduce cognitive task analysis to engineering practice and the difficulty of developing cognitive models (see next page). Additionally, there is the need to make widely available certain new knowledge representations (i.e., qualitative simulations) which will be more effective than those offered by first-generation expert system tools. An additional barrier is the lengthy development cycle required before a system can move from research lab to a salable product.

Instructional Design Issues

The first major issue addressed by this chapter is the need to identify instructional science principles at a level of granularity that supports the building of computational models of learning and teaching. Instructional design issues present serious challenges to the current generation of researchers. This section discusses such challenges and describes possible solutions to the representation of student intentions, the support of knowledge reflection, and the engineering of tools for diagnosis.

Cognitive Modelling

Cognitive modelling is a methodology for developing computational explanations of cognition. It seeks a low-level description of cognitive processes — in this case of learning and teaching — which permits the encoding of rules and principles in a computer. Increased use of modelling is supported for the building of knowledge-based intelligent tutors and its use has strong advocates among psychologists and computer scientists.

Cognitive modelling for building knowledge-based systems should be increased in three areas, primarily in 1) development of pedagogical and subject-matter theories, 2) design of instruction, and 3) delivery of instruction. Of these phases, the design of instruction is the one that seems to have achieved the most direct benefit for knowledge-based systems, including substantial benefits from modelling subject matter experts. For instance, Anderson et al. [3] attribute much of the success of their tutors to the cognitive task analysis of experts in Lisp, geometry, and algebra.

Work on modelling good teachers and tutors has only just begun (with the exception of a few early classics, such as the work of Stevens and Collins on Socratic tutoring [21]). VanLehn expects this line of investigation to pay off at least as well, if not better, than the modelling of experts and learners [30].

Of the three phases of pedagogical work, the actual delivery of instruction is the area where cognitive modelling has found the least fruitful application. Mostly, this is due to a historical accident. In most systems to date, teacher models have been weaker than expert models and student models. Although a good teacher model might compensate for an impoverished expert or student model, experience has shown that strong expert and student models require a decent teacher model for the system to be effective.

VanLehn underscores the fact that modelling is just good engineering practice, regardless of whether one is building a hydroelectric dam or a science course [30]. With tongue in cheek, he suggests that if students could sue malfeasant instructional developers, cognitive modelling would be much more common since it is so obviously effective.

Representing Student Intentions

Great instructional leverage will come from implementing student and domain models based on cognitive modelling. Where problem solving is seen as a primary learning activity, additional power will come from understanding the cognitive processes necessary to complete the task and then from reification of these processes in the domain and student models. Building such models and linking them to a powerful interface can only be accomplished after a thorough task analysis of the domain has been achieved.

Developing an effective instructional model of the domain implies that a designer has generated a conceptualization and structuring of the task and the learning process. This instructional model may lead to finding ways to represent abstract cognitive structures, such as student goals and plans, and representing these structures as concrete visual or textual objects that can be made the focus of student action and discourse [19].

For example, a system might maintain a list of student subtasks. In a geometry environment, it might advise a student to first discover if two sides of a triangle are equal and then show that the triangle is isosceles. In a calculus environment, it might suggest use of the chain rule and indicate the two subtasks: differentiate the first function, multiplying it by the second, and then differentiate the second, multiplying it by the first. In each environment, the system might post and display each subtask as boxed or shaded to indicate which subtasks are active and which have been satisfied, respectively [19].

Tools built into an interface should support a student in expressing his/her plan directly to the machine, and then these tools might become the structure of the tutorial discourse. Tools might be offered at varying instructional levels as in the case where an algebra tutor offers tools at a low level (e.g., commands to add, divide, or multiply terms) and also at a higher level (e.g., commands to group variables, simplify equations, or substitute values).

In this way, the system might infer the intentions of the student from expressed plans. To build such tools requires a deep understanding of the domain, and it may be difficult to find a transparent representation for goals and plans in some domains. Any system which requires that the student solve a problem by using a planning icon unrelated to the problem solving domain might be burdening the student with additional complexity and forcing the learning of a formalism that is nearly as difficult as mastering the domain itself.

Well-crafted tools, on the other hand, will support a student in operating in the physical problem space and will be fully integrated with that space [19]. Excellent tools will also permit improved knowledge reflection or meta-cognitive activities involving conscious surveillance and self regulation. Instead of facilitating the use of a series of questions and answers, the availability of appropriate tools will support a tutor in making the student's thinking public for discussion. Questions from the tutor might then refer to student plans and expectations. Alternative high and low level languages might accommodate a user's shift in understanding [8] and would facilitate a comparable shift in tutorial discourse.

Another unresolved instructional design issue is the effect of immediate feedback on learning. Corbett and Anderson [7] note that students seemed more confident with less feedback. (They also note that this confidence, at least in the domain of Lisp programming, was unrelated to competence, specifically in performance on a post test.) Schooler and Anderson [15] record several disadvantages associated with immediate feedback: 1) the student grows dependent upon feedback and hesitates to act without it; 2) the student does not develop error correction and detection abilities; and 3) the feedback competes for the student's limited short-term memory resources. The jury is still out on a final evaluation of the effect of immediate feedback.

Another instructional issue which requires attention is the identification of teaching goals for these systems. Difficult yet desirable goals include encouraging students to gain confidence, passion, and ownership of their work. Yet current systems are a long way from achieving this goal. Another goal might be to support students in becoming researchers capable of independent exploration through networks of available knowledge.

Student Models and Error Diagnosis

Student modelling, an essential component of any tutoring system, is still incompletely understood. Effective student models should be usable, faithful, and runnable. They should provide descriptions of learning at a level of granularity that facilitates the encoding of principles and rules in a teaching system.

Current student models are shallow representations of topics a student does or does not know, or those topics about which the system does not have enough information. In fact, a robust student model should record the role of context in student learning, student learning preferences, motivation, history while acquiring past learning, and meta-knowledge about learning. AI researchers will wait a long time for such descriptions to evolve; of course, they might participate with instructional designers in efforts to develop such computational models of learning.

Research into evaluating automatic diagnosis of common errors and plausible misconceptions is another instructional arena that currently receives insufficient attention. In limited domains we have accomplished diagnosis [2, 11], yet we still do not know how to use this diagnostic material in subsequent dialogue to empower students.

In general, researchers are moving away from building omniscient tutors capable of detecting all possible errors and misconceptions. Instead, research is now focussed more on building empathic partners that choose from among several forms of interaction based on the content of the communication and the needs of the student [26]. Possible communication styles include didactic explanation, guided discovery learning, coaching or coaxing, and critiquing. Although no one style is preferred, different tutorial applications will be better addressed with a given primary style.

Representing and Reasoning about Tutoring Knowledge

In addition to trying to develop cognitive models of teaching and learning, this chapter also addresses the need for computer scientists to clearly define the structure and design of their systems so that instructional scientists can become their collaborators in building knowledge-based tutoring systems. This section describes efforts at the University of Massachusetts along this line; it clarifies how tutoring can be understood in terms of the artificial intelligence paradigm of knowledge and control, and shows how to represent knowledge computationally and how to express it as strategies and rules. Architectures and tools are proposed for developing new systems and for supporting the knowledge representation and acquisition process. The tools are now used in a generic and consistent foundation which has enabled us to represent, acquire, and reason about tutoring knowledge across several domains and from within several sites. Our goal is to enhance this framework and ultimately to produce systems in which psychologists, instructional scientists, and domain experts can work as our colleagues to modify and upgrade tutors without the need for knowledge engineers.

This section describes tools that facilitate both identifying tutoring knowledge and representing it. *Knowledge representation* is explained in terms of modelling domain knowledge, human thinking, learning processes, and tutoring strategies. A uniform language is proposed for storing tutoring primitives, including lessons, topics, and presentations. *Knowledge acquisition* is described as a methodology for identifying and encoding the expertise used by teachers to reason about tutoring. *Control knowledge* is explained in terms of the machine's ability to select a topic or response for an individual student and then to customize its discourse and dynamically modify its examples, questions, or descriptions for that student.

Building a Tutoring System

We have evolved a generic and consistent foundation for representing, acquiring, and reasoning about tutoring knowledge. The big payoff has been that we can now apply the framework and evolving theory to several domains. We are not invested in promoting a particular tutoring strategy, nor do we advocate a specific knowledge-based tutoring system design. Rather, we build tools that allow for a variety of system components, teaching styles, and intervention strategies to be combined into a single framework. For example, Socratic tutoring, incremental generalizations, and case-based reasoning are just a few of the teaching strategies we have experimented with using this framework. Ultimately, we expect the machine to reason about its own choice of intervention method, to switch teaching strategies, and to use a variety of tactics and teaching approaches, while making decisions about the most efficacious method for managing one-on-one tutoring.

Development cycle for artificial intelligence systems. Development of knowledge-based tutors, like development of any artificial intelligence system, requires several iterative cycles: computer scientists and instructional designers first collaborate on the design and development of the system, additional collaboration is required to test the system with students, and then the original implementation is modified and refined based on information gained through testing. This cycle is repeated as time permits.

For example, a professor at City College of San Francisco used the statics tutor (described in the next section) in a classroom and noticed weaknesses in the simulation's ability to inform the student. She augmented the system with verbal discourse, adding examples or explanations, making diagnoses, and clarifying system response. She gave us a list of her additional discourse moves to be incorporated into the next version of the tutor.

Representation and control. Artificial intelligence programs require that a teaching expert define the knowledge to be used along with the control structures which define the way an interpreter will traverse that knowledge. Knowledge representation refers to how such knowledge is stored by a system to allow it to model the domain, human thinking, learning processes, and tutoring strategies. Knowledge bases might store concepts, activities, relations between topics, and other quantities needed to make expert decisions. In tutoring, they might store a variety of lessons, topics, presentations, and response selections available to the tutor (see Figure 1). Control refers to passage of an interpreter through those knowledge bases and its selection of appropriate pieces of knowledge for making a diagnosis, a prediction, or an evaluation. For tutoring, control structures might be specified at the four levels indicated in Figure 1, separately defining control for selection of lesson, topic, presentation, and response selection.

Currently, our control structures are motivated by specific instructional and diagnostic goals; thus, for example, one control structure produces a predominantly Socratic interaction and another produces interactions based on presenting incrementally generalized versions of new concepts or examples. Control structures are specific to a particular level of control and are used separately to define the reasoning to be used for selecting a lesson, topic, presentation, or response.

Acquiring and encoding this large amount of knowledge, or the knowledge acquisition process, is difficult and time consuming. We have built a number of tools that facilitate representing, acquiring, and reasoning about tutoring knowledge (see Figure 2). For each knowledge base (lessons, topics, presentation, or response) we consider the nature of the knowledge that must be accessed, such as the examples or questions (from the presentation knowledge base) or the activity the tutor must engage in, such as to motivate or teach a topic, or to provide follow-up. We have built tools, shown at the bottom of Figure 2, to support most activities listed in the figure. Only a few such tools will be described in this chapter, namely TUPITS, the Response Matrix, and DACTNs. We divide the discussion into two parts,

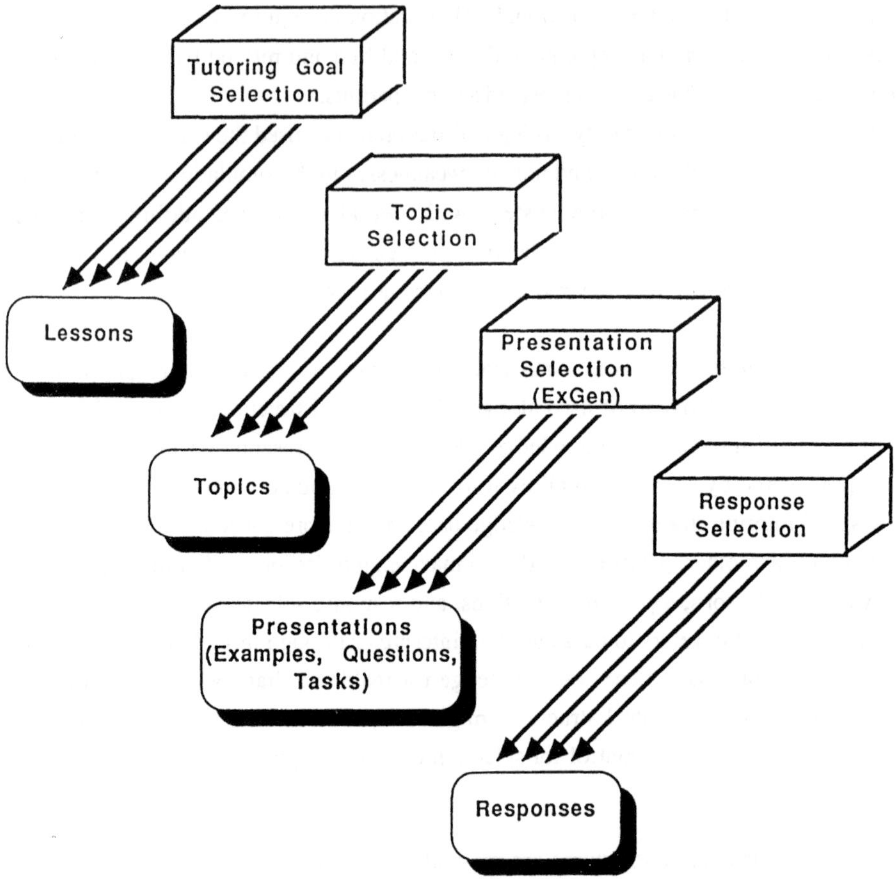

Figure 1: Representation and control in a tutoring system

separately describing tools for representing tutoring primitives (lessons, topics, and presentations) and then tools for representing discourse knowledge.

Tutoring Primitives

We define *tutoring primitives* as basic elements needed for communicating knowledge, such as topics to be taught, specific tutoring responses, and possible student errors. Our knowledge bases hold a variety of examples, knowledge types, tasks to be given to the student, and discourse states describing various human-machine interactions.

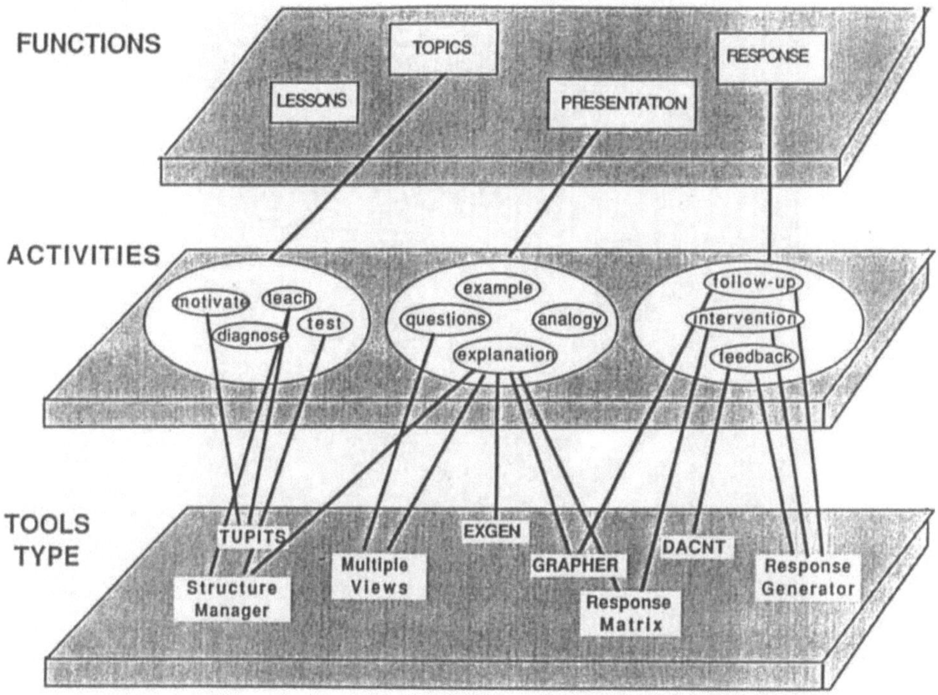

Figure 2: Tools for the representation and control of tutoring knowledge

As an example of how tutoring primitives are used, we describe a tutor built in conjunction with the Exploring Systems Earth (ESE) Consortium [9]. This tutor is based on interactive simulations that encourage students to work with "elements" of physics, such as mass, acceleration, and force. The goal is to help students generate hypotheses as necessary precursors to expanding their own intuitions. We want the simulations to encourage students to "listen to" their own scientific intuition and to make their own model of the physical world before an encoded tutor advises them about the accuracy of their choices. This tutor has been described elsewhere [27,28] and will only be summarized here.

Figure 3 shows a simulation for teaching concepts in introductory statics. Students are asked to identify forces and torques on the crane boom, or horizontal bar, and to use rubber banding to draw appropriate force vectors directly on the screen. When the beam is in static equilibrium there will be no net force or torque on any part of it. Students are asked to solve both qualitative and quantitative word problems.

If a student were to specify incorrect forces either by omitting force lines or by including the wrong ones, the tutor makes a decision about how to respond. There are many possible

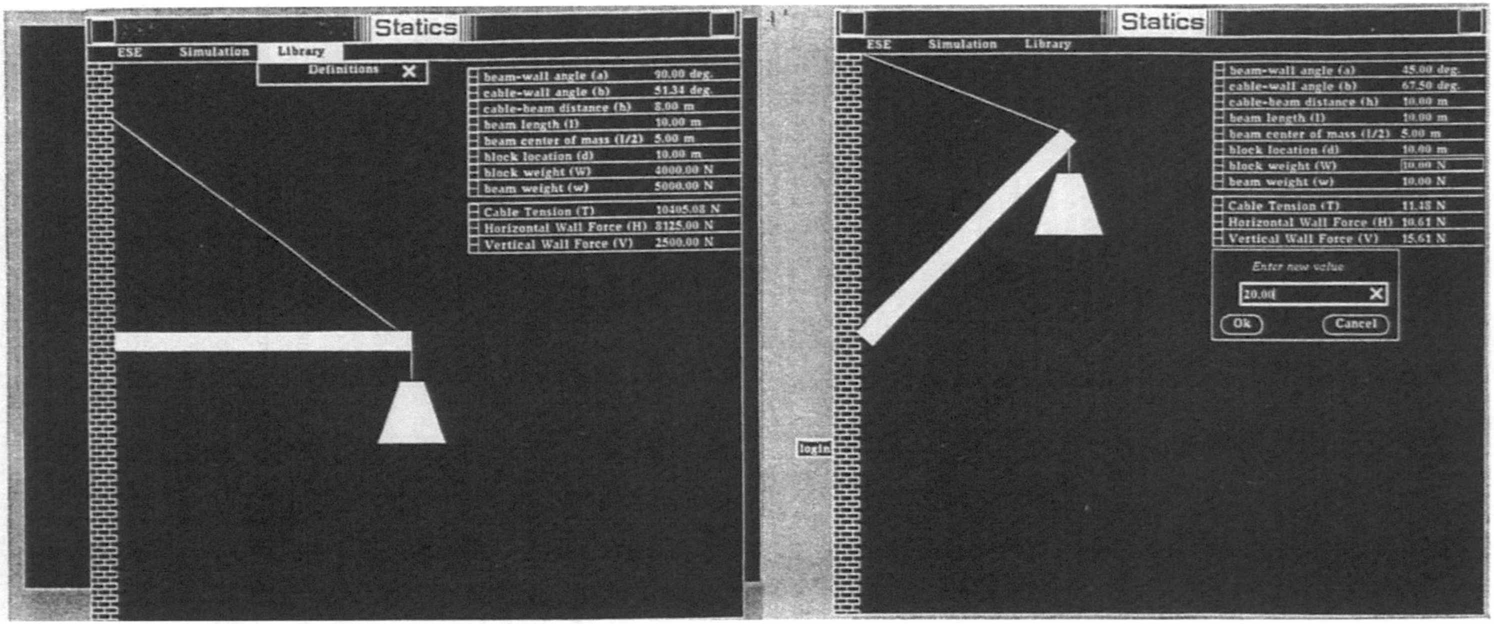

Figure 3: Statics tutor

responses depending on the tutorial strategy in effect. The tutor might present an explanation or hint, provide another problem, or demonstrate that the student's analysis leads to a logical contradiction. Still another response would be to withhold explicit feedback concerning the quality of the student's answer, and to instead demonstrate the consequence of omitting the "missing" force; i.e., the end of the beam next to the wall would crash down. Such a response would show the student how his/her conceptions might be in conflict with the observable world and to help him/her visualize both an internal conceptualization and the science theory.

Representing and reasoning about tutoring primitives. The four knowledge bases described earlier are used to represent topics, examples, explanations, and possible misconceptions. We use a network of Knowledge Units frames to explicitly express relationships between topics such as prerequisites, corequisites, and related misconceptions (Figure 4). An important notion about the network is that it is declarative — it contains a structured space of concepts, but does not mandate any particular order for traversal of this space.

The network describes tutorial strategies in terms of a vocabulary of primitive discourse moves such as teach, motivate, contrast, and summarize. It is implemented in a language called TUPITS[1] which was built as a framework to facilitate development of numerous tutors. It is an object-oriented representation language that provides a framework for defining primitive components of a tutorial discourse interaction. These components are then used by the tutor to reason about its next action.

As shown in Figure 4, each object in TUPITS is represented as a frame and each frame is linked with other frames representing prerequisites, corequisites, or triggered misconceptions. The primary objects in TUPITS are:

- lessons which define high-level goals and constraints for each tutoring session;
- knowledge Units (KUs);
- MIS-KUs, which represent common misconceptions, wrong facts or procedures, and other types of "buggy" knowledge;
- examples, which specify parameters that configure an example, diagram, or simulation to be presented to the student;
- questions, which define tasks for the student and how the student's behaviour during the task might be evaluated; and
- presentations, which bind an example together with associated questions.

MIS-KUs, or "Mis-Knowledge Units," represent common misconceptions or knowledge "bugs" and ways to remediate them. Remediation is inserted opportunistically into the

---

[1] TUPITS (Tutorial discourse Primitives for knowledge-based Tutoring Systems) was developed by Tom Murray and runs on both Hewlett-Packard Bobcats and Apple Macintosh IIs.

discourse. The tutoring strategy parameterizes this aspect of Knowledge Unit selection by indicating whether such remediation should occur as soon as the misconception is suspected, or wait until the current Knowledge Unit has been completed.

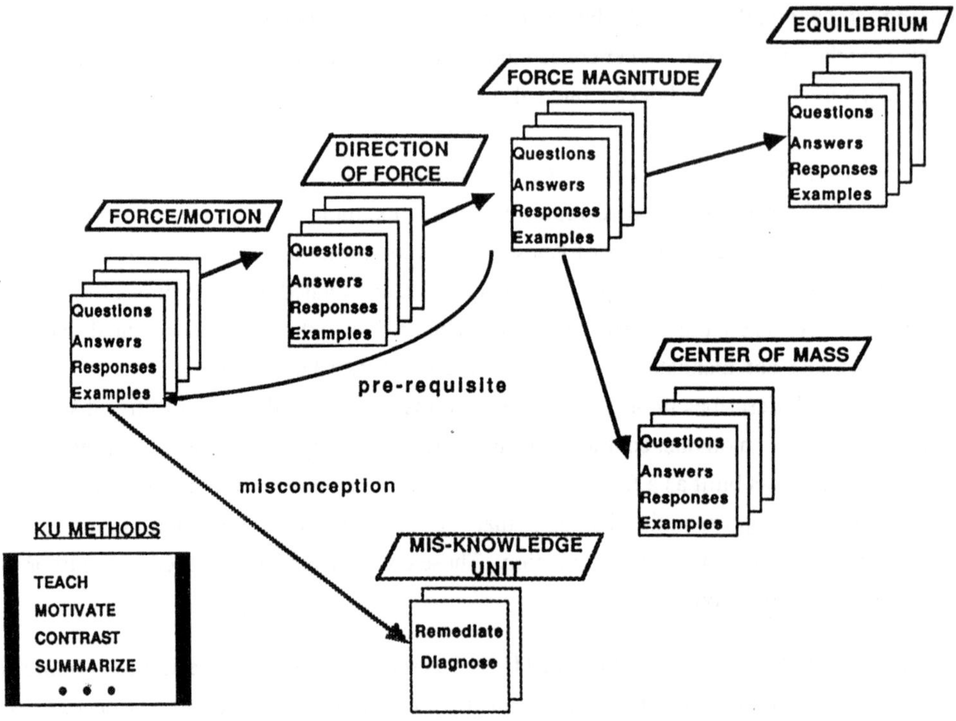

Figure 4: Hierarchy of frames

Control is achieved through information associated with each object which allows the system to respond dynamically to new tutoring situations. For instance, Knowledge Units, or topics represented as objects, have procedural "methods" associated with them that:

- teach their own topic interactively
- teach their own prerequisites
- explain knowledge didactically
- test students for knowledge of that topic
- summarize themselves
- provide examples of their knowledge (a substantiation of a procedure or concept)
- provide motivation for a student learning the topic, and
- compare this knowledge with that of other Knowledge Units.

A specific tutoring strategy manifests itself by parameterizing the algorithm used to traverse the knowledge primitives network based on classifications of and relations between knowledge units. Several major strategies have thus far been implemented. For example, the tutor might always teach prerequisites before teaching the goal topic. Alternatively, it might provide a diagnostic probe to see if the student knows a topic. Prerequisites might be presented if the student does not exhibit enough knowledge on the probe. These prerequisites may be reached in various ways, such as depth-first and breadth-first traversal. An intermediate strategy is to specialize the prerequisite relation into "hard" prerequisites, which are always covered before the goal topic, and "soft" prerequisites, taught only when the student displays a deficiency.

Discourse Analysis

Our tutors are beginning to represent and reason about alternative responses to the student. Choices are concerned with how much information to give and what motivational comments to make. For instance, the machine must decide whether or not to:

- talk *about* the student's response;
- provide *motivational* feedback about the student's learning process;
- say *whether* an approach is appropriate, *what* a correct response would be, and *why* the student's response is correct or incorrect;
- provide hints, leading questions, or counter-suggestions.

Motivational feedback may include asking questions about the student's interest in continuing or providing encouragement, congratulations, challenges, and other statements with affective or prelocutionary content. Control is modulated by which tutoring strategy is in effect, which in turn places constraints on what feedback or follow-up response to generate. The strategy may also specify that system action be predicated on whether the student's response was correct, or whether any response was given.

Reasoning about discourse level. As a start to this process we have defined the Response Matrix, which now encodes several high-level response strategies and tactics (see Figure 5). For example, we have designated an informative response tactic as one in which the machine will elaborate, give reasons, and congratulate the student. For each concept represented in the machine, some of these primitive responses are available and the machine will generate the requested tactic. However, we also advise the system about strategies such as Socratic tutoring, being brief, and being verbose. Here we indicate a priority ordering; thus to be Socratic, the machine must place highest priority on the tactic called coy, and secondary rating on the tactic to be informative. If there is a conflict between the checks and the crosses in the model shown in Figure 5, that notation with the highest priority will win.

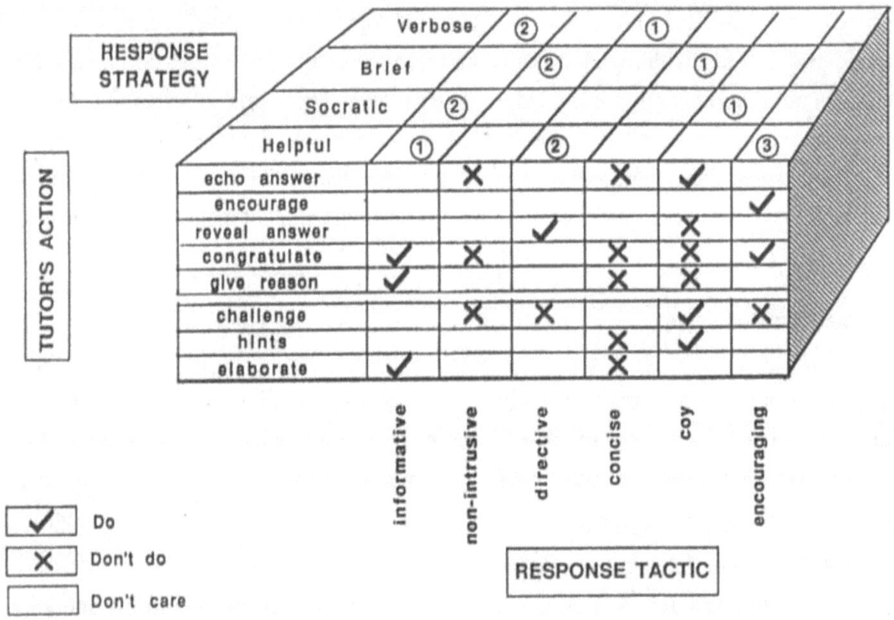

Figure 5: The Response Matrix: Reasoning about discourse

Managing Discourse

We realize that a more flexible and responsive discourse management technique is critical to a tutoring or consultant system. By discourse management, we mean the system's ability to maintain interactive discourse with a user and to custom-tailor its responses beyond the generalized discourse levels suggested above. Ideally, the system should tailor its response to the idiosyncrasies of a particular user. Machine discourse and response need not be in natural language to be effective [16].

For example, the system should ensure that an intervention relates directly to an individual's personal history, learning style, and on-line experience with the system. It should dynamically reason about a user's actions, the curriculum, and the discourse history. In doing this, the tutor should make each user feel that his/her unique situation has been responded to appropriately and sensitively. In this way, the system simulates one-on-one human tutoring behaviour. The mechanism we use to do this is called a DACTN, *Discourse ACtion Transition Network*,[2] which represents and controls human-machine dialogue. Figure 6 shows a DACTN for responding to a user about a question he/she asked.

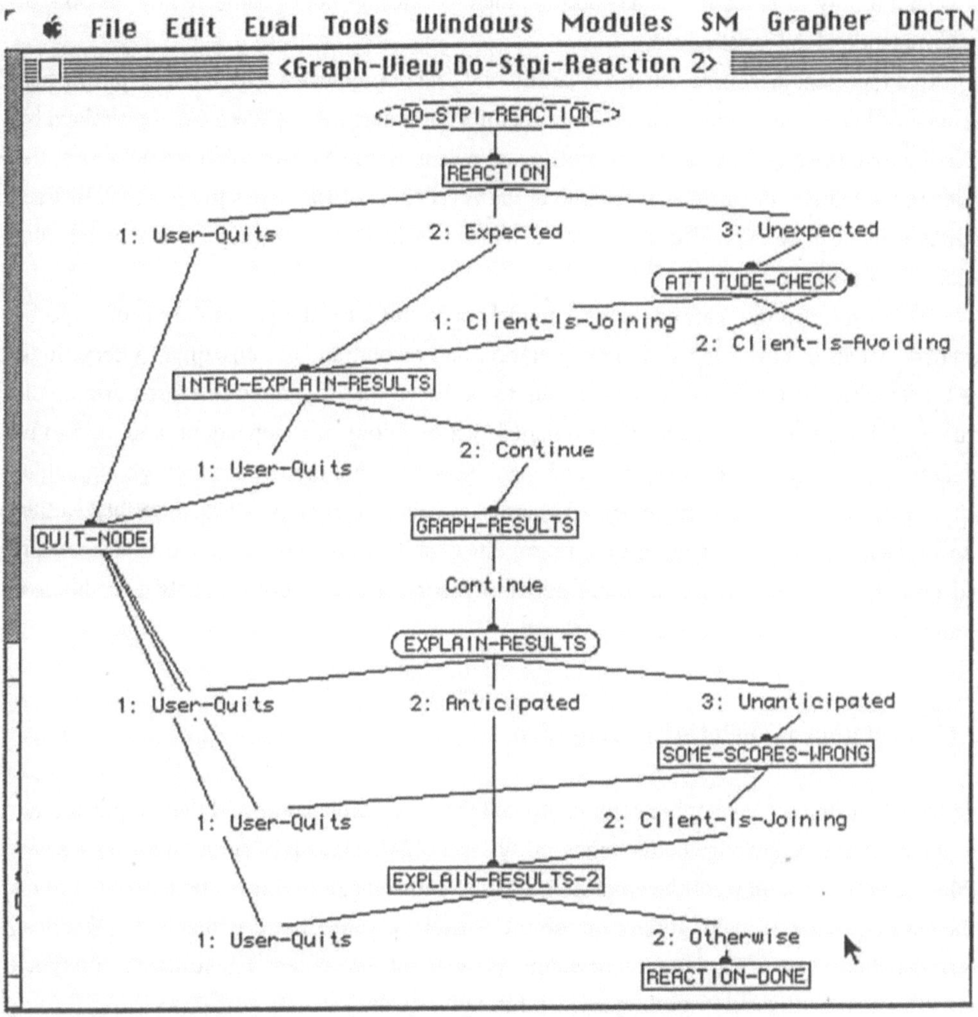

Figure 6: Discourse ACtion Transition Network: DACTN

Sometimes the intervention steps designated by a DACTN are based on a taxonomy of frequently observed discourse sequences which provide default responses for the tutor [28]. The discourse manager reasons about local context when making discourse decisions. Here, local context is an aggregate of the user profile and response history.

2 Rhymes with ACT-IN.

The DACTN represents the space of possible discourse situations; arcs track the state of the conversation and are defined as predicate sets while nodes provide actions for the tutor. The discourse manager first accesses the situation indicated by the arcs, resolving any conflicts between multiply-satisfied predicate sets, and then initiates the action indicated by the node at the termination of the satisfied arc.

Arcs represent discourse situations defined by sets of predicates over the user profile and the state of the system. For instance, the value of a particular arc in Figure 6 is determined by inferring over the current state of the profile and recent user responses. Placing actions at the nodes rather than on the arcs, as was done in the ATN [25], allows nodes to represent abstract actions which can be expanded into concrete substeps when and if the node is reached during execution of the DACTN.

Each user response causes the user model, or in this case the personality profile, to be updated, which in turn affects the interpretation and resolutions of subsequent interactions. DACTNs allow discourse control decisions to be based on a dynamic interpretation of the situation. In this way the mechanism remains flexible, domain-independent, and able to be dynamically rebuilt — decision points and machine actions are modifiable through a graphics editor. DACTNs have been implemented in three domains: the first is statics, described earlier, a second supports development of time management skills [20], and a third explains concepts and processes in elementary electrical network theory and is briefly described in the next section.

A Computational Model of Explanation

We have focussed on developing computational theories of explanation and their application to computer-based "knowledge communication systems" [24], e.g., advisory and tutoring systems which serve as a medium for the communication of knowledge. In this context, *explanation* is "the act or process of making plain or comprehensible; elucidation; clarification" (American Heritage Dictionary). Explanation research accounts for the content and structure of explicit communications, directed towards specific informative goals.

We claim that the most pressing research issues in explanation occur at an epistemological level of analysis. Such an analysis examines how the selection, organization, and presentation of the content of explanations are guided by three *epistemological sources of constraints,* namely:

- the internal structure of a domain's shared body of knowledge,
- the role of an individual's knowledge in understanding new concepts and situations, and
- the ways in which individuals are willing or able to transform their knowledge.

People will not understand an explanation, let alone retain, retrieve, and use it, if it does not make some contact with what they already know. Furthermore, there are restricted ways in which people are willing or able to transform the knowledge structures by which they understand the world. This means an explainer should identify pedagogically exploitable relations between the relevant knowledge and whatever guesses are available about the hearer's knowledge state, and structure the explanation to follow epistemological "gradients" along which he or she is likely to comprehend and integrate the new knowledge it contains. Thus, a theory of how to reason about the characteristics of knowledge when selecting and organizing the content of an explanation is necessary if we are to construct knowledge communication systems based on multi-use declarative knowledge bases.

The first application domain for our analysis of explanation is elementary electrical network theory. We emphasize the communication of an understanding of concepts such as "electricity," "current," and "resistance" within the context of reasoning about the operation of simple circuits and their components. We are building an explanation generation system to produce complex explanations and have described the system and the issues encountered elsewhere [22,23].

Knowledge Acquisition: Involving Teachers in the Process

As research into knowledge-based tutoring continues to produce increasingly more sophisticated systems and diverse representational paradigms, the gap between the computer science community and the instructional design community has widened. Educators' understanding, acceptance, and use of this research has been much slower than expected. Yet, as discussed in the first section of this chapter, educators are vital participants in the research collaborative to build knowledge-based tutors. Otherwise this research becomes increasingly academic and unconnected to the pragmatic aspects of teaching and learning. Clancey [6] says: "...the reality today is that the endeavor is one that only experienced programmers (or experts trained to be programmers) can accomplish. Indeed, research of the past decade has only further increased our standards of knowledge representation desirable to teaching, while the tools for constructing such programs lag far behind or are not generally available."

There are several concerns about how and when to involve instructional designers in designing and testing tutoring strategies. Practicing teachers do not have well-articulated theories of learning or instruction. In addition, relevant instructional and cognitive theories are not operationalized to a level easily implemented in a computer, nor do these theories anticipate practical factors and domain related idiosyncrasies.

As a small step towards including teachers and educational researchers in this work, we have developed a knowledge acquisition interface for the statics tutor described earlier. The tutor conveys a qualitative understanding of Newton's laws and an intuitive grasp of the relationship between forces and force components in static systems [28,29]. Part of its curriculum centers around a learning environment called the "crane boom" in which the student manipulates a simulated physical system and observes the resulting forces and force components. The knowledge acquisition interface was developed in part as a response to the combined need for more teacher participation and more collaboration in developing tutoring strategies [14]. The framework incorporates instructional design paradigms and facilitates rapid creation and manipulation of multiple tutoring strategies. Currently, teachers use this framework to incrementally add to and modify existing knowledge and to debug, update, and expand knowledge "pieces" for topics, examples, hints, prerequisites, etc. We also expect teachers to be able to create or modify tutoring strategies which determine how the tutor responds to the student.

The knowledge acquisition interface provides a view of the sum of the object types, attributes, relationships, and decision levels available to the tutor. This is a conceptual vocabulary for describing "what to teach" and "how to teach" it. The interface is designed to reify this framework for the teachers and others working with the system, making it possible for them to organize and encode their knowledge. Figure 7 shows a screen dump of the interface. The three menu bars at the top allow a teacher to select an object, instances of that object, and slots within the instance. The teacher might test, review, edit, or play any "object" in the system including any topic, summary, example, sound or graphic. Buttoning on one of these objects causes an editor to open along the bottom of the screen, which can be used by the teacher to change any text issued by the system. All changes are automatically entered into the Lisp code of the system. The teacher can then run a portion of the tutor to test his/her correction. In the figure, the wrap-up statement of the topic "intuition about linear-equilibrium" is being modified.

The interface facilitates both knowledge acquisition (in which a computer scientist interacts with the teacher to formalize his/her knowledge) and data entry and testing (in which the teacher adds to or modifies the knowledge base). This interface is further described [14].

Conclusion and Discussion

This chapter has documented some issues to explore enroute to creating an integration of instructional and computer science in service to developing knowledge-based tutoring systems. Several accomplishments in the field were noted along with areas targeted for further work. For instance, representation and control issues seem well understood, whereas research into student models and diagnosis remains incomplete. Deep issues also remain in developing cognitive models of learning and teaching.

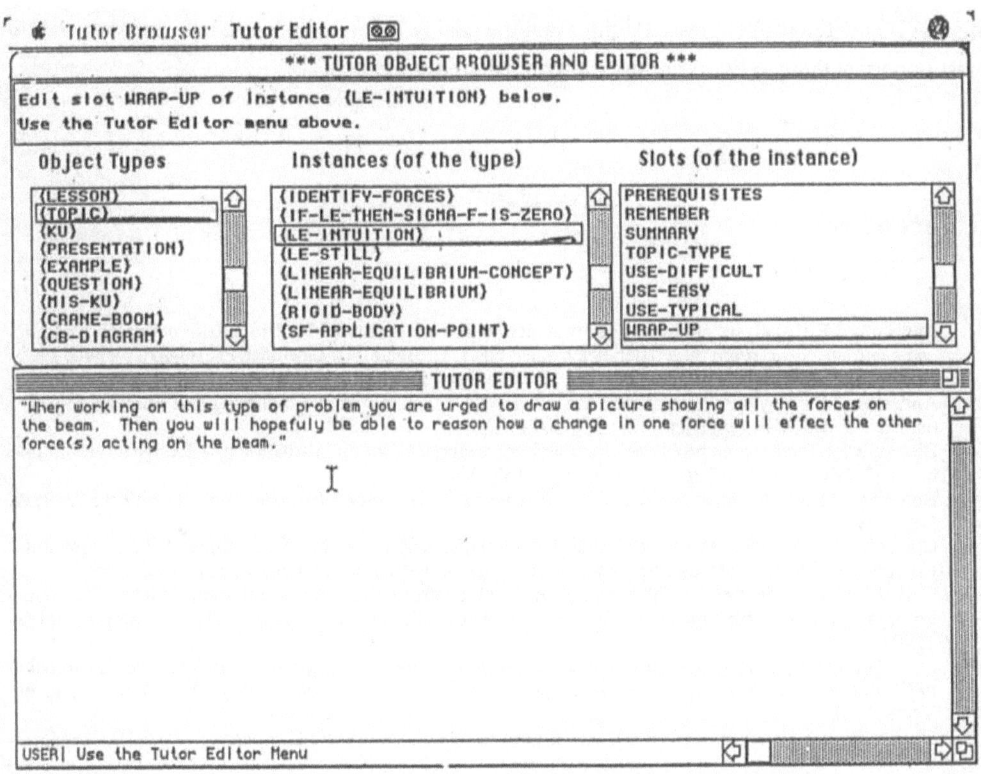

Figure 7: The Knowledge Acquisition Interface

Given the vision we defined for the field in the first two sections, a great deal of material remains for further study. However, we must also be aware of the needed context — i.e., repeated experimentation and exploration. As a field, our plate is very full. One small defeat, whether in a classroom or with regard to a single box, should not be considered a remarkable failure. Current limitations in cognitive modelling and understanding human learning should be placed in perspective. We ask a great deal of our science and engineering, and the technology may not yet be advanced enough to provide materials to solve our problems.

Winning or losing in a single subarea is not the point. Thus, if a system fails to achieve a powerful breakthrough we need not abandon the search. Rather, we should realize that a research effort might need to be redirected until such time as learning and teaching are more completely understood, or until technology permits a solution to problems currently beyond our ability. A more principled view of the field requires development of several broad-based research approaches in which success and failure are simply a part of the game. Coubertin, the founder of modern-day Olympics (of which Calgary was a recent host, as well as the host of this NATO conference) expressed it this way: the goal is "not to win, but to take part, just as the most important thing in life is not the triumph, but the struggle."

References

1. Anderson, J.R.: Analysis of student performance with the Lisp tutor. In: *Diagnostic monitoring of skill and knowledge acquisition* (N. Frederickson et al., eds.). Hillsdale, NJ: Lawrence Erlbaum Associates 1990
2. Anderson, J., & Reiser, B.: The Lisp tutor. *Byte* , 10, pp. 159-175 (1986)
3. Anderson, J.R., Boyle, C.F., Corbett, A.T., & Lewis, M.W.: Cognitive modeling and knowledge-based tutoring. *Artificial Intelligence,* 42, pp. 7-50 (1990)
4. Bloom, B.S.: The 2-sigma problem: The search for methods of group instruction as effective as one-to-one tutoring. *Educational Researcher,* 13., 6, pp. 4-16 (1984)
5. Bowscher, J.E.: *Educating America: Lessons learned in the nation's corporations.* New York: Wiley & Sons 1989
6. Clancey, W.J.: A practical authority shell for apprenticeship learning. Proceedings of the International Conference on Intelligent Tutoring Systems (ITS-88). University of Montreal, Canada, June 1988
7. Corbett, A., & Anderson, J.: The effect of feedback control on learning to program with the Lisp tutor. Proceedings of the 12th Annual Meeting of the Cognitive Science Society, pp. 702-708. Cambridge, MA 1990.
8. Dillenbourg, P.: The language shift: A mechanism for triggering metacognitive activities. In: *Foundations and frontiers in instructional computing systems* (P. Winne, & M. Jones, eds.). New York: Springer-Verlag 1991
9. Duckworth, E., Kelley, J., & Wilson, S.: AI goes to school. *Academic Computing,* pp. 6-10, 38-43, 62-63, November 1987
10. Goldman, H.D.: Instructional systems development in the United States Air Force. In: *Instructional development: The state of the art II* (R. Bass, & C. Dills, eds.). Dubuque: Kendall/Hunt 1984
11. Johnson, L., & Soloway, E.M.: Intention-based diagnosis of programming errors. Proceedings of the National Conference of Artificial Intelligence, pp. 369-380, Austin, Texas 1984
12. Lesgold, A., Laijoie, S.P., Bunzo, M., & Eggan, G.: A coached practice environment for an electronics troubleshooting job. In: *Computer assisted instruction and intelligent tutoring systems* (J. Larkin, R. Chabay, & C. Shefic, eds.). Hillsdale, NJ: Lawrence Erlbaum Associates 1990
13. Lewis, M., McArthur, D., Stasz, C., & Zmuidzinas, M.: Discovery-based tutoring in mathematics. In: Working notes: Artificial Intelligence Spring Symposium, AAAI, Palo Alto, CA 1990
14. Murray, T., & Woolf, B.: A knowledge acquisition framework facilitating multiple tutoring strategies. Working notes: Symposium on Knowledge-based Environments for Learning and Teaching, pp. 120-127, AAAI: Menlo Park, CA 1990
15. Schooler, L., & Anderson, J.: The disruptive potential of immediate feedback. Proceedings of the 12th Annual Meeting of the Cognitive Science Society, pp. 796-803, Cambridge, MA 1990
16. Servan-Schreiber, D.: From intelligent tutoring to computerized psychotherapy. Proceedings of the Sixth National Conference on Artificial Intelligence (AAAI-87), pp. 66-71, Los Altos, CA: Morgan Kaufmann 1987
17. Shute, V.: Rose garden promises of intelligent tutoring systems: Blossom or thorn? Paper presented at the Space Operations, Applications and Research (SOAR) Symposium (Contact V. Shute, AFHRL, Brooks Air Force Base, TX 78235-5601) 1990
18. Shute, V.J., Glaser, R., & Raghavan, K.: Inference and discovery in an exploratory laboratory. In: *Learning and individual differences* (P.L. Ackerman, R.J. Sternberg, & R. Glaser, eds.). New York: W.H. Freeman 1989

19. Singley, K.: The reification of goal structures in a calculus tutor: Effects on problem-solving performance. *Interactive Learning Environments,* 1, pp. 102-123 (1990)
20. Slovin, T., & Woolf, B. P.: A consultant tutor for personal development. In: Proceedings of the international conference on intelligent tutoring systems (C. Frasson, ed.). Dept. of Information, University of Montreal, Canada 1988
21. Stevens, A., & Collins, A.: The goal structure of a Socratic tutor. Proceedings of the Association for Computing Machinery Annual Conference (also available as BBN Report No. 3518 from Bolt Beranek and Newman Inc., Cambridge, Mass., 02138) 1977
22. Suthers, D.: The epistemological structure of explanation. In: Proceedings of AAAI 1990 Workshop on Explanation, Boston, July 1990
23. Suthers, D., & Woolf, B.: Accounting for the epistemological structure of explanation. In: Working notes of the AAAI 1990 Spring Symposium on Knowledge-based Environments for Learning and Teaching. AAAI, Menlo Park, CA, pp. 46-51. Also available as Technical Report 90-36, Computer and Information Science Dept., University of Massachusetts, Amherst, MA 1990
24. Wenger, E.: *Artificial intelligence and tutoring systems.* Los Altos, CA: Morgan Kaufmann 1988
25. Woods, W.: Transition network grammars for natural language analysis. *Communications of the ACM,* 13 (10), pp. 591-606 (1970)
26. Woolf, B.: Intelligent tutoring systems: A survey. In: *Exploring artificial intelligence* (H. Shrobe & the American Association for Artificial Intelligence, eds.). Palo Alto, CA: Morgan Kaufmann 1988
27. Woolf, B., & Cunningham, P.: Multiple knowledge sources in intelligent tutoring systems. *IEEE Expert,* Los Alamitos, CA, pp 41-54, Summer 1987
28. Woolf, B., & Murray, T.: A framework for representing tutorial discourse. International Joint Conference in Artificial Intelligence (IJCAI-87), Palo Alto, CA: Morgan Kaufmann, pp. 189-192 (1987)
29. Woolf, B., Murray, T., Suthers, D., & Schultz, K.: Knowledge primitives for tutoring systems. Proceedings of the International Conference on Intelligent Tutoring Systems (ITS88), University of Montreal, Canada, pp. 491-498 (1988)
30. Woolf, B., Soloway, E., Clancey, W.J., VanLehn, K., & Suthers, D.: Knowledge-based environments for teaching and learning. *AI Magazine,* 11, 5, pp. 74-77 (1991)

Phenomenographic Research and the Design of Diagnostic Strategies for Adaptive Tutoring Systems

Diana Laurillard

Institute of Educational Technology, Open University, Milton Keynes, England

Abstract: Adaptive tutoring systems require explicit information about the forms of misconception students have within the topic being taught. Phenomenographic research, which uses qualitative interview data to describe the "outcome space" for learning a specific topic, can provide that level of detail needed. The paper gives examples of this and argues that this approach is more tractable than student modelling and leads to a system architecture that combines knowledge of the student with the interactive interface to define a diagnostic strategy for an adaptive, though not intelligent tutoring system.

Keywords: phenomenography, phenomenology, qualitative research, student learning, diagnostic strategy, student modelling, Newtonian mechanics, adaptive tutoring system.

Introduction

There is a natural synergy between the outcomes of phenomenographic research and the requirements of adaptive tutoring systems. The latter require a detailed analysis of the different ways a topic is conceptualized, if the activities generated by the program are to address an individual's learning difficulties. Phenomenographic research provides the analysis of what students know about a topic, in a form that makes computer-based diagnosis possible, because it clarifies the logical relationship between the students' and the expert's conceptions of the topic. This paper illustrates these ideas with reference to a research and development project on students' conceptualizations of Newtonian mechanics.

NATO ASI Series, Vol. F 85
Adaptive Learning Environments
Edited by M. Jones and P. H. Winne

Student Modelling and Diagnosis

How can adaptive tutoring systems diagnose what a student needs to be taught? One strategy has been to use a student model. In a previous paper, I argued that generative student modelling of the type that generates possible faulty procedures from a complete expert procedure leads to unhelpful teaching [3]. Diagnostic systems built on generative student models will necessarily capture only the processing difficulties students have, or the gaps in their knowledge. In order to capture those misconceptions that are qualitatively different from the expert's knowledge, we need explicit descriptions of them, as they cannot be generated from expert knowledge.

Non-generative models of students are often little more than a log of what the student has done on the program so far — which topics they have met, their performance on tasks, their chosen route through the material, etc. These are useful, and all of them, especially performance data, can assist diagnosis. But this is no more than "dumb-CAL" aspires to. The attraction of student modelling is that it should enable the system to "know" the student in the way it "knows" the domain, via an explicit model. Any explicit model of student learning, however, would have to include components such as motivation, perception, and interpretation, and also cope with the instability of these across tasks (student learning strategies are highly context-dependent), the unknowability of how they interpret their perceptions, and the inconsistency of their beliefs and conceptualizations (students are known to hold incompatible beliefs, not unlike the rest of us).

The difficulties inherent in developing a usable student model make it a fascinating topic for cognitive science, but unsuitable for educational research and development. For the educationist there are fewer interesting spin-offs from the endeavour than there are for the cognitive scientist. There is a high risk that an explicit model of how students learn is unknowable and unlikely to be usable. For those with a mission to understand how students learn with a view to improving our ability to help them, the more fascinating problem is to make explicit *what* they know. The strategy is then to develop a diagnostic procedure that can discover what they know and use this to generate a suitable teaching strategy adaptive to the student's needs. The student model is then only a model of what they know, not how they came to know it.

Recent empirical studies in student learning have demonstrated that it is possible to determine the complete "outcome space" for a particular concept in terms of the possible ways it can be understood and misunderstood, i.e., all the possible learning outcomes. This current research paradigm has a natural synergy with the development of adaptive tutoring systems because the descriptions of misconceptions it supplies are exactly what is needed to develop a tutoring program that can perform systematic differential diagnoses of student knowledge. The completeness of the descriptions, their precision and the (so far) relatively small number of them for each topic area, make these empirically-generated findings invaluable for computer-based systems.

My aim in the next section is to show that this research methodology, now termed "phenomenographic," can supply the rigorous analysis of students' conceptions required by adaptive or intelligent tutoring systems.

Phenomenographic Methodology

Phenomenography derives its methodology from a phenomenological perspective on psychology. It describes (graphs) the phenomena of students' experience of learning a subject. As in phenomenology, it denies a dualism between the mental and the physical (see Marton's original paper [4]), and unites them in a "world-as-experienced" as the only reality we can have access to:

> From a phenomenographic perspective, then, knowledge is constituted through the internal relation between the knower (the subject) and the known (the object). Phenomena as experienced and understood are therefore what we should try to describe in our studies of learning [6].

One consequence of rejecting dualism is that we cannot expect there to be a consistent and coherent conceptual structure in the students' head, to be discovered and mapped for diagnostic purposes. For the individual, conceptions are embodied in an experience of an event, so they are context-dependent. However, by generalizing across a number of individuals' experiences of a topic through a set of tasks, it is possible to describe a consistent and coherent structure of understanding of that topic in all its possible forms:

> Presentation of logical relations between categories of description corresponding to different conceptions of the same phenomenon is the feature that most clearly distinguishes phenomenography from other kinds of qualitative analysis in social science and education [6].

The set of categories produced from a phenomenographic analysis should be generalizable beyond a particular group of subjects, and indeed has usually proved to be very easy to replicate in different institutions and different countries.

The value of this logically-related set of categories, or "outcome space," is that it offers an empirically-based and parsimonious description of how a topic is known. Most designers would agree that a tutoring system should be designed on the basis of empirical work to clarify students' conceptions of the subject. However, in spite of the considerable research into, for example, students' conceptions of Newtonian mechanics, it would be hard for a designer to derive a specific approach to the diagnosis and remediation of the topic. Clements [1] concludes that some students believe that "motion implies a force." Viennot [7] argues that students simultaneously hold Newtonian and non-Newtonian conceptions of force. He shows that for certain tasks students identify the correct Newtonian force, whereas for others, where the motion is in the opposite direction to the force, they impose a non-Newtonian force in the direction of motion — an elaboration of Clements' finding. Both used written answers. Watts and Zylberstajn [8] used interviews to derive similar findings, as did McDermott [5], who also found that students "lacked a consistent conceptual system" (ibid, p.30). There is universal agreement on the nature of the misconceptions, but for the tutorial designer these analyses give little help in suggesting how a computer might diagnose the form of misconception for an individual student. They provide evidence for the physics teacher that students do not understand force, but they do not present the teacher with a tool for diagnosis or for designing remedial teaching. The precise relationship between the different misconceptions is not defined, so it is not clear how they should be distinguished, and yet this is essential if remediation is to be properly targeted.

To illustrate the feasibility of diagnosing qualitative conceptions in an adaptive tutoring system, we can follow through a particular example based on research into students' conceptions in physics. It is a good area to choose for a contrastive analysis of methodologies, because it has been heavily researched in recent years, especially the domain of Newtonian mechanics, and yet the outcomes of the research have not fitted easily into the requirements of adaptive or intelligent tutoring systems, with the result that the research has made little difference to the design of such systems in that field.

Describing the Outcome Space

In order to describe the outcome space for a particular topic, the key steps are:

- decide on the topic
- generate questions to probe understanding
- pilot questions
- refine questions
- interview at least 20 students
- sort protocols into categories
- test reliability of categories with independent judges
- refine categories.

These simple statements belie the complexity of the process in action. Piloting the questions is most important because that is where the researcher discovers both the potential richness of the data, and the ease with which interviews could miss important data if questions are not put the right way, or if the interviewer is not tenacious enough in his or her probing. Similarly, sorting the protocols requires sustained concentration over a long period, as well as expert understanding of the topic, if the outcome space being generated is to accurately reflect the logical relations between student and expert conceptions. The following example illustrates the aspect of the process in action.

A current research project based at the University of Melbourne (see Note 2), is setting out to describe the outcome space for the concepts of Newtonian mechanics: speed, velocity, average speed, displacement, projectile motion, etc. Students at final school year and first year degree level are interviewed individually about how they conceptualize mechanics. The student is given a brief problem statement, such as the following:

> A ball inside a train is rolled backwards towards the back of the train. It travels 2m along the floor in 3 seconds, while the train travels forward at a constant speed of 10mps. Discuss the displacement of the ball in the 3 second interval of time.

Each student's response is audio-recorded. Up to five problems are covered within each interview lasting approximately one hour.

Once protocols are transcribed, two members of the research team independently analyze them, generating category descriptions of the qualitative differences in the students' conceptions for each problem. These categories are then discussed and finalized by the whole team.

Taking as an example, the interviews on Newton's Third Law, we can follow through the development of the outcome space, and the procedure for diagnosing a student's form of conception. In this section we consider the description of the outcome space.

For this problem students are first asked to state Newton's Third Law (if they cannot remember they are given a prepared statement of it). Their definitions are recorded, and sometimes referred back to later in the interview. Figure 1 shows three versions of the Law offered by students.

What is Newton's Third Law (the principle of action and reaction)? Please state it in your own words:

> When a body is at rest the forces on a system equal zero
>
> For every action there is an equal and opposite reaction
>
> Every force has an equal and opposite reaction at equilibrium

---

Figure 1: Students definitions of Newton's Third Law

Students are then asked to describe the forces acting on the two situations pictured in Figure 2. The protocols they generate, both oral and written, are recorded for analysis.

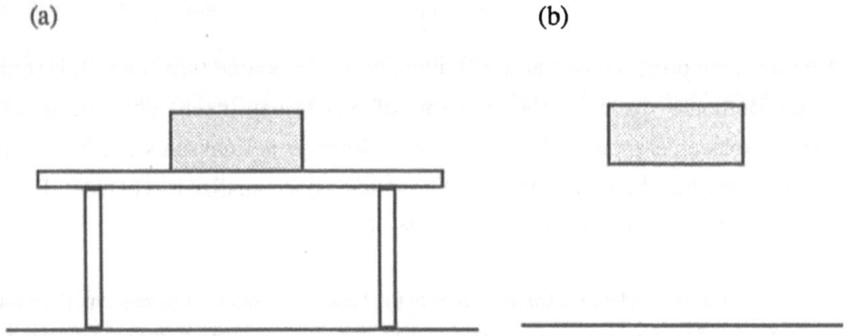

Figure 2: Students are asked to explain forces acting in each case

For this question the categories of conception have been defined in terms of the particular aspects of Newton's Third Law that they violate. Assuming that the Law can be stated in three parts:

L1 All forces are paired

L2 Paired forces are equal and opposite

L3 Paired forces act on different objects,

and using these definitions, categories of misconception can be defined as follows:

Category A describes the non-violation of all three. Protocols are often incomplete, in the sense that they miss out some obvious force pair, but since there are so many force pairs that could be named in the two diagrams, we could reasonably disregard omissions. There should be an absolute minimum, though; perhaps reaction forces could be named in the first diagram, and gravitational forces in the second.

Category B is equivalent to the violation of L3. This is most easily recognized as the pairing of different types of forces acting on the same body. Thus on the table, the box has equal and opposite gravitational and reaction forces acting on it. Equal and opposite forces are identified with equilibrium — it is not recognized that they are acting on two different bodies. Thus in free fall, gravitational and friction forces are both acting on the box. The imbalance between them leads to the violation of L2 and hence, to the logical conclusion that the Law does not apply to free fall. This worries some of these students and they tend to avoid that conclusion, though not always.

Category C is equivalent to a violation of L1 and L3. It logically entails the violation of L2 as well, but this is not always apparent. The main point is that this category fails to make sure that all forces are paired, and is most often manifested as only "mg" acting in the second diagram, with no paired and equal force on the earth. If asked, these students tend to draw the conclusion that the Law does not apply to free fall.

Examples of student protocols for Categories A, B, and C follow:

A: Forces are paired, are equal and opposite, and act on different objects.

"That's the attractive, well, gravitational force that's bringing the box towards the earth [mg on box acting down], . . . and this force here [F on earth acting up], well, it's got to be an opposite force, so this force here [mg] is the force exerted by the earth on the box . . . which has the same magnitude as that [F]." [MU72]

". . . they're all cancelling out each other, and here, um, the force of the earth, oh, box falling towards ground, yeah, the earth on the box is equal to the force of the box on the earth, but because the box's mass is so much less than the earth, it is the earth moves towards, I mean, not the earth moves, the box moves towards the earth." [UC13]

B: Forces are paired but do not act on different bodies.

"[The forces in the second case] are just the weight of the box acting down and there's air resistance acting up . . . if this box had been falling from an aeroplane it might have reached terminal velocity. As I said before, it's constant so that means, like, the forces could be equal because gravity pulling down and air resistance up, they could be the same. Then, like, if it just fell off the table, it hasn't got a chance to reach that. The force acting down is bigger so that's why it falls down to the ground." [MU71]

"There is a net force, um, which is, which is present, and that's what is causing the acceleration . . . the force of gravity which is the mg force minus the component which is the resistance." [MU89]

"It [Newton's Third Law] applies to when they're in equilibrium and at rest, but when the actual system is trying to reach equilibrium it doesn't apply." [MU1]

C: Forces are defined as equal and opposite, but are not always paired, and do not always act on different objects.

"The only force acting is the force of gravity which is making the box accelerate towards the ground at 9.8m/s, so there's movement because there's, um, an unbalanced force." [MU69]

"Ah, the second one, no table, so, ah, the box has still got gravity acting on it. Ah, force equals mg, and seeing there's no other forces coming from anywhere, ah, presumably, it doesn't tell us that there's no air resistance, but going by the others it's not going to worry too much, so it's just going to fall towards the ground with constant acceleration.... I'd only apply Newton's Third Law where there's no resulting acceleration for a thing, whereas this box is accelerating as it comes downwards, so I don't know, I wouldn't use Newton at all here." [MU3]

These categories provide us with a working definition of the "outcome space" for the concept of force as represented in Newton's Third Law.

The importance of finding a *complete* description of the outcome space is that if teaching is to be effective, then new ideas must be introduced in relation to existing ideas, compared with them, contrasted if necessary. Any description of new information will carry with it many unspoken assumptions, and the teacher must be aware that many incompatible, but unchallenged, assumptions might form the intellectual bed into which the new ideas are sown, and they may be very strange bed-fellows. If the teacher knows the possible ways in which an idea can be conceptualized, then it is possible to make explicit the assumptions which are not compatible with this new idea, and to challenge them directly.

We could look for inadequate learning skills on the part of the student to describe what is happening here. Certainly, if students were to employ a careful analysis of the teacher's spoken discourse they should be able to discern the internal problems with their initial unwarranted assumptions, and so achieve a concept qualitatively similar to the teacher's. But this is just one discourse among many, building on earlier ones, and possibly building on sand, if those too were inadequately understood. It is quite possible for even the conscientious student to be overburdened with so many ill-fitting ideas that it becomes more and more difficult to sort them out.

Consider the student trying to make sense of Newton's Third Law. It is frequently stated in its briefest form — "action and reaction are equal and opposite" — and not just by teachers, but by text-books as well. So the student may not be made aware of L1 and L3 in the first place. Applying just L2 to situation (a) the student recognizes that for it to work at all the forces must be paired, and so uses L1 implicitly in describing the situation. But which forces are paired? The words "equal and opposite" suggest a balance, and the student is inevitably reminded of "equilibrium," a familiar everyday concept that also balances equal and, in a sense, opposite forces. The box is in equilibrium because the weight force due to the earth is equal to the reaction force from the table. This is true, but it is not the application of Newton's Third Law. The problem is that this incorrect application appears to work in this, and indeed many other cases. It is easy for the mistake to go unchallenged.

If that is the way the student is thinking, then the challenge comes only with situation (b), which is not in equilibrium. Working still with L2, and applying that, it is clear that something has to oppose the force of gravity in the absence of the table, and that can only be air resistance. It must be something also acting on the box, since they still believe that equilibrium is relevant, i.e., the forces *on the box* must be equal and opposite. Because L3 has never been made clear, they are stuck with that notion, even though it is quite clear that the box is not in equilibrium; hence the desperate conclusion that Newton's Law applies once the system achieves equilibrium. In this situation, the student is struggling with incompatible assumptions and the key, L3, is simply not available to him/her.

Students with conception C have much less of an intellectual struggle because they do not insist on L1. For them, action and reaction are equal and opposite if there happens to be a reaction. So in case (a), clearly there is a reaction from the table, but in case (b) there is nothing to react, and they are perfectly happy to say that there is an unpaired force mg, and therefore, if pushed, that Newton's Law does not apply in this situation.

We have to acknowledge, therefore, that the student trying to learn Newton's Third Law is handicapped at the start, if the Law is not given in its full form. The misconceptions that arise do so from a reasonable, if not a rigorously logical, attempt to make sense of an incomplete formulation.

In generating computer-based teaching material around this topic, we have to be aware, therefore, that students bring not only ideas about equilibrium but also those reformulations, or misconceptions of the concept of force. If the teaching is to address these ideas, it must first diagnose which ones the student holds. It can be done by interview; can it be done by computer?

Diagnosing the Student's Conception

The problem of diagnosing the form of misconception can be tackled by analyzing the key questions in interview protocols that yielded answers clearly identifiable as belonging to a particular category. The form of dialogue cannot be the same as an interview when conducted by a computer, but it can mirror a lot of what happens if we analyze and can then formalize the structure of the interview.

Taking the 17 interviews carried out for this concept, those questions which elicited categorizable student answers were:

- What is Newton's Third Law?
- What forces are acting in (a)?
- What forces are acting in (b)?
- How does magnitude of forces compare (for each pair given)?
- How does the Third Law apply in (a)?
- How does the Third Law apply in (b)?

In many cases, the students' replies needed coaxing through use of follow-up questions such as "Could you say a bit more," "Could you describe that in more detail," etc. A computer-based dialogue would have to include these as well in order to be sure of generating sufficient student input to allow the diagnosis to take place.

When student answers to these questions are compared with the forms defined in the categories, we can generate the following analysis of the way the questions are likely to be answered for each type of conception.

1. What is Newton's Third Law?
   A: L1 All forces are paired
      L2 Paired forces are equal and opposite
      L3 Paired forces act on different objects
   B: L1 and L2
   C: L2

2. What forces are acting in (a)?
   A: 2 gravitational, 2 resistive
   B: 1 gravitational, 1 resistive
   C: ditto

3. What forces are acting in (b)?
   A: gravitational, may also state resistive
   B: pairs gravitational with resistive
   C: gravitational only (on box only)

4. How does magnitude of forces compare for each pair given?
   A: equal in all cases
   B: in case (b) leads to admission that g and r forces are not equal
   C: equal in (a); no paired forces in (b)

5. How does the Third Law apply in (a)?
   A: force of box on table equals force of table on box (and box/earth, earth/table)
   B: weight of box equals reaction of table on box
   C: ditto

6. How does the Third Law apply in (b)?
   A: force of box on earth equals force of earth on box.
   B: at terminal velocity / on hitting ground /when reaches equilibrium
   C: does not apply

Question 1 is important because it requires the student to articulate his/her view of what the Law says, and this can be referred back to later. It does not provide the final description for a student with conception A or B, because he/she frequently omits L1 and L3, although he/she turns out to be implicit in what he/she says elsewhere.

Question 2 allows us to discriminate A conceptions from B and C. Question 3 allows us to discriminate between B and C as well. However, without the context of Newton's Third Law having been set by Question 1, it is quite possible that B conceptions would lead to only gravitational forces being listed here.

Question 4 is important for leading the student with conception B towards a contradiction which prepares the way for remedial teaching.

Question 5 provides a student-constructed description of what he/she indicated in Question 2, which can be used later in further computer-generated descriptions of what is happening.

Question 6 serves a similar function for (b), and also provides the key to establishing that students with C conception have to confront the fact that the Law apparently sometimes does not apply.

Student-constructed input to these questions requires careful analysis for computer diagnosis to be possible. Existing interview protocols provide a valuable data-base for generating the forms the replies can take. In similar tutorial dialogues used in Open University courses, where student input is continuously monitored, it can take up to 50 developmental testers to give the program an acceptable level of diagnostic performance, i.e., (almost) never evaluating a right answer as wrong or a wrong answer as right. Managing this kind of dialogue is one of the areas where this approach to adaptive tutoring requires input from artificial intelligence projects [2].

We have now established sufficient certainty about the way a dialogue might be conducted, that it becomes possible to construct a program capable of determining how any individual conceptualizes this aspect of force. Figures 1-4 show how the dialogue might proceed. In each screen dialogue, student inputs are underlined. Figure 1 shows various possible versions of the Law. Figure 3 shows how Question 3 discriminates between all three forms of conception. Figure 4 shows how a student with conception B could be led to the non-viability of his/her application. The advantage of this kind of diagnostic procedure is that it relies upon the fact that the student's conceptual structure will be manifested in the form of his/her interaction with the system. It does not have to be known explicitly. The form of its manifestation in the context of a particular task does have to be known explicitly, and this *can* be known, through phenomenography. Furthermore, because phenomenography characterizes forms of conception, not types of student, it is possible to use the same categories in a different task context. It is not clear whether it would be possible to predict the form that the dialogue should

Conception A answer:

This shows a box falling towards the ground.

Place arrows to mark all the forces acting in the picture.

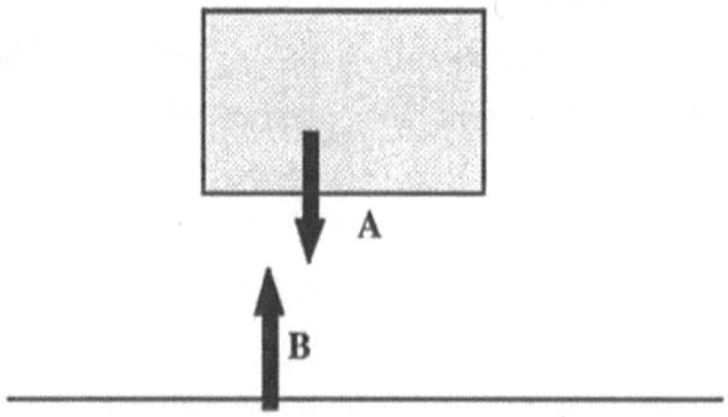

What is A?

Force of box on earth

Conception B answers:

This shows a box falling towards the ground.

Place arrows to mark all the forces acting in the picture.

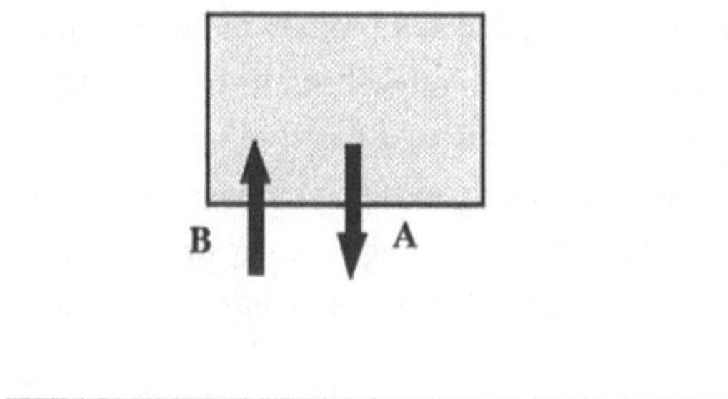

What is A?

Weight of box

What is B?

Air resistance

Conception C answers:

This shows a box falling towards the ground.

Place arrows to mark all the forces acting in the picture.

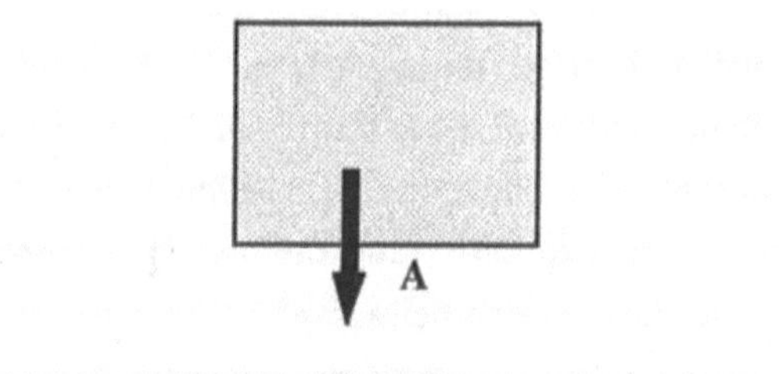

What is A?

Weight of box

Figure 3: Students' descriptions of forces acting

This shows a box falling towards the ground.

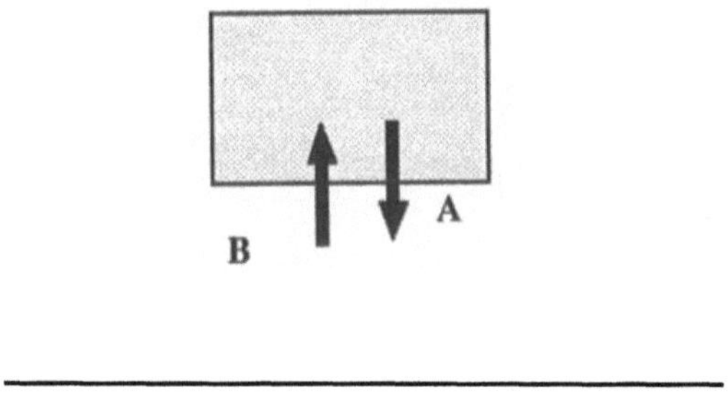

What is A?

Weight of box

What is B?

Air resistance

How do magnitudes of A and B compare?

A is greater, so the box falls to the ground

But you said for the Law to hold, action and reaction must be equal and opposite.

But not until equilibrium is reached

Figure 4: Conception B description of forces acting

take to reveal the forms of conception. This is an empirical question that has never been put to the test. If the research has to be done for every task in order to generate the form of dialogue, then this is a disadvantage of the method over the goals of the AI approach, which sets out to model the student precisely so that their conceptual structure in any context can be known to the system.

To summarize, then, the methods of phenomenography can be used to (i) derive diagnostic questions, (ii) ensure the completeness of the diagnostic procedure, (iii) remove the problem of student modelling to the form the dialogue interaction should take.

Concluding Points

The implication of the argument put forward in this paper is that the future for the design of adaptive tutoring systems will be determined by the type of preparatory empirical research that offers the best description of how students learn. There has been little success in the cognitive approach, building on psychological learning theories. Educational research has not produced a cognitive model of how students learn. On the other hand, it is increasingly recognized that descriptive studies of what students know produce usable and replicable findings. If a student model is not possible then the standard architecture for intelligent tutoring systems (Figure 5) will have to be revised.

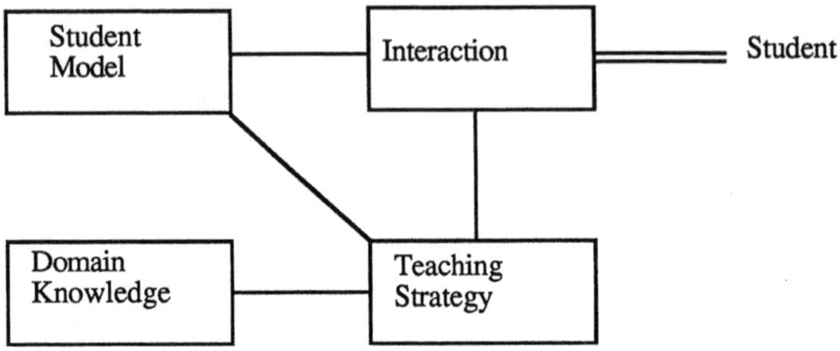

Figure 5: Standard architecture for intelligent tutoring system

It follows from the discussion on the form of the diagnostic process that the student model has to remain implicit, manifested in the way the interaction develops, and therefore the two should be combined, as in Figure 6. The teaching strategy used in the succeeding instructional phase would then make use of what the diagnostic phase discovers.

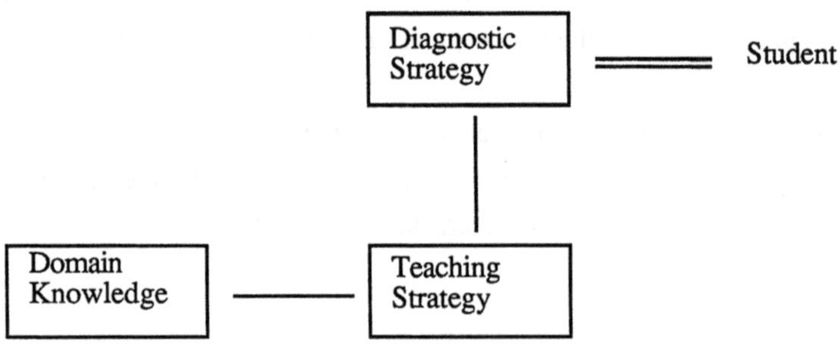

Figure 6: Revised architecture for intelligent tutoring system

In this paper I am proposing the combination of two well-established research areas, student learning and intelligent tutoring. The current phenomenographic paradigm for research on student learning, with its emphasis on exhaustive description of the phenomena, is precisely what the field of intelligent tutoring systems needs for further well-founded theory-development. Conversely, empirically-derived descriptions of student learning are most rigorously tested through implementation in well-defined tutoring systems. If we are ever to capture the intelligence of the teacher in tutoring systems, then perhaps we should begin to exploit the natural symbiosis between these two fields.

Notes

A version of this paper was given at the Third European Conference of Research on Learning and Instruction, Universidad Autonoma de Madrid, Spain, 4 - 7 September 1989.

The data described in this paper have been generated from a research project based at the Centre for the Study of Higher Education at the University of Melbourne, directed by Dr. Paul Ramsden. The author is an external collaborator on the project.

Acknowledgements

While the paper was written by the author, the following members of the project team (listed alphabetically) all contributed to the data collection and analysis: John Bowden, Gloria dall'Alba and Elaine Martin, ERADU, Royal Melbourne Institute of Technology; Ference Marton, Department of Education and Educational Research, University of Gothenburg, Sweden; Geoffrey Masters, Australian Council of Educational Research; Paul Ramsden and Andreas Stephanou, CSHE, University of Melbourne, Australia, and Eleanor Walsh, Latrobe University, Melbourne, Australia.

References

1. Clement, J.: Students' preconceptions in introductory mechanics. *American Journal of Physics*, 50, pp. 66-71 (1982)
2. Elsom-Cook, M.: Dialogue and teaching styles. Centre for Information Technology in Education, Technical Report No 62, Open University, UK 1988
3. Laurillard, D. M.: The pedagogical limitations of generative student models. *Instructional Science*, 17, pp. 235-250 (1988)
4. Marton, F.: Phenomenography — describing conceptions of the world around us. *Instructional Science*, 10, pp. 177-200 (1981)
5. McDermott, L.: Research on conceptual understanding in mechanics. *Physics Today*, pp. 24-32, July 1984

6. Ramsden, P.: Phenomenographic research and the measurement of understanding: An investigation of students' conceptions of speed, distance and time. *International Journal of Education Research*, 13 (1990)
7. Viennot, L.: Spontaneous reasoning in elementary dynamics. *European Journal of Science Education*, 1, pp. 205-221 (1979)
8. Watts, D., & Zylbersztajn, A.: A survey of some children's ideas about force. *Physics Education*, 16, pp. 360-365 (1981)

Part 5

Models of Students' Metacognition, Motivation, and Learning Strategies

Models of Students' Metacognition, Motivation, and Learning Strategies

Ellen Mandinach[1] and Jim Greer[2]

[1]Educational Testing Service, Princeton, NJ, USA
[2]ARIES Laboratory, Department of Computational Science, University of Saskatchewan, Saskatoon, Canada

The two papers presented in this section use the psychological construct metacognition as the substantive foundation for tutor development. However, the motivation for selecting the construct and its implementation in the design process reflect some fundamental differences between the backgrounds and perspectives of the two authors. Sharon Derry is an educational psychologist with extensive experience in the development of computer-based tutors. Pierre Dillenbourg has formal training in both educational psychology and artificial intelligence.

Let us approach the two papers first with some reflections on metacognition and some history of the construct. Metacognition gets at the very heart of one of education's primary objectives — the notion of transfer. It recently has been the focus of substantial research and theoretical attention (e.g., [17, 18, 19]). The construct also centers around an ongoing debate in the cognitive and instructional literature — the extent to which such skills are applicable across tasks or are specific to domains or content areas [8, 12]. Processes have been identified that are thought to organize a learner's cognition. These processes have been termed metacognitive [2, 6, 7], executive [1, 13], and self-regulated [3].

It is the hope of educators and researchers that these higher-order thinking skills are trainable and transferable. As Voss [15] notes, transfer is central to all learning. However, not all learners are equally likely to be able to transfer skills from one domain to another. Similarly, not all tasks [5, 10, 11], instructional programs, or skills are likely to engender transfer. Yet, according to some (e.g., [9]), the general processes are not sufficient to produce learning. They must be embedded within a content area to provide the appropriate environment in which to cultivate and apply the skills.

The two tutor projects described here address some of these theoretical and practical issues, one in terms of a concrete set of examples, and the other more in terms of a philosophical perspective. Derry's paper is very concrete, grounding her description of a cognitive-mentorship system (CMS) for arithmetic word problems in relevant psychological and instructional theories. She uses the techniques of artificial intelligence to implement these theories in her CMS. Dillenbourg, in contrast, uses formal language in providing a technical approach to the construction of a computer architecture that espouses a specific philosophical perspective. The psychological construct seems secondary to principles by which the

NATO ASI Series, Vol. F 85
Adaptive Learning Environments
Edited by M. Jones and P. H. Winne

architecture is delineated. Interestingly, both authors focus on the same two prominent theories in which metacognition is embedded, and they select different perspectives to implement. Derry selected a Vygotskian approach, whereas Dillenbourg opted for primarily a Piagetian orientation with some Vygotskian aspects.

The theoretical perspectives chosen directly influence the design and conceptualization of the two systems. Derry reviews both theoretical positions and describes the benefits and problems of each perspective. She notes that a Piagetian-based system would emphasize exploration with the tutor serving as a catalyst, whereas a Vygotskian tutor espouses cognitive apprenticeship, with the system serving as a mentor. A problem with the former orientation also is one of its strengths.

The Piagetian constructivist approach emphasizes the role of exploration without inclusion of explicit instructional strategies. Discovery learning can be a powerful method, particularly for abstract problems because it forces students to assume responsibility for their own learning. However, there are two problems endemic here. First, many students have difficulties with abstractions. They are unable to link such concepts to concrete entities. Instead, they need tasks that require real-world applications in order to benefit from instruction. Second is the problem of responsibility for learning. Fundamentally, this is an aptitude-by-treatment interaction (ATI) issue [4]. Not all students are able to assume the necessary responsibility and acquire knowledge through the discovery learning paradigm. They require more direct instruction. Thus, the constructivist approach may not be appropriate for some students.

The Vygotskian [16] orientation seeks to avoid this problem by implementing what is known as the "zone of proximal development" within a tutor. The emphasis here is on the mentor or tutor first modelling for the student appropriate cognitive behaviour. Through a sequence of shared activities, the tutor gradually shifts the requirements of performance to the student and begins to fade the modelling support. This seems like a much more logical and implementable theory for tutor design than discovery learning.

Indeed, this is the perspective that Derry implements in her system. She has three foci: (a) to describe the architecture of a tutor that can simulate decisions human mentors would make at various stages of instruction; (b) to implement this architecture within a specific content area such as arithmetic word problems; and (c) to design a system that addresses the acquisition and development of metacognition. Derry uses a three-part definition of metacognition that centers on transfer, intelligence about oneself, and the ability to regulate one's own behaviour. It is important to acknowledge that there are probably as many definitions of and subcomponents for metacognition as there are individuals conducting research in the field. For someone familiar with the field, Derry has narrowed her focus to a small set of components and a workable, operational definition. It is reflected in the discussion of what she calls her three decision-making points. Global planning, considered the most important, is in essence the system model for a student's knowledge. It is the knowledge of a student's performance with respect to the curriculum objectives. An important point Derry makes is the need for a holistic approach which relaxes the lock-step procedures often found in many tutors (see [14] for details). Such lock-step procedures fail to consider individual differences, instead maintaining the integrity of the tutorial sequence.

The other two decision-making points are local planning and local intervention. The former focusses on more immediate learning goals that lead to problem solving. The latter is concerned both with remediation and diagnosis. Intervention is not simply error correction, but includes meaningful instruction directed toward solutions. In keeping with the Vygotskian conceptions of modelling and the prominent role of the mentor, it is interesting to note that the very higher-order skills that Derry's system is designed to develop in students are mirrored in the architecture of the tutor.

Whereas Derry's tutor focusses on a domain dependent content area (i.e., arithmetic problem solving) per se, but also the more transferable skills of metacognition, Dillenbourg's system seems to be relatively generic. There is no domain imbedded within his proposed framework, nor is there really an operationalization of the metacognitive skills on which his system is said to focus. An example would help to concretize his proposed system.

Dillenbourg uses the metaphor of a lift or elevator within a pyramid as a system by which a student can acquire metacognitive skills. The computer helps students to learn and perform tasks they were unable to do previously. He views the system as a "constructorium" in which students observe their behaviour and construct a structure of their knowledge states. The metaphor comes into play in that there is an infinite number of hierarchically constructed levels within the pyramid. Levels of cognition or learning occur as the lift rises and falls. However, it is unclear from the paper how these transitions occur (i.e., gradually, in an all-or-none manner, etc.) and what they mean in terms of skill acquisition. Dillenbourg uses language shifts to clarify how the dynamics within the pyramid function. Such a language shift allows the learner to pass qualitative jumps in learning. Learning has quantitative and qualitative aspects that are difficult to integrate. We can improve qualitatively our skills, by compilation, until we reach some threshold related to the limits of our working memory. Beyond that, we need a qualitative change that provides us with more powerful concepts. The language shift supports this change by associating at each level the actions performed by the learner (command language) with representation (description language) that will be used as actions at the next level. The interest of the language shift idea is to translate a well-known psychological process (reflected abstraction, development), into something that can be understood by the system designer (command language, description).

Although Piagetian in its hierarchical, stage-like conceptualization, the Dillenbourg system also contains shades of Vygotsky's "zone of proximal development." The objective of the system is to transfer control of learning from the tutor to the student in a progressive manner. As the student moves up the lift, there is a subsequent reduction in the role played by the tutor as well as fading of the apprenticeship.

Dillenbourg advocates fully integrating learning theories with the design of computer-based learning environments. Not only does a particular learning theory affect the ultimate design of a computer system that attempts to provide learning experiences consistent with that theory, but the converse should also be considered. That is, computer-based learning environments have such a profound impact on instruction that learning theories must be enhanced to accommodate this new partner in the educational enterprise. An instructional scientist might take exception to this notion, holding the belief that computer-based learning systems are tools that merely deliver instruction and can never approach the subtlety of a teacher or tutor. On the other hand, Dillenbourg optimistically looks to representing and supporting the metacognitive components of abstraction, control, and transfer; in a sense redefining instructional theory to suit the computer-based learning environment .

It is important to realize that Dillenbourg does not propose a specific system, but rather a generic architecture for metacognition. As a complete "deployable" system, his preliminary design is overly simplified. He presents, instead, a formal language for examining educational actions. The important argument is whether or not the language is sufficiently expressive to describe the necessary educational actions, while at the same time being sufficiently constrained to gain computational advantage from its use. He goes on to demonstrate how this language can be applied to an analysis of the general components of metacognition. This contribution is one of representation and offers a requirements analysis of the sorts of functions (operations) that a computer-based learning environment must possess in order to reason about metacognitive issues.

Transfer is tied to the notion of lift ascension. Learning results from examples across which transfer can occur. Such transfer can be used to promote the acquisition of metacognitive skills. According to Dillenbourg, interaction patterns within a particular system define the metacognitive concepts. The notion of transfer is not sufficiently explored or operationalized in terms of a theory of learning or within the system. What really is needed is a precise definition of metacognition, its component processes, and what constitutes evidence of transfer in terms of a concrete example of a system. The architecture that Dillenbourg proposes will need to be refined further into an actual computer system before it can be evaluated fully.

We have here two very different papers that reflect the distinctions between the author's primary disciplines. Despite these differences, Derry and Dillenbourg touch on many of the same issues and concepts, each from their own perspective. The five main issues that seemed to have emerged are domain dependence, abstraction, control, transfer, and the operationalization within the two systems of metacognition and its subcomponents. All are based on the assumptions espoused by the theories of learning embedded in the tutors. They are both theoretical and technical decisions. Moreover, the design decisions are not all-or-none points. Instead, they must be seen as flexible points along a continuum. Derry provides a concrete example and a discussion of learning theories. Dillenbourg takes a more philosophical and abstract approach to the issue of metacognition per se, but contributes a precise, well defined formalism that can represent metacognitive action. Yet, both authors raise a number of interesting issues, complex design and theoretical decisions, and methods in their work. Perhaps what is most promising is that both Derry and Dillenbourg are working toward the lofty goal of integrating instructional and computer science. It is an objective for which they must be commended. The road will not be easy nor will the design decisions be straightforward. However, one day we hope that both of these systems will enable students to rise to the top of the pyramid of metacognitive skills.

References

1. Belmont, J. M., Butterfield, E. C., & Ferretti, R. P.: To secure transfer of training instruct self-management skills. In: *How and how much can intelligence be increased* (D. K. Detterman & R. J. Sternberg, eds.). Norwood, NJ: Ablex 1982
2. Brown, A. L.: Knowing when, where, and how to remember: A problem of metacognition. In: *Advances in instructional psychology* (R. Glaser, ed.). Vol. 1, Hillsdale, N.J.: Lawrence Erlbaum Associates 1978
3. Corno, L., & Mandinach, E. B.: The role of cognitive engagement in classroom learning and motivation. *Educational Psychologist*, 18, pp. 88-108 (1983)
4. Cronbach, L. J., & Snow, R. E.: *Aptitude and instructional methods*. New York: Irvington 1977
5. Doyle, W.: Academic work. *Review of Educational Research*, 53, pp. 159-199 (1983)
6. Flavell, J. H.: Metacognitive aspects of problem solving. In: *The nature of intelligence* (L. B. Resnick, ed.). Hillsdale, N.J.: Lawrence Erlbaum Associates 1976
7. Flavell, J. H.: Metacognition and cognitive monitoring. *American Psychologist*, 34, pp. 906-911 (1979)
8. Glaser, R.: Education and thinking. *American Psychologist*, 39, pp. 93-104 (1984)
9. Resnick, L. B.: *Education and learning to think*. Washington, D.C.: National Academy Press 1987
10. Rigney, J. W.: Learning strategies: A theoretical perspective. In: *Learning strategies* (H. F. O'Neil, Jr., ed.). New York: Academic Press 1978
11. Rigney, J. W.: Cognitive learning strategies and dualities in information processing. In: *Aptitude, learning, and instruction* (R. E. Snow, P. A. Federico, & W. E. Montague, eds.). Vol. 1, Hillsdale, NJ: Lawrence Erlbaum Associates 1980
12. Simon, H. A.: Identifying basic abilities underlying intelligent performance of complex tasks. In: *The nature of intelligence* (L. B. Resnick, ed.). Hillsdale, N.J.: Lawrence Erlbaum Associates 1976
13. Snow, R. E.: Aptitude processes. In: *Aptitude, learning, and instruction* (R. E. Snow, P. A. Federico, & W. E. Montague, eds.). Vol. 1, Hillsdale, NJ: Lawrence Erlbaum Associates 1980
14. Snow, R. E., & Mandinach, E. B.: *Integrating assessment and instruction: A research and development agenda*. Princeton, NJ: Educational Testing Service (In press)
15. Voss, J. F.: Cognition and instruction: Toward a cognitive theory of learning. In: *Cognitive psychology and instruction* (A. M. Lesgold, J. W. Pellegrino, S. D. Fokkema, & R. Glaser, eds.). New York: Plenum Press 1978
16. Vygotsky, L. S.: *Mind in society*. Cambridge: Harvard University Press 1978
17. Weinert, F. E. & Kluwe, R. H. (eds.): *Metacognition, motivation, and understanding*. Hillsdale, NJ: Lawrence Erlbaum Associates 1987

18. Zimmerman, B. J. (ed.): Self-regulated learning and academic achievement [Special issue]. *Educational Psychologist*, 25 (1990)
19. Zimmerman, B. J. & Schunk, D. H. (eds.): *Self-regulated learning and academic achievement: Theory, research, and practice.* New York: Springer-Verlag 1989

Metacognitive Models of Learning and Instructional Systems Design

Sharon J. Derry

Department of Psychology and Learning Systems Institute, Florida State University, Tallahasee, FL, USA

Abstract: This paper examines two currently popular models of interactive learning. While both emphasize the importance of acquiring metacognitive intelligence, each represents a different view of how metacognitive intelligence is best learned. The first is a neo-Piagetian model that views metacognitive learning as a by-product of interactions with an environment that has been carefully designed. This model characterizes the student as a "reflective explorer" and places instructional systems in roles as catalysts that support the student by making abstract ideas and thinking processes the objects of reflection, experimentation and argument. The second approach, based on Vygotskian psychology, places the student in the role of cognitive apprentice, while the system becomes a cooperating, empathic mentor. This approach characterizes metacognitive learning as a process of gradually assuming more responsibility for what initially is a shared problem-solving activity. Although the cognitive apprenticeship model is probably more powerful, apprenticeship interactions are complex and may be impossible to accomplish with computers given current technology. However, developing the required technology is a worthwhile long-term goal for instructional computing research.

Keywords: metacognition, Piaget, Vygotsky, constructivism, reflection, cognitive apprenticeship, artificial intelligence, computer-assisted instruction, instructional systems design.

Introduction

A reflective glance at headlines of almost any daily newspaper confirms that we live in a world fraught with costly slips and errors of reasoning that could be prevented. Consider the

NATO ASI Series, Vol. F 85
Adaptive Learning Environments
Edited by M. Jones and P. H. Winne

following excerpts from associated press stories appearing in the Tallahassee Democrat during July, 1990:

Red Cross may have failed to report AIDS-contaminated blood.

PHILADELPHIA -- The American Red Cross failed to notify federal authorities about 230 cases in which patients may have contracted AIDS through contaminated blood transfusions, The Philadelphia Inquirer reported Tuesday.

In at least four cases, patients died as a result of contaminated blood. . . .

It said the agency found that the Red Cross lacked procedures "for reviewing and tracking transfusion-associated AIDS cases by national (headquarters) . . . ."

The FDA report also said that national Red Cross officials have not updated their procedures for handling error and accident reports since July 1981, calling those procedures inadequate.

Kodak planned test run: Hubble mirror flaws were never caught

WASHINGTON -- An unsuccessful bidder for the manufacture of the Hubble Space Telescope mirrors proposed a test that might have detected any focussing flaw, but NASA chose a company that did not include testing in its proposal, a NASA official said Tuesday. . . .

NASA officials gave the optical systems contract to Perkin-Elmer Corp., now called Hughes Danbury Optical Systems Inc., which did not offer the testing. The space agency never ordered the tests on the ground they were too expensive.

In addition, consider the imaginary entry that could have appeared in my diary last week (if I actually kept a diary):

Mystery mail still missing: U.S. Post Office claims no responsibility

SEPTEMBER 17, 1990 — Have been in Pittsburgh since August 27, but have received no forwarded mail. I have run up what will surely be a huge phone bill speaking to various postal officials, but none can offer an explanation or a method for correcting, or even diagnosing, the problem. My old carrier does appear to be forwarding my mail to the correct address, but my new carrier is not receiving it. Mysteriously, some direct mail also is missing — including several much-needed reimbursement checks.

SEPTEMBER 18, 1990 — Finally received two envelopes of mail forwarded from former postman, who indicated that he would not send any more mail to the central markup unit, which appears to be losing it. Although he had confirmed my address with me over the phone, both envelopes were addressed incorrectly, one to the wrong street number (722 instead of 772) and one to the wrong apartment number (Apt. C instead of C-5)! I also received one long-lost check forwarded by my family to an incorrect street number (172). Still, no word on where my forwarded mail has gone. The incompetency crisis is upon us!

The stories cited above are similar in that they provide examples of the kinds of common, everyday mistakes that waste and destroy both the human and non-human resources of our world. In addition, they are alike because of what they do not represent. None of the stories illustrates any mistake that is due to misconception or lack of technical content knowledge. Rather, errors in these stories can best be described using terms such as *carelessness*, *lack of effort*, and *failure to "follow through."* These types of mistakes represent instances of *metacognitive failure*. My argument is that an important focus for schools and training programs is the avoidance of costly metacognitive failure.

Metacognition Described

Prior to defining the terms *metacognition* and *metacognitive failure,* a context will be supplied by sharing with the reader a little of my own theoretical world view of the mind and how it works.

My first assumption is that human-machine interactions of any complexity can appropriately be conceptualized as the output of some cognitive information-processing system X. Thus, the behaviour and thoughts of a student solving a mathematics story problem are the outputs of a cognitive system whose components work together for the purpose of solving mathematics story problems. If two students and a computer join together to solve story problems, then information processing system X consists of all the capacities and processes that are contributed by different players and that operate in concert in an effort to achieve that goal. Thus conceived, cognitive system X could represent a transient artifact of a current goal — the collection of capabilities mobilized for a particular problem-solving situation. This is my view of "situated cognition." However, whenever particular collections of capacities and processes frequently work together and call upon one another to solve problems and achieve goals, the result is a system that achieves a certain degree of stability and permanence. I follow the connectionist argument to some extent, for I do not believe that crystalized cognitive systems exist in the head as such, but rather that various fundamental capabilities evolve that gradually, through experience and learning, develop propensities for working together as coherent, intelligent entities. Because such higher cognitive systems are situated creations, their boundaries are appropriately viewed as fuzzy and imprecise.

Stable cognitive systems are like "bureaucracies" where, in service of their goals, higher-level cognitive "agencies" utilize and coordinate their lower-order "agents" [24]. A somewhat ill-structured hierarchy of capabilities is thus envisioned. In a stable system, one part of the glue that binds the bureaucracy together is the concept of a subject domain — that set of real-world problems that requires the system's bureaucratic services and for which the bureaucracy exists . However, agents can be conscripted and thus work for more than one bureaucracy, and when this happens "transfer" occurs. The ability to flexibly transfer agents from one bureaucracy to another is part of the phenomenon called *metacognition.*

As a concept, *metacognition* has two aspects: it represents both the system's intelligence about itself, and the system's ability to regulate and control its own operation. A system possessing self-knowledge about its own operation can ask and answer the following kinds of questions: How do I work? What knowledge do I need? What are my strengths and weaknesses, limits and error propensities? What skills can I borrow from other previously-learned systems? Which of my agencies require interaction with others? A system possessing the ability to regulate itself will raise issues like the following: Am I moving toward my goal? Are things going okay, or am I screwing up and breaking down? What kind of screw up did I make this time? Which of my agencies is responsible? How can I repair and continue?

This chapter pertains to the importance of metacognition — of designing better, more sophisticated metacognitive intelligence into the cognitive systems we create. Example stories about telescopes, post offices and AIDS-infected blood were introduced to support this hypothesis: that cognitive systems running today's world are fallible, inefficient, and unintelligent, largely because we have undervalued development of their metacognitive faculties. For lack of metacognitive intelligence our systems cannot understand themselves, and do not monitor their performance. This pertains not only to giant, complex cognitive systems such as post offices and telephone companies, but also to the cognitive systems that evolve within children, in homes and at school. Perhaps one major cause of ineffectiveness, of the incompetency crises that we face today, is lack of attention to metacognitive design.

Metacognition and Instruction

In *The Sciences of the Artificial*, Simon [40] suggested that human cognitive systems are appropriately viewed as constructions — artifacts resulting from adaptive interactions with a complex world. The only problem with this idea is that it can seduce us into believing that just as an architect or artist designs and creates an object, so parents and teachers might engineer learning environments that will mold the cognitive systems of their children into whatever they want them to be. This line of thinking leads us to conclude that if metacognitive intelligence is desirable for society, our problem boils down to one of figuring out how to design and engineer learning environments that will foster evolution of metacognitive processes.

This basic idea is sound to an extent, and thus provides a reasonable perspective from which to approach the conceptualization of instructional computing systems. However, it is possible to oversimplify the problem from this perspective, for complexities surround the notion of adaptive interaction. For example, we know that while students are in fact adaptive agents who may respond to purposefully-designed environments, they also have tenacious wills of their own and can often adapt their surroundings in accordance with goals of their own creation. Furthermore, there is every reason to encourage precisely this form of flexible, creative intelligence. Instructional design must therefore be something rather different from the behavioural engineering of fool-proof environments that resist tampering by the student.

The general view of instructional design proposed involves (1) the inventing of problem situations that invite mobilization of certain interacting groups of cognitive and metacognitive thinking skills, and (2) the invention of interactive learning environments that afford and encourage metacognitive thought processes. The remainder of this chapter will explore two different classes of instructional design models that meet these criteria: the reflection/ constructivist models based largely on the Genevan school of psychology; and the cognitive apprenticeship model, largely derived from Vygotskian psychology. The implications of these models for the development of intelligent computer-based instruction also will be described.

A Reflection/Constructivist Model for Instructional Computing

Perhaps the most significant contribution of the Genevan school of developmental psychology, which refers primarily to Piaget and his colleagues, was the focussing of attention on the acquisition of self-regulation as a key to understanding the process of intellectual development. Piaget believed that the child's propensity and capacity for self-regulated thinking evolves through stages. In early intellectual development, self-regulation amounts to the automatic, unconscious adjustment and fine-tuning of performance. In a second developmental phase, alternative theories about knowledge models and strategies are tested through trial and error, although the child still exhibits limited consciousness of the theories and the thinking process itself. The most sophisticated form of self-regulation occurs in the final stage of development, during which time the child exhibits conscious, reflective surveillance of thought, manifested in the ability to discuss and critique one's own problem-solving strategies and knowledge models [2, 29]. This final stage of intellectual development represents the highest form of metacognitive awareness and knowledge.

Piagetian theory has provided impetus for an instructional approach that aims to promote development of conscious self-regulation through environmental engineering and enrichment. In the Piagetian classroom, the student is given access to thoughtfully-selected "cognitive tools" and is encouraged to participate in social interactions that involve use of those tools in problem solving. Cognitive tools are objects in the environment that not only facilitate the problem-solving process, but also provide physical representations of the mental constructs that evolve. Such physical representations are believed to make aspects of the thinking process visible so that they can be inspected and discussed more easily, thereby encouraging metacognitive awareness.

Before computers and related forms of technology, cognitive tools were limited to concrete manipulatives, such as puzzles and blocks. Recently, the advent of modern technology has inspired a renewed interest in the Genevan approach to schooling, for the computer can produce forms of representation that could not be accomplished easily with other media. Neither pencil-and-paper, nor concrete manipulatives, nor standard video can approach the usability, versatility, and power of computer graphics for illustrating the concepts and processes of problem solving, making them visibly and physically accessible to students for reflection, exploration, and manipulation.

The currently popular reflection/constructivist movement in math and science education is a neo-Piagetian idea. In instructional environments designed from this perspective, the computer system typically serves as a sort of catalyst that helps make abstract ideas and thinking processes the visible objects of experimentation, reflection, and discussion. Such systems may supply graphics-based cognitive toolkits — representational objects that can be used in constructing models of problems, situations and ideas. Advanced computer graphics may permit students to reify even highly abstract concepts, dynamical systems, or problem-solving strategies. By using computer tools to construct and study graphical models and simulations, users receive feedback regarding the form and adequacy of their mental conceptualizations and formal mathematical models. Systems of this type can be employed in instruction in various imaginative ways, since explicit instructional strategies are not built in. However, many designers tend to favor using the computer as a point of focus in group problem-solving sessions that encourage scientific argumentation among peers.

Some example systems that fit within this category include ALGEBRALAND [5], HERON [33], The Envisioning Machine [34], and ANIMATE [25]. More complex examples are LOGO [27] and BOXER [11] which also fall within this general philosophical framework. A number of ideas associated with this philosophy are present in SHERLOCK I [22], a system used for technical training in the military. The system by Nathan, Kintsch, and Young [25] will be described as a prototype example.

ANIMATE is used by students for representing and solving algebra story problems. Tools provided by the system include a set of graphical diagrams characterizing simple set relationships that have been identified through research as being basic conceptual units for understanding algebra. The system presents a word problem for the user to solve. Using the system's graphics toolkit, the user selects, labels, and combines graphical diagrams to construct a complex model of the problem, which is displayed on the computer screen. In this way, the student translates the problem text into a formal conceptual structure that can then be represented as an equation. The student may "check" the adequacy of the conceptual representation by running animations. For example, one problem has a giant ant leaving California at one point in time and moving east toward Detroit at a certain rate of speed, while an Army helicopter leaves the east coast at another point in time, moving west at another rate of speed in an attempt to intercept the ant. The student's problem is to determine the time at which the two entities will collide. If the student's conceptual model is a good one, the animation run should depict the two bodies moving at relative speeds toward one another and colliding at a feasible meeting point. Animation of an inaccurate representation might result in the ant's moving too fast, moving in the wrong direction, failing to encounter the helicopter, etc. Thus, the computer environment supplies "feedback" that helps the student judge the adequacy of both conceptual and formal mathematical models.

In designing their system, Nathan et al. followed instructional principles that are very characteristic of the reflection/constructivist philosophy. There is little or no lecturing or explanation. The student is invited to explore the system and make errors in the process, for errors provide the primary learning opportunities. The student, rather than a tutor, is given responsibility for goal-setting, self-monitoring and error diagnosis. This method stands in contrast to intelligent-tutoring systems that build models of the student as a basis for controlling the instructional plan, diagnosing errors, and selecting feedback messages [1].

Strengths & Weaknesses of the Reflection/Constructivist Approach to System Design

The reflection/constructivist approach to instructional computing maximizes the importance of a sophisticated and imaginative graphical interface, and minimizes the importance of student modelling and diagnosis. Arguments in favor of this approach can be made on several levels. Relative to the intelligent tutor, the unintelligent constructivist system is less expensive to build. The engineering technology for unintelligent graphics-based systems currently exists, while intelligent systems technology is still evolving. Moreover, with respect to the goal of creating higher forms of metacognitive intelligence, the reflection/constructivist approach can be recommended on theoretical grounds. Unlike many intelligent tutors, the unintelligent constructivist system does not usurp responsibility for self-regulation, but places this responsibility on the student where it belongs. Finally, there is even some support for the constructivist approach in research showing that performance can be improved by the the mere act of verbalizing one's thinking [15], since using graphics tools to elaborate one's mental model might be very similar to explaining one's thinking process in detail. Brown [2] speculates that explaining one's thinking is effective because the verbalizing process itself promotes reflective self-monitoring.

Nevertheless, there are a number of unsettled design issues surrounding the development of reflection/constructivist systems, and a great number of reasons to be cautious about wholesale adoption of this approach as the primary method for schooling. If currently available systems are taken as standards for what is to come, there is ample reason to question the validity and power of the cognitive tools that they provide. Several issues can be raised.

First, it is not clear that current projects are following any sound methodology for determining what specific concepts should be incorporated into systems to serve as the basic building blocks for mathematical and scientific thinking. Are the selected core concepts in systems such as BOXER or The Envisioning Machine truly useful enough to justify the considerable attention they will be given in any school that adopts their use? The system-development side of the reflection/constructionist movement would appear to need better methods for defining problem domains that face tomorrow's citizens and for analyzing those domains to identify what important core ideas should be subject-matter content. It is not sufficient simply to identify this content based on analyses of current textbooks, for solutions to tomorrow's problems may not come from old curriculum. Nor should any major project move forward merely on the basis of a developer's intuitive notions regarding what ideas are important or interesting. Moreover, it is totally inadequate to dismiss the issue of subject content entirely on grounds that the thinking process itself is the primary curriculum. In sum, selection of content is an issue that has not been adequately addressed by developers.

A second area that must be tackled pertains to issues of mental representation and individual differences. Current graphics-based instructional systems contain forms of visual imagery that appeal intuitively to system developers, but that may not match the representation schemes of domain experts, teachers or students. Moreover, not all system users may be equally adaptive to visual imagery; indeed, some may actually have to translate the visual representations provided by image-based systems into verbal or other representational formats. If some students are forced to solve problems and reason with a representational system that is awkward for them and therefore must be translated during the problem-solving process, their performance will suffer in predictable ways [12]. There should be a better scientific basis for designing the representational graphics employed in reflection/constructivist systems.

Another issue pertains to the presence or absence of an audience to observe the problem-solving processes of students interacting with systems. Brown [2] cites empirical evidence indicating that students perform better when problem solving is monitored. Research with LOGO environments, described by Clements [4] and Scardamalia [36], indicates that giving students total autonomy leads to poor results. However, it is obvious that one teacher cannot closely observe the performance of every student user in a classroom.

These kinds of findings strengthen the case for designing artificially-intelligent tutors that can mimic human-like functions such as monitoring, observing, and interacting. However, the constructivist approach favors another alternative: placing the computer at the center of small-group interactions. Group instruction is attractive in part because it proffers a relatively inexpensive solution. Theoretically, lower-ability students can gain in such arrangements if older, more advanced students are placed in groups to serve as role models and mentors. Advanced students presumably gain as well since, by analyzing and explaining thinking processes to lower-ability students, they may be sharpening their own evaluative and critical thinking skills. But small group instruction centered around a reflection/constructivist system does have its drawbacks.

Some parents and educators feel that if multi-ability problem solving becomes the dominate mode of instructional delivery, better students will too frequently be cast in mentorship roles, thereby limiting their opportunities for rapid acceleration. Another problem is the implied assumption that most any student who understands subject material can, with little experience or training, be an effective, empathic tutor. Finally, in group problem solving, there is nothing to guarantee that the form of the interaction will be productive for all students. In fact, research by Kuhn [16] indicates that effective forms of argumentation are rare, even among adults.

Another weakness in the reflection/constructivist approach is suggested by scientific research into factors that promote transfer of cognitive-skills training. A well-designed reflection/constructivist tool may help students develop higher metacognitive awareness and knowledge, but unless conditions for transfer are met during learning, newly acquired metacognitive abilities are not likely to be carried outside the immediate instructional environment. To facilitate transfer of newly-acquired cognitive skills, Pressley et al.[30] argue for use of "informed training" procedures. Informed training explicitly describes the potential usefulness of any newly-acquired thinking skill, and describes the conditions that will warrant its use in the future. Derry and Murphy [7] argue that prompting is also necessary. Prompting involves the engineering of the practice environment so that students are reminded to apply newly-acquired thinking methods at appropriate times during problem-solving practice. The notions of informed training and prompting are consistent with recommendations by Saloman and Perkins [35], who believe that transfer is facilitated by creating conditions that will encourage a student to think forward at the time that a cognitive skill is acquired, and to reach backward at the time that transfer is desired. When the aim of instruction is to promote metacognitive awareness, research and theory on cognitive-skills transfer raise serious doubts regarding the validity of any instructional system that fails to establish conditions for both forward-reaching and backward-reaching transfer. It is uncertain how reflection/constructivist systems could be designed to attend to this issue.

A Cognitive-Apprenticeship Model for Instructional Computing

Another theoretical perspective currently influencing much educational research is the developmental psychology of L.S. Vygotsky [42]. Like Piagetian psychology, the Vygotskian school also places strong emphasis on the importance of self-regulation as an educational goal. Not surprisingly, instructional approaches suggested by Vygotskian theory are compatible with constructivist methods up to a point. However, Vygotskian methods differ primarily by placing the teacher, or "mentor," in a central role of great importance.

In Piagetian constructivist classrooms, the "discovery" of self-regulation is engineered through environmental planning and encouragement of social interaction. Similarly, Vygotsky's theory also suggests that metacognitive awareness evolves from internalization of self-regulatory activities experienced through interactions with the environment. However, Vygotsky believed that self-regulation is acquired by a process that involves first experiencing "other-regulation," which occurs during tutorial-like social interactions with mentors. Through this special form of social interaction, the form and content of self-regulation are gradually transferred from the mentor and internalized by the learner. Thus, the opportunity to internalize self-regulatory mechanisms is viewed as being dependent upon the frequent availability of special social relationships that today are frequently called "cognitive apprenticeships" [6].

Cognitive apprenticeship denotes the sharing of problem-solving experiences between a student and a tutor. A dialogue occurs exposing the thinking processes involved. The tutor provides overall direction and encouragement, but assumes only that portion of the thinking that currently is too advanced for the student to manage alone. In early learning, assistance from the tutor, or "scaffolding" [26], enables the student to devote limited working memory to internalization of critical skills, while also experiencing the higher-order problem-solving strategies and control processes modelled through the tutor's guidance. As the student's problem-solving abilities improve, the tutor gradually fades support, encouraging the student to think independently using strategies and control processes previously modelled.

Brown [2] has outlined a three-stage model of cognitive apprenticeship that specifies different roles for the mentor at each stage. In the first stage, the mentor serves as a model problem-solver, thinking aloud to demonstrate the forms of executive control involved. Stage two is a complex activity whereby the mentor and student work together. Control processes continue to be made public through dialogue, although the mentor guides only when the student falters. In the final stage, the mentor cedes control to the student, functioning primarily as a supportive, empathic audience.

The complex conversational style of problem sharing in phase 2 actually occurs quite naturally, without rehearsal or training, in healthy parent-child relationships. The following dialogue from Wertsch [43], cited in Brown [2], clearly illustrates this point. In this study, mothers and children were given the task of copying a wooden puzzle of a truck, supplied as a model. In completing their puzzle, mothers were told to encourage the child if necessary. The following interaction occurred between a mother and her 2-1/2 year-old daughter.

1. C: Oh (glances at model, then looks at pieces pile). Oh now where's this one go? (picks up black cargo square, looks at copy, then at pile).
2. M: Where does it go in this other one (the model)? (child puts black cargo square back down in pieces pile, looks at pieces pile).
3. M: Look at the other truck (model) and then you can tell (child looks at model, then glances at pieces pile.)
4. C: Well (looks at copy then at model)
5. C: I look at it.
6. C: Um, this other puzzle has a black one over there (child points to black cargo square in model).
7. M: Um-hm.
8. C: A black one (looks at pieces pile).
9. M: So where do you want to put the black one on this (your) puzzle? (child picks up black cargo square from pieces pile and looks at copy).
10. C: Well, where do you put it in there? Over there? (inserts black cargo square correctly in copy).
11. M: That looks good.

It is important to note the functions served by the parent in such interactions, for these are the kinds of roles that must somehow be served by any instructional system that attempts to provide intelligent, coached apprenticeship. In the preceding example, the parent intervenes to: (1) keep the child on task, (2) encourage comparisons with the model, and (3) show the child where to look at the model. These interventions are cued in two ways: by errors and by queries.

In conclusion, the Vygotskian school of developmental psychology proposes that apprenticeship interactions promote development of metacognitive intelligence, an important goal of schooling. It follows directly that educational environments should furnish frequent opportunities for cognitive apprenticeships to occur. Perhaps it is not possible to provide each student with a personal human mentor; however, with further research it may be possible to build intelligent instructional systems that capture essential features of cognitive apprenticeship interaction. But as the next section will demonstrate, this is a difficult and complex research goal.

Design for an AI-based Cognitive Mentorship System

The remainder of this article will describe, in fairly general terms, a proposed architecture for an artificially-intelligent cognitive mentorship system (CMS) that follows the Vygotskian approach. My research team is attempting to develop a system of this type on the NeXT microcomputer, although our work focusses on particular parts of the architecture and not on others. Our current instantiation of this general idea is called TAPS, which stands for "Training Arithmetic Problem-solving Skills." Since our implementation in progress employs the domain of complex arithmetic word problems as a testbed, the following discussion will be developed using examples from that domain. However, no particular domain or specific instructional knowledge is implied by the basic architecture.

The proposed architecture is essentially a framework for characterizing the types of decisions that human mentors make and the points at which they are made. In developing this framework, I have drawn from and amalgamated the views of several researchers who have conducted studies of the decision-making processes by which expert human mentors control the timing, content, and style of instructional intervention [1, 13, 14, 17, 18, 19, 20, 31, 38]. Studies indicate that tutorial strategies might reasonably be generated at the key decision-making points outlined below:

Global planning. At this level a broad curriculum plan or agenda is consulted and a student's abilities are estimated with respect to that plan. At the beginning of each instructional session, a goal (or goals) is selected that will challenge the student appropriately.

Local planning. Here the tutor considers both the student's history and the student's immediate learning goals, and devises problem-solving experiences to serve as a context for learning.

Local intervention. At this level the tutor interprets the meaning of a student's actions observed during problem solving, and uses these observations as a basis for entering into instructional dialogue.

Within this proposed framework, the knowledge-engineering problem can be characterized as one of deciding what "diagnostic" patterns are sought by expert tutors at each of these levels, and what tutorial decisions are made on the basis of the various patterns observed. It is assumed that the decisions made at each of these levels will be complex, requiring the mentor to obtain and interpret information from multiple sources of information.

The proposed CMS architecture requires development of separate knowledge bases at the three levels outlined above: global planning, local planning, and local intervention. No argument will be given here for any particular knowledge-representation scheme or inferencing system except to say that an expert-systems approach is being assumed.

The proposed architecture can best be understood by examining how information would flow through a system. The flow diagram is shown in Figure 1, which illustrates the major system components and data stores (rectangles), knowledge inputs (arrows), and processes (rounded boxes). Discussion of Figure 1 will specify points at which system processes attempt to emulate the decisions of human mentors. These are the points at which knowledge-engineering studies of human mentors might be conducted for the purpose of influencing design of the knowledge bases and their chains of inference.

Global Planning (Processes 1, 13 & 14)

Generally, the purpose of global planning is to move each student through a curriculum designed to promote acquisition and flexible utilization of critical "knowledge components" associated with an expert knowledge model for the target subject domain. Here the term *knowledge component* is used loosely in reference to any skill, concept, belief, or attitude associated with a subject matter.

Task analysis. Cognitive task analysis is believed to be the best method for deciding exactly what knowledge components should be included in a curriculum [21]. The result of such an analysis is a theory that identifies critical knowledge components required for performance in domain X, where domain X is often specified by a sampling of problem situations. All or, more often, a subset of these identified knowledge components become the learning objectives for the system — the subject-matter agenda.

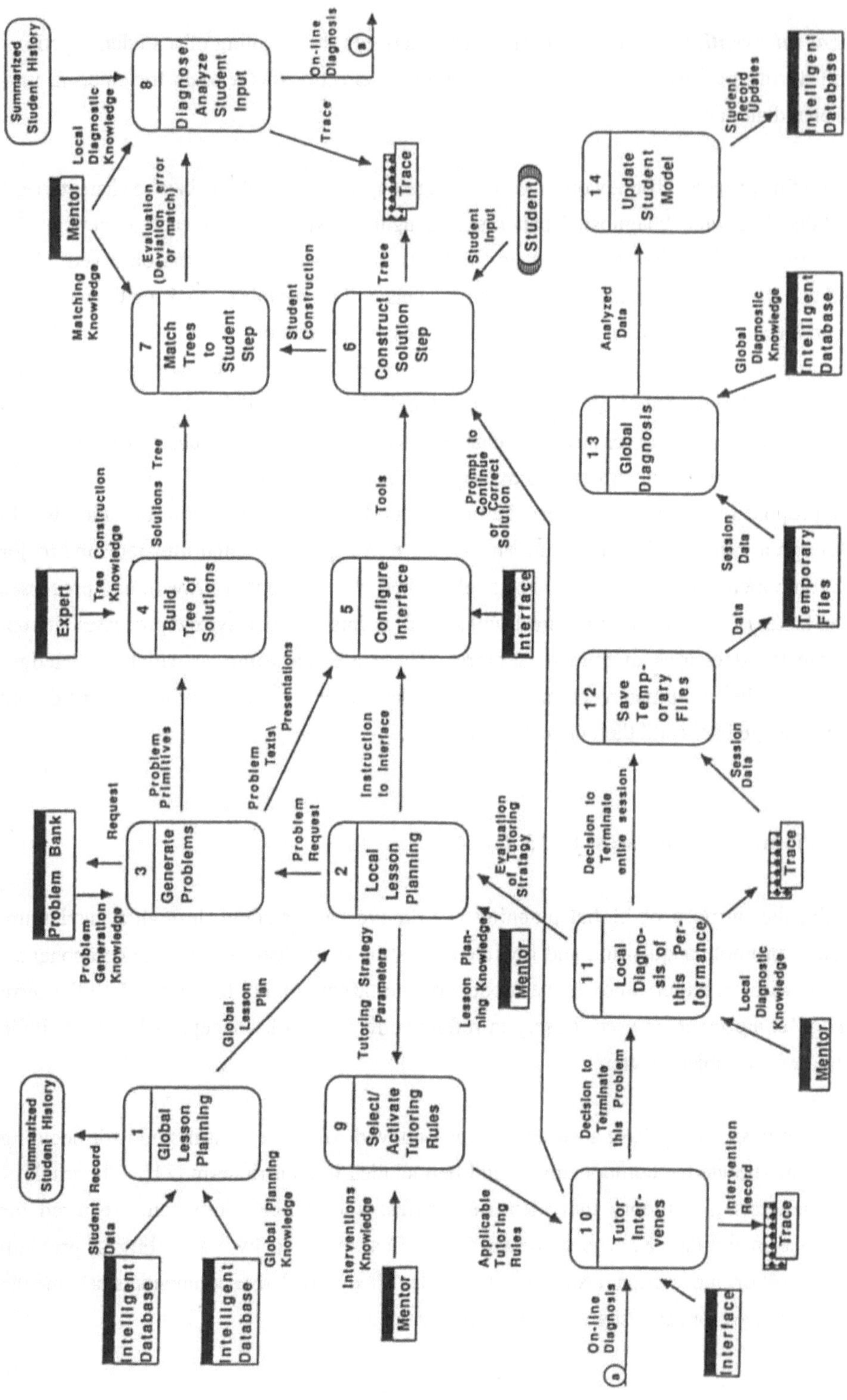

Figure 1: Overview of data flow

An example of a cognitive-style task analysis is illustrated by the TAPS theory for the domain of complex arithmetic story problems [8, 9]. Examples of the types of problems that specify the TAPS domain are given below in Table 1.

1. Mark needed 12 sheets of sandpaper to smooth off a tabletop. Now he wants to smooth off a tabletop that is just like the first one except that it is only half as wide and half as long. How many sheets will he need?
2. If 1/4 of the world's population is Chinese, and 1/5 of the remainder is Indian, then what percentage of the world is Indian?
3. Leon was offered two full-time jobs. The job at the grocery store pays $4.50 per hour, and one at the drug store pays $800 per month. How much money will Leon lose in a year if he takes the lower paying job?
4. At the beginning of April, Sam owed nothing on his Mastercharge card. He charged $35.00 worth of merchandise that month. Later he returned some of the merchandise and received $22.00 credit. He then paid his bill in full, but his check was mailed late and the Mastercharge company had already sent May's bill. His bill in May gave him the $22.00 credit, but it said he still owed $68.00. Sam now wants to pay his bill in full. For how much should he write the check?
5. Assume that there is a test for cancer that is 98 percent accurate; i.e., if someone has cancer, the test will be positive 98 percent of the time, and if one doesn't have it, the test will be negative 98 percent of the time. Assume further that .5 percent (1 out of every 200 people) actually have cancer. Now imagine that 10,000 tests for cancer are administered. Of these, how many will test positive? How many of these will be false positives?
6. The gang is sending Sam out for pizza. Dominoes sells its large pizza with three toppings for 12 bucks. Extra cheese is 2 bucks, and extra sauce is another 2 bucks. Additional toppings are $1.00 each. Sam is supposed to get two large pizzas. They want one with four and one with five toppings. Both pizzas will have extra cheese. Sam has a coupon that gets him 2 dollars off per pizza for an order of two or more. So far he has collected 20 dollars from the group. How much more must he collect?

Table 1: Example Problems used in TAPS

In agreement with other researchers [23], our task analysis led us to conclude that comprehension of these types of problems involves recognizing, linking, and operating upon semantic "schemas," simple conceptual models representing common set relationships that occur in problem situations. For example, consider the following situation: Jamie had $15.00, bought a pizza that cost $12.50, and now has $2.50 left. Many people appear to employ a "change schema" to represent such situations, which has a start set, a change set, and a final set that is a later version of the start set. In complex problem solving, people appear to combine many different types of schemas in formulating complex, higher-order problem representations.

The TAPS analysis also indicated that the process of combining schemas to form complex problem representations requires metacognitive knowledge. Metacognitive knowledge facilitates and monitors such processes as inferential comprehension, schema-chaining, planning, management of memory overload, error-detection, and repair. Certain motivational beliefs and attitudes associated with expertise also are forms of metacognitive knowledge that support complex problem solving. For example, problems solvers need to believe that complex problems aren't supposed to be solved quickly but that they can be "figured out." Such realistic beliefs about the domain and one's capabilities within it are important in helping students sustain the effort and persistence necessary for problem solving.

The TAPS cognitive task analysis served as the basis for selecting objectives for the TAPS curriculum agenda. Since most students entering TAPS already possess basic relational schemas, both simple and complex, the TAPS curriculum objectives focus largely on metacognitive awareness and knowledge as a basis for improving problem-solving performance. That is, the primary purpose of the TAPS system is to enhance students' metacognitive intelligence, specifically within the word-problem domain, but hopefully outside it as well. Examples of metacognitive skills taught in TAPS include self-monitoring, error-checking, and problem-solving strategies such as working forward and working backward.

Global tutorial planning. Global planning requires knowing the status of the student's current performance on each critical knowledge component identified in the curriculum agenda, including capability with complex problem types that require the student to combine these knowledge components in various ways. In TAPS, this evaluation of the student's domain capabilities will reside in an individual student record along with other data concerning the student's general motivational characteristics, achievement, interests, etc. Considered as a whole, this record constitutes the system's model of the student's knowledge.

Before the student's first session, initial scores in the student record are determined by testing and interviewing and are input directly to the student record by a teacher or researcher, or in some cases by the student. However, estimates must continuously be tuned and updated by the system following each tutorial session, just as a human tutor would form and revise general impressions of a student's capabilities as tutoring progresses. Revision and tuning are represented by processes 13 (global diagnosis) and 14 (updating student model), which, to increase system response times, are performed off-line.

Global diagnosis (process 13) is controlled by an intelligent database. We note parenthetically that associating intelligence with a database is an innovation in ITS design, as intelligence typically is confined to other system components. Input to process 13 includes trace data from a tutorial session and a set of inference rules for identifying performance patterns in session data and for relating those patterns to particular strengths or deficits in the student's knowledge model. In other words, process 13 reasons with available data in an attempt to assign credit and blame for current performance to particular knowledge components.

In process 14 (student model update), the evaluation obtained from process 13 is combined with historical information already contained in the student's record and an update of the student knowledge model is obtained. In addition to the evaluation from process 13, input to process 14 includes the student knowledge model and a set of inference rules for combining current with historical data. In general, these rules operate such that if a student exhibits a strong performance, and if this performance is associated (per process 13) with knowledge components X, Y, and Z, then scores for X, Y, and Z will be upgraded in the student's record. Conversely, if the student exhibits a poor performance, then scores for X, Y, and Z would be downgraded in the student's record. However, it is critical to weight both historical performance as well as recent evidence when updating the student knowledge model, since performance is not always consistent. Thus a single performance should not receive undue weight in the student's overall evaluation.

Output from process 14 is the updated student record that serves as input to global lesson planning, process 1 in Figure 1. The objective of this process is to holistically evaluate the student model and, based on this evaluation, decide upon suitable goals for an upcoming tutorial session. These learning goals target particular knowledge components that a student needs to strengthen, and particular types of problems that a student needs to tackle. Inputs to process 1 include the student model and a set of decision rules for selecting instructional goals. Both reside in the intelligent database system, which also controls process 1. Decision outputs from process 1 include a global lesson plan stated in terms of lesson objectives, which is passed to a local lesson-planning process, discussed later.

Decision rules for selecting instructional objectives in process 1 should reflect a cognitive perspective on how students should be moved through a curriculum agenda. This perspective can be contrasted with traditional instructional-design theory, which emphasizes the importance of organizing instruction so that elementary prerequisite competencies are mastered prior to presentation of more complex problem-solving tasks that employ them. As noted by Peterson, Fennema, and Carpenter [28], a persistent problem with this technology has been its inability to foster broad transfer and flexible problem solving outside the classroom environment. They blame this on the tendency of the traditional technology to overly "atomize" complex concepts. Thus, students often are required to practice minor subskills that have no meaning when considered apart from broader schematic contexts. For example, students frequently are required to learn basic mathematics operations prior to being introduced to word problems that give a situated semantic context and therefore meaning to the operations.

Like Peterson et al. [28], we advocate a more holistic approach to global planning in which knowledge is acquired not in isolation, but within the context of problem-solving situations that require its use in various combinations. Accordingly, we have conceptualized a global planning method based on a system of heuristics that can be adjusted to relax the lock-step requirements of traditional instructional design theory, yet constrain movement through a curriculum in a commonsense way [10]. The aim is to avoid both overatomizing and overshooting student capabilities, while achieving a decision-making style that resembles what a human tutor might do.

To facilitate the imprecise reasoning process we wish to emulate for global planning, variables in the TAPS student record are represented as scores on fuzzy linguistic intervals [39]. A complete discussion of fuzzy linguistic representation is not possible here, but an example will serve to illustrate the basic idea: assume that, dependent upon performance history, students are assigned performance scores ranging from 1 (very poor) to 5 (very good) for problem-type variable X. Assume further that problem-type X itself is characterized by a score on the following scale: 1 (very easy) to 5 (very difficult). This fuzzy representation system combines with the heuristic reasoning strategy to make possible planning rules of the following form: since student's last performance was "very good" on "moderately difficult" problems, select "difficult" problems for the current lesson.

In sum, we propose that a CMS must carry out processes associated with global planning: maintaining and updating a student knowledge model and selecting tutorial goals based on evaluations of that model. Global planning decisions can be handled by an intelligent database, which houses the student model as well as the knowledge base and inference capabilities required for updating and evaluating it.

Local Lesson Planning (Processes 2, 3, 5, & 9)

Research by Leinhardt and Greeno [17] has shown that expert teachers plan lessons using many different "instructional routines." *Instructional routines* are social scripts that organize problem solving activity and that, through frequent use, become familiar to teachers and students. Different routines serve different purposes, and the choice of which to use depends largely on the current goals of instruction. For example, Sweller and Cooper [41] have developed a routine for schema acquisition called "worked examples," whereby students are repeatedly asked to study an expert solution, then work a similar problem following the expert example. A routine for developing planning skill is "planning boards" [32], whereby students are asked to identify problem goals and subgoals prior to working each problem. A routine for developing representational skills is illustrated by Singley and Anderson's algebra tutor (viewed on visit to Carnegie-Mellon), which requires students to select a diagram that best represents each problem and then to label it during problem solution.

Regardless of which routine is chosen, local tutorial style can vary widely. In the version of Singley and Anderson's algebra tutor that I viewed, for example, there was no intervention other than feedback when the problem is successfully solved. In SHERLOCK I, an ITS for avionics troubleshooting [21, 22], the tutor supplies assistance at the student's request. However, research has shown that expert human tutors do not always wait for students to request assistance, nor do they interrupt to deliver unnecessary mini-lessons. Rather, good tutors typically intervene in response to indicators that the student is experiencing difficulty with the problem-solving process. Like routines, different intervention styles also serve different instructional purposes. For example, a non-specific coaching style (e.g., "Are your sure? Should you take another look?"), is likely to encourage reflective self-evaluation. Lepper and Chabay [20] have identified several specific local tutoring styles in their observations of human tutors: coach, cheerleader, collaborator, competitor, drill sergeant, lecturer, and Socratic teacher.

The idealized system outlined in Figure 1 is able to plan a variety of lessons by combining different instructional routines and tutoring styles according to rules established by a cognitive apprenticeship model. For example, in accordance with Brown's three-stage model of cognitive apprenticeship, routines involving modelling, and tutorial styles involving a high degree of mentor control, should be selected for true novices, as these students would be ready for stage-one cognitive apprenticeship. Students with mid-range performance scores, who would be classified as neither novices nor experts, should receive stage-two apprenticeships. Stage-two apprenticeships are characterized by shared problem solving and a moderate degree of system control. Intervention in stage two should be triggered by student errors or queries. Finally, students approaching expertise should be required to solve problems on their own and diagnose their own performance. Thus, at stage three, the system should intervene only to provide empathy and support.

In accordance with these ideas, process 2 in Figure 1, or local lesson planning, uses as input the instructional objectives and a summarized student history provided by process 1, and a set of lesson planning rules residing within the subsystem Mentor. One set of outputs from process 1 contains choices for a particular instructional routine and local tutoring style, which are passed to process 9. Based on these choices, process 9 then selects and activates the tutoring rules that guide the forthcoming lesson.

Mentor also instructs Interface to generate the appropriate screen and communication facilities to support the chosen tutoring strategy (process 5). The interface must provide concept-enhancing tools that will help the student perform problem-solving tasks on line while simultaneously creating an explicit solution representation that can be examined and judged by the Mentor. For example, if a diagramming and labelling routine is chosen, then the screen interface provides tools that will enable the student to build and label problem diagrams (TAPS screens illustrating this idea will be shown as Figures 3 - 5, discussed later). Obviously the basic interface design must be flexible and conveniently varied to permit its use with a range of tutoring strategies and instructional routines.

During lesson planning, Mentor also instructs Problem Bank to supply problems appropriate for this particular student and lesson plan (process 3). This storage bank is searched for whatever types of problems are needed for the session. For example, if the current instructional goal is to develop planning ability, complex problems containing multiple subgoals would be needed. Problems also should match the student on characteristics such as age, world knowledge, gender, and interests. For example, the problem generator could be asked to provide five-step problems containing various multiplicative operations and dealing with subjects of interest to young adult females.

The problem generator must deliver two types of output. The first comprises actual problem presentations, which will be viewed by the student. These are passed to process 5 (configure interface). Presentations may take various forms, ranging from word-problem text to video presentations containing problem situations for the student to identify. In fact, the basic system design is ideal for implementation of multi-media presentations. The second type of output is a parsed version of the embedded problem containing the primitives that will be needed by the system's expert. These are passed to process 4, described later.

Local Diagnosis/Intervention (Processes 4, 6, 7, 8, 10, 11)

Cognitive mentorship at the critical stage-two level is unobtrusive and either error-driven [19], or query driven [22]. A significant challenge for system development is enabling the machine mentor to detect and understand the different types of errors and queries that a student might make. When errors arise and remain unnoticed by the student, the machine mentor must be able to intervene in ways that support the student's metacognitive learning processes. That is, the intervention must not simply correct the error, but rather help the student learn something about his or her own error propensities. Similarly, when a query is made, the system must be able to interpret the student's current difficulty so that an appropriate answer can be given.

Error recognition. One method for enabling a machine to recognize student difficulties involves having an expert system solve the same problem that the student is solving, then comparing the student's emerging solution representation to that created by the expert. An error is detected whenever the student's solution path deviates from the expert path. However, this approach is complicated by the fact that the same problem can be approached in many different correct ways. Moreover, the student may not be expected to "solve" a stated problem in the traditional sense. For example, the instructional task may only require the student to find goals and subgoals. Thus, the tutoring expert must be more than an expert system; it must be able to produce all acceptable solution paths to any given problem for any given task statement.

There are several possible approaches to the implementation of the tutoring expert system. In our earlier version of TAPS we used an approach whereby the expert constructs an AND/OR tree consisting of all acceptable model solutions for the current problem. An example of an AND/OR tree for a simple word problem is provided as Figure 2. Such trees supply a knowledge source for each problem that can in fact be used by the Mentor in several ways. For example, in addition to using the tree as a basis for interpreting student moves, the tree can be used to help the Mentor produce model demonstration solutions. This approach, which has proved satisfactory for the domain of algebra and pre-algebra word problems, will be assumed for the present example, although other methods could be used here without disturbing other aspects of system design. Construction of the AND/OR tree is represented in Figure 1 as process 4.

Inputs to process 4 include a parsed version of each problem and other problem primitives required for tree construction, output by the problem bank during process 3. Other inputs include rules for tree construction, which are housed in the system Expert. Output from process 4 is an augmented AND/OR solutions tree that provides a basis for identifying primitive errors in the student's on-line solution strategy.

The student's emerging solution strategy appears on the screen (see Figures 4 - 8) and is compared to the AND/OR tree in process 7, using error-detection rules that reside in the subsystem Mentor. In addition to the expert tree, process 7 also receives input from process 6, in which the student employs interface graphics tools to explicitly construct steps in a problem solution. Each step in the student's solution is interpreted as a branch in a student solution tree. The first branch is matched to the AND/OR tree in an attempt to determine which solution strategy the student is trying to pursue. Locating the student's strategy in reference to the AND/OR tree is a non-trivial problem, since the student can begin a solution process at any point in any tree. Also, the student may flounder or abandon several approaches. The

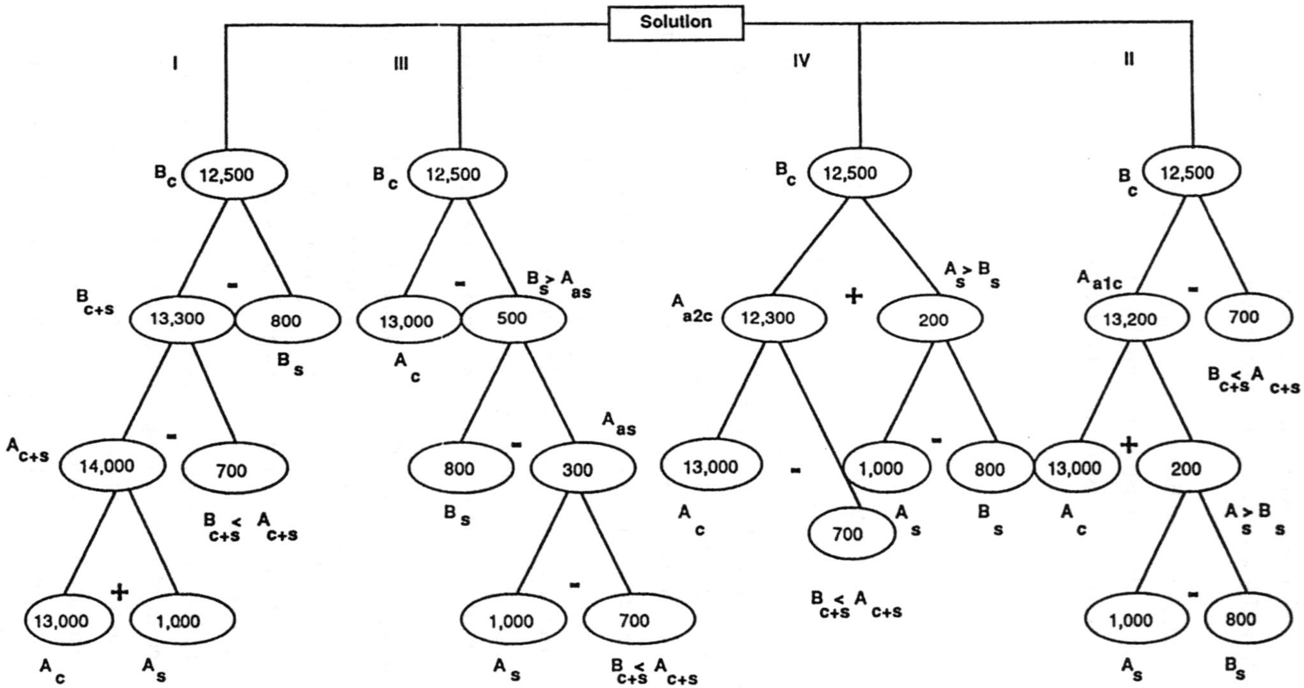

A_c : the cost of dealer A's car

A_s : the cost of dealer A's stereo

B_s : the cost of dealer B's stereo

B_c : the cost of dealer B's car

B_{c+s} : the cost of dealer A's car and stereo

A_{c+s} : the cost of dealer B's car and stereo

A_{as} : the adjusted stereo cost of dealer A such that $A + A = B$

A_{a1c} : adjusted car cost of dealer A such that $A_{a1c} + A_s = B_{c+s}$

A_{a2c} : adjusted car cost of dealer A if stereos are sold at the same price

Figure 2: Expert Solutions Module Solution Tree for Car Problem

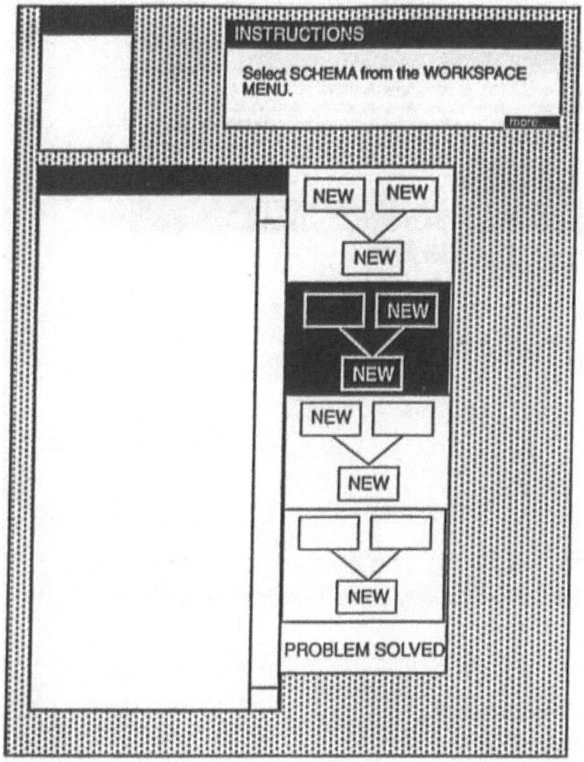

Figure 3: Part of a screen showing TAPS graphic tools for constructing problem trees. Students choose a schema by clicking on it with a mouse and moving it to the workspace.

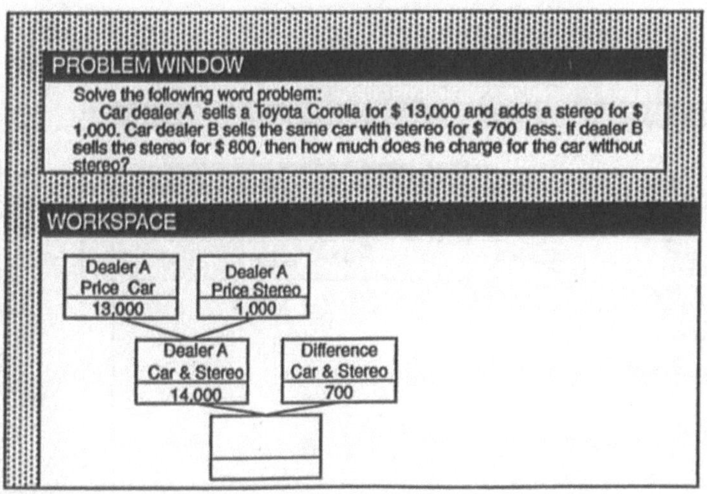

Figure 4: Part of TAPS screen showing text presentation of word problems and part of a student solution. The system is performing calculations for the student. The student is labelling sets and selecting operations. (Note that this student appears to be working forward without a plan.)

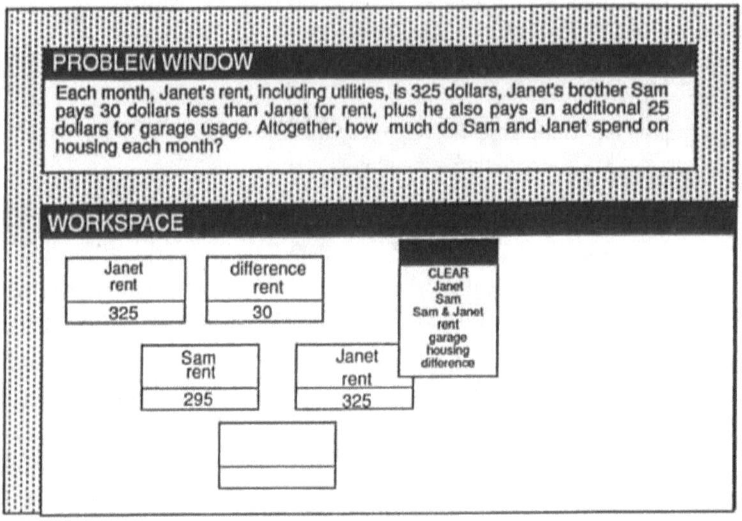

Figure 5: Sets are labelled by clicking on a box. A selection of labels appears and the student chooses by pointing with the cursor.

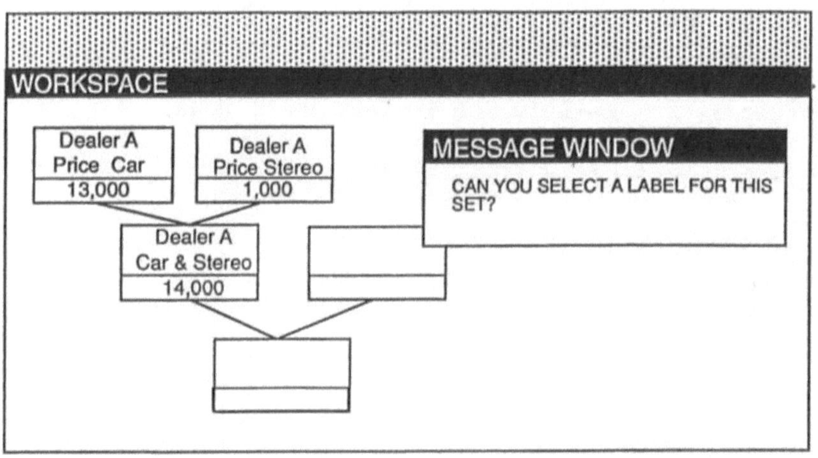

Figure 6: Here the system prompts the student to label a set. Labels help the system understand what the student is thinking.

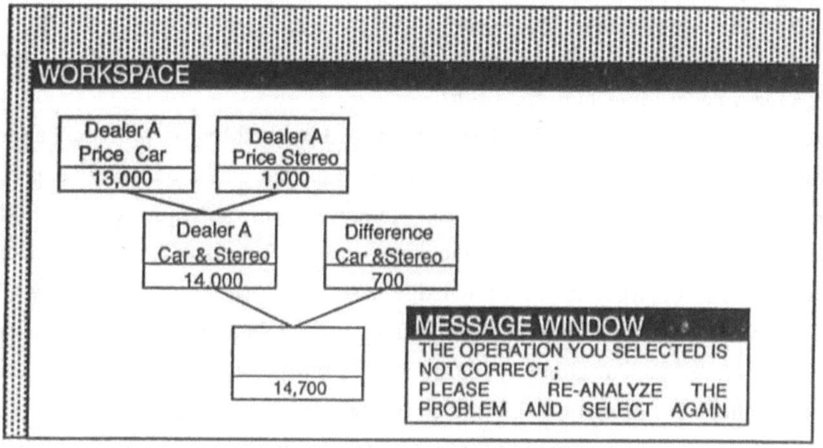

Figure 7: Here the system makes a specific correction.

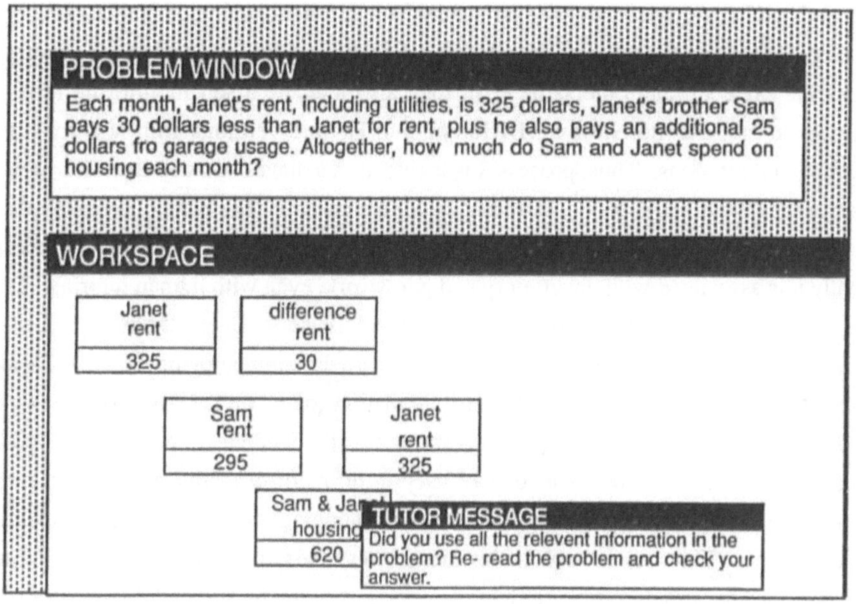

Figure 8: Here the system "sees" that a student has omitted a step.

uncertainty of this environment makes this an ideal task for imprecise reasoning methods. Several imprecise reasoning methodologies exist in the expert systems field. We happen to be exploring a fuzzy pattern-matching approach.

Once a student's solution path has been determined by the Mentor, process 7 attempts to detect student errors by matching the student's input to the correct branch of the expert tree to determine how the student's solution deviates. Interpreting errors requires that the Mentor's rule base incorporates knowledge of the the types of deviation errors known to occur in the target domain. To construct such a knowledge base, developers must conduct research to produce a taxonomy of deviation errors that actually occur in human protocols. Our previous research has produced such a taxonomy for the TAPS story-problem domain, which consists of eleven basic categories of errors. Examples of error types include: omission of a needed schema, inclusion of a schema not in the solution tree, forming a bad schema for determining a good subgoal. Using this taxonomy, trained humans can identify primitive errors with 90% reliability. We are currently working on the error-detection routine for the TAPS system. Examples of some error-detection capabilities are illustrated in Figures 6 - 8. Our hope is that the machine will eventually be capable of identifying basic errors with about the same degree of reliability as a trained human tutor.

However, simple error detection often will not lead directly to an adequate explanation of the student's difficulty, since the same error may have different meanings in different contexts. For example, a computational error detected as a deviation might indicate lack of a prerequisite calculational skill, although the same error may also indicate a self-monitoring failure or a breakdown in student motivation. Different tutorial interventions follow from different diagnostic interpretations. Thus, process 8 is included as a diagnostic step in which basic error data is combined with other system information for the purpose of drawing inferences about the presence of higher-order error models. Although this diagnostic step is useful and necessary, frequently it is associated with uncertainty and guesswork, even with human tutoring. Like the human tutor, the machine tutor must here rely on imprecise reasoning methods.

Responses to evaluated errors and error patterns are determined by process 10. Responses vary widely and may include demonstrations (simulations based on the AND/OR tree), explicit corrections, requests for clarification, suggestions that the student reflect upon the problem-solving process, etc. Responses also may vary in terms of empathy, with more empathic tutoring styles being quicker to offer support and encouragement at signs of frustration or discouragement. The way in which the mentor responds to a particular error pattern is constrained by the strategy activated in process 9 during the lesson planning phase. In accordance with Brown's cognitive mentorship philosophy, process 9 should produce a tutorial strategy characterized by control and modelling at stage-one apprenticeship interaction, a highly

highly interactive process characterized by shared problem solving at stage two, and finally, an empathic, non-intrusive tutor at stage three.

Sometimes the chosen intervention will represent a decision to terminate work on a particular problem. This decision serves as a signal to implement process 11, which performs a local diagnosis of the current tutoring session. If diagnostic indicators show that the student has been adequately challenged and appears to be making progress toward the desired goal, the current lesson plan continues until the allotted time for the lesson expires. If the problem exercise has been too difficult or easy for the student, the Mentor may choose to repair the current lesson plan by requesting the problem bank to alter problem difficulty. Under certain circumstances, a minor repair may not be possible. Such would be the case, for example, if the student is unable to solve even the easiest problems associated with the active lesson plan. In this case there is a decision to terminate the session and update the database, on the assumption that information from the current tutoring session will help determine a more adequate plan for the student's next session.

CMS Model: Brief Summary

The complexity of cognitive apprenticeship interaction makes the prospect of constructing a truly competent CMS system a challenging but distant research goal. It is apparent that any attempt to develop a truly interactive CMS must depend heavily on artificial intelligence technologies. Fox [13,14] has argued that such systems cannot presently be built due to the inadequacy of existing natural-language technologies. However, the system design overviewed here may be able to bypass this difficult natural-language problem.

Conclusions

In many traditional instructional systems, metacognitive knowledge is either ignored or treated as incidental to cognitive goals. This article considered some of the consequences of focussing our major efforts on metacognitive (versus cognitive) knowledge. This focus would require system designers to engage in a process of meta-metacognition — the deliberate development of metacognitive intelligence through engineering of the instructional environment. Two basic approaches to instructional systems design were identified: the reflection/constructivist approach based on Piagetian psychology, and the cognitive apprenticeship approach based on Vygotskian theory. Although the reflection/constructivist method has numerous weaknesses, it also has a great many strengths that can be leveraged by computer-based graphics technologies. Also, compared to the cognitive apprenticeship model, it is a relatively realistic and inexpensive model to implement on computer. Complexity is the major problem in employing the apprenticeship model as a basis for instructional systems design. However, it is a powerful model and its implementation is an important long-term goal for research in intelligent educational computing.

Acknowledgements

I am grateful to Lois Hawkes, Harald Kegelmann, Dawn Holmes, and Clark Quinn for their valuable contributions and insights. Funding for this project was provided by a grant from the Florida High Technology and Industry Council to Lois Hawkes and the author.

References

1. Anderson, J. S., Boyle, C. F., & Reiser, B. J.: Intelligent tutoring systems. *Science*, 228, pp. 456-468 (1985)
2. Brown, A. L.: Metacognition, executive control, self-regulation, and other more mysterious mechanisms. In: *Metacognition, motivation and understanding* (F. Weinert, & R. Klewe, eds.). Hillsdale, NJ: Lawrence Erlbaum Associates 1987
3. Brown, A. L.: Motivation to learn and understand: On taking charge of one's own learning. *Cognition and Instruction*, 5, pp. 311-322 (1988)
4. Clements, D. H.: Effects of Logo and CAI environments on cognition and creativity. *Journal of Educational Psychology*, 78, pp. 309-318 (1986)
5. Collins, A., & Brown, J. S.: The computer as a tool for learning through reflection. In: *Learning issues for intelligent tutoring systems* (H. Mandl & A. Lesgold, eds.). New York: Springer-Verlag 1988
6. Collins, A., Brown, J. S., & Newman, S. E.: Cognitive apprenticeship: Teaching the craft of reading, writing, and mathematics. In: *Knowing, learning and instruction: Essays in honor of Robert Glaser*. (L.B. Resnick, ed.). Hillsdale, NJ: Lawrence Erlbaum Associates 1989
7. Derry, S. J.: Strategy and expertise in word problem solving. In: *Cognitive strategy research: From basic research to educational applications* (C. McCormick, G. Miller, & M. Pressley, eds.). New York: Springer-Verlag 1989
8. Derry, S. J, & Murphy, D.: Designing systems that train learning ability: From theory to practice. *Review of Educational Research*, 56, pp. 1-39 (1986)
9. Derry, S. J., Hawkes, L. W., & Tsai, C.: A theory for remediating problem-solving skills of older children and adults. *Educational Psychologist*, 22, pp. 55-87 (1987)
10. Derry, S. J., Hawkes, L. W., & Ziegler, U.: A plan-based opportunistic architecture for intelligent tutoring. In: ITS-88 (Proceedings of international conference on intelligent tutoring systems) Montreal: University of Montreal, June 1988
11 Disessa, A.: A principled design for an integrated computational environment. *Human-computer Interaction*, 1, pp. 1-4 (1985)

12 Ericsson, K. A., & Simon, H. A.: *Protocol analysis: Verbal reports as data.* Cambridge, Mass: MIT Press 1984
13. Fox, B. A.: Repair as a factor in interface design. Technical Report, Boulder: Institute for Cognitive Science, University of Colorado 1988a
14. Fox, B. A.: Robust learning environments: The issue of canned text. Technical Report, Boulder: Institute for Cognitive Science, University of Colorado 1988b
15. Gagne, R. M., & Smith, M. C.: A study of the effects of verbalization and problem solving. *Journal of Experimental Psychology,* 63, pp. 12-18 (1962)
16. Kuhn, D.: The skills of argument. Colloquium presented at Carnegie-Mellon University, October 1990
17. Leinhardt, G., & Greeno, J. G.: The cognitive skill of teaching. *Journal of Educational Psychology,* 78, pp. 75-95 (1986)
18. Leinhardt, G., & Ohlsson, S.: Tutorials on the structure of tutoring from teachers. AERA Presentation, April 1989
19. Lepper, M. R.: Goals and strategies of expert human tutors: Cognitive and affective considerations. AERA Presentation, April 1989
20. Lepper, M. R., & Chabay, R. W.: Socializing the intelligent tutor: Bringing empathy to computer tutors. In: *Learning issues for intelligent tutoring systems* (H. Mandl, & A. Lesgold, eds.). New York: Springer-Verlag 1988
21. Lesgold, A.: Toward a theory of curriculum for use in designing intelligent instructional systems. In: *Learning issues for intelligent tutoring systems* (H. Mandl, & A. Lesgold, eds.). New York: Springer-Verlag 1988
22. Lesgold, A., Lajoie, S., Bunzo, M., & Eggan, G.: SHERLOCK: A coached practice environment for an electronics troubleshooting. In: *Computer assisted instruction and intelligent tutoring systems: Establishing communication and collaboration* (J. Larkin, R. Chabay, & C. Scheftic, eds.). Hillsdale, NJ: Lawrence Erlbaum Associates (in press)
23. Marshall, S. P., Pribe, C. A., & Smith, J. D.: Schema knowledge structures for representing and understanding arithmetic story problems. Contract No. N00014-85-K-0661, San Diego, CA: Center for Research in Mathematics and Science Education, March 1987
24. Minksy, M.: *The Society of Mind.* New York: Simon and Schuster 1985
25. Nathan, M. J., Kintsch, W., & Young, E.: A theory of algebra word problem comprehension and its implications for unintelligent tutoring systems. ICS Technical Report #90-02, Boulder: Institute for Cognitive Science, University of Colorado 1990
26. Palincsar, A. S.: The role of dialogue in providing scaffolded instruction. *Educational Psychologist,* 21, pp. 73-99 (1986)
27. Papert, S.: *Mindstorms: Children, computers, and powerful ideas.* New York: Basic Books 1980
28. Peterson, P., Fennema, E., & Carpenter, T.: Using knowledge of how students think about mathematics. *Educational Leadership,* 46, pp. 42-46 (1988/89)
29. Piaget, J.: *The grasp of consciousness: Action and concept in the young child.* Cambridge, MA: Harvard University Press 1976
30. Pressley, M., Borkowski, J. G., & O'Sullivan, J. T.: Memory strategy instruction is made of this: Metamemory and durable strategy use. *Educational Psychologist,* 19, pp. 94-107 (1984)
31. Reiser, B.: Pedagogical strategies for human and computer tutoring. AERA Presentation, April 1989
32. Resnick, L. B.: Treating mathematics as an ill-structured discipline. In: *Research agenda for mathematics education: Teaching and assessment of mathematical problem-solving* (R. Charles, & E. A. Silver, eds.). Hillsdale, NJ: Lawrence Erlbaum Associates (in press)
33. Reusser, K., Kampfer, A., Sprenger, M., Staub, F., Stebler, R., & Stussi, R.: Tutoring mathematical word problems using solution trees. Research report No. 8., Switzerland: University of Bern, April 1990
34. Roschelle, J.: Mental models from computer models: How do students do it? AERA presentation, April 1990
35. Salomon, G., & Perkins, D. N.: Rocky roads to transfer: Rethinking mechanisms of a neglected phenomenon. *Educational Psychologist,* 24, pp. 113-142 (1989)
36. Scardamalia, M. E., Bereiter, C., McLean, R. S., Swallow, J., & Woodruff, E.: Computer-supported intentional learning environments. *Journal of Educational Computing Research,* 5, pp. 51-68 (1989)
37. Schoenfeld, A. H.: Episodes and executive decisions in mathematical problem solving. In: *Acquisition of mathematics concepts and processes* (R. Lesh & M. Landau, eds.). New York: Academic Press 1983
38. Schoenfeld, A. H.: What's all the fuss about metacognition? In: *Cognitive science and mathematics education* (A. Schoenfeld, ed.). Hillsdale, NJ: Lawrence Erlbaum Associates 1987
39. Schwartz, D. G.: Outline of a naive semantics for reasoning with qualitative linguistic information. Proceedings of IJCAI-89, pp. 20- 25 (1989)
40. Simon, H.: *The Sciences of the Artificial.* Cambridge, MA: MIT Press 1981

41. Sweller, J., & Cooper, G. A.: The use of worked examples as a substitute for problem solving in learning algebra. *Cognition and Instruction*, 2, pp. 59-89 (1985)
42. Vygotsky, L. S.: *Mind in society: The development of higher psychological processes* (M. Cole, V. John-Steiner, S. Scribner, & E. Souberman, eds. and trans.). Cambridge, MA: Harvard University Press 1978
43. Wertsch, J. V.: Adult-child interaction and the roots of metacognition. *Quarterly newsletter of the institute for comparative development*, 1, pp. 15-18 (1978)

The Language Shift: A Mechanism for Triggering Metacognitive Activities

Pierre Dillenbourg

Faculté de Psychologie et des Sciences de l'Education, University of Geneva, Switzerland

Abstract: This chapter presents a metaphor for designing educational computing systems (ECSs) that progressively transfer to the learner an increasing amount of control in the problem solving process. The continuous variation of learner's control is segmented into a few levels. The transition from some level i to the next higher level i+1 results from the internalization of the concepts necessary to control the activities at level i. The use of reflection tools is proposed for supporting the internalization process. These reflection tools reify the control features of the learner's activities, i.e., they make concrete some abstract features of his or her behaviour. The next level is reached when the learner is able to use aspects reified at level i to interact with the system at level i+1. The same control concept is first used as a description language (by the system) at some level i, and then as a command language (by the learner) at the level i+1. This language shift mechanism elevates the learner's level of control and the level of abstraction. It is described by analogy with an elevator that would move inside a pyramid. A floor of the pyramid corresponds to some control level. We use a formal notation to look inside the language shift mechanism and relate it to various psychological theories and current ECSs.

Introduction

Metacognition refers to "understanding of knowledge, an understanding that can be reflected in either effective use or overt description of the knowledge in question" [5]. This definition covers the two main facets of metacognition: regulation of action and knowledge about knowledge. Metacognition is a very complex concept because it touches on many fundamental issues in cognitive psychology, such as learning, understanding, reading, consciousness, self-

NATO ASI Series, Vol. F 85
Adaptive Learning Environments
Edited by M. Jones and P. H. Winne

image, etc. This over-extended meaning may lead to giving the word "metacognition" the image of an empty concept.

The complexity and looseness of this concept does not question its importance [41]. This complexity corresponds to a particular stage in research; the various mechanisms that exist under the "metacognition" label have still to be isolated and labelled [5]. We do believe that metacognition research has the potential to improve actual classroom practice. Schoenfeld [41], and Palincsar and Brown [37] have demonstrated concrete and efficient forms of metacognitive training. Metacognitive research has "reawakened an interest in the role of consciousness, or awareness, or understanding, in thinking and problem-solving" [8]. This is not for scientific pleasure; it concerns thousands of children who are wasting their lives at the back of some classrooms. Learning disabilities appear to be connected with poor metacognitive skills [53] and can be reduced by metacognitive development programs [8].

What is the link between metacognition and design of an ECS? If metacognition is related to learning, it is still more closely related to self-instruction [48], and therefore to learning with an ECS. The debate about student control that opposes LOGO defenders with partisans of strong tutoring is typically a metacognitive issue. Moreover, metacognition is also related to motivation — through the self-image [48] — and to the issue of transfer, two key issues in ECS evaluation.

The development of the ECS field is still obstructed by narrow-minded people that can only consider two possibilities: 1) you build a very directive teaching system that will be very efficient and centred on some specific content, or 2) you leave the students playing around, roughly speaking, learning nothing but vague cognitive skills. Metacognitive investigations go beyond this stupid discrimination and open the door on ECSs that acknowledge the context-dependency of knowledge and the importance of basic procedural skills.

This chapter is based on a continuous view of metacognition: there is no one single cognition level plus a control level, but instead an (infinite) tower of levels, each level controlling the hierarchically inferior level [5, 33]. Recursion is the only way to implement this infinite tower within a finite device, the human brain. We hence discard the idea of having some metacognitive box that controls some other cognitive box. Metacognition is rather the emergent property of our cognitive system when it processes information about itself. In this contribution, we analyze the metacognitive processes in terms of inductive, deductive and analogical processes that are not specific to metacognitive activities.

This chapter will focus on an important concept in metacognition: reflection. The word "reflection" has two meanings. The psychological reflection is the cognitive activity that leads to some consciousness of one's own knowledge. The physical reflection consists of returning to something its own image. This chapter investigates how the computer's physical reflection can support the learner's psychological reflection by presenting him or her with some reified description of his or her behaviour [6, 11]. *Reification* means making concrete abstract aspects of behaviour, or, in Wenger's terms [50], creating a written notation for a process. We won't consider the computer's reflection in the psychological sense, i.e., a field of research better known under the label "computational reflection" [33].

Framework for Interaction Design

It is our ambition to present a discussion that goes beyond the simple description of systems that care about metacognition or the enumeration of a few empirical rules. We have attempted to describe our approach in a formal way. The result of this attempt, although incomplete, constitutes a first step in the long-term development of *computational mathetics*, i.e., a computational formalization of the learning process and of the ECS design process [42]. The specificity of our discipline is precisely the relationship between the learning process and the design process. So far, these processes have been separated: on one hand, we have some theories about learning, and, on the other hand, we have some principles about how to design an ECS that promotes learning. The latter are supposed to be consistent with the former, but they are still separated. The challenge is to integrate the latter into the former; the ECS features have to be incorporated into the theory of "learning with an ECS." The quest for such an integrated theory is the major difference between research efforts and development work. Computational mathetics aims to be just such a unified theory, under some computational form. We have already attempted to develop a similar framework in the domain of student modelling approaches [19].

This formal notation is not completed in the sense that, at the end, reasoning with the proposed notation is not simpler than reasoning on real problems. Theorems are not available for formal deductions; however, we believe it is still worthwhile to present this proposed notation as a first step towards computational mathetics. We will first describe the notation and then the language shift mechanism with the associated pyramid metaphor. An example, theoretical foundations and relations with similar work will be described later on.

Terminology and Notation

This section introduces some minimal notation that will be used in this attempted framework. We restrict ourselves to a few concepts related to metacognition and learner-system interaction.

We use uppercases to represent sets and lowercases for elements. Variables will be denoted _variable.

The atoms of the framework are actions. An *action* is any act performed by a agent through the interface: a sentence typed in by the learner, a window opened by the system, a button pushed by the learner, etc. An action will be noted by a predicate:

action (_agent, _problem, _level, _time)

An *agent* is a cognitive system able to use an interface. In this framework, we restrict ourselves to two agents, the learner or student and the system or computer. This framework may be extended to multi-agent systems such as systems with several real learners or systems where the computer plays the role of a collaborative learner [20]. Hence, we have:

action (**learner**, _problem, _level, _time) or
action (**system**, _problem, _level, _time)

A *problem class* is a set of problems that have similar intrinsic features, i.e., the knowledge required to solve the problem, the solution process, etc. A class may be subdivided into several subclasses. Within each *subclass*, problems have similar extrinsic features, i.e., a similar expression, being within a similar context, etc. The solution of each problem requires activating knowledge specific to its subclass plus the knowledge shared by the whole class. For instance, if the class is "fault diagnosis," we can have many subclasses such as "car engine diagnosis," "hard disk diagnosis," "water pump diagnosis," etc. The first subclass can again be subdivided into "Porshe engine diagnosis," "Fiat engine diagnosis," etc. This distinction between problem classes and subclasses will be necessary later for discussing the transfer issue. Each class can obviously be considered a subclass of some larger set of problems. It is considered as a class if it is the largest subclass among the pedagogical objectives. A problem class is noted **P** and its subclasses $\mathbf{P_i}$. A problem is associated with a number in subscript:

Example : action (_agent, $\mathbf{problem_1}$, _level, _time)

The "level" slot refers to the agent's reasoning. For the purpose of this paper, we define the agent's reasoning as a *hierarchy of control levels*. This hierarchy looks more like a pyramid than an inverted tree (with roots in the sky) because each decision at one level does not necessarily map to a few at the inferior level. Sometimes, control may be more global, e.g., when choosing a main approach to some problem. An example of segmentation in control levels is presented later in the MEMOLAB Example. Levels will be noted by an integer that counts the levels from the bottom of the pyramid. It must be said that the concept of control level is broader than in the chunking theory; the internalization of some concept requires some abstraction in addition to a simple compilation process.

Example : action (_agent, _problem, **level-1**, _time)

The *time* is here defined as the position of an action within a sequence of actions. We do not represent the length of intervals. Time is represented by an integer.

Example : action (_agent, _problem, _level, **5**)

For the simplicity of writing, this complex predicate will sometimes be denoted simply by writing its time slot in subscript:

$action_5$ = action (_agent, _problem, _level, **5**)

The *action space* is the set of actions from which some agent may select its actions. The action space is defined by a triplet:

Action-Space (agent, level, pedagogical-approach)

The set of actions available varies according to the agent, the level, and the pedagogical approach. The learner's action space is determined by the system according to its current pedagogical approach. For instance, the action "consulting the dictionary" may be accepted at some stage of the interaction, and forbidden during the evaluation stage. The system's action space is defined by the designer and the interaction. Determining the learner's action space is important for the purpose of this paper since it represents the system's ability to tune the learner's control of the system. Roughly speaking, the complexity of the student's control increases with the size of his/her action space. The choice of pedagogical methods will not be discussed in this framework, but it could be introduced in relation to the action space concept.

An action space can be viewed as a language with a set of basic actions as vocabulary and with a few syntactical rules that govern sentence building. According to the *grain-size* of analysis, an action may be one word long (such as a key press or a click) or some more complex sentence (e.g., click on object A, drag it on top of object B and select the "connect" menu option). We will specify later on different kinds of language.

A *behaviour* of an agent X is a subset of X's action space, i.e., a set of actions that have the same agent-slot X and have been performed for the same problem:

Behaviour ($agent_X$, $problem_i$) =
{ action ($agent_X$, $problem_i$, _level, 1),
action ($agent_X$, $problem_i$, _level, 2),
action ($agent_X$, $problem_i$, _level, 3),
action ($agent_X$, $problem_i$, _level, 4),
... }

The *interaction* is a sequence of actions performed by agents through the interface. Each action belongs to the current action space of each agent. We only consider student-computer interactions but the notation leaves the gate open for other classes of interactions, e.g., interaction between two learners. The interaction between two agents X and Y for some problem Z is as follows:.

Interaction (agent-X, agent-Y, problem-Z)

Example: Interaction (learner, system, $problem_i$) =
{ action (learner, $problem_i$, _level, 1),
action (system, $problem_i$, _level, 2),
action (learner, $problem_i$, _level, 3),
action (system, $problem_i$, _level, 4),
... }

Finally, the representation that some agent has of some object is:

Representation (agent, object)

The "Lift in the Pyramid" Metaphor

Figure 1 shows the metaphor we will use in this chapter: a lift within a pyramid. The pyramid represents the hierarchy of controls described in the previous section and each floor corresponds to some level of control. The ground floor is called floor 1. The lift cabin represents the activity of the learner. The lift position within the pyramid represents how the reasoning is shared between the learner and the system. The area above the lift is the part of the reasoning process which is regulated by the system (the tutor component). In the area below the lift, one finds the functionalities offered by the system to solve problems, e.g., basic calculus tools. The size of the lift represents the number of decision levels assumed by the learner, i.e., the cognitive load on the learner's shoulders.

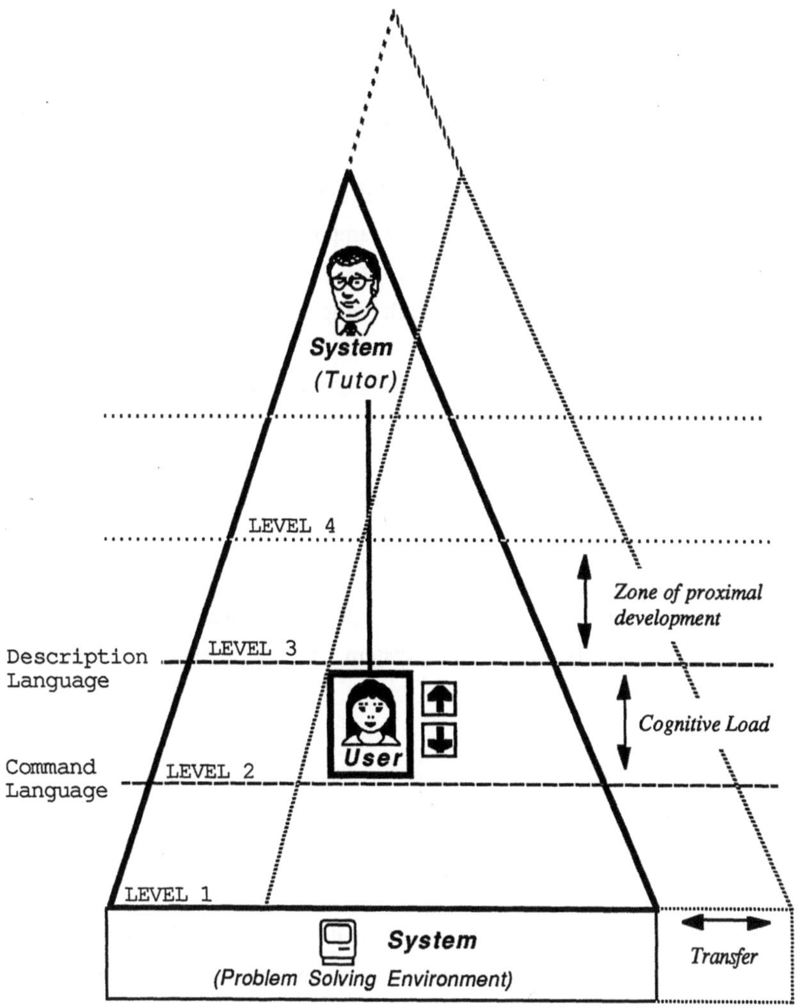

Figure 1 : The "Lift in the Pyramid" metaphor

It is always possible to imagine a level beneath or above the level considered. The definition of a ground floor is context-dependent and arbitrary. The ground floor of an ECS that teaches equation-solving may, for instance, be the top floor of another system on elementary calculus.

The *command language* defines the learner's action space: the words of the language determine the available actions and the language syntax sets the possible combinations of actions. At the outset, this command language defines the baseline of the pyramid, but this paper will show that we can elevate the command language to higher floors. The *description language* is a set of words and syntactical rules used by the computer to present a representation of the learner's action. A representation language is not neutral but emphasizes some features. The description language is supposed to be some graphical language, composed of objects and relations between objects. The objects represent the learner's actions. The relations between objects hence reify the relations between actions, i.e., the control performed at the lower floor.

The system action space is composed of direct answers to learner's commands plus sentences from the description language. For example, in Algebraland [6], if the learner uses the command "distribute" on the equation 3(x -5) = 7 , then the system will have two actions: returning the new equation 3x - (3*5)= 7 and drawing a line that reifies the transformation link between these states.

In our notation, the action spaces can hence be defined as follows:

(Action-space (learner, level_N, π)) =
{ action (learner,_,level_N,_) | action (learner,_,level_N,_) $\in$ command-language}

(Action-space (system, level-N, π))=
{action(learner,_,level_N,_)| action(learner,_,level_N,_) $\Rightarrow$ action(system,_,_,_)} U
{action(system,_,level_{N+1},_)|action (system,_,level_{N+1},_)$\in$ description-language}

The Ascending Mechanisms

Teachers aim for learners to perform better in higher levels of control and abstraction. Metaphorically, the goal is that the lift reaches the highest floors. It must be said that, for many tasks, it is probably difficult to imagine more than three or four levels and that the relationship between two levels is probably not identical all through the pyramid. "Nature may not always be theoretically aesthetic" [50]. We examine the mechanisms of shifting to the next level (up), which can recursively lead to this goal.

The Structure of Experience

Let us imagine that the learner has to solve a problem, 1, at the first floor of the pyramid. His behaviour is:

Behaviour (learner, $problem_1$) =
{ action (learner, $problem_1$, $level_1$, 1),
action (learner, $problem_1$, $level_1$, 2),
action (learner, $problem_1$, $level_1$, 3),
action (learner, $problem_1$, $level_1$, 4),
... }

where actions are sentences of the command language.

The microworld may give an answer to each learner's action. If the action is simply typing text into a window, then the answer is neutrally bringing characters on the screen. But if the action consists in using some facility offered by the microworld, then the system response may be the result of some longer computation. The action of the computer may also be to do nothing:

Interaction (learner, system, $problem_1$) =
{ action (learner, $problem_1$,$level_1$, 1),
action (system, $problem_1$, $level_1$, 2),
action (learner, $problem_1$, $level_1$, 3)
action (system, $problem_1$, $level_1$, 4),
action (learner, $problem_1$, $level_1$, 5),
... }

For reifying the learner's behaviour, the system has supplementary actions, expressed with the description language. These actions describe the relation between the last **n** learner's actions, where n varies according to the problem, the level, and the time. In the simplest case, the description language reifies the relation between the two last learner's actions and the intermediate system's action. The reification actions belong indeed to a higher level, here level

2, since they represent the control feature of the lower level. Subsequently, an interaction with systematic reification of the control aspects of the learner's behaviour becomes something like:

Interaction (learner, system, $problem_1$) =
{ action (learner, $problem_1$, $level_1$, 1),
action (system, $problem_1$, $level_1$, 2),
action (learner, $problem_1$, $level_1$, 3),
action (system, $problem_1$, **$level_2$**, 4),
action (system, $problem_1$, $level_1$, 5),
action (learner, $problem_1$, $level_1$, 6),
action (system, $problem_1$, **$level_2$**, 7),
... }

where the level-2 actions are a sentence from the description language, and in this example:

action (system, $problem_1$, **$level_2$**, 4) =
Representation (system, relation ($action_1$,$action_2$,$action_3$))

and action (system, $problem_1$, **$level_2$**, 7) =
Representation (system, relation ($action_3$,$action_5$,$action_6$))

The description language sentences constitute the punctuation that enables the learner to split the interaction sequence into *interaction segments*. An interaction segment is a subset of the interaction described by a description language sentence:

Interaction-Segment (learner, system, $problem_i$, i) =
{ ...
action (learner, $problem_i$, $level_{N-1}$, M-3),
action (system, $problem_i$, $level_{N-1}$, M-2),
action (learner, $problem_i$, $level_{N-1}$, M-1),
action (system, $problem_i$, **$level_N$**, M)
... }

If we imagine that the problem is to add fractions, here is an example of an interaction fragment:

Interaction-Segment (learner, system, "(2/3 + 4/9)", i) =
{ ...

action (learner, "(2/3 + 4/9)", $level_2$, 5) =
clicks on fraction 2/3 and asks "mult-den-by" with arg.3

action (system, "(2/3 + 4/9)", $level_2$, 6) =
replaces 3 by 9

action (learner, "(2/3 + 4/9)", $level_2$, 7) =
clicks on fraction 2/3 and asks "mult-num-by" with arg.3

action (system, "(2/3 + 4/9)", $level_3$, 8) =
graphical representation of "make-equivalent-fraction"
... }

This segment should be preceded by another one where the learner determines the common denominator and followed by other ones where he or she performs the addition and eventual simplification. This example is at level 2 since the learner does not perform the arithmetic operations by him or herself, but asks the system to do it via the command language. At a higher level, this segment would become a part of a segment called "reduce-to-the-same-denominator."

The length of an interaction segment may vary. The system action between the learner's two actions ($action_{m-2}$) is necessary to understand the relationship between the learner's actions only if this system's action brings new information necessary for the choice of the learner's second action. Otherwise, this action can be removed from the segment. This model further simplifies reality by the fact that the student's actions are considered to constitute a flat set. Things may be more complex (e.g., $action_3$ resulting from $action_1$ instead of resulting from $action_2$). It is clear that a model needs to make some simplifications to be useful; it is indeed these simplifications that create its heuristic power.

This interaction will be repeated for successive problems of P. After some time, the learner has observed a large set of interaction segments. The learner's experience is a collection of these segments, denoted E:

E = { Interaction-Segment(learner, system, $problem_i$, n)
Interaction-Segment(learner, system, $problem_i$, m)
Interaction-Segment(learner, system, $problem_j$, p)
Interaction-Segment(learner, system, $problem_k$, q)
... }

The Induction Postulate

The interaction gives the learner the opportunity to observe the computer's representation of control features. The aim is that the learner can build his or her own representation as a result of the internalization process:

(internalization
  (Representation
    (system, relation (..., $action_{M-3}$, $action_{M-2}$, $action_{M-1}$))
$\Rightarrow$
(Representation (learner, relation (..., $action_{M-3}$, $action_{M-2}$, $action_{M-1}$))

This section and the next ones analyze how reflection can help this internalization process. The role of reflection is to organize and structure experience. We base our work on the postulate that this process is mainly inductive. Campbell and Bickhard [7] proposed the concept of environmental *interaction patterns* as a basis for cognitive development. In the current problem, interaction patterns are sets of similarities between segments. These patterns will be internalized as metacognitive concepts. But this induction process is very difficult since it concerns relational concepts (concepts describing relations between actions).

We will see how the computer can help this induction. This inductive process includes two stages: 1) clustering, i.e., grouping segments into classes, and 2) pure induction, i.e., searching for similarities between objects within each cluster. In natural learning-concept-from-example situations, clustering and inducing are intertwined. Making classes is guided by the common properties of the objects in the classes, and discovering these properties is oriented by some idea of what the concept could be. Educational settings make the learner's life easier by artificially separating these two stages — the tutor classifies objects into positive and negative examples of the concept to be acquired or sets up an environment in which this classification appears clearly to the learner. Then, in a third stage, the integration of the acquired concept can be improved by constraining the learner to use the description language as a new command language. These three stages are described in the next sections.

Clustering Stage

In our case, clustering means regrouping segments that correspond to a similar relation between the student's actions. The description language includes the information necessary to perform this task. Remember that elements of E_S (to be clustered) are of the form:

{ ...
action (learner, $problem_i$, $level_{N-1}$, M-3),
action (system, $problem_i$, $level_{N-1}$, M-2),
action (learner, $problem_i$, $level_{N-1}$, M-1),
action (system, $problem_i$, **$level_N$**, M)
... }

According to our definition of the syntax of the description language, the last element of this segment is a representation of the relation between the previous elements.

action (system, $problem_1$, **$level_N$**, M) =
Representation (system, relation (...,$action_{M-3}$,$action_{M-2}$,$action_{M-1}$))

This equation reduces the complexity of the clustering stage because induction is performed on a single element ($action_m$) instead of on whole segments, and also because this element has concrete (visual) features (provided that $action_m$ belongs to a graphical description language).

If the description language must guide the clustering process, its syntax should be designed to ease this process. Let us imagine a description language composed of objects. Any pair of objects (o_1, o_2) can be connected according to four rules: up, down, left, right. Then the learner's experience may be partitioned as follows:

E = { $E_{s.up}$, $E_{s.down}$,$E_{s\cdot left}$,$E_{s.right}$} where

E_{up}={Interaction-Segment (learner,system,_,n)| $action_m$ = up(o_1,o_2)}
E_{down}={Interaction-Segment (learner,system,_,m)| $action_m$ = down(o_1,o_2)}
E_{left}={Interaction-Segment (learner,system,_,p)| $action_p$ = left(o_1,o_2)}
E_{right}={Interaction-Segment (learner,system,_,q)| $action_q$ = right(o_1,o_2)}

or in short: E={$E_{rel.1}$,$E_{rel.2}$,...$E_{rel.x}$={Interaction-Segment(learner,system,_,n) | $action_m$ =rel.X(o_1,o_2)}}

Given that the syntax of the description language has to guide the clustering process, the designer has to choose a syntax that is sufficient but simple. If the possible relations are numerous or complex or not easy to perceive, the clustering process will be more complex.

Inducing Stage

The task of the learner is now to perform induction on each cluster of E_1. One cluster is:

$E_{rel.x}$={Interaction-Segment(learner,system,_,n)|$action_m$ =rel.X(o_1,o_2)}

where

$rel_x(o_1,o_2)$= representation (system, relation(...,$action_{m-3}$,$action_{m-2}$,$action_{m-1}$))

Since machine learning has passed through its "glasnost," we know pure induction does not exist, because the role of background knowledge is very important [16]. We use, in induction, a lot of knowledge from the context, from the usefulness of the concept to be acquired, from our previous experiences, etc. The learner does not perform induction in a knowledge-free environment. An ECS is precisely an environment in which the amount of available knowledge can be partially controlled.

The semantics of the description language may or may not contain a concrete (visual) relation between objects which represents metaphorically the real relation between the learner's actions. If this metaphor is very obvious, the learner can deduce the common features that he or she is expected to find within the cluster. For instance, in figure 2a, it can be logically deduced that this pattern includes A ⇒ B action sequences while figure 2b describes a pattern where the relation between A and B is that they both result from a third action X.

Figure 2.a

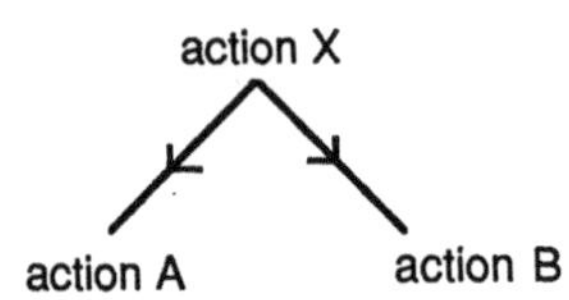

Figure 2.b

In other words, the design of the description language must take into account its analogical role in guiding induction. This analogy does not exempt the learner from induction; analogy is far from being an error-free process [26]. The learner has to check on the cluster objects and consider the context in order to give a particular meaning to a relation described by the language.

Integration: The Language Shift Mechanism

When the learner has acquired a new concept about his or her own behavioural regulation, the system should constrain him or her to use this concept for later problems. This can be done by using the description language as a new command language (and offering a new description language). This is what we call the "*language shift.*" This mechanism is defined by the following equation:

$$\text{description language at level}_n = \text{command language at level}_{n+1}$$

After the language shift, the learner has new tools for solving the problem, i.e., the solution process is changed. The new tools can be implemented by means such as new options in menus. Naming a new concept (as a menu item) anchors this concept in the learner's memory. In the pyramid metaphor, this language shift corresponds to the lift moving one level up, when one constrains the learner to describe his or her behaviour in terms of how it is regulated instead of by performing the actions directly.

A corollary of the above equation is that the system has to perform the actions the learner performed at the previous level:

$$\text{Action-Space (system,level}_N,\pi) = \text{Action-Space (learner,level}_{N+1},\pi)$$

The learner's cognitive effort necessary for reaching the next floor is somewhat lessened by the fact that the bottom boundary of the learner's activities goes up simultaneously — he or she no longer has to perform the computation required by his or her actions since the computer does it for him or her. The learner now has more cognitive resources available for concentrating on the control aspects. This is represented metaphorically on the pyramid by the fact that the lift remains the same size. The final goal of an ECS is obviously that the learner becomes able to perform alone all the control covered by the pyramid. However, by allocating the automatization of subskills to the system instead of to the learner, the focus on metacognitive aspects can be made sooner and more efficiently. An alternative approach to the computer-made automatization of subskills is the learner-made automatization of these subskills, i.e., the systematic practice of these skills, until they are compiled in quasi-automatic procedures.

Inside the Language Shift: Action Subspaces

We have described the language shift as an all-or-none process. This process can be analyzed more finely if we stratify the learner's action space into ordered subsets. We have empirically determined five subspaces according to the kind of activities that the learner is allowed to perform on the description of his or her behaviour:

observing	the learner just looks at the description
editing	the learner has some tools to edit the description
orienting	the learner uses the description to select a problem state
composing	the learner creates the description by combining items
creating	the learner builds the description from scratch

If the interaction description is a tree, the levels of activities might be:

observing	looking at the tree
editing	annotating nodes by justifications
orienting	selecting a node for backtracking or ask for replay
composing	building the tree from a bank of parts
creating	drawing the tree with lines and boxes

These action subspaces constitute successive steps within the language shift mechanism. The observation level clearly corresponds to the description language, while the orientation activities begin to use the description as a new command language.

The Role of Problem Variations

Transfer and lift ascension are viewed as two facets of a similar inductive mechanism, built around the description language.

In the pyramid metaphor, focussing on transfer means working on partially overlapping pyramids that correspond to new problem subclasses (or classes in case of far transfer). The union of two pyramids forms a new one. The height of the new pyramid is proportional to its breadth. We try now to analyze this intuitive rule and to relate it with the mechanisms of lift elevation previously described.

In learning concepts from examples, differences between examples are very important because they enable one to eliminate features that are not relevant to the concept. For instance, for teaching the concept of a square, the examples set must include non-horizontal squares; otherwise, learners will consider that a square may have only horizontal and vertical sides.

Varying the subclass of problems has the same effect on interaction clusters as non-horizontal squares, to guarantee that features shared by examples are relevant components of the concept, i.e., they insure eliminating non-relevant similarities.

Let us consider two segments:

Interaction-Segment(learner, system, $problem_i$, n)
Interaction-Segment(learner, system, $problem_j$, m)

Remember that the last element of each segment represents the relationship between the previous ones:

$action_n$ = representation (system, relation (...,$action_{n-3}$,$action_{n-2}$,$action_{n-1}$))
$action_m$ = representation (system, relation (...,$action_{m-3}$,$action_{m-2}$,$action_{nm-1}$))

The condition for transfer is that the learner detects some isomorphism between the two segments (..., $action_{n-3}$, $action_{n-2}$, $action_{n-1}$) and (..., $action_{m-3}$, $action_{m-2}$, $action_{nm-1}$). This isomorphism is represented in the description language by the concrete similarities between the actions in the left term:

relation ($action_n$, $action_m$) =
representation
(system, relation
((...,$action_{n-3}$,$action_{n-2}$,$action_{n-1}$),
(...,$action_{m-3}$,$action_{m-2}$,$action_{nm-1}$))

This equation has important corollaries for the relation between the transfer process and the description language. If the description language does not include elements specific to some subclass P_i , we have:

$action_n$ = $action_m$

In this case, the learner is directly informed by the system of the opportunity for transfer. If the representation used for the description language contains elements specific to some subclass but these elements can be easily isolated from those that are shared, the transfer will be guided by searching for ($action_n \cap action_m$) since:

$$(action_n \cap action_m) =$$
$$representation$$
$$(system,(...,action_{n-3},action_{n-2},action_{n-1}) \cap$$
$$(...,action_{m-3},action_{m-2},action_{nm-1}))$$

Reciprocally, transfer mechanisms are important for the description language. The learner will demonstrate that he or she has integrated the description language when he or she will use it explicitly to perform transfer. This is important to detect the right time to start a language shift.

The MEMOLAB Example

We are currently designing a system that applies the language shift mechanism to the complexity of a real world problem: "nobody grows up by solving the tower of Hanoï problem!" [21]. This learning environment is called MEMOLAB. The pedagogical goals are that students acquire the fundamental concepts necessary to perform experimentation in psychology. These concepts are experienced by designing and running experiments on human memory, in an artificial lab. The four-floors pyramid is built around the concepts of experimentation. Peripheral concepts from statistics and human memory are built around these core concepts. The four floors are:

1: building non-comparative experiments (single sample)
2: building simple comparative experiments (one factor, several samples)
3: building uni-dimensional experimental plans, and
4: building multi-dimensional experimental plans.

Building an experiment means assembling concrete events on the lab workbench. An event is the association of some subjects with some task and a measurement device. A task is defined by an activity, a material and a few parameters. Building a plan means creating a non-instantiated single experiment on the workbench and generating the experiment by defining an n-dimensional table of factors (n being the number of independent variables).

At level one, the dumb beginner will sequence event-frames on the lab workbench. Each event-frame includes some part of the information that defines the event (subjects,task,.etc.).

The learners decide what information has to be displayed in each event frame. The elevation to the second floor implies that students understand that observing an effect means creating a variation between groups and that these inter-group variations must be more important than the intra-group variations. The description language will reify the differential nature of the experimental method. The system will regroup experiments that can be compared and redisplay the events in order to enlighten the differences.

The differentiation nature of the first floor description language defines the second floor command language. At the second floor, learners will use these differences to build experiments. For instance, they will describe the whole sequence of activities for a first sample. Then, the second sample sequence will be built by editing the first sample sequence (e.g., augmenting the length of words that subjects of the second group have to memorize), i.e., it will be defined by its difference with the first sequence.

The passage to the third floor implies a new discrimination by the learner between the concrete structure of the experiment (a sequence of events) and the variables (dependent and independent) that instantiate this structure. The description language will redisplay the experiments by separating the paradigm and its associated plan. The third floor command language will then offer two workbenchs, one similar to lower floors, to build experimental paradigms, and a new one, to define experimental plans. Finally, the concept of interaction between effects is necessary to reach the fourth floor. This concept will be suggested by comparing plans of the third floor, in the same way that experiments have been compared at the floor1-floor2 transition.

Theoretical Bridges

This framework can be read from several theoretical and practical perspectives. We review related work in psychology, in machine learning and in research on ECSs.

Psychologists Visiting the Pyramid

Metacognition and reflected abstraction (Piaget). The mechanism of language shift is closely related to the piagetian concept of *reflected abstraction* [39]. Reflected abstraction is a process by which properties that are implicit at some level of knowledge can be abstracted and explicitly accessed at a higher level. The general relationship between metacognition and reflected abstraction is a complex issue of genetic psychology that goes beyond the scope of this paper [4]. However, Campbell and Bickhard [7] — although rather in conflict with the piagetian structuralism — proposed an interesting analysis of this relationship that pertains to our approach. Let us remember that the induction of interaction patterns which is the basis of the language shift is a key notion of Campbell and Bickhard's theory.

These authors describe developmental stages in terms of going through a hierarchy of *knowing levels*, where each level "knows" the properties of the subordinated level. For Campbell and Bickhard, reflective abstraction is a mechanism of *knowing-level ascension*. Such an ascension through a hierarchy of levels matches our definition of the language shift mechanism. This parallelism is emphasized by the following paragraph (where the authors use the word "system" for referring to a cognitive system, i.e., an agent in our terminology):

> Suppose that a system could learn to create external indicators of various points in and aspects of its own internal process — as it was actually engaged in those processes. Then the indicators would manifest properties of the organization and functioning of those internal processes. Being external, the indicators would be available for examination by the system itself. From the indicators, the system could then abstract the properties of the processes that yielded those indicators. That is, using such indicators, a system could reflectively abstract its own properties [7, p. 86].

If we stay in the piagetian lineage, the lift metaphor is very close to the neopiagetian theories developed by Robbie Case [9]. In this approach, the process of stage transition consists in integrating independent control structures into a more complex one, in a way very similar to our metaphor. In the MEMOLAB example, the objects of one floor are reorganized in order to reduce the task complexity. A group of single-group experiments (level 1) is re-unitarized into comparative experiments (level 2). Sets of comparative experiments are re-unitarized as experimental plans (level 3) and groups of plans are re-unitarized as multi-dimensional plans (level 4). The mechanism that triggers this re-unitarization process is partly linked to the limits of working memory. Interestingly, we know the limits of working memory are related to the issue of awareness through the concept of focus of attention, more precisely the control function that actively maintains information in working memory [27].

Internalization of regulation processes (Vygotsky). According to Vygostsky [47], the development of higher psychological processes results from the *internalization* of inter-individual processes. Metacognition would also have social origins, self-regulation being viewed as the result of adult-child regulation [51]. The vygotskian concept of "zone of proximal development" (ZPD) is present in our framework as the stage just above the lift position. This stage includes control activities that the learner is not able to perform alone but can do with the help of the computer:

$$\text{ZPD} = \text{Action-space (system+user,level}_{N+1}\text{,coaching)}$$
$$\text{if we have Action-space (learner,level}_{N}\text{,\_)}$$

Vygostky outlined the linguistic nature of the internalization mechanism when he declared that "verbal thought is the transferral of speech to an internal level" and that "reflection is the transferral of argumentation to an internal level" (Vygotsky, quoted in [51]). This linguistic dimension is important for our purpose because it relates the type of user-computer interaction to our interest for metacognitive issues. Models of mental activities are indeed generally identified through verbs such as to think, to know, to ignore,.etc. [49]. These linguistic aspects of internalization have been analyzed by Wertsch [51]. He suggested that some linguistic mechanisms allow the performance of intra-psychological processes at some stage of the inter-psychological level. Wertsch observed mothers monitoring their children solving a puzzle. He found that a mother would change her referential perspective according to the child's skills. When identifying a piece of the puzzle, the beginner's mother would refer to piece attributes that both agents could observe (e.g., "a green piece"), while later, the mother tended to refer to the strategy used (e.g., "a piece with another colour"). According to Wertsch, *strategy-based* referential means that "an understanding of the strategy was required to interpret a referring expression appropriately." In the pyramid metaphor, the role of the description language corresponds to the mother's discourse, i.e., it describes the learner's behaviour in terms of the underlying strategy [18].

Transfer and metacognition. Several researchers have analyzed the relationship between reflection and transfer. Rozin (quoted in [5]) related reflective access to knowledge (the key to metacognition) and multiple access of knowledge (the key to transfer). This link supposes that "accessing is connecting previously isolated components, or mental faculties, and passing information between them" [7, p. 89]. Ann Brown [5] reports research on transfer between isomorphic problems by three- and four-year-old children. These children exhibited a greater transfer when, after each problem, they were required to describe their solution to "Kermit the frog" so that he could reproduce it. Multiplicity and reflection hence become central issues in the design of ITS. The difference between Brown's experiments and our approach is that we explore the reflection-transfer link in the opposite direction — how transfer can be used to promote metacognition.

The framework may also be related to Anderson's theories of transfer within the ACT* framework [44]. Each segment of the learner's experience can be expressed as a production rule:

{ ...
action (learner, $problem_i$, $level_{N-1}$, M-3),
action (system, $problem_i$, $level_{N-1}$, M-2),
action (learner, $problem_i$, $level_{N-1}$, M-1),
action (system, $problem_i$, **$level_N$**, M)
... }

corresponding to the production rule:

IF ...
AND action (learner, $problem_i$, $level_{N-1}$, M-3)
AND action (system, $problem_i$, $level_{N-1}$, M-2)
THEN action (learner, $problem_i$, $level_{N-1}$, M-1)

This rule is represented by:

action (system, $problem_i$, **$level_N$**, M)

The control aspects are compiled in these rules. Conversely, the raison d'être of action (system, $problem_i$, **$level_N$**, M) is precisely to give some access to these underlying control features. The lift ascension, in other words, corresponds to a process that inverts Anderson's compilation process. The student task would be rather to extract the hidden metaknowledge in a similar way to a knowledge engineer [10] attempting to build a deep expert system [45]. This fundamental difference of approach implies another measure of transfer. Singley and Anderson estimate the difficulty of transfer as proportional to the overlapping between the production sets corresponding to the source and target problems. This overlapping is quantified in terms of the number of identical productions (with some weighting). In our approach, the overlapping includes not only identical segments but also segments sharing the same representation, i.e., the same abstraction. This view is also supported by computational applications in the so-called *abstraction-based analogy* field [25, 43].

Computers Scientists Looking at the Pyramid

With the last subsection, we touched on the relation between the pyramid and production systems. Several machine learning systems attempt to learn from some representation of experience called "problem solving path" [30]. It is a trace of the operators applied during the solution process, associated with the state of the problem and some measure of the operator efficiency. *Learning from the problem solving path* has already found applications in the design of ECSs such as ACM [31] and PROTO-TEG [17]. Interestingly, Klahr [28] relates this kind of machine learning with the concept of reflected abstraction. By time line, Klahr refers to something similar to the solution path or what J.S. Brown [6] called "audit trail":

> The time line and its associated analyzers can be viewed as an attempt to further specify Piaget's appealing but mysterious notion of "reflective abstraction"; it provides a means for the system to ruminate about the efficacy of its own processing episodes [28, p. 117]

These systems learn by searching for conditions that improve the efficiency of operators, i.e., they aim to improve control skills involved in operator selection. For that, they attempt to induce the features that characterize states where the operator X has been efficient, and discriminate these states from those where the same operator has failed. The key of this inductive process is the *generalization hierarchy*, i.e., a graph that informs the system that two different features can be induced as instances of a more general concept. This generalization hierarchy is often encompassed in the language used to describe the instances and the concepts. Researchers agree on the crucial role of this description language in inductive learning [3, 29, 46]. This language determines the concept search space by selecting the object features that will be taken into account and how features can be generalized.

The role of the description language in the pyramid corresponds to the role of the description language in machine learning. The set of instances is the sequence of command language sentences, i.e., the first three elements of each triplet in E_S. The description of these instances is provided by the description language, i.e., the last element of each segment.

The semantics of the description language provide the deductive component necessary for induction. For many years, machine learning theorists mistakenly believed that learning could be purely inductive and neglected the deductive aspects involved (e.g., the description language role). Later the deductive aspects were overestimated by the explanation-based learning stream [13, 35]. Today, the complementarity of inductive, deductive, and analogical sources of knowledge is well accepted. According to their relative weight, these sources of knowledge paint the learning process a more-inductive colour or more-deductive colour. Implementations differ on the scale of the task distribution between knowledge sources. Devi [15] proposed to combine inductive and deductive main phases while Dillenbourg and Self [20] view learning as a complex and built-on-the-fly sequence of small inductive, deductive and analogical steps. This *microscopic* view of learning fits with the learner task in his or her lift. The meaning of some action (system, $problem_i$, $\mathbf{level_N}$, M) can help to find similarities between interaction patterns or, inversely, interaction patterns can help to understand the meaning of representational aspects. Both mechanisms occur probably in parallel or iteratively.

ECSs Around the Pyramid

In the field of ECSs, several pieces of work may be related to the pyramid lift metaphor. Two ECSs are often quoted when speaking about reflection: ALGEBRALAND [6] and the GEOMETRY tutor [1]. ALGEBRALAND may be described within our framework as a lift locked at the second floor. The users have to solve linear equations. They have a command language at their disposal that performs the ground floor computations: add-to-both-side, distribute, expand, etc. The description language is an inverted tree whose nodes are the intermediate transformations of the equation. Branches correspond to applications of an operator. This representation reifies the heuristic aspects of a solving process: the multiple solution paths, the backtracking steps, etc.

To extend ALGEBRALAND along the pyramid metaphor, we should add a ground floor where the learner types in some equation (command language = set of algebraic symbols). Learners have access in ALGEBRALAND to some editing activities (e.g., annotating the tree) that constitute the basis for adding a third floor to this system. At this third floor, the command language would, for instance, act directly on the description tree with commands such as "Select the node with the fewest occurrences of x." Such a command would compel the learner to make his or her strategy more explicit.

This approach of an ECS is based on fundamental issues that distinguish it from the first generation of CBT material; designers pay more attention to the process of learning than to its products [6]. The holy law of immediate feedback, inherited from the behaviourist grounds of CBT, is called into question in the interest of giving the learner time to inspect his or her behavioural trace [24, 50]. The pyramid metaphor emphasizes the complementarity of immediate and delayed feedback. Immediate feedback is necessary to install low-level skills that need to be automated, while delayed feedback is necessary when the focus is the learner's consciousness of some features of his/her own behaviour.

The framework is also very close to the work of Derry and her colleagues on the TAPS II system [14]. In TAPS II, the students concentrate on the representation of the word problem to solve, instead of on the representation of the problem solving strategy. As the author points out, these representations are intertwined:

> ...a person's conceptualization of a problem may actually emerge as a by-product of the problem-solving strategy itself. Simultaneously, the way in which a problem is conceptualized will suggest a strategic ordering of problem-solving operations that can be applied to solve the problem. It is precisely this sort of reciprocal, dynamic interaction between representation and operation that must be supported if computers are to serve as conceptualizing tools in instruction [14, p. 4].

Learners are invited to build a schema of the problem solution by selecting general schemas into a bank and instantiating them with the problem data ("composition" level of activities). TAPS II occupies the three first floors of the pyramid. Simple arithmetic operations may be performed by the system at the ground floor; the assembled schemas are used as a description language of the second floor but also as a command language of the third floor. This results from the fact that the learner has to build the representation of his or her activity. Some self-monitoring strategies are available at the top of the third floor for guiding the student but do not form a new description language.

The major difference between the "lift in the pyramid" metaphor and the systems described here is that it concentrates on the *dynamic* aspect of a system. This system can be thought of as a sequence of microworlds. The learner's metacognitive development (for a particular task) parallels his or her road through these increasingly abstract worlds. Let us note that this sequence may be nested within a sequence of increasingly complex tasks (e.g., considering the number of parameters affecting problem difficulty) or within a larger-scale sequence that covers various parts of the curriculum.

The progressivity defined by the pyramid metaphor instantiates the apprenticeship paradigm [50]: the tutor assumes the part of control that the learner cannot yet perform and progressively transfers control to the learner. This approach has growing popularity both in education — in the vygotskian line — and in machine learning [52].

According to Cumming and Self [12], one major challenge of ECSs is to decouple the *task level* and the *discussion level*. At the task level, the student works to solve the particular problem or task proposed by the system. At the discussion level, he or she reflects on the task level and interacts with the system about some aspects of this reflection (e.g., plans, failures, etc.). The language shift mechanism recursively exploits this discrimination at each level of the pyramid.

Let us, for instance, consider the concept of knowledge negotiation system [36], created by opposition to the paradigm of knowledge communication that dominated our field during two decades [50]. In our understanding, the terms "knowledge negotiation" refers to some relationship between the task and the discussion level. The multiplicity of equally valid viewpoints at the task level requires the existence of some discussion level where explicit negotiation or articulation of viewpoints can occur. This explicit negotiation movement is attested to within the literature by a significant shift in focus from "tutorial discourse" to "tutorial dialogue" [38, 2].

Finally, we believe that the pyramid is consistent with the idea of *constructorium*, i.e., the conception of the computer as a lab where learners observe the construction of their own knowledge [18]. After many years of passive schooling, students naturally acquire a passive model of learning. Learning comes to mean listening to a teacher, reading a textbook, or repeating a definition. ECSs would gain an innovative power by removing this baneful image, by reflecting to the learner a better image of its learning activities. This image should emphasize that learning is an active process of constructing knowledge.

Conclusions

ECSs can advantageously offer tools for reflecting to the learner some abstract aspects of his or her behaviour. However, educationalists have, for a long time, been confronted with the issue that presenting some information to the learner does not mean that this information will be processed and assimilated. Assimilation results in transforming this information during some activities. The fact that the computer enables such activities does not imply that learners do actually perform these activities! The idea behind the language shift is to compel the user to perform such activities; the assimilation of the concepts of the description language is the premise of their use as a new command language.

The detailed implementation of the language shift is beyond the scope of this paper. It raises problems that have been with us for many years (e.g., the psychological validity of the description language (and all the related student modelling issues) and who decides the language shift). Our current work on MEMOLAB [23] aims to bring answers to these questions and to confront the consistency of the pyramid and language shift ideas to the complexity of real world problems. It is clear, however, that the pyramid metaphor does not describe a complete learning environment, but only its core structure. Around the pyramid, one needs to implement complementary tools that stimulate the necessary internalization process and introduce the peripheral concepts. In MEMOLAB, for instance, these tools will constitute a complex learning society, including soft coaching agents, statistical tools, specialized counsellors, reflection tools and an encyclopedia of human memory (written in some hypertext form). If the scientific interest of learning is related to the aesthetics of its design principles, its pedagogical power is related to the richness of multiplicity of experiences.

Acknowledgements

This research is partially funded by the Swiss NRP23 research program on AI and robotics. Thanks to A. Brandeis, P. Mendlsohn, D. Schneider, J. Self and all the workshop participants for their comments on previous drafts.

References

1. Anderson, J.R., Boyle, C.F., & Yost G.: The geometry tutor. Proceedings of the Ninth International Joint Conference on Artificial Intelligence, Los Angeles Vol.1 (1985)
2. Baker, M.: A model for tutorial dialogues based on critical argument. Proceedings of the 4th AI and Education Conference, IOS. Amsterdam,.pp. 2-8 (1989)
3. Banerji, R.: Solving the linguistic problems in learning. *Fundamenta Informatica XII*, pp. 51-78 (1989)
4. Blanchet, A.: Abstraction réfléchissante et metacognition. Paper presented at the "Archives Jean Piaget," Geneve, April 23, 1990
5. Brown, A.: Metacognition, executive control, self-regulation and other more mysterious mechanisms. In: *Metacognition, motivation and understanding* (F.E. Weinert & R.H. Kluwe, eds.). Hillsdale, NJ: Lawrence Erlbaum Associates 1987
6. Brown, J.S.: Process versus product: A perspective on tools for communal and informal electronic learning. *Journal of Computing Research*, 1 (2) (1985)
7. Campbell, R.L., & Bickhard, M.H.: *Knowing levels and developmental stages*. Basel: Karger 1986
8. Campione, J.C.: Metacognitive components of instructional research with problem learners. In: *Metacognition, motivation and understanding* (F.E. Weinert & R.H. Kluwe, eds.). Hillsdale, NJ: Lawrence Erlbaum Associates 1987
9. Case, R.: *Intellectual development, birth to adulthood*. New York: Academic Press 1985
10. Clancey, W.J.: The knowledge engineer as student: Metacognitive bases for asking good questions. In: *Learning issues for intelligent tutoring systems* (H. Mandl & A. Lesgold, eds.). New York: Springer-Verlag 1988
11. Collins, & Brown, J.S.: The computer as a tool for learning through reflection. In: *Learning issues for intelligent tutoring systems* (H. Mandl & A. Lesgold, eds.). New York: Springer-Verlag 1988
12. Cumming, G., & Self, J.: Collaborative intelligent educational system. Proceedings of the 4th AI and Education Conference, IOS, Amsterdam,.pp. 73-80 (1989)

13. DeJong, G., & Mooney, R.: Explanation-based learning: An alternative view. *Machine Learning*, 1, pp. 145-176 (1986)
14. Derry, S.J.: Flexible tools for problem solving instruction. Paper presented at the AERA Symposium, Computers as Cognitive Tools. Boston, MA 1990
15. Devi, R.: Machine learning and tutoring systems. CITE Report 61, UK: Open University 1989
16. Dietterich, T.G.: Learning at the knowledge level. In: *Machine Learning*, Vol. 1, 3, pp. 287-316 (1986)
17. Dillenbourg, P.: Designing a self-improving tutor: PROTO-TEG. *Instructional Science*, 18, pp. 193-216 (1989)
18. Dillenbourg, P.: The computer as a constructorium: Tools for observing one's own learning. In: *Knowledge Negotiation* (R. Moyse & M. Elsom-Cook, eds.). London: Paul Chapman (in press)
19. Dillenbourg, P., & Self, J.A.: *A framework for learner modelling*. TECFA Document 90-5, University of Geneva 1990
20. Dillenbourg, P., & Self, J.A: Designing human-computer collaborative learning. In: *Computer-supported collaborative learning* (C.E. O'Malley, ed.). Wiley & Sons (in press)
21. Dillenbourg, P., Mendelsohn, P., & Schneider, D.: The Geneva manifesto of intelligent learning environments. Document TECFA 90-3, Université de Genève 1990a
22. Dillenbourg, P., Hilario, M., Mendelsohn, P., & Schneider, D.: Training transfer: A bridge between the theory-oriented and product-oriented approaches to ITS design. Document TECFA 90-3, Université de Genève 1990b
23. Dillenbourg, P., Hilario, M., Mendelsohn, P., & Schneider, D.: The MEMOLAB project. Document TECFA 90-4, Université de Genève 1990c
24. Foss, C.: Acquisition of error management skills. Paper presented at Third International Conference on Artificial Intelligence and Education, Pittsburgh, p. 27 (1987)
25. Greiner, R.: Abstraction-based analogical inference. In: *Analogical reasoning* (D. H. Helman, ed.). Doordrecht, The Netherlands: Kluwer Academic Publishers 1988
26. Hall, R.P.: Computational approaches to analogical reasoning: A comparative analysis. *Artificial Intelligence*, 39, pp. 39-120 (1989)
27. Jackendoff, R.S.: *Consciousness and the computational mind.* Cambridge, MA: MIT Press 1987
28. Klahr, D.: Transition processes in quantitative development. In: *Mechanisms of cognitive development* (R.J, Sternberg, ed.). New York: Freeman & Company 1984
29. Kodratoff, Y., & Ganascia, J.G.: Improving the generalisation step in learning. In: *Machine learning* (R.S. Michalski, J.G. Carbonell & T.M. Mitchell, eds.). Vol II, Los Altos, CA: Morgan Kaufman 1986
30. Langley, P.: Learning search strategies through discrimination. *International Journal of Man-Machine Studies*, 18, pp. 513-541 (1983)
31. Langley, P., & Ohlsson, S.: Automated cognitive modelling. Proceedings of the National Conference on Artificial Intelligence, Austin, Texas, pp. 193-197 (1984)
32. Lochhead, J.: Teaching analytic reasoning skills through pair problem solving. In: *Thinking and learning skills: Vol. 1: Relating instruction to research.* (J.W. Segal, S.F Chipman & R. Glaser, eds.). Hillsdale, NJ: Lawrence Erlbaum Associates 1985
33. Maes, O.: Issues in computational reflection. In: *Meta-level architectures and reflection* (P.Maes & D. Nardi, eds.). Amsterdam: Elsevier 1988
34. Michalski, R.S: Understanding the nature of learning: Issues and research directions. In: *Machine learning* (R.S. Michalski, J.G. Carbonell & T.M. Mitchell, eds.). Vol II, Los Altos: Morgan Kaufman 1986
35. Mitchell, T.M., Keller, R.M., & Kedar-Cabelli, S.T.: Explanation-based generalization: A unifying view. *Machine Learning*, 1, pp. 47-80 (1986)
36. Moyse, R.:Knowledge negotiation. Working Paper, IET, UK: Open University 1989
37. Palincsar, A.S., & Brown, A.L.: Reciprocal teaching of comprehension-fostering and comprehension-monitoring activities. *Cognition and Instruction*, vol. 1, 2, pp. 117-175 (1984)
38. Pertrie-Brown, A.M.: Discourse and dialogue: Concepts in intelligent tutoring interactions. *Journal of Artificial Intelligence in Education*, Vol.1, 2, pp. 21-30 (1990)
39. Piaget, J.: *Biology and knowledge.* Chicago, IL: The University of Chicago Press 1971
40. Reimann, P.: *Problem solving models of scientific discovery learning process.* Frankfurt: Peter Lang 1990
41. Schoenfeld, A.H.: What's all the fuss about metacognition? In: *Cognitive science and mathematics education* (A.H. Schoenfeld, ed.). Hillsdale, NJ: Lawrence Erlbaum Associates 1987
42. Self, J.A.: An introduction to computational mathetics. Working paper, Computing Department, University of Lancaster 1990
43. Shinn, H.S.: Abstractional analogy: A model of analogical reasoning. Proceedings of a Workshop on Case-Based Reasoning, Florida, pp. 370-387 (1988)
44. Singley, M.K., & Anderson, J.R.: *The transfer of cognitive skills.* Cambridge, MA: Harvard University Press 1989

45. Steels, L.: Components of expertise. *AI Magazine*, vol. 11, 2, pp. 28-49 (1990)
46. Utgoff, P.E.: Shift of bias for inductive concept learning. In: *Machine learning* (R.S. Michalski, J.G. Carbonell & T.M. Mitchell, eds.). Vol II, Los Altos, CA: Morgan Kaufman 1986
47. Vygotsky, L.S.: (written in the 30's, but edited by M. Cole, V. John-Steiner, S. Scribner & E. Souberman) *Mind in society: The development of higher psychological processes.* Cambridge, MA: Harvard University Press 1978
48. Weinert, F.E., & Kluwe, R.H.: *Metacognition, motivation and understanding.* Hillsdale, NJ: Lawrence Erlbaum Associates 1987
49. Wellman, H.M.: The child's theory of mind: The development of conceptions of cognition. In: *The growth of reflection in children* (S.R. Yussen, ed.). Madison, WI: Academic Press 1985
50. Wenger, E.: *Artificial intelligence and tutoring systems: Computational and cognitive approaches to the communication of knowledge.* Los Altos, CA: Morgan Kaufman 1987
51. Wertsch, J.V.: Adult-child interaction as a source of self-regulation. In: *The growth of reflection in children* (S.R Yussen, ed.). Madison, WI: Academic Press 1985
52. Wilkins, D.C.: Apprenticeship learning techniques for knowledge based systems. Doctoral dissertation report, STAN-CS-88-142, Stanford University, CA 1988
53. Wong, B.Y.L.: Metacognition and learning disabilities. In: *Metacognition, cognition and human performance* (D.L. Forrest-Presley, G.E. MacKinnon & T.G. Waller, eds.). Vol. 2, New York: Academic Press 1985

Part 6

Student-System Interactions

Student-System Interactions

Benedict du Boulay[1] & Peter Goodyear[2]

[1]School of Cognitive and Computing Sciences, University of Sussex, Falmer, Brighton, England
[2]Department of Educational Research, Lancaster University, Lancaster, England

Despite the explicit pairing of papers both at the Calgary Institute and in this volume, the paper by Stephano Cerri is best regarded as being in the same general area as that by Laurillard. Cerri describes a methodology (and software system that embodies that methodology) for the gradual elaboration of a generative student model in some domain. By contrast with Laurillard who proposes a carefully controlled, cyclic, empirical process to be completed prior to the design of the resultant tutor/diagnoser, Cerri's methodology involves a cyclic refinement process involving an expert, the evolving tutorial/diagnostic system and students, all linked through the design tool. For Cerri, there is rather less obvious distinction between knowledge acquisition and system implementation in that the two processes are intertwined. Cerri also subscribes to the standard view of student modelling within the intelligent tutoring systems community and certainly does not make the kind of distinction between classifying a student's conceptions and modelling the student which is of concern to Laurillard.

There are similarities between Cerri's approach and that of others in this volume, including Winne. Cerri is concerned with reducing the amount of effort needed to implement an intelligent tutoring system, and talks about using software tools as a way of involving educationalists and psychologists with system builders.

Cerri offers us the notion of an "inverted dialogue" to capture the essence of his methodology. This is a dialogue where conventional participant roles are exchanged; for example, the expert becomes "the student" and the student model becomes "the teacher." In fact, there will be several different dialogues and inverted dialogues between the various "participants" during the production of the fully-realized student model.

The basic idea is that the system starts out with an impoverished, but generative, student model provided by the expert. What follows falls into two main phases. In the first phase, the system is allowed to interact with students using its impoverished student model and, no doubt, making a rather bad job of being a teacher/diagnoser. So there will be aspects of student behaviour that are not predicted correctly or covered properly by the partial model. These failures of coverage are examined by the human expert. The expert analyzes the transcript of the record of the system's interactions with the students with a view to hypothesizing the underlying causes of the students' surface errors as observed. At this point, the expert is free to take note of whichever part of the transcript he or she wishes. In the final stage of this first phase, the development system presents the expert with selections from the recorded transcripts

NATO ASI Series, Vol. F 85
Adaptive Learning Environments
Edited by M. Jones and P. H. Winne

to help ensure that the expert has considered all the surface evidence in sufficient breadth. Here, the system still has only its impoverished student model but the human expert has a rich set of hypotheses about student errors. A difficult issue for the system at this final stage of the first phase is how it can do better than simply presenting every part of every transcript.

In the second phase of the interaction, the expert employs his or her hypotheses from the first stage to elaborate the impoverished student model. The system tries to assist by presenting the expert with that part of the existing impoverished model that most closely predicts the observed error. This model is presented as a kind of prototype that the expert can form into a more accurate version. Cerri acknowledges the difficult issue of "attribution of blame," i.e., how will the system make a decision of what counts as "most closely predicts." The system thus helps the expert to refine the model in various ways, to broaden its coverage or increase its discriminability. In the final stage of the second phase, the expert runs the elaborated models, using the system to ensure that they behave as intended.

In a way, the methodology described by Cerri is similar to work in machine learning, in particular to the fully automatic elaboration of algebraic expertise embodied in LEX [2], except that in Cerri's system, there is a human at a crucial point in the loop.

The notion of an inverted dialogue together with the possibility of a variety of agents filling student and teacher roles is carried through into the Nobile prototype. The prototype makes use of a whole raft of contemporary AI representation techniques and languages, particularly object-oriented systems. The basic routines have all been written using the generic place holders "teacher" and "student" where each may be filled by a range of entities. Thus, the same routine can be used without modification to interrogate a real student, a student model or even a student record. Of course, one gets answers different in kind in each case, but (as with Woolf) it all helps with the push towards modularity and generic systems.

Phil Winne's paper is also perhaps more usefully contrasted with those of Woolf and Laurillard than with that of Cerri. Winne offers a more skeptical view of the current "success stories" of intelligent tutoring systems than Woolf, and points out their lack of general availability. He has three main aims. First, he wishes to derive the desirable characteristics of an intelligent tutoring system from theoretical considerations of a cognitively-orientated educational psychology. This is a highly ambitious and admirable objective. Second, he proposes the design of a system that embodies these characteristics and which could be built using techniques currently available. Finally, he is concerned that the field itself should progress scientifically and sketches some of the ways of moving forward.

A crucial notion for Winne is that learners bring a great deal to the learning situation by way of existing knowledge and skills. Of course, those working in the mainstream of intelligent tutoring system research acknowledge this. But the systems that they build (necessarily, alas) tend to treat whatever is novel in the instructional material in a vacuum, and leave it to the learner to integrate the new ideas with existing ones largely unaided. This "principle of the role of aptitudes" is similar to what underpins Laurillard's view of the learner. For both of them, the crucial issue is not just how well one structures or presents some new tutorial material in its own terms, but how well one can integrate or embed the new into the old.

At first sight, the theory of cognition embodied in the duality of "primitive" and "artificial" cognitive operations and in the acronym SMART is a general cognitive theory from which one may derive conclusions for good teaching practice (or other social interactions). Indeed, the use of an acronym at all as an educational device falls within the scope of the theory. However, it may be useful to think of Winne's cognitive theory more as an outcome of analysis of effective teaching than as an independent predictor of it. Of course, the theory is useful in offering constraints (derived from the learner's cognitive processing) on reasonable teaching behaviour, but its focus and level of granularity is best applied to educational interactions rather than to other aspects of behaviour.

Winne draws a distinction between knowledge "of" a domain and knowledge "about" a domain which is related to the notion of embedding, mentioned earlier. Clearly, along with many in intelligent tutoring systems research, he is happy with the concept of a "domain." When someone offers an instance of a domain (such as "the history of chemistry") the reader is prepared to think, "Okay, I'll go along with you; I'll join in your fiction that there is such a thing, let's see what you do with the idea...", so it is unreasonable for us to object to any specific usage of this kind, but that does not prevent the basic idea from being fundamentally suspect. A "domain" is a human invention, created for a particular purpose (a fiction with which we happily and unavoidably connive). The danger comes when one starts attributing a "domain" with an independent existence of its own. One slips from a mode of saying, "For present purposes, this is how I want to describe the world" to a mode of saying, "This is how the world is." It is worth emphasizing the arbitrariness of the notion when considering Winne's distinction between knowledge "of" and knowledge "about." In particular, we could choose to redefine the domain in such a way that his given examples of knowledge "about" actually become knowledge "of."

This issue of the boundaries of a domain also arises in Ohlsson's paper where he defines his domain as mathematics principles and is then surprised that teaching for a conceptual understanding of mathematical principles does not ease the learning of mathematical actions. Instead, his domain should be defined as "doing subtraction", in which case there is a further conceptual basis which may be taught and which may reasonably be supposed to facilitate the learning of the required action.

Winne reminds us of the importance of the episodic and situated aspects of what we know, and asserts that intelligent tutoring systems need to assist that aspect of knowledge integration where they can. He also emphasizes the importance of motivation and its role in helping the learner pay attention to relevant parts of what they already know. The importance of this becomes more obvious when one considers the relative "sizes" of what a learner already knows and whatever new knowledge and skill is being taught. Surprisingly, one thing missing from Winne's list of aptitudes is anything which embraces what we think of as "world knowledge," "naive/alternative conceptions," or "entrenched beliefs" [3]. Now, one could say that *alternative* beliefs are not aptitudes. Nevertheless, they do count as prior knowledge and they are often all the learner has with which to make sense of the new (scientific) accounts of the world being presented to them. Winne seems to be happy to talk about knowledge integration as if it is a neat marrying of the new to the old, and as if the old is fundamentally correct. The "sense making" that goes on in learning is generally much messier than this [Laurillard,this volume] and we scrabble around for all sorts of bits of existing knowledge that might help us make sense of the new — in ways which would horrify and mystify folk who may be happy talking about "domains" and which (alas) are just too hard to deal with in artificial intelligent terms as yet.

A valuable facet of Winne's theory is its taxonomy of causes of instructional failure. In particular, he draws attention to the fact that what the teacher may regard as "instructional cues" only become so when the learner interprets them as cues. This emphasis on the learner's interpretation of the educational interaction (as opposed to its "raw" content) is reminiscent of Laurillard's argument against student modelling, namely that it is impossible to capture the student's perception and interpretation of what is happening. It is also reminiscent of her distinction between student modelling and mapping students' conceptions in which the notion of "how" something is known plays a central role.

Only a small part of Winne's taxonomy is devoted directly to what we may call "domain content" issues; most of it is about the learner's failure to embed, or failure to engage with, the material. This must be a crucial lesson for intelligent tutoring system design, which thus far has tended to concentrate its efforts in knowledge of the domain rather than in knowledge "about" the domain (modulo the discussion above) or in motivational or attentional issues. A notable exception is Anderson, whose LISP tutor (at least in its early version: [1]) has been criticized precisely because it dealt with attentional issues by trying to remediate errors at the time they were committed, so giving rise to a rather officious, interventionist tutorial style. Remediating at the point of error would be in accordance with Winne's theory, but it is clear that too much tutorial intervention can (in some cases) be counter-productive and unmotivating. We need a theory that could predict the tradeoff (if any) between attention and motivation.

The second part of Winne's paper is a design for an achievable intelligent tutoring system that embodies the best of current thinking in educational psychology — as in Winne's theory outlined in the first part of his paper. The system is at pains to help the learner construct knowledge about the domain though the domain itself (economics) is relatively unimportant in the paper. What is important is that the domain is conventionally taught with text-based resources and is mostly concerned with teaching facts, terms, concepts and principles rather than decomposable sub-skills. This can be contrasted with the coding part of programming, geometric theorem proving or algebraic simplification, for which model-tracing technology might be appropriate. Far from being merely an expensive automated page-turner, Winne's system shows how an intelligent tutoring system might really be able to offer much more than a book (except portability) for the study of text. He is also concerned that systems should be developed for material that is part of mainstream curricula rather than for narrow esoteric specializations fit only to show the technology off in the best light. He does not make the case quite as strongly as that.

In its design, the system shares some objectives with those of Cerri's Nobile, in that it would be constructed to gather data about its users, which can be used to improve later versions. There is, however, no explicit commitment to anything like Cerri's inverted dialogue methodology for the evolution of the system. The concern with data-gathering links to Winne's third objective, namely how the field as a whole is to progress. Indeed, he sees intelligent tutoring systems technology offering the possibility of extensive and fine-grained data gathering, as well as the possibility of relatively easily running pedagogic experiments over realistically complex subject matters.

Whether or not one subscribes to the details of Winne's theory, a value of the checklist that it provides becomes clear in the second part of the paper. He argues, for example, that his proposed system would require the student to negotiate explicit learning goals with the system. Designers of other intelligent tutoring systems may wish to omit such a step, but they had better think through their reasons, as Winne offers persuasive empirical evidence for his position.

Winne styles his system "state of the art" in that it would need all the same kinds of AI facilities that go to construct either Cerri's Nobile or the tools which Woolf describes elsewhere in this volume. Some things still look very hard, though — e.g., the ability of the system to track and comment on the student inputting a diagrammatic network as a synopsis of the piece of text being studied.

Finally, Winne offers a prescription for the development of the field which nicely complements those of Woolf and Cerri. Where they are trying to assist communication within the field and its related fields via the use of standardized software tools, Winne argues for more careful data gathering and more extensive data sharing across different teams.

References

1. Anderson, J.R., & Reiser, J.: The LISP tutor. *BYTE*, 10, p. 4 (1985)
2. Mitchell, T.M., Utgoff, P.E. & Banerji R.: Learning by Experimentation: Acquiring and Refining Problem-Solving Heuristics. In: *Machine Learning: an Artificial Intelligence Approach* (R.S. Michalski & J.G. Carbonell, eds.). Berlin: Springer-Verlag 1984

3. Vosniadou, S & Brewer, W.: A cross cultural investigation of children's conceptions about the earth, the sun and the moon. In: *Learning and Instruction* (H. Mandl et al., eds.). Oxford: Pergamon Press 1990

Nobile: User Model Acquisition in a Natural Laboratory

Stefano A. Cerri, Elena Cheli & Angus McIntyre

Dida*Lab, Via Lamarmora 3, Milano, Italy

Abstract: A recurrent problem in the design of intelligent tutoring systems is the difficulty of obtaining the student models required by the systems. This paper describes a prototype knowledge acquisition system under development for use in an experimental program (the European Delta project Nat*Lab) intended to evaluate and refine a proposed methodology for performing student model acquisition. The requirements of the methodology and the way that they are realized in the prototype are discussed in detail.

Keywords: student models, intelligent tutoring, knowledge acquisition.

The Natural Laboratory

The Problems of User Model Acquisition

A majority of current intelligent tutoring systems (ITSs) are characterized by the way in which they attempt to meet the requirements of individual users by constructing and using models of the user. In general, these models, or at least the components out of which they are constructed, must be prepared in advance, an activity that requires a considerable outlay in terms of time and expertise. Additionally, user model acquisition, like any other knowledge acquisition activity, carries with it the risk that the specialist knowledge required (in this case didactic expertise as well as knowledge in the field of study of the tutoring system) will be only imperfectly captured, possibly because the context in which the knowledge acquisition is performed is unnatural to the experts consulted, as well as the risk that the knowledge provided will not prove robust or consistent with the system in which it is to be used.

Clearly, the process of designing and developing intelligent tutoring systems would be made considerably easier and more efficient, and the quality of the final system would be

NATO ASI Series, Vol. F 85
Adaptive Learning Environments
Edited by M. Jones and P. H. Winne

improved, if some way could be found of overcoming the "model acquisition bottleneck." It is for this purpose that the *Natural Laboratory* methodology [5,6,7] has been proposed.

The Natural Laboratory

The Natural Laboratory approach aims to fulfill the following requirements, which we consider essential to any effective knowledge acquisition system, whether in the domain of intelligent tutoring or elsewhere:

1. Permitting specialists to use the terms and concepts that they are familiar with, in the context of a familiar activity, and performing any necessary transformations from the framework used by the specialist into the formalism required by the system.
2. Constraining the form in which the expert can express himself or herself as little as possible, and, ideally even allowing the experts to choose their own way of working.
3. Taking an active part in the interaction with the expert and providing contexts for the application of the expert's knowledge, in order to recover the kind of intuitive or unformalized knowledge which would otherwise be missed.

Specifically, the methodology proposes to avoid, as far as possible, involving the expert in direct construction of models, by the use of what might be described as "indirect programming techniques", in particular, one such technique known as the *inverted dialogue* technique.

The purpose of the Natural Laboratory methodology is the acquisition of formal representations (that is, models) of student misconceptions (sometimes termed bugs, after the work of Brown and Burton [1,2]) which can be used to identify the typical errors associated with those misconceptions. The basic methodology proposed for achieving this can be summed up as follows:

1. Definition (by the system designer in consultation with domain experts) of the formal knowledge base representing the field of study to be taught by the system.
2. Construction (by the system designer) of an initial model base, optionally including a limited set of models encoding plausible student misconceptions.
3. Incremental refinement and extension of the model base (by domain specialists) by means of a series of inverted dialogues conducted using the existing models in the model base.
4. Incorporation of the final set of validated models in the completed tutoring system.

A key aspect of the methodology is that step 3 is iterative, the result of each cycle being used as the input to the next. Model acquisition is thus not a once-and-for-all activity, but rather a process of gradual refinement and extension. While we cannot avoid the initial overhead of constructing the domain representation and an initial model set "by hand", the incremental nature of the methodology allows a steady increase in the system's knowledge. Rather than having to construct a complete model set for the domain from first principles, the system designer may define only a minimal set of possible errors, and then use the cycle of interactions as a kind of "bootstrapping" process for refining and enlarging this set of errors, with the results of each interaction serving as the basis for future interactions.

Inverted Dialogues

An Introduction to Inverted Dialogues

The term *inverted dialogue* is used to mean an interaction in which the usual roles of the participants are reversed or altered. For instance, while the standard interaction between an ITS and a user puts the user in the role of student, and the system in the role of teacher, the inverted dialogue counterpart of this standard interaction would involve the user acting the part of teacher, and the system taking the part of the student. Similarly, during the design phase of a system, the domain specialist may be said — by a small abuse of language — to be a teacher, and the system, a student. The equivalent inverted dialogue would require the specialist to assume the role of the student, while the system plays the part of teacher.

The inverted dialogue approach has numerous applications in the domain of intelligent tutoring. Teachers can practise diagnosis by identifying and then simulating student errors in a two-stage dialogue. Advanced students may learn to reason about possible misconceptions in the field of study by the same process, and less advanced students may use inverted dialogues as the basis for a kind of discovery learning, posing questions about a domain to the "perfect student" encoded in the system's model base.

Model Acquisition Using Inverted Dialogues

For the purposes of model acquisition, inverted dialogues are generally considered to take place in two stages. In the basic methodology, the aim of the dialogues is to allow the expert to inspect and verify some of the initial set of error models proposed by the system designer. To achieve this, the expert must first identify the misconception represented by the model (from the errors that it generates), and then confirm that he/she has correctly identified and understood the misconception. Models verified in this way can be accepted for inclusion in the final version of the tutoring system.

The first stage, identification of the misconception, is realized by an inverted dialogue in which the expert assumes the teacher's role, and examines the responses produced by the model. This should lead the expert to formulate some hypotheses about the misconception(s) underlying the surface errors so that in the second stage of the dialogue, in which the expert plays the part of a student answering questions put by the system, he/she may simulate those errors. If the expert's simulation matches the predictions of the model, it indicates that the expert has (probably) identified and understood the misconception represented. If the expert considers this a plausible model, it may then be marked as accepted. The interchange of roles is summed up in Figure 1.

The dialogues provide a means for confirming the models proposed by the system designer; more importantly, they also provide a basis for the extension of the set of models. To see how this can take place, it is necessary to consider the use of inverted dialogues in model acquisition as a process of negotiation between the system and the domain specialist, whose purpose is to reach an agreement on the nature of a model for a particular misconception. When the system and the expert find themselves in disagreement, the terms of the negotiation must become more specific, with each side attempting to justify their viewpoint.

When the expert disagrees with the system, it indicates that the two participants in the dialogue are using different models. What we would like to do is to allow the system to acquire the model that is being used by the expert, and add it to the set of models available to the system. The expert may choose to withdraw his/her prediction on seeing the system's prediction, he/she may ask the system to justify its prediction before being ready to give up his/her own, or he/she may wish to provide a justification for his/her own prediction — which is to say, describe a new model. This model can then be tested by means of a further inverted dialogue to ensure that it conforms to the expert's expectations of it, and if it proves satisfactory, be added to the base of models available to the system .

The methodology envisages a mechanism or mechanisms by which the system may explain the predictions it makes, and a means by which the expert may enter a model or modify an existing model. Explanation mechanisms and the provision of habitable knowledge editing facilities are not trivial problems, but they are areas that have been extensively studied and there is no reason to consider that the requirement for such facilities poses insuperable problems to the methodology. In addition, the state of the inverted dialogue itself may provide a context which can make the explanations more coherent, and facilitate the expert's task by narrowing down the area of the model on which explicit alterations must be carried out.

The Natural Laboratory methodology proposes an account in which user model acquisition is seen as a cooperation between the system and the domain specialist in which the objective is

Figure 1: Inverted dialogues in the basic methodology

for the two participants to arrive at an agreement on the possible variations of the knowledge associated with a domain. Given that the system is likely to begin with incomplete or inaccurate knowledge, it must acquire the knowledge possessed by the domain specialist, by asking him/her to provide explicit justifications for the predictions that he/she makes.

Student Sessions and the Natural Laboratory

The basic methodology presented above is heavily model-driven, which is to say that it is dependent on the initial set of models encoded by the system designer. It may well be that the system designer can, with a reasonable effort, create a large enough initial model base to serve as a platform for the development of a complete set of models by the domain specialist, either by the process of negotiation sketched above, or because the specialist is inspired by some existing model to use the model editing facilities to create a similar but distinct new model.

Nevertheless, there is a risk that the limitations of the initial set may cause the specialist to overlook some important misconceptions or omissions characteristic of the field of study, thus missing some model or group of models from the final set to be made available to the tutoring system. Moreover, the system designer is still obliged to spend an amount of time — probably considerable — designing the initial model set in isolation.

What we would like to do is to simultaneously reduce the system designer's workload and make it more likely that the final set of models will give good coverage of the significant misconceptions associated with the field of study. Nevertheless, it is important that in doing so, we should not simply transfer the system designer's work to the domain specialist.

A proposed solution is to extend the methodology to make use of the tutoring system under development as a mechanism for collecting real errors. The system is run with real students, and the Natural Laboratory environment monitors and records their behaviour in different situations. The same two-stage inverted dialogue mechanism as before is then used, with the difference being that, instead of basing the dialogues on a misconception model, the system uses the actual recorded student behaviours. In the first stage of the dialogue, the expert is allowed to examine the student's behaviour exactly as in a normal first-stage inverted dialogue, in order to form an impression of the kind of error being made. In the second stage, the system chooses situations from among those recorded for the student to test how well the expert has understood the mistakes that the student made.

Diagnosing the causes of errors made by students is a task that should be within the competence of a domain specialist, so that the expert should be able to diagnose and simulate the misconceptions represented in the behaviours of real students. Simulation is not enough, however, because we still lack a model of the student's behaviours that we can insert into the model base of the tutoring system. Without such a model, the expert's ability to recognize and reproduce the student's mistakes serves no purpose.

To provide such a model, the system must appeal to the expert. It can assist the expert, however, by attempting to identify among the models that it already possesses, the one which most closely approaches the behaviours observed in the student. This can be achieved easily enough, by simply matching the predictions of each model with the observed behaviours of the student whose responses have been recorded[1]. This closest-matching model can then be used as a basis for the creation (using the model editor) of a new model, which may then be evaluated through the inverted dialogue mechanism to see if it conforms to the observed student behaviours. The assignment of roles in this procedure is shown in Table 1.

1. Record acquisition	Teacher	Tutoring system strategy
	Student	Human student
2. Record inspection	Teacher	Human expert
	Student	Student record
3. Confirmation of diagnosis	Teacher	Inverted Dialogue Manager (using student record)
	Student	Human expert
4. Model acquisition	Teacher	Inverted Dialogue Manager (using student model)
	Student	Human expert
5. Model confirmation	Teacher	Human expert
	Student	Student model

Table 1: Dialogue roles in model acquisition

The initial pair of inverted dialogues serves to familiarize the expert with the student's behaviours, and to demonstrate that the expert has understood the behaviour. During the next stage, using a model instead of a transcript, the expert continues to simulate the behaviour of the student. Any disagreement with the predictions made by the model indicates a point at which the model diverges from a correct model of the student, and prompts an editing session intended to adapt the model to produce the correct behaviours. The final inverted dialogue, a dialogue in

[1]This approach may be too simplistic; one objective of the experimental program in which the Natural Laboratory methodology is being tested is to attempt to determine some strategies for model-selection.

which the expert puts questions to the model, allows the expert to verify that the model performs as he/she expects.

The advantage of this approach is that we can severely restrict the set of initial models, perhaps to a single model — the system designer's conception of a correct account of the knowledge of the system. With each new interaction, the system will extend the set of models at its disposal, providing a basis for further editing in future interactions with the expert — and possibly for interactions with the student — in order to direct the error collection process. Furthermore, this approach offers the possibility of capturing the misconceptions of real students, but does so in such a way that the expert is helped to identify the cases in which the model proposed by the system fails to predict the appropriate behaviour, and where the expert's intervention will be necessary.

Models in the Natural Laboratory

Requirements Of Models

The Natural Laboratory imposes some requirements on the nature of models. Most of these requirements come under the heading of good model design, but it is worth mentioning briefly why these particular requirements have been stipulated. Ideally, models for use in the Natural Laboratory should be:

1. generative
2. explanatory
3. explicit
4. decomposed

Generative models, which is to say models that are capable of actively producing behaviours rather than passively recognizing them, are required by the inverted dialogue modality in which the system must simulate the behaviour of a student. Generative models may also be adapted to act as recognizers more easily than passive models may be used for generation.

Models are also required to be explanatory — that is, they should be designed with a view to serving as the basis for an explanation of the predictions that they make. This is clearly necessary, if the model is to be able to provide a justification of its predictions during the negotiation phase.

This requirement, in turn, partially motivates the succeeding requirement. A model must be explicit — that is, representing the knowledge of the domain overtly, rather than by implication — in order to support explanation. Other reasons for the explicitness requirement are that the model must be able to support reasoning by the system as well as the user, and that if the model is to be edited, the editing task will be considerably simplified if the model is expressed in a precise high-level form, rather than in terms of arbitrary code.

A final requirement or guideline proposed is that models should be realized in terms of a decomposition of the domain, a decomposition made according to some structure appropriate to the domain, whether a supposed "cognitively real" representation of the user's reasoning in the domain, or some natural pattern present in the domain (for example, the causal or functional structure of the field, as proposed in [11]). This requirement is obviously related to the need for explanation and explicitness, but a decomposed model carries the additional advantage that it allows areas of difficulty to be resolved into sub-areas, narrowing down the area within which diagnosis must be performed, and permitting the identification of those cases which are strictly relevant to the misconception under study.

Effectively, models are equivalent to small expert systems, whose domain of expertise is that of the field of study taught by the tutoring system. This is not to say that a particular representation is obligatory; for instance, production rules, common in current expert systems, or the task-method approaches proposed for "second-generation" expert systems [8, 10], but rather that many of the issues important in expert system design, such as explanation and representation, are also relevant to the design of user models.

Nobile

Implementation of the Nobile System

The Nobile prototype[2] has been developed as part of the European Delta project Nat*Lab (P7004/D1016), whose major objective is the definition, evaluation and refinement of the Natural Laboratory methodology described above. The evaluation of the methodology depends on the use of the prototypes developed in the project (including Nobile) in a program of carefully planned experiments intended to determine how the methodology performs in practice, and to identify refinements or improvements to the methodology and the tools suggested for it.

---

[2]NOBILE = Nat*Lab Object-Based Interactive Learner Environment.

Nobile has been implemented using Common LISP, and the LISP-based knowledge representation languages KRS [9, 12, 13] and GTE [14]. The existing system was developed using Macintosh Allegro Common LISP on Apple Macintosh computers, making use of the object-oriented Object LISP provided by MACL for implementation of the user interface. Work is in progress to port the prototype to other environments, Sun UNIX and MS-DOS machines being the current intended targets.

The choice of the high-level languages KRS and GTE was motivated by the desire to make the knowledge used by the system and encoded into the tutoring systems under development as precise and explicit as possible. KRS, an object-oriented representation language based in intentional logic, is used to represent the factual knowledge available to the tutoring system, and also for describing concepts in the field of intelligent tutoring systems — models, domains, topics, exercises and so forth. GTE, which is based on KRS, and was intended for instructional applications, provides a mechanism for describing activities in terms of tasks and methods. It is used to represent the instructional strategies utilized by the tutoring systems under development, and in the encoding of one type of student model supported by the system — a process-based account of student activities in a domain. Both languages are based on Common LISP and allow access to the full power of the language. The languages used to realize the various components of the system are shown in Figure 2.

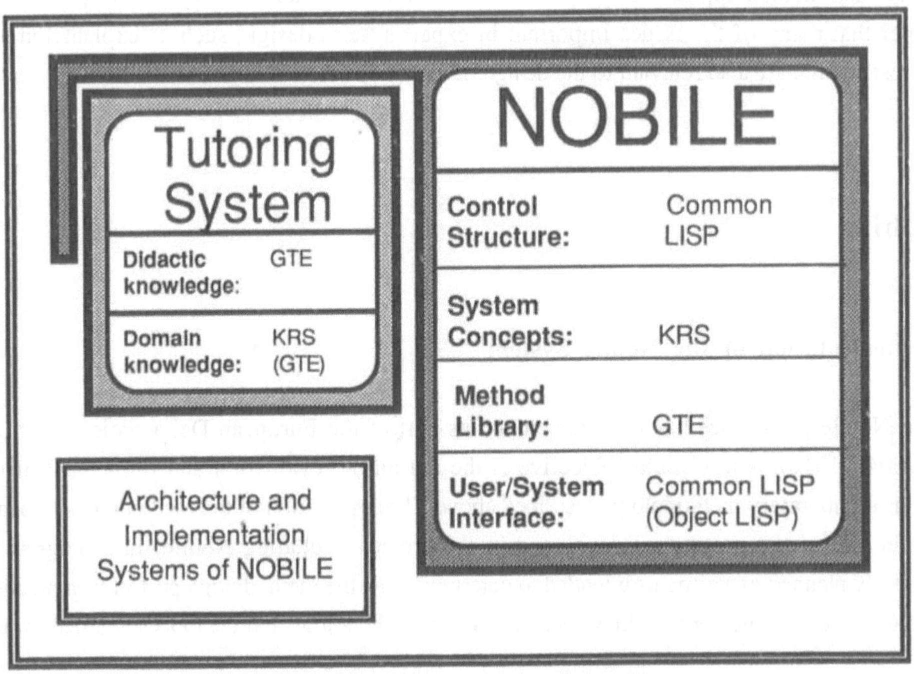

Figure 2: NOBILE Implementation Systems

The Nobile Knowledge Acquisition Shell

The Nobile system is conceived as a shell for knowledge acquisition, realizing the methodology of the Natural Laboratory described previously. Tutoring systems under development may be inserted into this shell in order to acquire student models for use in the systems. At present, these tutoring systems must be purpose-written according to certain guidelines in order to run under the Nobile shell, which also provides interface facilities and GTE method libraries for use by the systems. Future Nobile-like systems, however, are envisaged as being integrated with an authoring environment to allow fully general tutoring systems to be constructed and developed.

The current main requirements of tutoring systems for use with Nobile have to do with the languages which are used to implement the system. Primarily, a Nobile-compatible tutoring system must be a GTE program in order to allow the execution of the system to be monitored by the Nobile shell. Additionally, Nobile provides standard definitions for use by the tutoring system. Some, such as the library of instructional methods and the interface routines, are optional, while others such as the definitions of tutoring concepts (including domains, models, problems and so forth), are required. The most significant constraint on the design of tutoring systems, the notion of dialogue agents, will be discussed in the following section.

The Nobile system is intended both for the collection of student behaviours, and for the analysis of these behaviours by an expert, leading to the construction of models for the behaviours. In addition to implementations of the inverted dialogues described above, the full system will include tools for inspecting student session transcripts, editing models, and on-line note-taking. Before describing in detail how the system works, however, it is worth examining some of the concepts underlying the implementation, in order to make the functionalities of the system clearer.

Dialogue Agents: Realizing Inverted Dialogues with OOP

As mentioned above, the Nobile system is implemented using KRS, which is an object-oriented knowledge representation language incorporating notions such as inheritance and context maintenance. In this section, we will outline how the object-oriented programming style supported by KRS can be used to implement inverted dialogues in an elegant and economical manner.

In the description of inverted dialogues given earlier, the dialogues were depicted in terms of the roles (teacher and student) involved in the dialogues. We can make this description explicit by stating that there are two abstract dialogue roles, each of which may be taken by some specific entity, such as a human expert, or a human student, or a student model, and so on. The nature of the dialogue is defined by the participants, and, as an exact converse, the nature of each participant is defined by their role in the dialogue.

Taking the second point first, let us consider the nature of a student in an ordinary interaction with a tutoring system. In the interaction, the student must answer particular questions: "What is your name?", "What is the answer to problem <x> in context <y>?" and so forth, and must be presented with certain information, such as "The answer was correct." or "The rule for this problem is <x>." and so on. A student, then, is defined by the interactions that can happen between the student and the tutoring system. In the same way, a teacher is defined by a similar set of interactions: "Which problem should be presented to the student?", "In which context?" and so on.

We can thus provide an abstract account of teachers and students in terms of the interactions that they are able to participate in, and make use of this in defining our tutoring system. Rather than defining a complete tutoring system with an integrated strategy and user interface, we abstract out the teacher and student aspects of the system, and define only the core of the system, and the way that that core interacts with the teacher and student in terms of high-level interactions.

To make this example a little clearer, the following code is taken from the "Alice" tutoring system implemented under Nobile:

```
(defconcept ALICE-CHOOSE-AREA-METHOD
    (an implementation-method
       (action
          [method-condition (teacher) ()
             (put-in-context
                context
                'current-area
                (ks-request
                  teacher
                  (get-next-area context)))])))
```

The code defines[3] a GTE method for choosing the next area to teach to the student. Leaving details of the implementation aside, the important part is that the new area is found by making a "knowledge source request" to whichever entity is currently represented by the variable "teacher", asking he, she or it to evaluate the request "get-next-area" with respect to the current context. The tutoring system has no presuppositions about how this request[4] is to be

[3]Partially — some parts have been removed for the sake of simplicity.
[4]Readers familiar with KRS may recognize that the syntax of the request is not true KRS, but is in fact a GTE construct. This is 'syntactic sugar' — the same mechanism could easily be implemented using KRS subjects with arguments.

carried out; it simply makes the request, and expects to receive an appropriate response. Interactions with the student are handled in the same way.

The advantage of this is that the tutoring system can be executed without prejudice as to the real identities of the entities known to it as "teacher" and "learner," provided that they can handle the interactions it makes with them. The way that these interactions are to be realized is then defined for each possible entity or type of entity that can participate in an interaction. For instance, the request "What is the answer to problem <x> in context <y>?" would be handled in different ways depending on whether the "learner" to whom the question was addressed was a real human student, a record of such a student, or a generative student model. In the case of a real student, the problem might be presented on-screen with a menu, and the response given via the keyboard, or using a mouse. If the "learner" role happened to be filled by a record of a past student session, the response would result from a look-up in a table; if the "learner" was a student model, the response would be found by executing the student model. In every case, the way in which the request is performed would be transparent to the tutoring system.

If we define the tutoring system to make use only of high-level requests to abstract dialogue agents (teachers and learners), and then define how these requests are to be carried out by specific agents, we are in a position to use the same tutoring system, unmodified, with whatever combination of real agents we want. For instance, we might have a real student (interacting with the system through a screen and keyboard) in the learner role, and a teaching strategy written in KRS or LISP in the teacher role. This is effectively equivalent to the situation in a normal tutoring system. Alternatively, we can fill the learner role with a student model, and the teacher role with a human expert user, thus realizing the first inverted dialogue in the basic model acquisition methodology. Not all the possible combinations are sensible — there would be little value in using the system strategy (as teacher) with a prerecorded student session (as learner) — but some may have advantages that are not immediately apparent. For instance, instantiating both agents to be human users (and, for the sake of convenience, arranging things so that they can use different workstations) may help the system designer observe how a human expert chooses questions to diagnose particular misconceptions.

Because KRS is an object-oriented language, this kind of abstraction is easy to implement. The inheritance system also allows us to take advantage of the natural structure of the agents, as shown in Figure 3 and Figure 4. For instance, the system descriptions of the human teacher and the strategies used by the tutoring system both inherit some information from the abstract teacher agent, while their more specialized domain-dependent realizations inherit in turn from each of them, and the normal tutoring strategy and the specialized strategy used by the inverted dialogue manager both have interactions in common that they inherit from the general strategy defined for the tutoring system as a whole.

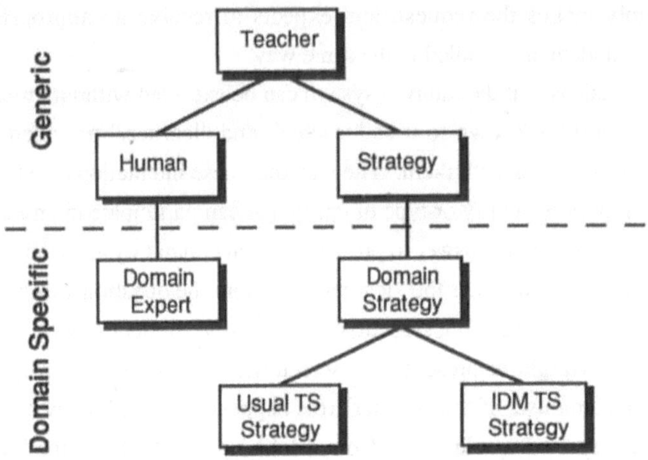

Figure 3: A hierarchy of teaching agents

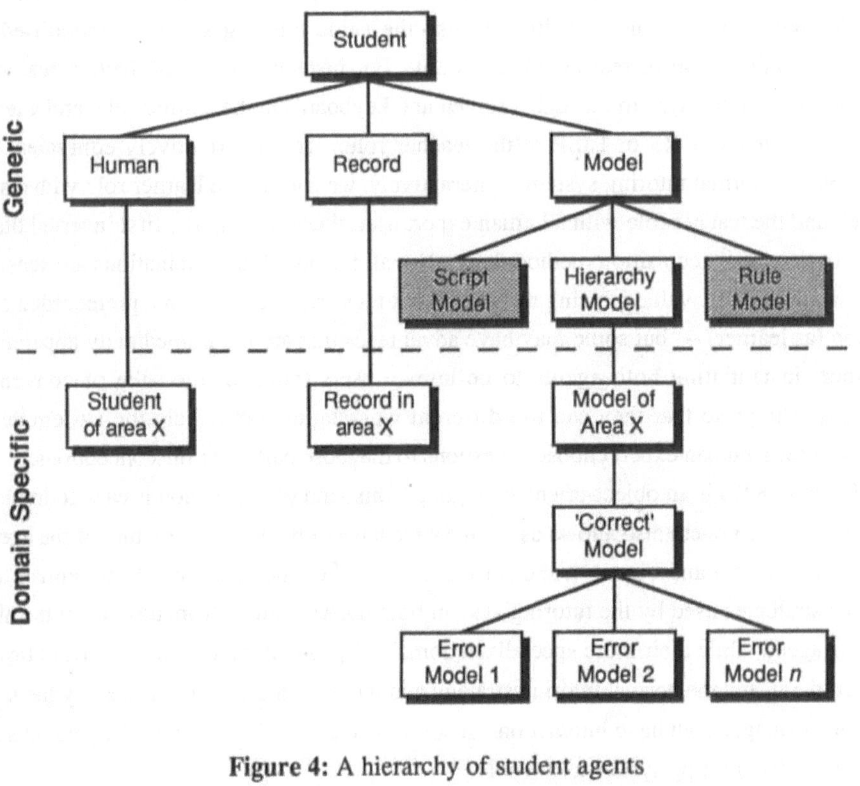

Figure 4: A hierarchy of student agents

In the same way, our set of possible filters for the learner role is composed of human students, records of their interactions, and student models. Student models in turn decompose into different types, with inherently very different underlying representations, but all are able to respond to the same requests made to them by the tutoring system. The hierarchy is shown in Figure 4[5].

The Nobile system offers the user the opportunity to select the agents to insert into the teacher and learner roles through means of a control panel, shown in Figure 5. In the left hand section, the buttons serve to select an agent (if there is more than one agent of the given type, then the user is offered a menu of the available agents). Pressing the "Run" button will then execute the tutoring system using the current combination of agents.

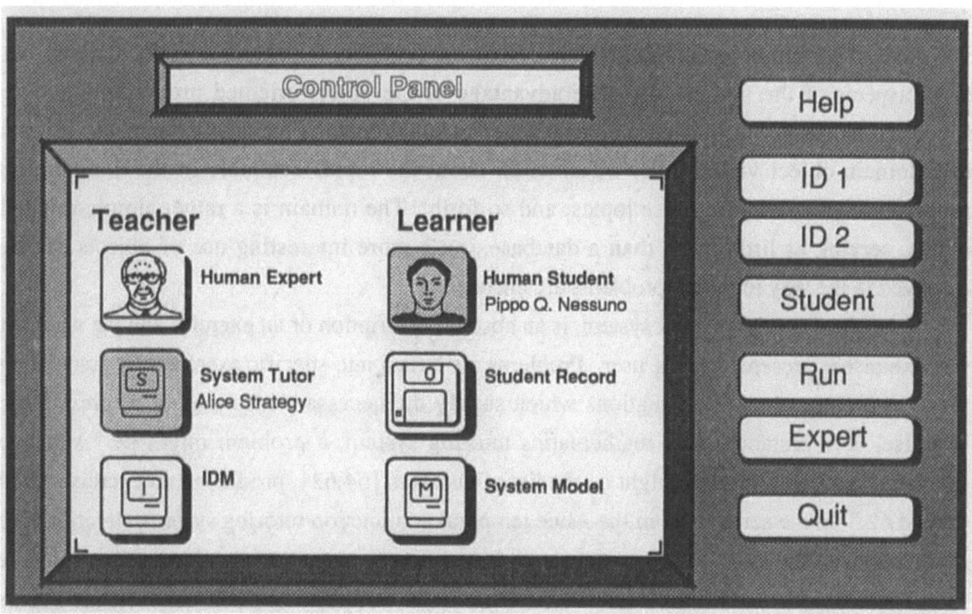

Figure 5: The Nobile Control Panel

The other left-hand buttons include program buttons for executing the tutoring system with dialogue roles changed automatically under system control. For instance, the button labelled "ID 1" in the diagram will execute a knowledge acquisition dialogue of the type described in the section on the basic methodology — first with the teacher instantiated to the human expert and the learner selected from among the models available to the system, next with an inverted

[5]At present, only models based on hierarchies of GTE tasks and methods, termed 'Hierarchy models,' have been implemented, but other models — for instance, based on production rules or scripts — could be built in the future.

dialogue manager strategy (using the same model) as teacher, and then a human student. Similarly, "ID 2" evokes the more complex acquisition dialogue, including a total of four inverted dialogues sequenced and managed by the system, while the button marked "Student" runs the system with the standard tutoring system strategy as teacher and a human student as learner. The other buttons offer access to the help facilities of the system, or to the system maintenance tools (including the model editors) in isolation from the inverted dialogue mechanisms.

Other Objects in Nobile

The most important objects in the Nobile system are probably the agents described above, but other aspects of the system also take advantage of the object-oriented programming style supported by KRS. As an example, the teacher agents (human or encoded) can make requests to a domain object which gives information about the topics available in the domain, the problems associated with those topics, and so forth. The domain is a rather simple-minded object, serving as little more than a database, but a more interesting use of objects can be observed in the way in which problems are encoded.

A problem[6], in the present system, is an abstract description of an exercise and the way that that exercise is presented to the user. Problems are turned into specific exercises by associating them with contexts called situations which supply the necessary information to present the exercise. For instance, in a mathematics tutoring system, a problem might be "Add two numbers," and the situation might be the list of numbers {54,62}, producing an exercise "Add 54 and 62." In the same way, in the Alice temporal conjunction tutoring system, situations are descriptions of the same sentence translated into different languages, while problems include "Find the conjunction in this sentence," "What is the temporal relation between the events described in the sentence?", and "Translate this sentence into language X."

Problems are defined in a hierarchical manner, with the specific problems used by each tutoring system inheriting from more generic problems, which in turn inherit from the general object problem. The Alice "Find temporal relation" problem referred to above is a concept[7] of type ALICE-MENU-PROBLEM, which is in turn of type MENU-PROBLEM, which inherits from the problem type SIMPLE-PROBLEM. At the highest level in this hierarchy, SIMPLE-

[6]During development of the current Nobile system, the testbed tutoring systems have tended to be of a rather unimaginative question-and-answer type, so one of the fundamental objects is a 'problem' (in the sense of an exercise, rather than a misconception). In an extended system, however, we hope to move away from this approach, and develop a general classification of interaction types, of which the kind of question-and-answer situation prevalent in the existing system would be merely one instance of a range of possibilities.

[7]The primitive objects of KRS are called concepts.

PROBLEM defines a name and comments, and indicates that a problem should be able to handle requests to present itself, to get an answer from the learner, and to verify the answer. MENU-PROBLEM defines how the presentation is to be made and the response received (as the name suggests, by means of a menu), while the tutoring system specific concepts that inherit from MENU-PROBLEM define what information is actually presented to the user, i.e., what should be shown on the screen, and what the contents of the menu should be. An example of a problem being presented is shown in Figure 6[8].

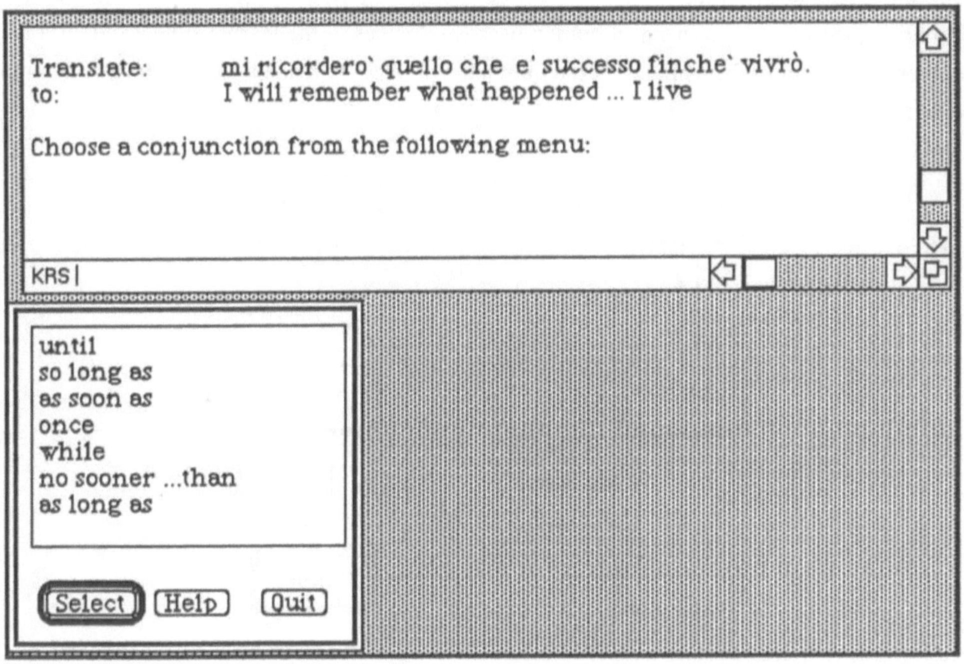

Figure 6: Alice's "Translate Conjunction" problem

The definition of problems benefits from the object-oriented approach of KRS in two ways. The inheritance mechanisms described above allow instances of problems to be defined economically, without needing to redefine, for example, the mechanisms for presenting a menu for every new problem. In this way, a tutoring system designer can simply specify the domain-specific aspects of a problem (generally, what information to present to the user, and how to determine if a user's answer is correct), while ignoring the details of the implementation. Secondly, the problem definitions make use of requests in the same way as agents, so that

---

[8]All example screen images are taken from the Macintosh SE version of Nobile.

problems can be made to present themselves, or to get and verify responses without any need for the calling object to know about the internal structure or the implementation of the problem.

The request mechanism is extensively used inside Nobile, so that the execution of the tutoring system tends to result in a small forest of exchanged messages. To give an example, consider the case of a method for finding a problem and presenting it to a learner. The method passes a request to the teacher to provide the problem, and the teacher in turn requests the domain to supply the available problems. This process is represented in the left-hand column of Figure 7. The actual presentation to the user is made by requesting the learner to see the problem. Because the learner is a human user (in this case), the learner object requests the problem to present itself, which in turn requires the problem to make a request to its context in order to recover the information to present to the user.

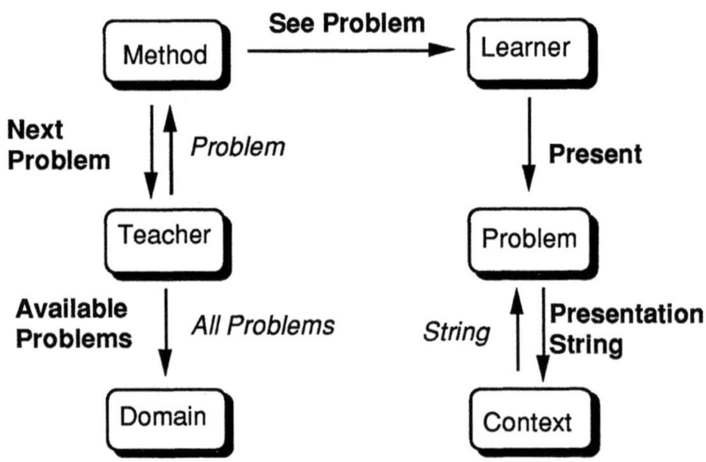

Figure 7: An example of request passing in Nobile

That the implementation of Nobile has been simplified by the adoption of an object-oriented approach should not surprise proponents of object-oriented programming, but OOP has advantages for Nobile that are specific to the nature of the system itself. Nobile is required to be heavily modular, at several levels: the system's aim of knowledge acquisition for different tutoring systems requires that it should be possible to insert different systems into the shell, the implementation of inverted dialogues requires a similar interchangeability among agents, and, to a lesser extent, modularity of problems and situations is desirable if not essential. This modularity would be much harder to achieve with conventional programming techniques.

Also, it is intended that the development of tutoring systems for use with the Nobile shell should be carried out by authors who may not be familiar with the implementation of the shell. The inheritance of properties and functions among objects and the abstraction of data mean that new systems can be developed based on the predefined facilities offered by Nobile without requiring the author to reimplement relatively low-level definitions, such as mechanisms for presenting material or verifying solutions. If the author can describe problems simply in terms of the questions asked to the learner, and the way to verify the solutions, rather than concerning him/herself with the lower-level design of the system, the design process will be considerably simplified.

GTE: Tasks and Methods for Modelling and Control

The preceding sections have described the way that the object-oriented approach supported by KRS has been used in the implementation of Nobile. The system also makes extensive use of the instructional design language GTE, which allows processes to be described in terms of tasks (activities to be performed) and methods (the means to perform these methods). This section will briefly describe the main ways in which GTE is used.

The first, and more conventional, use of GTE is to represent the instructional strategies of the tutoring systems. This is the kind of use for which GTE was developed, and a Nobile-compatible tutoring system is much like any other GTE program, except perhaps for a greater reliance on the use of knowledge sources and request passing (as described above). However, GTE is a new language, and has yet to evolve a characteristic style, so it may be that future systems developed in GTE will also make heavy use of the knowledge source facilities provided by the language.

The use of GTE for implementing the instructional strategies in Nobile is not controversial: GTE has been designed with this kind of use in mind. However, there is another advantage in the use of GTE, which is that the activity of the GTE task processor can be monitored from the Nobile shell. The negotiation procedure used in the inverted dialogues depends on the shell being able to observe the execution state of the tutoring system and intervene when a particular condition arises such as when the expert's prediction disagrees with that made by the system model. The GTE monitor is also used to implement the bookkeeping procedures that record the student's responses for later examination by the expert.

The second use for GTE in the current system is for the implementation of a class of student models called "hierarchy models." It is intended that Nobile should eventually support a variety of different model types, based, for example, on scripts or production rules, or any other formalism that appears suitable for student modelling, with a view to experimentally determining the advantages and disadvantages of each type. The current system, however, supports only a single model type, in which the procedural knowledge that underlies the student's behaviours is modelled in terms of the processes that he/she must carry out in order to resolve a particular problem.

These processes are represented in the system by a simplified set of GTE tasks and methods, which are intended to be relatively easy for non-programmers to understand and edit. Rather than using the full power of the GTE language, hierarchy models are defined using restricted versions of the standard GTE task and method types, effectively a subset of the language which permits the expert to decompose processes into sub-processes, to pass information, and to refer to the factual knowledge component of the user model, represented by KRS concepts. These methods, although restricted, can still be monitored for the purposes of providing the expert with a view of the system's reasoning towards a conclusion[9].

The choice of GTE methods as a representation base for the student models was motivated by a desire to give an explicit and understandable account of the knowledge involved in a model. The hierarchy models of Nobile are effectively small second-generation expert systems, expert in the production of correct (or incorrect) responses to particular problems in a given domain of study. The representation has the advantage of encouraging an explicit account of the knowledge involved in an activity, which makes explaining the model's reasoning easier, and which should also mean that models developed will have long term value, rather than just constituting *ad hoc* temporary solutions to the problem of representing student behaviours.

Other Tools

As discussed above, a Natural Laboratory system will need to provide editing tools to allow the expert to create and alter models. In Nobile, each model is capable of responding to an "Edit" request by invoking an appropriate model editor. The model editor shown in Figure 8 is used for editing hierarchy models, taking full advantage of the structure of the models to display them to the expert in such a way as to help her/him visualize the structure of processes and sub-processes. The editor was implemented on the development system using an object-oriented LISP, called Object LISP, provided as part of the current Macintosh Allegro Common LISP. The editor provides the expert with the opportunity to view the tree of tasks and methods, resize it, and inspect and edit individual components of the tree by clicking on the nodes of the tree. Work is in progress to provide cut and paste facilities so that elements can be moved from one model to another, together with selective inspection of sub-parts of the tree and visual editing facilities for the factual part of the knowledge base.

---

[9]See [4] for an account of explanation in second-generation expert systems. [3] describes explanation in the context of task- and method-based systems.

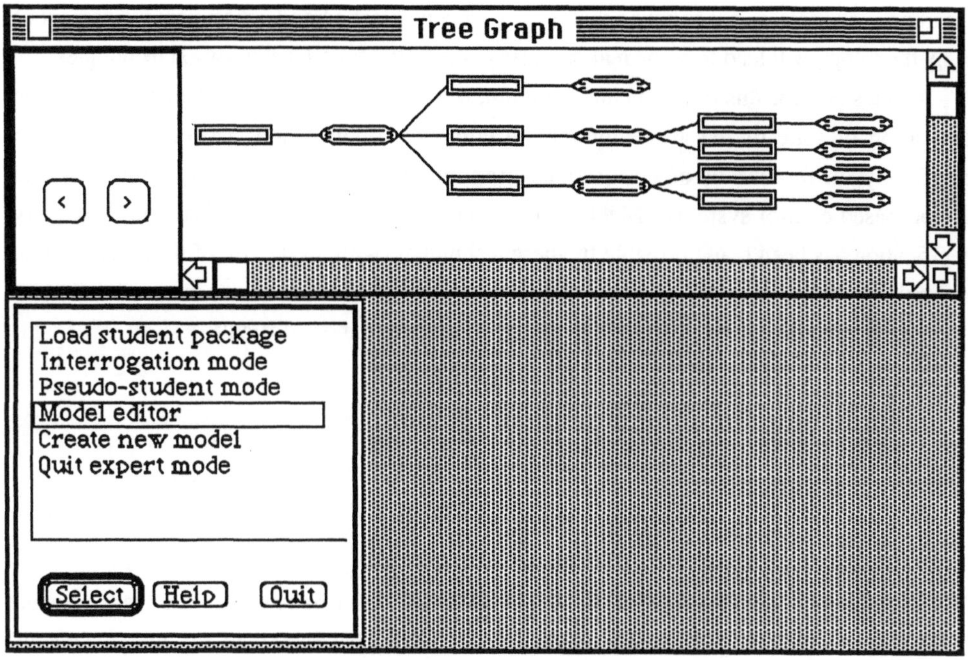

Figure 8: The Nobile hierarchy model editor

Other tools include the ability for experts to see transcripts of the student's sessions with the tutoring system, with the complete text of the interaction. The various contributions of the tutor, the shell, and the student to the dialogue are indicated in the development version by the use of different fonts. An "intelligent" notepad facility will also be provided so that the expert can record observations about the student's misconceptions or the system's predictions, with information about the context in which the observation was made provided automatically by the shell.

Summary

The development of user models for intelligent tutoring systems is a time- and labour-intensive process, which could well benefit from the use of computational tools intended to reduce the effort involved in developing models and improve the quality of the models produced. The Natural Laboratory methodology described in the first part of this paper is a possible means of providing such tools, and it is hoped that the experimental testing and subsequent refinement of the methodology will lead to some real progress in the field of model acquisition techniques.

As a testbed for this experimental program, the Nobile prototype has benefited from the application of state of the art techniques in computer science and artificial intelligence; specifically, in the use of object-oriented programming, message-passing, and task- and method-based control systems. Meeting the special requirements of the Natural Laboratory specification has been made possible by these techniques; without the use of these techniques, the implementation of many central elements of the methodology, such as inverted dialogues and modular tutoring systems, would have been considerably more difficult.

Acknowledgements

This paper, and the development of the Nobile prototype described herein were made possible by the support given to the Nat*Lab project (Delta P7004/D1016) by the CEC, and by Dida*El s.r.l. The authors would also like to thank the developers of the Laboratorio Naturale project (in particular Prof. S. A. Cerri, Prof. G. Magi, and Dott.ssa L. Saetti), the other members of the Nat*Lab consortium — Knowledge Technologies & the Vrije Universiteit Brussel (B), IDSIA (CH), Siemens AG (D), HiTec (GR), the Universities of Udine and Trieste (I) and the Universities of Lancaster & Leeds (UK), and past and present workers at Dida*Lab (including Philippe Alcouffe, Anna De Censi, Nur Erol, Claudio Guggiari, Marina Salvato, Roberto Serra and Kris Van Marcke) who have given help and suggestions.

References

1. Brown, J.S., & Burton, R.R.: Diagnostic models for procedural bugs in basic mathematical skills. *Cognitive Science*, 2, pp. 155-192 (1978)
2. Burton, R.R.: Diagnosing bugs in a simple procedural skill. In: *Intelligent tutoring systems* (D. Sleeman & J.S. Brown, eds.). 1982
3. Deknock, L.: *A knowledge-level approach to explanation.* VUB AI-Lab Memo, 90-4, 1990
4. Kassel, G.: Systèmes experts de seconde génération et explication du raisonnement. In: Proceedings of the ninth international workshop on expert systems and their applications, Avignon 1989
5. McIntyre, A., & Cheli, E.: Inverted dialogues and the natural laboratory in user model acquisition. Dida*Lab internal technical report TR90-14, 1990
6. The Nat*Lab Consortium: Nat*Lab: Student model acquisition in a natural laboratory. Technical Annex Part A, CEC Delta Project P7004/D1016

7. Saetti, L, & Cerri, S.A.: Maestro! e il "laboratorio naturale." Dida*Lab TR-88-29-00, Internal publication of Dida*El srl, Milano, Italy 1988
8. Steels, L.: Second generation expert systems. In: *Future generation computer systems.* North Holland, Amsterdam 1985
9. Steels, L.: The KRS concept system. VUB AI-Lab Technical Report 86-1, 1986
10. Steels, L.: Components of expertise. *AI Magazine*, 11, 2, Summer 1990
11. Stevens, A., Collins, A., & Goldin, S.E.: Misconceptions in students' understanding. *International Journal of Man-Machine Studies*, 11 (1979)
12. Van Marcke, K.: KRS: An object-oriented representation language. *Revue d'Intelligence Artificielle*, 1, 4, Hermes 1988
13. Van Marcke, K.: KRS user manual. VUB AI-Lab Memo 88-15, 1988
14. Van Marcke, K.: A generic tutoring environment. Proceedings of ECAI-90 (forthcoming) 1990

State-of-the-Art Instructional Computing Systems that Afford Instruction and Bootstrap Research

Philip H. Winne

Faculty of Education, Simon Fraser University, Burnaby, Canada

Abstract: Research and development of instructional computing systems (ICSs) are exploring the frontiers of knowledge in both computing and instructional sciences. While these efforts are slowly advancing knowledge, they have not yet produced practical ICSs that can be readily used in educational settings. I propose a retreat to regions where knowledge is relatively more firmly established, regions I call "merely" state-of-the-art. Specifically, a state-of-the-art ICS would be built on knowledge of computing systems and instruction that is available now rather than on knowledge in the process of being found by research at the frontier. I propose developing a state-of-the-art ICS that teaches learners how to read so that their comprehension exceeds that gained by reading a superior textbook. I sketch a theory of instruction that underlies the instructional features of a state-of-the-art ICS focussed on this objective. Then, I illustrate in "paperware" form what this ICS might look like. I conclude by describing how work at the frontier of ICSs can be advanced by using a state-of-the-art ICS to bootstrap knowledge needed.

Keywords: instructional computing systems, tutoring systems, instructional psychology, learning, motivation.

A Modest Retreat from the Frontier

Research and development in the field of instructional computing systems (ICSs) is a beginning for prototypic systems that tutor learners and that support learning through interactive discovery. One significant result of efforts on these fronts is that researchers, teachers, and even students are being stimulated to revise their conceptions of education. Beyond revitalizing notions of education, research on ICSs also is spurring innovations in and, recently, active

NATO ASI Series, Vol. F 85
Adaptive Learning Environments
Edited by M. Jones and P. H. Winne

collaborations among the field's parent disciplines of media technologies, artificial intelligence and computing science generally, and instructional psychology. Although many and complex challenges are found at the frontier of research on ICSs (e.g., see [8]), there seems little debate that efforts to break through these frontiers offer enormous promise.

Four Bottlenecks

The gap between promises made by pioneers at the frontier of research and realizations of those promises is, however, very wide. Today, no intelligent ICSs are widely available to schools. A very tiny number of well designed, interactive discovery-learning environments are in use at a very few sites. For the immediate future, the picture of supplementing, not to say replacing, traditional forms of instruction with ICSs does not appear likely to develop. At least four reasons can be cited for this prediction:

1. Basic research is now only at the threshold of exploring the nature of learning with ICSs and the means for providing effective instruction using ICSs. Pushing back ignorance in these areas, and then developing ICSs that efficiently implement knowledge that we are just now in the process of gaining, will inevitably take time.
2. ICSs that have been developed almost always remain closetted in researchers' laboratories. This prevents the communities of scientists from learning more about the advances embodied in particular systems. It also ensures that not enough data can be gathered about how learning proceeds in the special environment of ICSs. Knowledge needed for developing demonstrably effective ICSs depends, in my view, on (a) sharing systems among researchers in the field to accumulate gains in knowledge, and (b) bootstrapping successively small gains in our understanding of learning by placing ICSs in settings where they can be widely used by students to generate data continuously.
3. Even when ICSs have been developed and field tested to a point where they could be implemented widely in schools, considerable delays will ensue as the vast spectrum of schools' curricula are reformatted for presentation using ICSs. Other large-scale reforms in educational curricula have proven that change of this magnitude is a convoluted and slow process.
4. Once these three initial hurdles have been cleared, significant practical issues will need to be addressed. Two of the more prominent of these are the cost of installing ICSs in classrooms and the shock that ICSs may deliver to traditional forms of teaching and learning in schools.

"Merely" State-of-the-Art Research on ICSs

This chapter proposes a plan for research on ICSs that, in some respects, retreats modestly from the frontier that many researchers are now exploring. Specifically, I propose creating ICSs that are "merely" state-of-the-art. This species of ICS is considerably less audacious than pioneering systems that have invited revolutionary reconceptualizations of education and that have supplied grounds for radically different views of learning and the learner. Instead, the target of producing a merely state-of-the-art ICS is closer and easier to hit: design and implement an ICS that is much like a common textbook and its accessories (e.g., worksheets, a study guide, films) but that is demonstrably more instructionally effective than the best textbook available. A state-of-the-art ICS not only would present text to students and interact with them to foster understanding and develop knowledge, it also would extend students' skills for achieving understanding in general and elaborate their means for learning effectively by reading.

Opening bottlenecks. There are six reasons why a merely state-of-the-art approach may speed progress relative to pioneering research on ICSs at the frontiers of knowledge of computing and the instructional sciences:

1. State-of-the-art ICSs are founded on research findings from instructional psychology and computing that are available now rather than requiring knowledge that is in the process of being created. The main challenges facing state-of-the-art systems are to apply what is known now, and to make small refinements and extensions to the present edition of the encyclopedia of knowledge about ICSs.
2. Researchers may be more prone to share state-of-the-art ICSs and place them in real-life learning settings because state-of-the-art systems do not represent as big a scientific gamble as do pioneering systems at the frontier.
3. State-of-the-art ICSs, in the form of textbooks and their accessories, do not require radically different forms for representing knowledge. Hence, formatting the bulk of existing school curricula for instruction by an ICS is not as high a hurdle to clear as it is with pioneering systems. The tradeoff for finessing this problem is that not all tasks important to education can be included in state-of-the-art ICSs. By definition, only those tasks that are approached by reading a text and working with its traditional accompaniments can be included.
4. Hardware for state-of-the-art ICSs is already in place in some schools and is widely available in colleges, universities, and many industrial training settings. Thus, state-of-the-art ICSs are practical.
5. Reading a text and working with accompaniments, such as exercises in a study guide, are tasks that fit comfortably with today's patterns of schooling. Disruption to extant

educational systems can be minimized by supplementing them with state-of-the-art ICSs to merge the best of both approaches to education.

6. Even when research at the frontier of ICSs bears fruit, I predict that reading will remain a prominent means for learning. This makes it worthwhile to build and install state-of-the-art ICSs in a majority of educational settings.

First steps in a plan for progress. The plan I propose for implementing a state-of-the-art ICS retreats from the frontiers of pioneering research on ICSs to states of the arts in computing and instructional sciences. As a first step toward creating state-of-the-art ICSs, the next major section lays out principles that provide a theoretical foundation for understanding learning from instruction. As the next step, I describe a "paperware" prototype, state-of-the-art ICS. This illustrates what such a system might look like in general.

The plan I envision does not halt with implementing a state-of-the-art ICS. Remaining steps are presented as the conclusion to this chapter.

In favor of plural strategies. To the extent that the distinction I draw between frontier and state-of-the-art research on ICSs is meaningful, neither style of research should be pursued to the exclusion of the other. Singlemindedly pursuing frontier research alone is likely to be frustrating because the problems it addresses are intrinsically hard. Slavishly following a strategy of state-of-the-art research would surely curtail our visions for the future. In my view, vigorously pursing both sorts of research simultaneously, preferably in a collaborative way, will be most profitable.

A Theory for Designing ICSs that Afford Learning

Although it is rather presumptuous, I intend to sketch in this section the outline of a theory of instruction that provides a platform for designing ICSs. As a short working description of the term theory, I adopt this: a theory is an invention of human thought, comprised of a consistent set of propositions that is falsifiable in whole or in part, and that provides grounds for explanations and predictions. Two other terms play important roles in this section and merit definition (selected from *Webster's Ninth New Collegiate Dictionary*):

afford *vt* to make available, give forth, or provide naturally or inevitably
principle *n* the laws or facts of nature underlying an artificial device

I suggest that four main domains underlie a theory for designing ICSs that afford learning: the learner, learning, what is learned, and instruction. In the following, I've formatted critical information about each domain in terms of principles and elaborations on them. Each principle deserves much more consideration than I can provide in this chapter. My objective is to present main features in each domain that lead toward a justification for *why* an ICS (or any other medium for instruction) can teach.

The Learner

It is unfashionable today to view the learner as an empty vessel, or as clay in the hands of an instructor who shapes what a learner comes to know and how a learner is motivated. I, too, reject such views of learners. Rather, I believe that each learner brings to every instructional interaction broad and deep knowledge that has been acquired over the course of innumerable previous experiences. Some of these experiences arise circumstantially; others are self-consciously made self-instructional; yet others were purposefully crafted by a teacher (or surrogate, such as a book or an ICS) to instruct the learner.

Unlike the metaphor of an empty vessel, a description that I find worthy casts the learner as artisan. Below are links between features of this description and topics that are central to learning from instruction.

A learner is an artisan ...

in whose hands	in whose mind
raw materials	knowledge of the world
are fashioned	is cognitively processed
to create vessels	to create structures of knowledge
that are valuable as such, and	that are valid and useful representations of the learner's world, and
that can hold other raw materials.	that encompass future experiences of perceiving, being motivated, and learning.

The view of learner as artisan suggests that two components are critical in every event where learning is guided by instruction: cognitive processes and prior knowledge. Cognitive processes are the subject of the next section on learning. Prior knowledge is a generic label. It refers to an array of instructionally relevant aptitudes that learners call on as they participate in instruction (and, in all other interactions with the world). Aptitudes are comprised of a learner's: (a) specific knowledge of the topics under consideration, (b) knowledge about the environment in which instruction is occurring, (c) intellectual skills and cognitive strategies for partaking in learning, and (d) motivation and related personality characteristics (e.g., cognitive styles; see [7]) that initiate, shape, and sustain interactions with information.

Human beings are born with a cognitive system that affords enriching one's aptitudes. Since aptitudes can be enriched, they are incremental rather than fixed entities or stable capacities. Aptitudes develop naturally, as the result of a learner's everyday experience, and planfully, as a result of instruction (including a learner's self-directed instruction).

> THE PRINCIPLE OF APTITUDES. Aptitudes that learners call on as they participate in instruction are results of prior learning.
>
> THE PRINCIPLE OF THE ROLE OF APTITUDES. Every learner brings to every instructional event an array of aptitudes that are central — but not sole — determinants of how learning is carried out.

These two principles point toward two conclusions. First, to optimize instructional effectiveness, an effective ICS must take account of aptitudes in adapting instruction to the learner. Second, aptitudes themselves should be targets of instruction so that learners become successively more capable of learning. Because aptitudes are incremental, they are targets that may move during instruction. To take account of changes in aptitudes, ICSs must monitor them during instruction and adapt.

Learning As Cognitive Processing

The word "learning" can be used as a noun and as a verb. In this chapter, I emphasize characteristics associated with the verb form: learning is actions that a subject — a learner — performs on objects, knowledge that has been acquired (prior knowledge) and information in the midst of being processed. Typically, actions that a learner performs in the mind are called cognitive processes. Engaging cognitive processes is thinking, and thinking is axiomatically critical to learning from instruction. Thus, my view of learning is a view of activity, of action, of *thoughts in process*.

To begin to understand learning as process, it is necessary to explore further what information is, and to examine the mental actions that learners perform on or with information. A treatment of information appears in a subsequent section titled "A Model of Achievements Gained by Learning." Here, I describe properties of the processing of information that are critical in learning.

Information in process is active. Information that learners are processing at a given instant is *active*. Active information has the potential to be consciously inspected. Active information is described metaphorically as residing in a mental location called the working memory. Without further processing, information remains in an active state only for brief periods, typically a few seconds to tens of seconds.

Knowledge is information that the learner has achieved by cognitively processing information at an earlier time. Not all of one's knowledge is active at a given instant. Inactive knowledge is inert and is considered to be located in a metaphorical place called the long-term memory. The life span of inert knowledge seems, in most instructionally relevant cases, to correspond approximately to the life span of the learner.

There are limits to the amount of information that can be active at one time. This limit is a joint function of two features [4]. One is a family of variables describing the information that is active, such as its degree of organization. The second is a parameter of each learner's cognitive system, the capacity of working memory. Both variables are blended into a notion of the capacity of working memory. The capacity of long-term memory appears, for instructionally relevant purposes, to be limitless.

> THE PRINCIPLE OF INFORMATION IN PROCESS. Information in the act of being processed — active information — is limited in amount and, without further processing or external representation, is available to the learner's conscious mental inspection only for a few to a few tens of seconds.

Cognition as process. Cognition is commonly referred to by the phrases "cognitive process" and "information processing." As a process, cognition must have three features. First, every process operates on raw materials or input. A process cannot operate on nothing. Input to cognitive processes is information from either or both of two sources: the external world (e.g., a textbook, a peer's explanation) or memory (a thought). Second, carrying out a process takes time. There are no instantaneous cognitive processes. Third, each process yields output or a product. In the case of cognitive processes, outputs are information active in memory.

> THE PRINCIPLE OF COGNITIVE PROCESS. A cognitive process involves prior knowledge, new information, or both as input; it takes time; and it outputs information.

The significance of this principle is that instructional effectiveness varies, in part, with the degree to which an ICS is successful in coordinating the informational input to thinking and the time learners take or have to think. Once in process, however, output is a function of input(s) and time. Interruptions punctuate and distractions abbreviate the time a learner engages a given kind of processing.

Two main kinds of cognitive processes. Debates rage about the number and the kinds of cognitive processes. I postulate two fundamental species of cognition: primitive cognitive operations and artificial cognitive processes [29].

Primitive cognitive operations are primitive in three critical senses. First, they cannot be analyzed into subprocesses. They are fundamental in the sense of fundamental particles such as quarks. Second, these operations are primitive in the sense that they are intrinsic to the human cognitive system. There is very little instructionally relevant variance in the facility with which neurologically normal learners carry out primitive cognitive operations. Third, the primitive cognitive operations are primitive in the sense that they become incorporated in higher-order thinking. They are one kind of building block comprising aptitudes. I theorize that there are five primitive cognitive operations: stimulating, monitoring, assembling, rehearsing, and translating. Referring to each operation by its first letter allows the set to be labeled the SMART operations.

Stimulating activates inert knowledge so that it is available for cognitive processing [1]. Input to this operation is information currently active (in working memory). This information may have originated in the world or it may be an output of other cognitive processing. Output of the operation is a chunk of knowledge that was inert (in long-term memory) and is now active (in working memory). Stimulating is an involuntary and effortless operation. If a teacher says "quiz," students may involuntarily become nervous [35]. If an ICS suggests, "Let's review," sophisticated learners may automatically and effortlessly activate a set of rules for strategically processing information that the ICS displays next [31].

Monitoring compares two chunks of information that are currently active (in working memory). One chunk supplies a profile of attributes or a prototype that serves as a standard against which the other chunk is evaluated [13]. Input to monitoring is information that specifies features of a chunk of information. Output is a list of notations about the presence of attributes or about the degree of correspondence between the target chunk and the standard. Monitoring has received much attention by instructional researchers as a simple comparison operation upon receipt of feedback [9] and as a process for tracking the use of complex cognitive strategies in learning [11]. Most learners need to be taught what to monitor, that is, what standards to use in monitoring, and they need to be cued to monitor [20].

Assembling takes two chunks of information that are active (in working memory) as input. Output from assembling is a relation or an informational predicate that links these chunks. The kinds of relations produced by assembling can be semantic, figural (images), or both. All of these relations are associated with increased achievements [21]. Learners may assemble on their own, and they can be cued to assemble with positive effects [34].

Rehearsing sustains information in an active state (in working memory). Multiple rehearsals elevate the likelihood that information will be acquired [10], but there are diminishing returns for multiple rehearsals [1] and rehearsing by itself (maintenance rehearsal) appears to be insufficient to acquire knowledge. Supplementing rehearsing with assembling, monitoring, or translating substantially boosts the chances of acquiring new knowledge.

Translating takes information as input and outputs fundamentally the same information in a second representation or a different mode of representation. An example of creating a second representation is paraphrasing a definition. An example of changing mode of representation is developing a figural representation (e.g., a graph) of a symbolic definition (e.g., the equation defining a parabola). A particularly critical kind of translating is recoding declarative representations that describe how to perform tasks into procedural forms that accomplish those tasks [2].

Artificial cognitive processes are the second species of cognition. These are, first, processes according to the definition of a process given earlier. They are cognitive because they take place in a mind. They are artificial in Simon's [24] sense; that is, they are "produced by art rather than by nature." Thus, artificial cognitive processes are procedures in which primitive cognitive operations are fused with knowledge. Production systems for heuristically monitoring one's evolving comprehension of a text or for judging the appropriateness of reviewing information when studying for a test illustrate artificial cognitive processes. Strategies for solving problems in physics and smoothing social relations also satisfy this definition of artificial cognitive processes [25].

Two main kinds of artificial cognitive processes can be distinguished — pattern recognizing and action taking. Both kinds can be represented as procedures or rules in which conditions (IFs) refer to properties or states. Pattern recognizing processes have a single consequent (a THEN) that names a category or class. A thing or event having the properties contained in a pattern recognizing rule receives a label when the rule's conditions are all active (in working memory) and when monitoring reveals appropriate correspondences between that thing or event and properties referred to in IFs. Action-taking rules work the same way except that they can have multiple consequents. The distinguishing feature of action-taking rules is that at least one consequent transforms information by applying a cognitive operation or artificial cognitive process either to information that is active (in working memory) or to inert knowledge (in long-term memory).

Knowledge is an intrinsic component of every artificial cognitive process, appearing in both IFs and THEN(s). Hence, these processes are achievements of learning rather than "hard-wired" elements within a learner's cognitive system. Individual differences in learners' artificial cognition — e.g., facility in solving algebra word problems, writing coherent compositions, and anticipating test questions for a lecture in a college course — are differences due to prior opportunities to learn. Artificial cognitive processes also are distinguished from primitive operations because they can be analyzed into components [2]. However, like primitive cognitive operations, artificial cognitive processes are building blocks in aptitudes, or they may be aptitudes per se.

> THE PRINCIPLE OF TWO KINDS OF COGNITIVE ACTIVITY. Primitive cognitive operations and artificial cognitive processes are two species of cognitive acts involved in learning from instruction.

This principle has two important consequences. First, many objectives of instruction focus on knowledge that is expressed in the form of artificial cognitive processes. Second, the bulk of individual differences among learners that give rise to variance observed in the evolving forms of interaction between an ICS and a learner are manifestations of artificial cognitive processes. Therefore, to guide learners toward particular achievements (i.e., outputs), an ICS needs to take account of which artificial cognitive processes (and cognitive operations) a learner applies to which input(s). Since inputs change as instruction proceeds, this is another reason justifying the need for ICS to track what learners do during instructional sessions.

Self-regulation is a central feature of learning. A common thread weaving together many contemporary theories of human learning is that the learner, more so than the environment, regulates cognition. As learners achieve knowledge — propositional and procedural — about learning in a particular instructional setting, they use this knowledge to govern when and which kinds of cognition are engaged. Self-regulation is therefore *metacognitive*; that is, it is an artificial cognitive process — a monitoring operation elaborated by prior achievements — that searches for and uses other knowledge in the service of learning. A host of recent studies have documented that self regulative cognition can be taught [25, 34,36], and that learning processes are facilitated in a wide variety of subjects when self regulative competence is achieved and applied to govern cognition [22]. Indeed, self-regulation appears to be intrinsic to hierarchically organized systems in general [3].

What constitutes self-regulation? Zimmerman and Pons [37] propose a ten-dimensional description of self regulative, artificial cognitive processes that meld both prior knowledge plus information afforded by an instructional environment (Table 1).

Self-regulation is often misconceived as signifying that the learner consciously directs all cognition. This seems subjectively wrong when we examine our own thinking, and it has been demonstrated experimentally not to be the case. Anderson's [1, 2] ACT* theory proposes a mechanism, proceduralization, by which complex sets of rules governing cognition can be submerged in action so as to become relatively inscrutable to consciousness. Recent research into the nature of expertise attests to the prevalence of complex proceduralized systems in fluent performance [5]. These studies also suggest that the availability of cognition to conscious inspection generally correlates inversely with the learner's expertise in the artificial cognitive processing being carried out.

Dimension	Description
Self-Evaluation	Monitoring qualities of or improvements in work on a task
Organizing and Transforming	Re-assembling information to enhance achievements
Goal-Setting and Planning	Identifying goals or subgoals Planning a pattern of acts and setting time limits
Seeking Information	Efforts to secure information relevant to the task at hand
Keeping Records and Monitoring Progress	Recording information about events in a task and the results of those events
Environmental Structuring	Selecting or arranging the physical setting of studying to enhance learning
Self-Consequences	Arranging to receive or imagining rewards for success or penalties for failure
Rehearsing and Memorizing	Practice; review
Seeking Social Assistance	Soliciting help
Reviewing Subject Matter	Re-examining prior work

Table 1: Dimensions of Self-Regulation

THE PRINCIPLE OF SELF-REGULATION. Learners can self-regulate thinking and can learn how to regulate learning, but they may not be fully conscious of information involved in self-regulative cognition.

The principle of self-regulation has two important implications. ICSs can become more effective if they support and guide learners' self-regulation during instruction. And, since self-regulation is central in learning to learn, it is an important achievement to be sought.

Summary about learning as a process. Learning is processing information under constraints which limit the quantity of information that can be in process at a given moment. Inputs to learning processes are information in the instructional environment that has entered the learner's cognitive system by mechanisms of perception, plus information that has been activated from a vast store of inert, prior knowledge. Since different inputs and different processing, primitive or artificial, create different outputs, the effectiveness of an ICS depends on guiding learners in thinking. Ultimately, one goal of an ICS is to transfer to learners the knowledge underlying such guidance so that learners themselves become more adept at self-regulating the cognitive events of learning. For learners to achieve self-regulative cognition and to understand how to use this knowledge, the ICS and the learner require terms with which to communicate about this topic. A main contribution of recent research in instructional psychology has been to invent concepts that describe thinking and to coin terms with which to communicate about thinking (cf. [12]).

> THE PRINCIPLE OF THE NECESSITY OF PROPOSITIONAL KNOWLEDGE. To communicate about any topic, with another or with oneself, requires terms — propositional knowledge — in which to express information about the topic.

A Model of Achievements Gained by Learning

Outputs of learning processes are information. When that information corresponds to goals for learning set by an instructional designer, an artificially intelligent ICS, or the learner; and if the information is later available for recall and subsequent use — that is, it is lodged in a learner's long-term memory and can be stimulated by pattern recognizing procedures — I call the output an achievement.

Today, it is common in the fields of curriculum and instructional psychology to speak of domains. The label connotes a body of information whose boundary is permeable to information from other domains. There is, for example, a domain of facts about the history of chemistry and another, somewhat separate, domain of skills for solving chemistry problems. Intruding into these domains is information found in a domain of affect, how one feels about these several domains of knowledge about chemistry. The concept of a domain is prototypic rather than stipulative; that is, it is difficult to list features that satisfactorily stipulate what a domain is, but one can identify instances of domains rather reliably.

I theorize that achievements can be usefully divided into three broad types of domains. To illustrate these divisions, in the following, consider two regions from the domain of chemistry, say, the periodic table of the elements and balancing oxidation-reduction equations.

Knowledge of a domain. Knowledge of the domain in my example is information explicitly presented by the periodic table. Here are examples: hydrogen is the first element in the table. One dimension of the table represents the number of electron shells in an atom. Inert materials are found toward the right in the table. Knowledge of a domain, in general, is not restricted to declarative forms — propositions, schemata, frames, and so forth. Rules or procedural forms also can be knowledge of a domain, as would be necessary for solving problems that involve balancing oxidation-reduction equations.

Knowledge about a domain. Here are examples of knowledge about one part of the domain of chemistry, the periodic table: the periodic table is in the back of my chemistry text; mnemonics are useful in memorizing some information in the table; principles that underlie an organization of information, such as the dimensions of the periodic table, provide limited grounds for making predictions.

None of these propositions is knowledge of chemistry per se, knowledge of the domain. Rather, knowledge about a domain is information that a person believes to be true about knowledge of the domain of chemistry. Knowledge about a domain is metaknowledge; literally; it is after knowledge of the domain. Metaknowledge about a domain contains "regions" of knowledge within the domain of chemistry, and it also stretches beyond the domain of chemistry into other domains of knowledge.

Since the definition of domain is not stipulative, the distinction between knowledge of a domain and knowledge about a domain is fuzzier yet. My last example of knowledge about the periodic table of elements was this: principles that underlie organization provide limited grounds for making predictions. This proposition can be a separate target for instruction [19]; when it is, it would be considered knowledge of a domain labeled critical thinking or reasoning. When knowledge of a domain called reasoning is imported into and applied within the domain of chemistry, the status of the imported information is simultaneously knowledge of the domain of reasoning and knowledge about the domain of chemistry. Grasping the distinction between these two sorts of knowledge — knowledge of and knowledge about — and being able to employ them conjointly are major developmental achievements for learners [15].

Knowledge that establishes grounds for motivated action. Everyone has had the experience of trying to remember a bit of inert knowledge. How might this motivated event be characterized in mental terms? How might one account for the behaviour of *trying* to recall or, in general, seeking any goal?

Knowledge is inert (in long-term memory) until it becomes active in (working) memory due to being stimulated. Suppose information presently active in memory is a rule about how to balance oxidation-reduction equations plus a partial answer just developed in a step of trying to solve a particular chemistry problem. By electing to inspect (monitor) this information, a self regulative act, the learner can stimulate other particular inert knowledge and thereby make it active. Anderson [1] labels stimulating inert knowledge as the result of "paying attention" an act of spreading activation.

What spurs a learner to inspect information, to pay attention? The answer is other information, in this case, a heuristic that is information about solving problems. Antecedents in this heuristic match the pattern of information about a problem like the one being worked out. (Note that the information represented by these antecedents is *not* specific information *of* chemistry.) The consequent is to monitor currently active information, thereby creating a pattern of correspondences between the present case and a prototypic case of solving an oxidation-reduction problem. If this pattern satisfies a pattern recognition rule for the next step on a path toward solution, it is stimulated and the learner has "remembered" what to do next. The complete event is an intentional or motivated act because knowledge in memory was monitored (inspected, paid attention to) at the learner's discretion. Less technically, the learner seems to an observer to be motivated to remember something.

In general, if the only contents in the mind are bits of knowledge plus other information in the midst of being cognitively processed, and if motivated actions that we observe originate in mental events, motivation has a clear description.

> THE PRINCIPLE OF MOTIVATION. Motivation is a state of knowledge. This state accounts for a learner's selections among alternative acts, qualities of behaviour, and persistence at tasks. Except for autonomic responses (e.g, digestion), innate reflexes (e.g, blinking when a puff of air strikes the eye), and unintended recall (due to stimulating), all human behaviour is motivated.

What kinds of information in the mind could supply these accounts, could explain the learner's discretion, such as purposefully directing attention in the preceding example about balancing an oxidation-reduction equation? Current theory suggests that five kinds of information establish grounds for motivated acts [30, 32]. Labelling each kind of knowledge by its first letter allows this set to be referred to mnemonically as AEIOU. The full complement of these five kinds of knowledge together define a motive.

Attributions are propositions that explain why an event has the outcome that it does. Attributions can be categorized using a 3-dimensional scheme. Locus concerns whether the reason that explains an event's outcome is within oneself or originates in the external world (e.g., ability versus a hint from the ICS). Stability addresses whether the cause is always the same for this situation or whether it applies inconsistently (e.g., a resource always available in the ICS's interface versus luck). Controllability is about whether the cause is governed by oneself or is beyond one's influence (e.g., learner control versus system control).

Efficacies are thoughts about one's competence or capability to achieve goals. When a task is first addressed, an *efficacy expectation* predicts the likelihood of being able to perform the task. When a task has just been completed and outcomes are precise and clear, learners usually reflect on how accurate their efficacy expectation was, that is, whether goals have been achieved. A learner's information about efficacy can derive from memories of past experiences with similar tasks (this is prior knowledge), from observing how and how well another (a peer or an ICS) achieves goals, from one's level of arousal, and from persuasion or exhortation.

Incentives are the values that outcomes (see below) or products satisfy if they can be attained. Almost all incentives important to learning with an ICS are learned values. These can be categorized according to a bewildering variety of systems, but I favor one that has just three categories. *Mastery* incentives reflect a value of learning for learning's sake. One hypothesis is that learners hold mastery incentives for tasks that offer opportunities to expand one's information about efficacy. *Performance* incentives refer to how much learners value demonstrating, to themselves or to others, that they are able or "smart", as well as how much they value avoiding the appearance of incompetence. Tasks perceived as having high performance incentives are ones that a learner views primarily in terms of validating an already held efficacy expectation, be that expectation positive or negative. *Social* incentives focus on values learners hold about relations between themselves and other people in the context of a task. Social incentives generally involve balancing two potentially competing values: value in being accepted by peers or accepting guidance from an authority versus values about having liberty to be oneself and the autonomy to perform tasks in one's own preferred ways.

Outcome expectations are predictions the learner makes about the results of engaging in a task. Each expected outcome has an incentive to the learner, including no incentive. Outcomes are immediate triggers for attributions.

Utility judgments are information that result from monitoring profiles of the preceding four motivational thoughts where each profile characterizes an alternative set of actions that might be taken in addressing a task. Every instructional task allows the learner some selection — at the least, disengaging or continuing to interact with the ICS. The alternative with the highest utility implies which alternative the learner will pursue, the vigor with which it will be pursued, and persistence in carrying out this alternative.

Intelligence is knowledge <u>for</u> learning. Under these views of cognition and knowledge, it follows (arguably; see [17]) that intelligence is embodied as knowledge and, hence, that intelligence is an achievement. Like aptitudes, intelligence is therefore incremental. Notably, intelligence must be manifest in action to be counted as intelligence. That is, intelligence is apparent only when knowledge is applied.

> THE PRINCIPLE OF INTELLIGENCE. Intelligence is: (a) a capacity to store new information in memory as knowledge; (b) aptitudes — prior knowledge of and about a domain — that can be made active in appreciating a situation and in cognitively processing information; and (c) motives to apply aptitudes.

Where does intelligence originate? This is not the place to raise and attempt to resolve the nature-nurture debate. Instead, I simply assert that knowledge is created in the process of learning, and that learning is situated predominantly in interactions between a learner and the environment. When instruction is offered by a person — a teacher; a surrogate for a teacher, such as a text or an ICS; or a tool, such as the computing language Logo, that constrains how a learner interacts with information — it follows that the learner's achievements are shaped importantly by someone else.

> THE PRINCIPLE OF THE ORIGIN OF INTELLIGENCE. Intelligent agents infrequently invent knowledge for themselves. More commonly, they borrow

information from others and then monitor, translate, and assemble it with prior knowledge to create aptitudes that express intelligence.

These two principles about intelligence apply not only to learners but also to an ICS that strives for artificial intelligence.

Summary about achievements. Tasks that present opportunities for achieving knowledge can be posed by an ICS. Such tasks also may be recalled or designed by the learner. Domains of knowledge are defined relative to a particular task. Prior knowledge *of* a domain is knowledge that a learner has achieved by earlier experience. Knowledge *about* a domain, achieved through previous learning as well, is aptitudes that have potential to shape means for achieving knowledge of a domain. Knowledge that *establishes grounds* for engaging in learning is previously learned information that accounts for motives about learning.

THE PRINCIPLE OF KINDS OF ACHIEVEMENTS. Achievements can be knowledge of a domain, knowledge about a domain, or knowledge that establishes grounds for engaging in learning. All three kinds of achievements comprise intelligence.

Achievements play dual roles in learning from instruction. First, they can be viewed as achievements in the past tense, as prior knowledge or aptitudes that, if active, facilitate learning. Second, they can be seen as achievements in the future tense, as goals to be attained during and after a learner participates in instruction.

A Model of Instructional Events that Afford Learning

I analyze instructional events in terms of tasks presented to learners for them to carry out. Table 2 identifies five facets that typify an instructional task. To understand how a learner performs an instructional task, each facet needs to be mapped in detail, and all five facets need to be considered in relation to each other over the course of carrying out successive tasks in an instructional session.

The ICS designer's aim is to arrange facets of instructional tasks so that, when a learner works through tasks, the learner achieves particular products of cognition in a fashion that affords recall of (stimulating) those achievements at appropriate times in the future. The simplest design for instructional tasks is to tell content that the learner is to acquire. Beyond this barest form of instruction, the instructor (or surrogate, such as an ICS) has four options, as suggested by the features of instructional tasks (Table 2) that an instructor can control. It is important to recognize that these same four options can be exercised by learners as they self regulate their own learning.

THE PRINCIPLE OF INSTRUCTIONAL OPTIONS. Beyond telling content to be achieved, an instructor may: prompt inert knowledge, cue cognitive operations, provide evaluations, and attempt to match demands imposed by a task's setting to the learner's prior knowledge, aptitudes, and limited cognitive capacity.

Facet	Description
Conditions	Information afforded in the presentation of the task Inert knowledge (prior achievements, aptitudes) Features of and tools afforded by the environment that influence the learner's ability to compensate for limited cognitive capacity
Operations	Primitive cognitive operations (SMARTs) and artificial cognitive processes (rules, heuristics, and so forth) applied to active knowledge (in working memory) and to newly perceived information
Product(s)	Updates to active knowledge (in working memory) Potential achievements created by operations
Evaluation(s)	Information about ... 1. standards, or 2. prior knowledge to be activated ... that is afforded by the environment or activated from inert knowledge 1. during the "steps" in the task and 2. upon quitting or completing the task
Standards	Criteria applied to intermediate and final achievements to be gained Criteria applied to how the task is performed (e.g., duration, displays of motivation, allowances for backtracking, and so forth)

Table 2: Facets of Instructional Tasks

Why instruction fails. Instructional tasks provide opportunities for learners to learn, but merely being exposed to such tasks does not guarantee that a learner incorporates new information as knowledge. How might an ICS guide a learner's engagement with instruction to invite learning and foster achievements? One approach to answering this question is to list what should be avoided, to identify conditions that block learning guided by instruction. Upon re-examining the facets of an instructional task listed in Table 2 in light of earlier sections about the learner, learning as cognitive processing, and achievements gained by learning, five primary reasons for ineffective instruction can be identified.

THE PRINCIPLES OF FAILED INSTRUCTION. Instruction fails when:

1. New content is not made available (told) to the learner.
2. The learner can not appreciate new content in terms of prior knowledge because
   a. prior knowledge is not recalled (made active by stimulating it) or

b. new content can not be assembled with prior knowledge.

3. The learner's cognition is not guided by instructional cues because the learner
   a. does not register the cue as information, or
   b. misinterprets cognitions that are cued, or
   c. is unable to carry out cognitions that make information into achievements, or
   d. is not motivated to engage in and complete the instructional task.
4. Evaluations are ineffective because
   a. they exclude information about products' deficiencies or errors, or
   b. the learner is not guided by cues in evaluation messages (see #3).
5. Cognitive capacity is exceeded.

The importance of these five principles of failed instruction is this: to increase the likelihood that instruction will be effective, prevent instruction from failing to engage the learner in learning that can gain achievements.

Summary: A Theory of Instruction

The foregoing is partially summarized as follows. The learner is the agent who engages in learning new information. The results of learning activities that correspond to goals, be they an instructor's or a learner's, are achievements. Achievements can be knowledge about all manner of things, but three fundamental categories circumscribe the essential kinds of knowledge to be learned, as well as aptitudes for learning from instruction: knowledge of a domain, knowledge about a domain, and knowledge that establishes grounds for motivation. Each is intrinsic in learning new information that is incorporated into a learner's store of knowledge.

Cognition refers to dynamic mental activities that handle and create information. It can be represented in terms of structures of knowledge plus a minimal set of primitive cognitive operations. The complexities of cognition, therefore, arise from complexities of human knowledge.

Under this view, instruction is, in principle, guiding or controlling knowledge with which a learner thinks and accommodating this to limits of the amount of knowledge the learner can think with during a limited span of time. To the degree that an ICS encourages and supports specific cognition — specific primitive cognitive operations and particular artificial cognitive processes applied to select items of knowledge — and avoids exceeding the limits of the learner's cognitive system, instruction will promote achievement. The key to making an ICS that is more effective than, say, pure discovery environments where learner control is absolute, lies in taking into account two main items: achievements the learner already has gained that are relevant to reaching instructional objectives set for a current session, and forms of cognition that engage those prior achievements and add new information to them. These two items specify, as fully as contemporary research can, how instruction works.

Affording Learning and Bootstrapping Research Using State-of-the-Art ICSs

In this second major part of this chapter, I sketch preliminary designs for a state-of-the-art ICS that is built on the theoretical foundation just developed. For ease of presentation hereafter, I refer to the ICS as IT and assign an androgynous name to a learner, Pat. The next section outlines goals sought in designing IT to interact with Pat. The two sections following describe briefly how Pat and IT interact, and how an instructor configures IT. In concluding sections, I focus on how IT simultaneously affords learning and bootstraps research so that the field can advance beyond state-of-the-art ICSs toward the frontier of intelligent tutoring systems.

IT's Interface Serves Two Goals

IT's interface is the channel for communications between Pat, the instructor, and a surrogate for the instructor, IT. In IT's interface, Pat can view and manipulate information relating to the domains being studied. Note that domains is plural in the previous sentence. In a state-of-the-art ICS, students will simultaneously study knowledge *of* a subject matter domain — elementary economics in my following examples — and knowledge *of* a second domain, strategies for reading to comprehend and for recalling what has been read. This second domain is knowledge for using IT to read, comprehend, and extend achievements in a subject matter domain like economics. This dual focus, on economics and on learning strategies, is essential if IT is to hit the target I set for state-of-the-art ICSs. A consequence of this dual focus is that knowledge *of* learning strategies plays a double role in communications between Pat and IT: these communications address knowledge *of* learning strategies per se and, simultaneously, are knowledge *about* knowledge in the domain of economics.

Affording Learning. As Pat uses features in IT's interface and every time IT intervenes in Pat's studying activities, instructional options are implemented that, according to presently available research, afford Pat's learning. Specifically, if Pat chooses to manipulate information in the manner provided by a particular feature, this kind of manipulation of information is presumed to correspond to cognition that research suggests will engage Pat in productive learning. The rules that govern when and how IT intervenes in Pat's studying redirect Pat's cognitive processing of content in ways that research suggests will afford learning. Examples of these affordances will be presented later in a section describing details of IT.

> THE PRINCIPLE OF AFFORDING LEARNING. Features in the interface of a state-of-the-art ICS are tools for the learner to manipulate information. A state-of-the-art ICS's interactions with the learner are governed by rules that describe contingencies between cognitive activities. Each action, by the learner or by the ICS, engages the learner in cognition that, according to research, affords learning that creates achievements.

Bootstrapping Research. Students are inventive. As they learn, their approaches to learning evolve, and these variations are raw materials for forging new understandings of learning. Thus, as Pat manipulates information in IT and engages with IT's interventions, IT will record these events. These data provide a window into Pat's learning by *tracing* observable reflections of Pat's cognitions and the information manipulated by these cognitions [28, 29]. Thus, IT can support research into how to afford learning directly and how to avoid conditions that cause instruction to fail. As patterns in these data are uncovered and understood, IT bootstraps the research on which IT is based.

> THE PRINCIPLE OF BOOTSTRAPPING RESEARCH. A state-of-the-art ICS is a tool that researchers use to investigate learning. Data gathered by a state-of-the-art ICS can help frame and test hypotheses about learning per se and about how to afford learning when a student interacts with an ICS.

On the Face of IT: Overview

Figures 1, 2, and 3 display main panels of IT's interface. Figure 1 illustrates a screen at the beginning of a session. Figures 2 and 3 show screens that are displayed simultaneously at a middle point in this same instructional session. These figures are introduced now to provide a basis for upcoming discussion. Select features illustrated in the figures will be examined in detail later.

Pat studies, in part, by selecting and manipulating information in IT's interface. When Pat first begins to work with IT, a 1-button mouse and a numeric keypad are the only input devices Pat needs. Placement of the cursor at screen locations, button clicks at locations, and drags over regions of the screen (continuously pressing the mouse button while moving the cursor over a rectangular region of the screen) send messages to IT about Pat's studying. For instance, Pat can select a menu item such as I'm Learning It in the **How Come?** menu of Figure 2

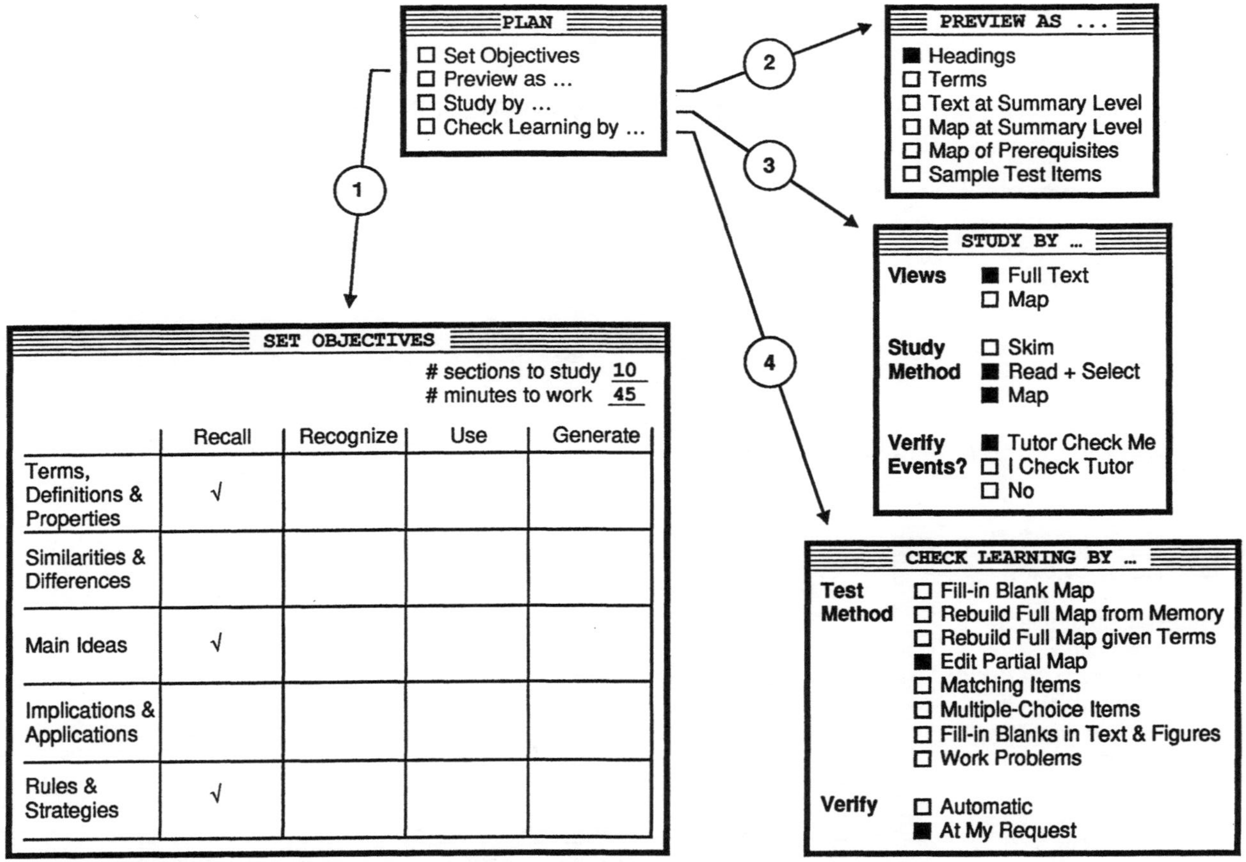

Figure 1: The Beginning of a Session with IT

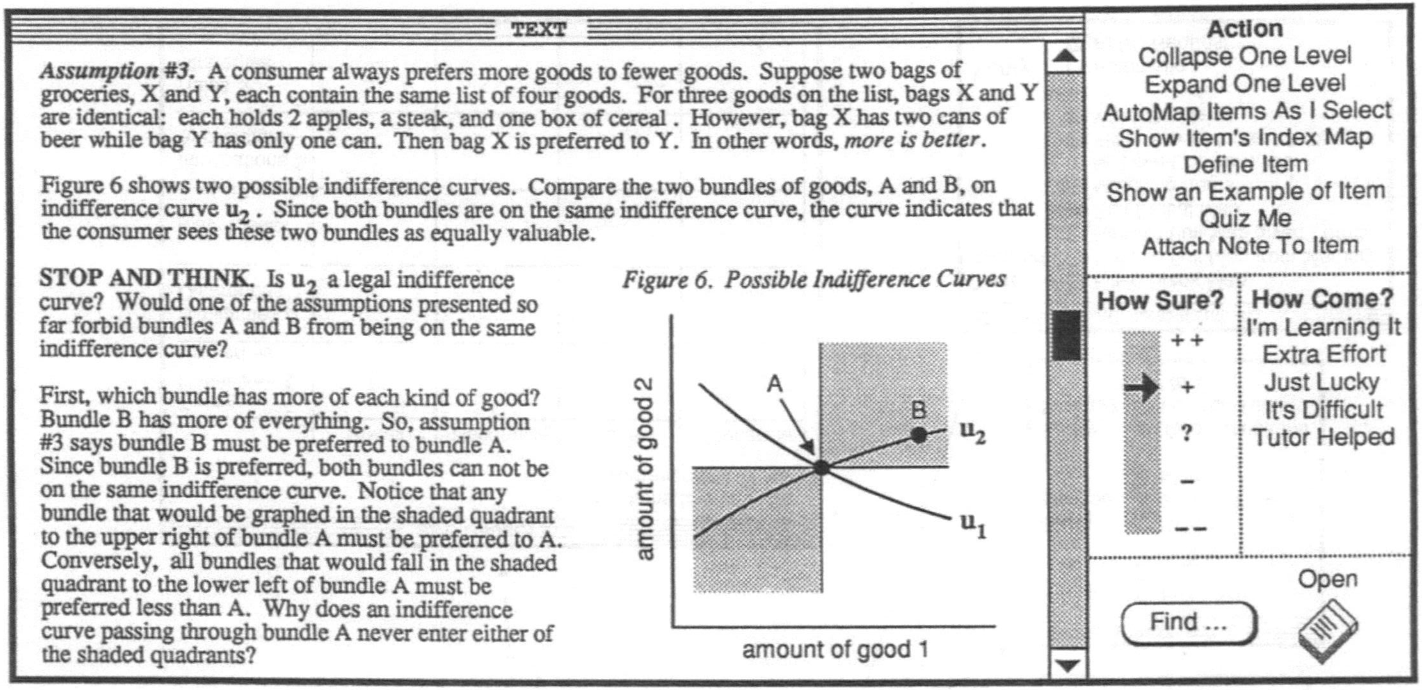

Figure 2: During a Session with IT

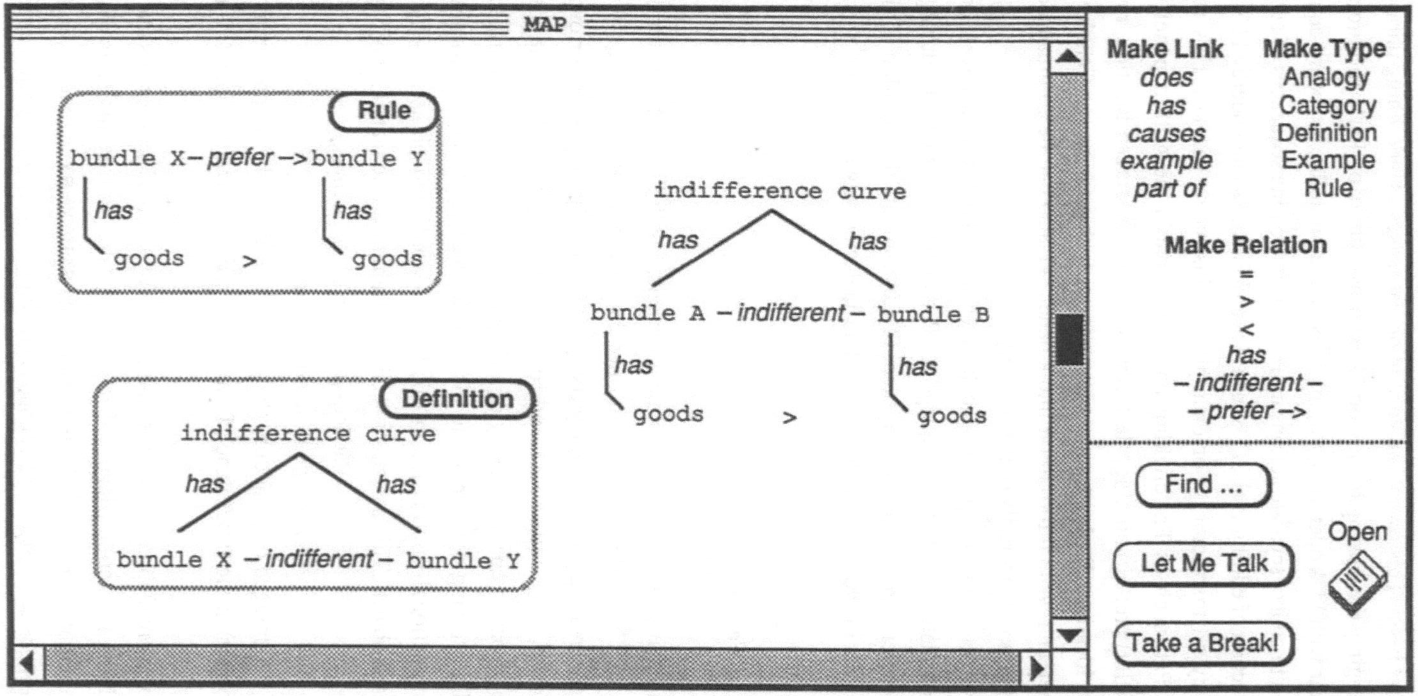

Figure 3: During a Session with IT

by clicking on that item. This reveals an attribution Pat makes. Underlining phrases in a text, imitated by dragging the cursor over words, exposes output of Pat's monitoring. After becoming familiar with IT's operation, Pat might be taught to define keyboard equivalents for mouse events and to collect separate actions into macros for routine sequences of actions.

Using a collection of editing tools, IT's interface and the rules that underlie IT's interactions are configured by an instructor. For example, the instructor can key IT's responses to messages from Pat, such as Pat clicking on Define Item in the **Action** panel (Figure 2). Responses (initially) are: do nothing, flash reverse video at a screen location, reverse video permanently at a location, display text in a box with or without a menu of choices, reveal or erase a new panel, and write information into a panel. IT also can be commanded to disable features of the interface temporarily or permanently .

IT tracks every event that Pat performs in the interface and indexes each event on a timeline. This creates a complete record of the sequence of Pat's interactions with IT during each study period. Because events are temporally indexed, IT can compute the duration of single events (e.g., non-movement of the cursor, a drag) as well as latencies between events.

Preparing IT to Teach

Before Pat first begins to study an assignment presented with IT, an instructor uses tools to define features in IT's interface and to edit rules that govern how IT interacts with Pat. The tools are shells for creating content displays (windows of text, graphics, or borrowing displays from anthologies of, say, animations), and for designing menus, sliders, buttons, and rules. For instance, to prepare a content display of a chapter of text that Pat will read, the instructor imports a word processing document into the shell for **TEXT**. The instructor then identifies "objects" of instructional importance in this text — words and phrases — by clicking or dragging over each object. This presents a shell for a framing a rule that has this base form:

IF Pat does *action* on *object* at $time_j$

THEN do *IT-action* at $time_k$

For instance, if Pat dragged over (action) the phrase "consumer always prefers more goods to fewer goods" (object) in the **TEXT** panel, IT might immediately reverse video (IT-action) those words.

Rules can be more elaborate than this base form. A pattern of prior events can supplement the single condition for action illustrated in the base rule. For example, an instructionally relevant pattern might be that Pat selected Skim in the **STUDY BY** ... panel (Figure 1) at the beginning of the study session and, 45 seconds ago, dragged over some phrase appearing in the text. Pat has just dragged over another phrase only two sentences later. Pat's reading rate in this session can be computed. If IT had data, gathered during previous study sessions, that Pat reads at a normal rate of X words/minute, IT can infer whether Pat is thinking about the information at this point in the text more deeply than just skimming it.

Multiple *IT-actions* also can be placed in a rule. For example, the rule that reverses video might be elaborated by, "... and write *object* in window #2 at location x, y." If panel #2 is a graphic representation of text that Pat has selected, a semantic network like that shown in the **MAP** display of Figure 3 is built up by IT as Pat successively selects text that the instructor tagged and labeled. This elaborated rule, programmed to fire if Pat clicks on AutoMap Items As I Select in the **Action** panel of Figure 2, has IT model a cognitive operation for Pat — IT automatically translates and assembles Pat's selections of text into a semantic network representation.

To give Pat options about whether IT mirrors cognition that Pat might carry out without IT's help, the instructor uses a shell for menus to build the menu labeled **Action** in Figure 2. Pat's clicking on the menu item AutoMap Items as I Select in **Action** before starting to study enables the rule just described. This configures IT to translate information from prose to figural format as Pat selects each object and, since IT records this menu selection, reveals information about Pat's self-regulation of studying in this session.

On the Face of IT: Details

This section describes a selection of IT's features as Pat would use them, as an instructor might design IT to afford learning, and as a researcher would use IT's records of data to bootstrap research. Limitations of space preclude a complete treatment of every feature shown in Figures 1–3, but the general picture of how a state-of-the-art ICS would function should be clear. For ease of discussion, assume that Pat has used IT for several weeks in an introductory economics course and, so, is familiar with IT's features. Also, recall that all of IT's behaviour has been fashioned by Pat's instructor.

As Pat begins this study session, IT first displays the **PLAN** panel (Figure 1) and requires Pat to make at least one selection in each of this panel's four subpanels. This affords acquiring course content and boosts incentive, according to a study by Morgan [18]. He found that having students set specific goals at the beginning of each study session in a university course boosted achievement and increased students' interest in the subject of the course.

Pat elected to preview this reading assignment by surveying headings in the chapter, headings that the instructor tagged while tailoring IT's instructional environment. A study by Wilhite [26] found that students who surveyed headings boosted their achievement of main ideas, but not of details, when achievement was measured by multiple-choice questions.

Importantly, this effect emerged only for students who had taken a previous university course in the domain of the topic studied, that is, for students with prior knowledge of the topic. Consequently, the instructor also would program IT to retrieve measures of Pat's prior achievements, gathered in preceding tutorials that related to the current topic. If Pat's prior knowledge was sufficient, IT would merely record Pat's selection of this form of preview.

If Pat's achievement was underdeveloped, several issues need to be researched. First, it is not clear what level of prior knowledge is insufficient for Pat to profit from previewing text headings. With data gathered from Pat and peers in this course, studies can be carried out to identify a generic cut off. Second, IT may afford Pat repairs for this deficiency while Pat studies the body of the text. For instance, Pat has directed IT to verify selections of items from the text in the **Verify Events?** section of the **STUDY BY** ... panel. Thus, as Pat "underlines" material in the text while reading, IT compares these selections to canonical selections that the instructor tagged. Depending on how IT is programmed to respond to (a) canonical selections that Pat omits and (b) non-canonical selections that Pat makes, IT may be able to compensate for Pat's low aptitude. Aptitude-treatment interaction studies of this sort, performed with Pat and peers, would bootstrap research about instruction. As a third illustration, IT might suggest to Pat that the preview of today's material be preceded by a recap of content covered in previous sessions at Text at Summary Level. Studying summaries, instead of studying the full text, can produce equal and even increased levels of achievement of subject matter with considerable gains in efficiency [23]. Thus, examining summaries of prerequisite knowledge might elevate Pat's low prior knowledge before Pat proceeds to preview headings for today's session. In addition, IT might be programmed to explain to Pat why the review has been suggested, thereby telling Pat information in the domain of self-regulation. Other means whereby IT affords self-regulation are listed in Table 3.

In the **TEXT** panel, Pat reads, selects items from the text as well as regions in graphic supplements that adjoin the text, and can direct IT to perform any of several functions listed in the **Action** panel. At any point, or as requested by IT, Pat can reveal certitude about learning by positioning the pointer in the **How Sure?** slider. IT monitors Pat's selections from the text, comparing them to a canonical set that the instructor identified, as well as to Pat's certitude.

Suppose Pat selects canonical items #1 – 6 and #8 but not #7, and the instructor designed IT's rules to recognize occasions where Pat bypassed a canonical item. Perhaps Pat is not paying sufficient attention to the text? Or, could Pat be using an inappropriate list of criteria for monitoring comprehension of the text's information? IT might request Pat to select a response in the **How Come?** panel to differentiate these: It's Difficult would trace that Pat is paying attention but may be unclear about criteria against which to monitor information for comprehending the topic being studied.

Dimension of Self-Regulation	Feature Indicating Dimension of Self-Regulation
Self-Evaluation	Verify options in STUDY BY ... CHECK LEARNING BY ... and option chosen in **Verify** **How Sure?**
Organizing and Transforming	Collapse One Level Expand One Level, AutoMap Items As I Select **Make Link** among elements and **Make Type** to cluster elements in MAP
Goal-Setting and Planning	PLAN & its submenus: SET OBJECTIVES plus # sections __ and # minutes __ STUDY BY ... PREVIEW BY ... CHECK LEARNING BY ...
Seeking Information	Show Item's Index Map Show an Example of Item **Find ...**
Keeping Records and Monitoring Progress	Dragging over objects in TEXT **Make Link** between objects in MAP Quiz Me CHECK LEARNING BY ... **How Sure** **How Come**
Self-Consequences	**Take A Break** (free reading; games; video disk)
Rehearsing and Memorizing	Scrolling to re-display information in TEXT or MAP Quiz Me I Check Tutor in **Verify Events**
Seeking Social Assistance	Tutor Check Me in **Verify Events**
Reviewing Subject Matter	Scrolling to re-display information in TEXT or MAP

Table 3: Some Features in IT's Interface that Afford Self-Regulation

Research is not yet clear about how IT should provide feedback in instances like this [33]. A model proposed by Kulhavy and Stock [16] suggests that Pat's certitude may provide a criterion to incorporate rules about feedback and, as these researchers note, an environment such as IT is ideal for carrying out such research. IT's **How Sure?** slider provides means for Pat to record certitude and contribute data that might refine Kulhavy and Stock's model.

Recall that, in step 3 of Figure 1, Pat elected to use a **Study Method** that involves a map, such as the one displayed in Figure 3. Mapping is an activity that involves Pat in: monitoring text using knowledge of indifference curves plus knowledge about learning in this domain to identify elements to be mapped [6]; selecting items and copying them to the **MAP** panel, thereby tracing Pat's monitoring of comprehension; assembling ideas by choosing links from the **Make Link** panel to join items; and translating information from prose to figural representations. Provided that Pat selects canonical items to map, mapping affords achievement of the subject matter [14]. In the right hand area of the graphic portion of **MAP**, Pat has mapped information about the bundles of goods labeled A and B from the **TEXT** panel's Figure 6. This affords Pat a clear, organized translation to use in monitoring information about indifference curve $\mathbf{u_2}$ in the **TEXT** panel relative to information about indifference curves that Pat had mapped and classified as a **Definition** type. By tracking Pat's mapping, IT can pinpoint whether Pat's memory contains active information necessary to answer the question posed in the text. The instructor could have designed IT to refresh information that Pat needs if this comparison shows that Pat's map is incomplete. Research is almost entirely silent about how to guide Pat's learning using this feedback-like intervention [33].

Next Steps in a Plan for Progress

In the introduction to this chapter, I described first steps to take in advancing research on state-of-the-art ICSs. To this point, I have taken the steps of: (a) proposing a theoretical framework describing about how learning is afforded, (b) sketching an ICS that affords learning as well as we currently know how, and (c) illustrating a few researchable topics in instructional psychology that could be bootstrapped using a state-of-the-art ICS. In closing, I expand on the need to bootstrap research. Then, I lay out the remainder of a plan for sustaining progress.

New Research Is Essential

Research in instructional psychology and cognate fields has amassed considerable knowledge about how to afford learning. Some of these principles were illustrated earlier. Although trite, it is nonetheless true that more research must be done before it will be possible to design an ICS that affords learning as fully as everyone would like. Scores of topics need researching and, in the spirit of favoring plural strategies for advancing research on ICSs, I endorse exploring as many of these as possible. Rather than offer my idiosyncratic list of "important" topics that merit study, I describe instead a non-trivial rationale justifying why more research *must* be done and why it will be *progressive*.

Prior gains notwithstanding, knowledge available for designing state-of-the-art ICSs is importantly deficient in at least nine ways. I separate these nine issues into two sets: a set of five characteristics that have limited the appropriateness of past research as a basis for designing instruction for real classrooms, and a set of four features that have reduced the internal and construct validities of experiments.

First, it simply has been too expensive, for researchers and for students alike, to carry out studies that involve more just a few hours of instruction. As a consequence, second, even "lengthy" studies (those lasting more than an hour) have limited the amount of information students' study to fewer than 1000 propositions or less than a dozen rules. This is considerably less than content covered in a book chapter and certainly far less than material in a semester-long course. Third, the achievements students gain in research have no real life consequences for them — neither intrinsic nor external rewards hinge on achievements gained in experiments. Fourth, students participating in research have studied information that is disconnected from any ongoing, cumulative curriculum. This makes learning in research settings unnatural because learning is separated from aptitudes that are critical in real instructional situations. Fifth, except for studies that focus directly on feedback, learners rarely have been provided feedback during instruction or following tests of achievement(s). This, too, is unlike learning in a real environment where students receive feedback of many sorts from teachers and peers. These characteristics of the vast majority of research in instructional psychology are not characteristic of learning in school or, especially, in self-directed settings. Using a state-of-the-art ICS in real settings, as a supplement to teaching a regular school subject or to lectures in a survey college course, supplies a means to redress each of these five shortcomings.

The remaining four deficiencies of extant research all relate to issues of collecting data about learning over time. First, researchers have been forced to aggregate data about an individual student's learning over different chunks of knowledge in a text. This practice ignores variance that describes achievements in developmental terms, variance that is critical to theories of learning from instruction. Second, researchers have been forced to adopt an unnecessary and overly restrictive *a priori* assumption that nominally similar instructional events (for example, the several headings in a text) are functionally equivalent (are all cognitively processed by a reader in equivalent ways; [27]). ICSs provide means, in the form of traces, for testing such assumptions empirically rather than having to accept them in the absence of data. Third, it has rarely been possible to study fine-grained interactions between a learner and an instructor. Yet, these interactions are precisely those corresponding to the cognitive activities that theoretically comprise learning-as-process. The capacity of a state-of-the-art ICS to track events remedies this shortcoming. And, fourth, researchers heretofore have generally been unable to gather enough data to justify thorough analysis of patterns among interventions and the understandings these patterns may afford to the study of learning. A state-of-the-art ICS provides a tool for gathering and analyzing these patterns.

In general, these issues sum up to three main concerns: (1) Experimental control has been inadequate. (2) Data has been gathered at too large a grain size relative to constructs in theories that account for gaining achievements by learning. (3) Aptitudes central to learning have been inappropriately relegated to nothingness, either statistically by random assignment or by other control, whereas theory considers these aptitudes to be the primary source of variance in learning. These are problems that must be addressed to increase theoretical power.

What Next?

The state-of-the-art ICS that I sketched earlier retreats somewhat from the frontier of knowledge about computing science or instructional psychology. IT can be implemented now given research presently available in these fields. As well, hardware is available to install IT in hundreds of schools and colleges. As was demonstrated, however, there is much more to be gained by creating a state-of-the-art ICS. Results forthcoming from expansive research *in situ*, made possible by building state-of-the-art ICSs, can bootstrap knowledge needed to design progressively more effective and more useful systems.

To reap real profit from state-of-the-art ICSs, five simple steps need to be taken away from the pursuit of only frontier research on ICSs. These five steps comprise my final principle:

THE PRINCIPLE OF STRATEGIC DEVELOPMENT IN ICS.

1. Build a state-of-the-art ICS editing environment so that instructors can customize ICS shells by using a collection of tools and templates.
2. Choose subject matters to teach that are regular subjects in schools and colleges or that, like learning to read with more comprehension, are pan-curricular.
3. Use the ICS extensively in real-life educational settings.
4. Share data and distribute running ICSs among teams of researchers.
5. Recycle to step #1 based on knowledge bootstrapped in this process of strategic development.

Although this principle calls for a retreat from the frontiers of research, it offers challenge enough and promise. In conjunction with research at the frontier, the joint efforts of state-of-the-art research and frontier research may succeed where either alone can not.

Acknowledgements

The author would like to acknowledge the financial support of the Natural Sciences and Engineering Research Council of Canada, and the Social Sciences and Humanities Research Council of Canada, Grant #410-90-0414.

References

1. Anderson, J. R.: *The architecture of cognition*. Hillsdale, NJ: Lawrence Erlbaum Associates 1983
2. Anderson, J. R.: Skill acquisition: Compilation of weak-method problem solutions. *Psychological Review*, 94, pp. 192-210 (1987)
3. Carver, C. S., & Scheier, M. F.: Origins and functions of positive and negative affect: A control-process view. *Psychological Review*, 97, pp. 19-35 (1990)
4. Chase, W. G., & Ericsson, K. A.: Skilled memory. In: *Cognitive skills and their acquisition* (J. R. Anderson, ed.). Hillsdale, NJ: Lawrence Erlbaum Associates 1981
5. Chi, M. T. H., Glaser, R., & Farr, M J.: *The nature of expertise*. Hillsdale, NJ: Lawrence Erlbaum Associates 1989
6. Cook, L. K., & Mayer, R. E.: Teaching readers about the structure of scientific text. *Journal of Educational Psychology*, 80, pp. 448-456 (1988)
7. Corno, L., & Snow, R. E.: Adapting learning to individual differences among learners. In: *Handbook of research on teaching* (M. C. Wittrock, ed.). 3rd ed., New York, NY: Macmillan 1986
8. Frasson,, C., & Gauthier, G.: *Intelligent tutoring systems: At the crossroads of artificial intelligence and education*. Norwood, NJ: Ablex 1990
9. Getsie, R. L., Langer, P., & Glass, G. V.: Meta-analysis of the effects of type and combination of feedback on children's discrimination learning. *Review of Educational Research*, 55, pp. 9-22 (1985)
10. Gettinger, M.: Time allocated and time spent relative to time needed for learning as determinants of achievement. *Journal of Educational Psychology*, 77, pp. 3-11 (1985)
11. Ghatala, E. S.: Strategy-monitoring training enables young learners to select effective strategies. *Educational Psychologist*, 21, pp. 43-54 (1986)
12. Gregory, B.: *Inventing reality: Physics as language*. New York: Wiley 1988
13. Holland, J. H., Holyoak, K. J., Nisbett, R. E., & Thagard, P. T.: *Induction: Processes of inference, learning, and discovery*. Cambridge, MA: MIT Press 1986
14. Holley, D. D., & Dansereau, D. F. (Eds.): *Spatial learning strategies: Techniques, applications, and related issues*. Orlando, FL: Academic Press 1984
15. Kuhn, D.: Children and adults as intuitive scientists. *Psychological Review*, 96, pp. 674-689 (1989)
16. Kulhavy, R. W., & Stock, W. A.: Feedback in written instruction: The place of response certitude. *Educational Psychology Review*, 1, pp. 279-308 (1989)
17. Lohman, D. F.: Human intelligence: An introduction to advances in theory and research. *Review of Educational Research*, 59, pp. 333-373 (1989)
18. Morgan, M.: Self-monitoring of attained subgoals in private study. *Journal of Educational Psychology*, 77, pp. 623-630 (1985)
19. Nickerson, R. S.: *Reflections on reasoning*. Hillsdale, NJ: Lawrence Erlbaum Associates 1986
20. Paris, S. B., & Meyers, M.: Comprehension monitoring, memory, and study strategies of good and poor readers. *Journal of Reading Behavior*, 13, pp. 5-22 (1981)
21. Peters, E. E., Levin, J. R., McGivern, J. E., & Pressley, M.: Further comparison of representational and transformational prose-learning imagery. *Journal of Educational Psychology*, 77, pp. 129-136 (1985)
22. Pressley, M., et al.: *Cognitive strategy instruction that really improves children's academic performance*. Cambridge, MA: Brookline Books 1990

23. Reder, L. M.: Techniques available to author, teacher, and reader to improve retention of main ideas of a chapter. In: *Thinking and learning skills: Vol. 2. Research and open questions* (S. F. Chipman, J. W. Segal, & R. Glaser, eds.). Hillsdale, NJ: Lawrence Erlbaum Associates 1985
24. Simon, H. A.: *The sciences of the artificial* (2nd ed.). Cambridge, MA: MIT Press 1981
25. Weinstein, C. F., & Mayer, R. E.: The teaching of learning strategies. In: *Handbook of research on teaching* (M. C. Wittrock, ed.). 3rd ed. New York, NY: Macmillan 1986
26. Wilhite, S. C.: Headings as memory facilitators: The importance of prior knowledge. *Journal of Educational Psychology*, 81, pp. 115-117 (1989)
27. Winne, P. H.: Minimizing the black box problem to enhance the validity of theories about instructional effects. *Instructional Science*, 11, pp. 13-28 (1982)
28. Winne, P. H.: Why process-product research cannot explain process-product findings and a proposed remedy: The cognitive mediational paradigm. *Teaching and Teacher Education*, 3, pp. 333-356 (1987)
29. Winne, P. H.: Theories of instruction and of intelligence for designing artificially intelligent tutoring systems. *Educational Psychologist*, 24, pp. 229-259 (1989)
30. Winne, P. H.: Motivation and teaching. In: *Research on teaching* (H. Waxman, & H. J. Walberg, eds.). 2nd ed. Berkeley, CA: McCutchan 1990
31. Winne, P. H., & Marx, R. W.: Students' and teachers' views of thinking processes for classroom learning. *Elementary School Journal*, 82, pp. 493-518 (1982)
32. Winne, P. H., & Marx, R. W.: A cognitive processing analysis of motivation within classroom tasks. In: *Research on Motivation In Education: Volume 3. Goals and Cognitions* (C. Ames, & R. Ames, eds.). San Diego, CA: Academic Press 1989
33. Winne, P. H., & Walsh, J.: *Feedback, learning, motivation, and instruction.* Proposal to the Social Sciences and Humanities Research Council of Canada 1989
34. Wittrock, M. C.: Students' thought processes. In: *Handbook of research on teaching* (M. C. Wittrock, ed.). 3rd ed. New York: Macmillan 1986
35. Zajonc, R. B.: Feeling and thinking: Preferences need no inferences. *American Psychologist*, 35, pp. 151-175 (1981)
36. Zimmerman, B. J.: A social cognitive view of self-regulated academic learning. *Journal of Educational Psychology*, 81, pp. 329-339 (1989)
37. Zimmerman, B. J., & Pons, M. M.: Development of a structured interview for assessing student use of self-regulated learning strategies. *American Educational Research Journal*, 23, pp. 614-628 (1989)

Part 7

Synthesis

Synthesizing Instructional and Computational Science

Marlene Jones[1], Jim Greer[2], Ellen Mandinach[3], Benedict du Boulay[4], Peter Goodyear[5]

[1]Advanced Computing and Engineering, Alberta Research Council, Calgary, Canada
[2]ARIES Laboratory, Department of Computational Science, University of Saskatchewan, Saskatoon, Canada
[3]Educational Testing Service, Princeton, NJ, USA
[4]School of Cognitive and Computing Sciences, University of Sussex, Falmer, Brighton, England
[5]Department of Educational Research, Lancaster University, Lancaster, England

Abstract: This chapter is based on various discussions which took place at the Advanced Study Institute in Calgary during July 1990. In particular, this chapter reflects the synthesis sessions presented by Benedict du Boulay, Peter Goodyear, Jim Greer and Ellen Mandinach. The chapter starts by addressing the issue of why synthesis of two traditionally distinct research areas is a worthwhile goal, examines impediments to such a synthesis, and suggests that by addressing our differences, we can begin to understand them and bridge them. To assist in bridging our differences, the chapter contains a discussion of several common themes that are interwoven within the six topics of this book. We also discuss the need for stronger collaboration between the participating research areas. The chapter also contains a discussion of collaboration and research goals, steps we are taking towards success, and steps toward achieving recognition as a field of study.

Keywords: instructional science, computational science, AI/Education, research goals, Adaptive Learning Environments (ALEs), Interactive Learning Environments (ILEs), Intelligent Tutoring Systems (ITSs).

Introduction

In any attempt at synthesizing traditionally distinct (and diverse) research areas, one must consider why such synthesis is a worthwhile goal. The Advanced Study Institute that spawned this volume explored differences and sought common ground between the instructional and computational sciences. Instruction is an intriguing area of application for computational scientists, especially those interested in artificial intelligence. Through computer-based

NATO ASI Series, Vol. F 85
Adaptive Learning Environments
Edited by M. Jones and P. H. Winne

instruction one can explore many aspects of machine intelligence and test computational theories related to representing and reasoning about changing knowledge. On the other hand, the computer is an appealing tool for instructional scientists, as a means both to enhance instruction and to conduct controlled research into learning and instruction. The intersection of these computational and instructional research quests roughly defines the terrain of Adaptive Learning Environments (ALEs) [5].

From the early 1960's, Computer-Based Learning (CBL) systems capitalized on the capacity of the computer to deliver modestly individualized content to learners. Artificial Intelligence (AI) researchers hastened to point out that traditional CBL suffered from the inability to reason about its own knowledge of the domain, about its ability to instruct, and about the learner; and hence, in principle could never deliver instruction as well as a human teacher or tutor. CBL was accused of being built on a behaviourist paradigm of learning. AI interest in instruction led to increased research in Intelligent Tutoring Systems (ITSs) during the late 1970's and early 80's. ITS research projects and ITS researchers can claim to their credit many interesting general AI advancements as well as many challenges that will fuel AI research for some time to come. More recently, educators, anthropologists, and sociologists have begun to argue that ITSs suffer, in principle, from an inability to reason about the learner's construction of knowledge because ITSs fail to consider the context of learning and social interactions fundamental to learning processes. In other words, ITS research has assumed an overly-restrictive view of pedagogy. This has lead to the investigation of situated learning [1] and the development of Situated Learning Environments (SLEs). Others are focussing on the development of Interactive Learning Environments (ILEs) [14], computer-design environments in which the learner builds artifacts (from book reports to mini robots).

There are many tensions among the various approaches that comprise ALEs. The fact that the growing interest in ITSs seems to have tarnished basic research in CBL has not inhibited the continued development of CBL systems. The challenges raised by ITSs, to consider domain knowledge and the student, in many ways strengthened the CBL paradigm. ITSs provided the forcing function to justify the simplifications and assumptions CBL had made and to bring to the forefront CBL's successes. Interest in SLEs and ILEs may have a similar impact on ITS research, relieving it of its responsibility as the "be-all and end-all" of Adaptive Learning Environments. The challenge to consider context and social interaction in the ITS paradigm can act as a forcing function to evolve the ITS paradigm. These tensions increase the challenges and the gains of forging a synthesis of instructional and computational sciences.

So, what is the nature of possible syntheses of instructional and computational sciences? Is there common ground? Is there potential to define a common research agenda? Is there an emerging research discipline? This chapter explores the impediments, challenges, and paths to a synthesis of instructional and computational sciences.

Impediments to Synthesis – The Abyss

The ultimate goal of research into ALEs is to develop computer systems that provide or support effective learning experiences for a wide range of learners across a broad spectrum of knowledge domains. Nevertheless, a wide gulf seems to exist which separates instructional and computational science research efforts. There are differences in research goals and development goals; there are differences in terminology, in research methodologies, in the specificity and precision with which theories are described, and in what is considered to constitute proof of a theoretical result. Attempts to reach a synthesis across these issues require identifying and resolving problems that constitute this abyss. We have to deal with the difficulties in reconciling vastly different research goals, subtle terminologies, and divergent research methodologies and heritages.

Probably the greatest impediment to reaching common ground between the instructional and computational sciences is that many computational scientists are amateur educators and many instructional scientists are amateur programmers. This partial knowledge can lead to diminished respect for colleagues on "the other side of the abyss." It is tempting for each to think that the other is easily understood, and that the other should be quite satisfied to take a subservient role in joint research ventures.

The naive instructional scientist views the computational scientist as a professional computer programmer, who as such must be interested in building application software for education and training. However, many computational scientists have little interest in the details of programming computers *per se*. Principled research into constructing better computer hardware and software involves developing techniques and tools based on sound theoretical foundations of computational science. Viewing a computational scientist as a glorified application programmer is inaccurate.

The naive computational scientist views the instructional scientist as a professional educator who, as such, should be interested in planning lessons and delivering instruction to students. However, many instructional scientists have little desire to teach in classroom situations common to today's educational system. Principled research into teaching and learning leads toward developing techniques and tools based on sound theoretical foundations of education and cognition. Viewing an instructional scientist as a glorified teacher is also wrong.

Not only do researchers on "the other side of the abyss" have goals other than we might expect, they also have many misconceptions about ourselves.

Research and Development Goals

The basic goal of both instructional and computational scientists reading this chapter is to enable the development of computer systems that provide effective learning experiences for a wide range of learners across a broad spectrum of knowledge domains. A variety of more specific and diverse subgoals delineate the abyss. This, in conjunction with the difficulty of pursuing truly equitable, collaborative research, is a distressing situation. For either the instructional scientist or the computational scientist, we have learned that the results, techniques, or findings of researchers across the abyss are valuable. However, we also have come to understand, through first-hand experience, that results generated on each side of the abyss may be misunderstood, unappreciated, and inappropriately applied by those on the other side of the abyss.

Although one may initially view the abyss as being defined by the diverse goals of instructional and computational scientists, the situation is actually more complex than that. We identify at least five different orientations to research, each with its own subgoals, that illustrate the diversity of existing approaches to addressing this basic goal of constructing better ALEs. Each subgoal delineates a unique and relatively independent class of researchers.

1. the "traditional AI/computational scientist," whose principle goal is to advance the state of knowledge about AI/computational science; but who uses Education as an application domain that offers interesting and challenging problems that stretch established computational methods.
2. the "techie," whose main objective is to construct effective working instructional systems using available techniques from AI or Education without blindly adhering to or being blinkered by any particular paradigm or computational research agenda.
3. the "instructional scientist," who uses AI and computer technology to facilitate experimentation in advancing knowledge about instruction.
4. the "teacher," whose main objective is to provide effective instructional and learning support computer systems, using available results from AI and Education without specifically adhering to, or being blinkered by, any particular paradigm or educational research agenda.

5. the "cognitive scientist" who uses both AI and Education theories and techniques for the purposes of modelling and experimenting with cognition.

Researchers motivated by one of these subgoals must be aware of the existence and validity of the other, possibly conflicting, subgoals that may motivate their colleagues.

Research Methodology

Research paradigms and methodologies are rather different across the abyss, variance that stems from different notions of what is considered a research advance. Computational scientists are concerned with translating theory into detailed computational representations and algorithms, constructing detailed computational models that can be simulated with computer programs, evaluating the fidelity of the computational models, and managing and monitoring the tractability of algorithms. In computational science, proof in formal mathematical terms is preferred, although proof by construction or by implementation is frequently accepted. Empirical studies are relatively infrequent, although case study research is not uncommon.

Computational science is a very young science, in many ways struggling to evolve research paradigms and to select appropriate research methods. The discipline suffers a real sense of insecurity when compared with the "natural sciences." In fact, there has been a long-standing battle to establish the discipline as a respectable science. Unfortunately, this insecurity is often manifested in an attitude of apparent arrogance, especially toward the social sciences.

Instructional scientists are primarily concerned with proposing relatively coarse-grained, domain-independent theories, and proving these theories through experimental and quasi-experimental studies. These studies are used to measure the effects of interventions and to demonstrate the adequacy of a particular theory to describe some phenomenon. Studies with small samples, phenomenological research, and case-study research are gaining prominence and proving useful for theory formation and model construction.

Many technical terms overlap our research disciplines. However, the subtle connotations and even the denotations of many of these terms can differ when used by instructional versus computational scientists. For example, the terms *model*, *diagnosis*, *learning*, *planning*, *implementation*, and even *knowledge* have different connotations in education versus AI literature.

We hope that through focussing on our differences, we can begin to understand them and eventually reconcile them. The next section briefly mentions why we should bridge the abyss and then proceeds to discuss some of the common themes that arose at the Advanced Study Institute and hence in the chapters within this book. This is followed by a discussion of collaboration and research goals and steps we must take toward success. The final section of this chapter discusses Adaptive Learning Environments as a field of study. In these ways, we provide some suggestions for how we can begin to bridge the abyss.

Bridging the Abyss

Why should we try to bridge the abyss? The field of ALE research and development is large and complex, building upon diverse domains of expertise. No one researcher or developer can work in isolation. Knowledge is required from the other side of the abyss. Moreover, if we focus our research endeavours, we will likely move forward more efficiently and hence more rapidly. The six preceding sections of this book represent areas in which overlapping interests already exist and in which bridging the abyss will assist in furthering the research interests of both computational scientists and instructional scientists. Bridging the abyss will also result in the development of more sophisticated and, we hope, more effective instructional systems.

The critical supplementary question is *how* do we bridge the abyss? An essential step is that we understand the other side. That was one of the intents of the Advanced Study Institute. What we propose to do in this section is to summarize three of the common themes that arose at the Institute and that are interwoven in the chapters within this book. The three themes, which are not mutually exclusive, are

1. simplifying assumptions
2. the role of the learner
3. a shift in perspective on pedagogical knowledge.

Simplifying Assumptions

When communicating one's viewpoints, it is important to be explicit about one's assumptions. In order to undertake research and to develop ALEs, one must make simplifying assumptions. Implicit and unstated assumptions often are sources of much debate. Moreover, assumptions themselves are one of the unifying themes.

Simplifying assumptions regarding intended uses. The first simplifying assumption concerns the intended use of ALEs. Does the designer visualize a world in which such systems will be used sparingly, one component in a rich educational environment? Or does the designer believe that ALEs will be so pervasive that a student will be interacting with many such systems throughout the day? Each viewpoint implies further simplifying assumptions.

In the former case, which is perhaps more realistic, the ALE is not the entire educational context but rather one portion of it. There are several consequences of this perspective. First, there is no attempt to usurp the teacher's central role. Second, it allows the designer to ignore certain issues. For example, the learner can seek outside assistance regarding system use. The subject matter need not be comprehensive, allowing the designer to focus on smaller amounts of content. But more importantly, the designer can ignore many pedagogical issues or at least simplify the manner in which they are handled. One might limit the instructional strategies to be employed by the system. Similarly, the issue of motivation might be pushed aside, claiming that the teacher will provide this missing ingredient. If assumptions are unstated, the neglect of certain issues is viewed as exactly that, neglect, rather than as an understanding that other agents will continue to play important roles in the instructional process and that certain activities or processes can be ascribed to them.

A common simplifying assumption is that motivation need not be incorporated explicitly within an ALE. Because an ALE is embedded in a larger educational context, many designers feel that fostering motivation can be left as a responsibility for others within the larger context of education. Yet, too often we, the designers, do not make the necessary effort to incorporate the instructor. As many at the Institute observed, it is wise, if not critical, to involve the teacher. It is not sufficient to simply place a box in the classroom.

Simplifying assumptions regarding knowledge. One of the threads that runs through the preceding chapters and the presentations at the Institute concerns views of knowledge, the acquisition of knowledge, and the learner's role in that acquisition. Does one view knowledge as chunks of information or expertise to be acquired by the learner or as the mortar binding the chunks together? Phrased in this manner, one will likely answer "both." However, an examination of methodologies proposed and systems built illustrates that we often assume a particular viewpoint of knowledge, which then influences the methodologies that we propose for knowledge acquisition, either from the learner or by the learner.

Two diverse views of knowledge acquisition exist in the research literature: the designer working as an engineer, manipulating pieces of knowledge (hence the term knowledge engineer), and the designer as an anthropologist, analyzing the signs and signals as to what the underlying cognitive processes are. These two models also appear with the development of ALEs, and typically are not explicitly stated. There is also a subtle interplay between knowledge construction and knowledge deconstruction[1] or analysis, as is illustrated by the chapters within this volume.

The work of Laurillard, Derry, and Dillenbourg concerns the deconstruction of knowledge from the anthropological perspective. Laurillard presents a method for capturing the contexts within which a learner is applying specific knowledge. Derry and Dillenbourg investigate the use of knowledge (rules of thumb) in the application of facts and procedures within the problem-solving process. The investigations of both Derry and Dillenbourg are complicated by the fact that the roles of instructional agents and learners evolve over the course of interaction. The goal is for the learner to assume increasing responsibility for the problem-solving process over time. For all three, Laurillard, Derry and Dillenbourg, the designer acts more as an anthropologist than as an engineer in examining contexts, tasks, and situations.

In contrast, Cerri and Woolf are more concerned with the engineering aspects of knowledge acquisition and knowledge representation of deconstructed knowledge. Both recognize the importance of computational tools to assist in the process. In Cerri's case, a means of building up layers of descriptions is provided. The need for adequate tools was indicated several times at the Institute, and is discussed later in this chapter.

In examining the construction of knowledge, various models of how the learner acquires knowledge can be adopted, including transmission, negotiation, apprenticeship, exploration, and guided construction. Often the model adopted in an ALE is not implemented in pure form. For example, an exploration approach could be guided or an approach could be primarily based on transmitting knowledge with allowance for negotiation on the part of the learner. Shuell suggests that guided construction is the approach most compatible with current theories of learning. In any case, choice of a model has an impact on the assumptions and decisions that we make regarding the learner's role, learner control, and pedagogical knowledge required within the system.

In the shift from a view of the learner as an empty vessel waiting to be filled (transmission theory) to a view of the learner as meaningfully engaged in the learning process (artisan), there has been increasing emphasis on investigations of metacognition. By making records of student-system interactions available to the learner as well as the system, the learner has opportunities to reflect upon previous actions. Furthermore, there has been a realization by designers that metacognitive activities should not be left to chance. In addition to providing tools which allow reflection, the instructional agent must be aware that metacognitive processes are to be engaged by the learner, and must strive to facilitate such engagement. Metacognition should be on the instructional agenda. This reflects back to a lesson learned from

---

[1] The term "knowledge deconstruction" has a more precise meaning in certain circles such as literary criticism. We use the term here to mean the analysis of knowledge.

experimentation with the programming language LOGO — if one wants students to learn about problem-solving, have problem-solving explicitly on the agenda. In other words, specific foci should be embedded in a larger agenda.

This philosophy is reflected in the work of Derry, Dillenbourg, and Winne. Derry and Dillenbourg emphasize the encouragement of metacognitive processes. Winne proposes a theory of cognitive processes and empirical data, moving towards several theories of instruction. He presents a commitment to the idea that if the learner is going to engage in the activity of learning, this has to be embedded for that learner. The concern here is how one embeds knowledge in an ALE or how the learner gets to embed knowledge.

One's view of how the learner constructs knowledge juxtaposed with one's view of how the ALE will be used (sparsely versus overlapping) both influence the domains chosen. Most domains are still small and extremely dense. Examples include the work of Wasson[2], Laurillard, and Ohlsson. Yet, systems that span domains can be developed, as proposed by Winne. It is time to work toward scaling up, which will raise further issues of complexity, breadth, and timing. Once systems are capable of dealing with an educational interaction that spans more than a few hours, summaries, rest-breaks, recaps, and speed of delivery all become relevant issues, as they are for human teachers.

The Role of the Learner

Throughout the Institute, the role of the learner and learner modelling were recurring themes. Designers often make simplifying assumptions about the learner or style of learning.

A common simplifying assumption is that the ALE will be used by one individual at a time. Although designers talk as if interactions are one-to-one, this restriction is not always adhered to. ALEs are often used in small groups (for example, see Woolf's experience with the Recovery Boiler Tutor [17]), although this may not be part of the ALE's design. This will change. Researchers recognize that one does not just learn from experts who know more than oneself, one also learns from peers. Researchers are starting to examine the power of collaborative learning and to determine how best to facilitate it [cf. 6, 7, 10].

A learner is both an active constructor of knowledge as it is acquired and an interpreter of the learning environment. Designers feel comfortable with the learner constructing knowledge, but have often neglected the learner's interpretive role within the instructional interaction. Shuell points out that there is no optimal way to teach to all students. Learners are good at

[2] A discussion of Wasson's research is contained in the chapter by McCalla in this volume.

learning from suboptimal environments. We need to get away from the fetish of optimizing instruction and develop a broader pedagogical repertoire for our systems. The typical learner is able to learn from different styles of instruction and cope with suboptimal instruction, function with less than ideal resources, and work productively with poor instructional materials and presentations not individualized to the learner. The learner will adapt to the available approaches, constructing and interpreting interactions, regardless of whether the instructional agent intervenes. There exists a substantial amount of ethnographic educational research concerning learners' interpretation of their learning environments [12]. Instructional systems should not ignore the interpretive aspect of what the student does.

A debate regarding what we mean by *meaningful* learning was sparked by Ohlsson's presentation. Learners are habitual meaning-makers; they are continually doing interpretive work. Yet our models of acquisition of knowledge tend to ignore this aspect of what the learner does. We need to examine how the learner makes sense out of instruction. Learners make the instruction meaningful to themselves, but perhaps not in the manner intended by the instructor.

Related to the role of the learner is the continuous debate about the role of the learner model. Much of the discussion can be summarized with the following observations. The role of the learner model is not disappearing. Rather, it is either being moved off-line or into other components of the ALE. One view, as demonstrated in Laurillard's chapter, is that one employs knowledge of the student to build good artifacts to use in education. The artifacts themselves may not need an internal model of the learner, but the designer needs a model of the learner to build the artifact. This distinction has been clearly drawn in the human-computer interaction literature [15, 16]. A question related to this is, "How does the design of a good tool differ from the design of a good system?" Soloway proposes critiquing the work produced by the student, rather than critiquing the student directly. However, the same types of issues regarding learner modelling still exist. Hartley moves the learner model into a dialogue system, but the learner model does not go away. Rather, the system has to have an idea of what the argument or dialogue is about to determine a reasonable response to the argument.

A Shift in Perspective On Pedagogical Knowledge

During the course of the Institute, synthesizers raised issues that they felt were in danger of neglect. As mentioned earlier, one concerned the learner's contribution to educational interactions. A second revolved around the topic of modelling pedagogical knowledge.

During the last few years, there have been many discussions regarding the benefits of various instructional approaches and the desired locus of pedagogical decision making. It is not the case that tutoring is always better than exploration or visa versa. What is needed is a theory that decides appropriate instruction given the context, the educational situation. Decision making and control should not be viewed as a dichotomy but rather as a continuum from system control to learner control. This continuum was dubbed the *Elsom-Cook line*[3] at the Institute. A given system should be able to move along this line as required by the context. To decide where to position ourselves, we need a theory of how the agent selects an appropriate point on the Elsom-Cook line. We need to determine what types of knowledge support such decision making. Our scientific understanding of teaching, whether by human or computer, is seriously deficient if we do not understand how an instructional agent can reason about or come to a decision about an appropriate teaching style.

There is also a shifting role within the classroom which ALE designers are not yet reflecting. The teacher is adopting the role of facilitator rather than a dispenser of knowledge. A facilitator does more than transmit knowledge. A facilitator plans, monitors, repairs, intervenes and reshapes directions of activities for individual learners and for groups. The issue for the teacher is to design activities and engage students in the activities so that the students construct new knowledge and skills for themselves. This is different from simply attempting to "transmit" knowledge or skills directly. We should be investigating types of knowledge which enable instructional agents — teachers and ALEs — to do these things [4]. Teachers are constrained by ethics and physical resources, yet they manage to present acceptable alternatives in the face of these constraints. We need to identify the pedagogical knowledge that allows them to replan activities and find alternatives as they reason about goals, attributes of the learner, and pedagogical resources.

We need to move beyond a theory or science of instruction toward a theory of learning from instruction. The work of both Shuell and Winne illustrates this shift in perspective. Rather than settling for theories of cognition or theories of learning, they build on this knowledge, striving for theories of learning from instruction. From there we can move toward prescriptive theories of instruction which are informed by theories of learning from instruction.

The issue of the required granularity of knowledge recurred several times during the Institute, initially sparked by the comparison of Shuell's and Ohlsson's presentations. The presentations and the corresponding chapters illustrate differing viewpoints that exist regarding the granularity at which knowledge is required. Some argued that Shuell's work lacked the specificity required and that Ohlsson's demonstrated the granularity required for implementation within an ALE. Perhaps we are looking at this issue from the wrong perspective. One can argue that all levels are required. For some tasks, detailed representation at a fine granularity,

[3] For an illustration of where certain systems might be situated on the Elsom-Cook line, see Figure 10.1 in [3].

as is presented by Ohlsson, is required. Yet for others, the coarse-grained sizes will suffice. At issue is the interpretive power of the instructional agent. It has sufficed for educational theories to be coarse-grained or "underspecified" because of human ability to interpret such theories. In order for an ALE to interpret such theories, we need to examine the kinds of pedagogical knowledge that allow human instructional agents to make sense of what initially appear to be underspecified theories and prescriptions. What high-level model of learning and instruction allows an agent to reason across layers or grain sizes?

Two things seem to be required. As mentioned earlier, we need to scale up so as to deal with more realistic size chunks of the domain that we want students to learn. At the same time, we need to scale down to develop clearly articulated theories specifying the intended psychological outcomes of each small aspect of instructional activity. In the process of scaling down, we need to examine the pedagogical knowledge which allows teachers to interpret and apply existing educational theories.

Collaboration and Research Goals

There are three basic steps to collaboration that we need to undertake:

1. learn about each other's terminology, goals, history, and literature

2. through dialogue, negotiate mutually acceptable goals

3. co-ordinate our research efforts to ensure that we are not working at cross purposes.

There is, of course, more than one type of research goal, which we should consider. The following two categories were suggested at the Institute:

1. practical, applied, utilitarian goals

2. scientific, intellectual goals.

There is not universal agreement about the goals or types of goal which should be pursued. There are those who see the development of ALEs for educational or industrial use as one route for establishing collaborative research teams. The research team then pursues a specific research agenda within the context of practical development. Others argue that real scientific collaboration is difficult if the project is very practically oriented. Computational scientists do not want to be used as overpaid hackers; nor do instructional scientists want to be seen merely as providing a socially useful project for the testing of computational theories. The argument, then, is that real collaboration in our field is best rooted in the scientific goal of building and understanding intelligent teaching agents, the key elements in the functionality of an ALE. It is further argued that we need to build systems to test pedagogical hypotheses, and so advance the state of our scientific knowledge about learning and instruction. Such systems can also have practical applications as is the case with Winne's proposed ALE.

To further our scientific understanding of intelligent teaching agents, we must undertake system evaluation. Such system testing must evaluate one or more pedagogical hypotheses embedded in the system design. Ohlsson [9] argues that only then does system evaluation advance our scientific understanding.

The approach proposed at the Institute for illuminating our research goals was to start by asking the purpose of education. Is the purpose the acquisition of content or is it the acquisition of skills for life-long learning and problem solving? Or, as Soloway put it, should the goal of education be to instill confidence and passion? In each case, the teacher is an intelligent agent whose general goal is to facilitate the desired learning. We need to construct a computational theory of teaching which is not technology dependent. Shifts in the technology will show how we can get to the goal, but the goal itself is independent of the technology. By examining the functionality of intelligent teaching agents, we can generate research subgoals. For example, we might ask what is the scope and form of knowledge needed by the intelligent teaching agent? What are appropriate ways to partition that knowledge?

In assessing these research goals, we must come to terms with the revolution that is happening around us: the exploding quantity of information, the increasing access to technology, and changes reshaping the education system. Dickson warned that, without this awareness, we will continue to teach in the same manner as our parents and grandparents.

Soloway and Woolf argued that technology integration will change us. With 200 MIP machines, the questions and issues change, and how we interface with information changes. There will be too much information available at our finger-tips. We will have access to encyclopedias, databases, expert systems. As computing power increases, we need more intelligent management of information so that we are presented with a selection of information which is appropriate for us. Consequently, we will need to provide the learner with tools which can intelligently manage vast amounts of information. Some claim, on this basis, that the learner of the future will be cast in the role of researcher or independent explorer, with the teacher or instructional system assisting in the management of information.

As we look at changes in educational technology, we realize that there is a proliferation of educational software such as games for personal/home computers. The alarming aspect, as Woolf pointed out, is that less than 20% of educational software has *any* pedagogical input. We need to invert this ratio. Educational software is being developed for everyday use by persons outside of the field of research regarding ALEs. Woolf argued that we need to push for what we want. There is money for the development of AI-based systems in medicine; there is money for the development of AI-based systems in geology. As yet, similar funding does not exist for AI-based systems for education. We must lobby to bring about a change in the funding situation. She further argued that to do so, we will have to undertake more thorough independent evaluation of the educational systems that we develop in order to establish their worth in the eyes of potential sponsors.

Hence, our common goals must include lobbying for further funding and increasing the awareness of the educational benefits of ALEs in terms of what they can and do deliver. We need to convince industry that they must be the benefactor to education as a first step toward becoming the benefactor of powerful systems of education.

Steps Towards Success

There are steps toward success on both sides of the abyss that should be acknowledged. Two prime examples are the development of tools and the integration of instructional systems. Computational scientists know how to build computational tools to assist in the development of ALEs. Similarly, instructional scientists have years of experience in the implementation or integration of instructional systems. In both cases, there is expertise which needs to be shared for the successful development of ALEs.

The Need for Tools to Facilitate Research and Development

Throughout the Institute, the topic of tools recurred several times, and is apparent in several of the chapters within this book. We, as researchers and developers, require several types of tools. McCalla raised the need for knowledge engineering tools to ease the burden of system development in areas such as domain development, curriculum development, and learner model acquisition. The latter need was also addressed by others including Cerri, Laurillard and Hartley. Woolf stressed the need for qualitative modelling tools for the development of simulations (in conjunction with knowledge elicitation tools) and cognitive modelling.

Cerri pointed to other application areas which support a plethora of tools, such as mathematics, and asked why a similar situation has not yet emerged in our own field. This highlights the fact that we have not yet standardized our requirements, our computing platforms, or our philosophies. All of this makes the sharing of software and the development of standard tools unlikely. We need a unifying framework, such as that proposed in the PETE[4] and CTA[5] aspects of the European DELTA[6] program [2], to facilitate the development of common tools and the use of such tools. As yet the field lacks the financial incentive for the development of standard tools that has existed for some time in the area of mathematical applications. Increased interest from industrial and military sectors will eventually facilitate the development of tools, by providing such an incentive.

In addition to providing tools for developers, there is a need for tools which instructional scientists can use in further research, to develop and refine the theories upon which ALEs can be developed. This is nicely illustrated in Winne's chapter.

There is a third target audience for which tools should be built, and that is the learner. The image of AI-based instructional systems in the 1970's and 80's was that of artificial private tutors for the learner. The shift is now towards providing tools as well as guidance for the learner, tools by which the learner can construct knowledge, reflect on actions and artifacts, and inspect what the system believes about the learner.

We have seen the impact that appropriate tools have had on other fields of research. A prime example is the field of expert systems. Applications did not abound until a variety of development shells and environments were created to ease the burden of development. Likewise, we cannot expect the proliferation of high quality AI-based educational software until we have the tools to support development in a timely, cost-effective manner.

Integration of ALEs into Instructional Environments

With the growth of educational software, it is time that the developers of ALEs face another important issue: the integration of ALEs within existing learning environments such as schools, universities, and corporations.

Although integration into an existing learning environment such as a classroom is not the foremost consideration for system developers, it is an issue that they should not ignore. There are many factors which influence the ultimate use or non-use of instructional systems. Instructional scientists possess a wealth of knowledge regarding the implementation of instructional programs. Awareness of the relevant factors should be considered early in the development of an ALE, preferably at the preliminary design stage. Early involvement of practitioners within ALE projects should lead to greater consideration of pedagogical styles,

---

4 Portable Educational Tools Environment
5 Common Training Architecture
6 Developing European Learning through Technological Advance

educational objectives, and the organizational constraints under which such systems will be deployed.

Many factors can facilitate or impede the effective use of technology in instructional settings. Such factors are briefly discussed by Dickson. Research has shown that these determinants fall into three categories: money, flexibility, and time. Such constraints have the potential to alter design decisions, components of system development, and ultimately, system use.

Monetary issues present a challenge regardless of the potential instructional benefit of the ALE. One area of concern is the provision of physical resources and facilities. First, there are major gaps between the equipment that researchers use for system development and the equipment that is typically found in school settings. Second, if hardware is donated or acquired, it is critical that it be appropriate for the instructional institution's educational objectives, not just for a given project. At face value, the donation of hardware is extremely generous. However, even a straightforward donation has hidden costs and responsibilities that must be incurred by the institution.

A second issue concerns the lack of flexibility found in most school settings, partially an outgrowth of concerns for accountability. Teachers are held accountable for students' scores, supervisors for teachers' performances, and so on. Technology-based curriculum innovations do alter both teaching and learning activities [8, 13] and may oppose existing standards of achievement maintained by teachers, schools, the government, and the general public. Institutions need to re-examine some of the existing standards and to question the pressures to achieve such standards.

The lack of flexibility within curricula is a formidable obstacle. The closer the match with pre-existing educational objectives, the easier the integration of an ALE is likely to be. Mandated curricula are frequently so constrained and predefined that it is difficult to introduce instructional technology. Requesting that teachers integrate a system into their curriculum generally means that something else must be omitted. That "something else" is a topic for which they will be held accountable with respect to their students' achievements.

A related issue is that teachers' time is limited. Anything new requires change, and change requires both time and effort. A partial solution to the time problem is to provide opportunities for uninterrupted work, such as intensive training during the summer. Training is a vital component in the successful implementation of technology. Teachers are the critical link in making a system function effectively in the classroom. Hence, it is paramount that teachers have intensive training as well as on-going support.

A Field of Study

It is our belief that the research and development associated with ALEs is energetic and a worthwhile field of study. What the field of study should be termed is still open to debate. There are several aspects of the field that continue to make it challenging. The first challenge is that the field is not represented by a single research paradigm, as is often the case with a field of study. Rather, it has several research paradigms, and will continue to do so.

Second, research within this area is not entirely scientific. It involves both art and science. The difficulty remains as to how we, members of this research field, recognize this dichotomy in our endeavours and integrate art and science. At times, it appears that we want to deny our artistic side, and aim to operationalize all aspects of instruction. But successful interaction with the learner does involve artistry. We recognize this when a teacher facilitates, monitors, delivers instruction, and replans. We also believe that there are underlying principles which can guide these processes. We should certainly continue to study those principles.

Our third challenge is that this field of research must build on its interdisciplinary nature and foster collaboration. We need to develop interdisciplinary research teams such as those at the Institute for Research on Learning (IRL) and the Institute for Learning Sciences (ILS), among others. In order to focus energies into a unified direction, individual research teams may choose to adopt a particular research paradigm or methodology.

Related to collaboration are fundamental concerns raised by Pea and Soloway [11] in their report to the United States Office of Technology Assessment. These concerns have yet to be fully addressed by the research community or sponsoring government agencies. Pea and Soloway argued for the development of Centers for Interactive Technologies in Education (CITEs) which were to incorporate researchers, developers, and "front-line" teachers. They suggested associating each CITE with a K-12 school as well as linking it to commercial sectors. The CITE was to encourage visitors, give workshops to educators, and facilitate dissemination of information and collaboration. Many of these goals can be addressed on a smaller scale by the research community. Interdisciplinary research teams can incorporate computational scientists, instructional scientists, teachers, programmers and others. Educational programs can be developed by which teachers join research teams for particular projects or sabbaticals or even a few weeks in the summer. One example is the Alberta Teachers' Research Experience Program which allows science teachers to spend six weeks during the summer at the Alberta Research Council (ARC), and undertake a technology-based project with the guidance and assistance of ARC staff.

As a field of study, we need to develop a curriculum of study which, rather than being viewed as a standard carved in stone, can be adopted as a broad guide for the training of graduate students and future researchers. A group of participants from the Advanced Study Institute agreed to investigate this further and to develop suggested reading lists and a core curriculum. Such information is not just of value to students, but also will provide one more bridge between the two research areas of instructional psychology and computational science. We must continue to grow in understanding each other, and we must recognize our research as interdisciplinary and act accordingly.

Acknowledgements

The authors would like to thank Mary Mark and Philip Winne for their comments on an earlier draft of this chapter.

References

1. Brown, J. S.: Toward a new epistemology for learning. In: *Intelligent tutoring systems: At the crossroads of artificial intelligence and education.* (C. Frasson and G. Gauthier, eds.). Norwood, NJ: Ablex 1990
2. DELTA: *R&D on telematic systems in flexible and distance learning.* DGXIII CEC, Brussels 1991
3. Elsom-Cook, M.: Guided discovery tutoring and bounded student modelling. In: *Artificial intelligence and human learning: Intelligent computer-aided instruction* (J. Self, ed.). Chapman and Hall Computing 1988
4. Goodyear, P. (ed.): *Teaching knowledge and intelligent tutoring.* Ablex 1991
5. Goodyear, P., & Pain, H.: very private communication 1990
6. Johnson, D., Johnson, R., & Stanne, M.: Effects of co-operative, competitive and individualist goal structures on computer assisted instruction. *Journal of Educational Psychology,* 77, pp. 668-677 (1985)
7. Light, P., & Colbourne, C.: The role of social processes in children's microcomputer use. In: *Computer assisted learning in the social sciences and humanities* (W. Kent and R. Lewis, eds.). Oxford: Basil Blackweil 1989
8. Mandinach, E. B., & Cline, H. F.: *Implementing technology-based learning environments: Systems thinking and curriculum innovation.* Hillsdale, NJ: Lawrence Erlbaum Associates (In press)
9. Ohlsson, S.: System hacking meets learning theory: Reflections on the goals and standards of research in artificial intelligence and education. *Journal of Artificial Intelligence in Education,* 2, 3, pp. 5-18 (1991)
10. O'Malley, C. (ed.): Computer supported collaborative learning. Springer-Verlag (in press).
11. Pea, R., & Soloway, E.: The state of the art in educational technology R&D: Policy issues and opportunities. Proceedings of the International Conference on Intelligent Tutoring Systems (ITS-88), pp. 16-17, Montreal 1988
12. Rogoff, B., & Lave, J. (eds.): *Everyday cognition: Its development in social context.* Cambridge, MA: Harvard University Press 1984

13. Sandholtz, J. H., Ringstaff, C., & Dwyer, D. C.: *Classroom management: Teaching in high-tech environments: Classroom management revisited first-fourth year Findings.* ACOT Report #10, Cupertino, CA: Apple Computer, Inc., Advanced Technology Group, Apple Classroom of Tomorrow 1990
14. Soloway, E.: Log on education: Quick, where do the computers go? *Communications of the ACM,* 34, 2, pp. 29-33 (1991)
15. Streitz, N.: Mental models and metaphors: Implications for the design of adaptive user-system interfaces. In: *Learning issues for intelligent tutoring systems* (H. Mandl and A. Lesgold, eds.). Springer-Verlag 1988
16. Whitefield, A.: Human computer interaction models and their roles in the design of interactive systems. In: *Cognitive ergonomics: Understanding, learning and designing human-computer interaction* (P. Falzon, ed.). London: Academic Press 1990
17. Woolf, B.: Multiple knowledge source in intelligent teaching systems. *IEEE Expert,* pp. 41-54 (1987)

Contributors

Subject Index

NATO ASI Series F

Including Special Programmes on Sensory Systems for Robotic Control (ROB) and on Advanced Educational Technology (AET)

Vol. 1: Issues in Acoustic Signal - Image Processing and Recognition. Edited by C. H. Chen. VIII, 333 pages. 1983.

Vol. 2: Image Sequence Processing and Dynamic Scene Analysis. Edited by T. S. Huang. IX, 749 pages. 1983.

Vol. 3: Electronic Systems Effectiveness and Life Cycle Costing. Edited by J. K. Skwirzynski. XVII, 732 pages. 1983.

Vol. 4: Pictorial Data Analysis. Edited by R. M. Haralick. VIII, 468 pages. 1983.

Vol. 5: International Calibration Study of Traffic Conflict Techniques. Edited by E. Asmussen. VII, 229 pages. 1984.

Vol. 6: Information Technology and the Computer Network. Edited by K. G. Beauchamp. VIII, 271 pages. 1984.

Vol. 7: High-Speed Computation. Edited by J. S. Kowalik. IX, 441 pages. 1984.

Vol. 8: Program Transformation and Programming Environments. Report on a Workshop directed by F. L. Bauer and H. Remus. Edited by P. Pepper. XIV, 378 pages. 1984.

Vol. 9: Computer Aided Analysis and Optimization of Mechanical System Dynamics. Edited by E. J. Haug. XXII, 700 pages. 1984.

Vol. 10: Simulation and Model-Based Methodologies: An Integrative View. Edited by T. I. Ören. B. P. Zeigler, M. S. Elzas. XIII, 651 pages. 1984.

Vol. 11: Robotics and Artificial Intelligence. Edited by M. Brady. L. A. Gerhardt, H. F. Davidson. XVII, 693 pages. 1984.

Vol. 12: Combinatorial Algorithms on Words. Edited by A. Apostolico, Z. Galil. VIII, 361 pages. 1985.

Vol. 13: Logics and Models of Concurrent Systems. Edited by K. R. Apt. VIII, 498 pages. 1985.

Vol. 14: Control Flow and Data Flow: Concepts of Distributed Programming. Edited by M. Broy. VIII, 525 pages. 1985.

Vol. 15: Computational Mathematical Programming. Edited by K. Schittkowski. VIII, 451 pages. 1985.

Vol. 16: New Systems and Architectures for Automatic Speech Recognition and Synthesis. Edited by R. De Mori, C.Y. Suen. XIII, 630 pages. 1985.

Vol. 17: Fundamental Algorithms for Computer Graphics. Edited by R. A. Earnshaw. XVI, 1042 pages. 1985.

Vol. 18: Computer Architectures for Spatially Distributed Data. Edited by H. Freeman and G. G. Pieroni. VIII, 391 pages. 1985.

Vol. 19: Pictorial Information Systems in Medicine. Edited by K. H. Höhne. XII, 525 pages. 1986.

Vol. 20: Disordered Systems and Biological Organization. Edited by E. Bienenstock, F. Fogelman Soulié, G. Weisbuch. XXI, 405 pages. 1986

Vol. 21: Intelligent Decision Support in Process Environments. Edited by E. Hollnagel, G. Mancini, D. D. Woods. XV, 524 pages. 1986.

NATO ASI Series F

Vol. 22: Software System Design Methods. The Challenge of Advanced Computing Technology. Edited by J. K. Skwirzynski. XIII, 747 pages. 1986.

Vol. 23: Designing Computer-Based Learning Materials. Edited by H. Weinstock and A. Bork. IX, 285 pages. 1986.

Vol. 24: Database Machines. Modern Trends and Applications. Edited by A. K. Sood and A. H. Qureshi. VIII, 570 pages. 1986.

Vol. 25: Pyramidal Systems for Computer Vision. Edited by V. Cantoni and S. Levialdi. VIII, 392 pages. 1986. *(ROB)*

Vol. 26: Modelling and Analysis in Arms Control. Edited by R. Avenhaus, R. K. Huber and J. D. Kettelle. VIII, 488 pages. 1986.

Vol. 27: Computer Aided Optimal Design: Structural and Mechanical Systems. Edited by C. A. Mota Soares. XIII, 1029 pages. 1987.

Vol. 28: Distributed Operating Systems. Theory und Practice. Edited by Y. Paker, J.-P. Banatre and M. Bozyiğit. X, 379 pages. 1987.

Vol. 29: Languages for Sensor-Based Control in Robotics. Edited by U. Rembold and K. Hörmann. IX, 625 pages. 1987. *(ROB)*

Vol. 30: Pattern Recognition Theory and Applications. Edited by P. A. Devijver and J. Kittler. XI, 543 pages. 1987.

Vol. 31: Decision Support Systems: Theory and Application. Edited bv C. W. Holsapple and A. B. Whinston. X, 500 pages. 1987.

Vol. 32: Information Systems: Failure Analysis. Edited by J. A. Wise and A. Debons. XV, 338 pages. 1987.

Vol. 33: Machine Intelligence and Knowledge Engineering for Robotic Applications. Edited by A. K. C. Wong and A. Pugh. XIV, 486 pages. 1987. *(ROB)*

Vol. 34: Modelling, Robustness and Sensitivity Reduction in Control Systems. Edited by R.F. Curtain. IX, 492 pages. 1987.

Vol. 35: Expert Judgment and Expert Systems. Edited by J. L. Mumpower, L. D. Phillips, O. Renn and V. R. R. Uppuluri. VIII, 361 pages. 1987.

Vol. 36: Logic of Programming and Calculi of Discrete Design. Edited by M. Broy. VII, 415 pages. 1987.

Vol. 37: Dynamics of Infinite Dimensional Systems. Edited by S.-N. Chow and J. K. Hale. IX. 514 pages. 1987.

Vol. 38: Flow Control of Congested Networks. Edited by A. R. Odoni, L. Bianco and G. Szegö. XII, 355 pages. 1987.

Vol. 39: Mathematics and Computer Science in Medical Imaging. Edited by M. A. Viergever and A. Todd-Pokropek. VIII, 546 pages. 1988.

Vol. 40: Theoretical Foundations of Computer Graphics and CAD. Edited by R. A. Earnshaw. XX, 1246 pages. 1988.

Vol. 41: Neural Computers. Edited by R. Eckmiller and Ch. v. d. Malsburg. XIII, 566 pages. 1988.

Vol. 42: Real-Time Object Measurement and Classification. Edited by A. K. Jain. VIII, 407 pages. 1988. *(ROB)*

NATO ASI Series F

Vol. 43: Sensors and Sensory Systems for Advanced Robots. Edited by P. Dario. XI, 597 pages. 1988. *(ROB)*

Vol. 44: Signal Processing and Pattern Recognition in Nondestructive Evaluation of Materials. Edited by C. H. Chen. VIII, 344 pages. 1988. *(ROB)*

Vol. 45: Syntactic and Structural Pattern Recognition. Edited by G. Ferraté, T. Pavlidis, A. Sanfeliu and H. Bunke. XVI, 467 pages. 1988. *(ROB)*

Vol. 46: Recent Advances in Speech Understanding and Dialog Systems. Edited by H. Niemann, M. Lang and G. Sagerer. X, 521 pages. 1988.

Vol. 47: Advanced Computing Concepts and Techniques in Control Engineering. Edited by M. J. Denham and A. J. Laub. XI, 518 pages. 1988.

Vol. 48: Mathematical Models for Decision Support. Edited by G. Mitra. IX, 762 pages. 1988.

Vol. 49: Computer Integrated Manufacturing. Edited by I. B. Turksen. VIII, 568 pages. 1988.

Vol. 50: CAD Based Programming for Sensory Robots. Edited by B. Ravani. IX, 565 pages. 1988. *(ROB)*

Vol. 51: Algorithms and Model Formulations in Mathematical Programming. Edited by S. W. Wallace. IX, 190 pages. 1989.

Vol. 52: Sensor Devices and Systems for Robotics. Edited by A. Casals. IX, 362 pages. 1989. *(ROB)*

Vol. 53: Advanced Information Technologies for Industrial Material Flow Systems. Edited by S. Y. Nof and C. L. Moodie. IX, 710 pages. 1989.

Vol. 54: A Reappraisal of the Efficiency of Financial Markets. Edited by R. M. C. Guimarães, B. G. Kingsman and S. J. Taylor. X, 804 pages. 1989.

Vol. 55: Constructive Methods in Computing Science. Edited by M. Broy. VII, 478 pages. 1989.

Vol. 56: Multiple Criteria Decision Making and Risk Analysis Using Microcomputers. Edited by B. Karpak and S. Zionts. VII, 399 pages. 1989.

Vol. 57: Kinematics and Dynamic Issues in Sensor Based Control. Edited by G. E. Taylor. XI, 456 pages. 1990. *(ROB)*

Vol. 58: Highly Redundant Sensing in Robotic Systems. Edited by J. T. Tou and J. G. Balchen. X, 322 pages. 1990. *(ROB)*

Vol. 59: Superconducting Electronics. Edited by H. Weinstock and M. Nisenoff. X, 441 pages. 1989.

Vol. 60: 3D Imaging in Medicine. Algorithms, Systems, Applications. Edited by K. H. Höhne, H. Fuchs and S. M. Pizer. IX, 460 pages. 1990.

Vol. 61: Knowledge, Data and Computer-Assisted Decisions. Edited by M. Schader and W. Gaul. VIII, 421 pages. 1990.

Vol. 62: Supercomputing. Edited by J. S. Kowalik. X, 425 pages. 1990.

Vol. 63: Traditional and Non-Traditional Robotic Sensors. Edited by T. C. Henderson. VIII, 468 pages. 1990. *(ROB)*

Vol. 64: Sensory Robotics for the Handling of Limp Materials. Edited by P. M. Taylor. IX, 343 pages. 1990. *(ROB)*

Vol. 65: Mapping and Spatial Modelling for Navigation. Edited by L. F. Pau. VIII, 357 pages. 1990. *(ROB)*

NATO ASI Series F

Vol. 66: Sensor-Based Robots: Algorithms and Architectures. Edited by C. S. G. Lee. X, 285 pages. 1991. *(ROB)*

Vol. 67: Designing Hypermedia for Learning. Edited by D. H. Jonassen and H. Mandl. XXV, 457 pages. 1990. *(AET)*

Vol. 68: Neurocomputing. Algorithms, Architectures and Applications. Edited by F. Fogelman Soulié and J. Hérault. XI, 455 pages. 1990.

Vol. 69: Real-Time Integration Methods for Mechanical System Simulation. Edited by E. J. Haug and R. C. Deyo. VIII, 352 pages. 1991.

Vol. 70: Numerical Linear Algebra, Digital Signal Processing and Parallel Algorithms. Edited by G. H. Golub and P. Van Dooren. XIII, 729 pages. 1991.

Vol. 71: Expert Systems and Robotics. Edited by T. Jordanides and B.Torby. XII, 744 pages. 1991.

Vol. 72: High-Capacity Local and Metropolitan Area Networks. Architecture and Performance Issues. Edited by G. Pujolle. X, 536 pages. 1991.

Vol. 73: Automation and Systems Issues in Air Traffic Control. Edited by J. A. Wise, V. D. Hopkin and M. L. Smith. XIX, 594 pages. 1991.

Vol. 74: Picture Archiving and Communication Systems (PACS) in Medicine. Edited by H. K. Huang, O. Ratib, A. R. Bakker and G. Witte. XI, 438 pages. 1991.

Vol. 75: Speech Recognition and Understanding. Recent Advances, Trends and Applications. Edited by P. Laface and Renato De Mori. XI, 559 pages. 1991.

Vol. 76: Multimedia Interface Design in Education. Edited by A. D. N. Edwards and S. Holland. XIV, 216 pages. 1992. *(AET)*

Vol. 77: ComputerAlgorithms forSolving LinearAlgebraic Equations. The State of the Art. Edited by E. Spedicato. VIII, 352 pages. 1991.

Vol. 78: Integrating Advanced Technology into Technology Education. Edited by M. Hacker, A. Gordon and M. de Vries. VIII, 185 pages. 1991. *(AET)*

Vol. 79: Logic, Algebra, and Computation. Edited by F. L. Bauer. VII, 485 pages. 1991.

Vol. 80: Intelligent Tutoring Systems for Foreign Language Learning. Edited by M. L. Swartz and M. Yazdani. IX, 347 pages. 1992. *(AET)*

Vol. 81: Cognitive Tools for Learning . Edited by P. A. M. Kommers, D. H. Jonassen and J. T. Mayes. X, 278 pages. 1992. *(AET)*

Vol. 82: Combinatorial Optimization. New Frontiers in Theory and Practice. Edited by M. Akgül, H. W. Hamacher and S. Tüfekçi. XI, 334 pages. 1992.

Vol. 83: Active Perception and Robot Vision. Edited by A. K. Sood and H. Wechsler. IX, 756 pages. 1992.

Vol. 84: Computer-Based Learning Environments and Problem Solving. Edited by E. De Corte, M. C. Linn, H. Mandl and L. Verschaffel. XVI, 488 pages. 1992. *(AET)*

Vol. 85: Adaptive Learning Environments. Foundations and Frontiers. Edited by M. Jones and P. H. Winne. VIII, 408 pages. 1992. *(AET)*

Vol. 86: Intelligent Learning Environments and Knowledge Acquisition in Physics. Edited by A. Tiberghien and H. Mandl. VIII, 285 pages. 1992. *(AET)*

FSC
www.fsc.org
MIX
Papier aus verantwortungsvollen Quellen
Paper from responsible sources
FSC® C105338

If you have any concerns about our products,
you can contact us on
ProductSafety@springernature.com

In case Publisher is established outside the EU,
the EU authorized representative is:
Springer Nature Customer Service Center GmbH
Europaplatz 3, 69115 Heidelberg, Germany

Printed by Libri Plureos GmbH
in Hamburg, Germany